Sing Not War

CIVIL WAR AMERICA • Gary W. Gallagher, editor

Sing Not War

The Lives of Union & Confederate Veterans in Gilded Age America

JAMES MARTEN

The University of North Carolina Press • Chapel Hill

All rights reserved. Set in Ruzicka with Clarendon display by Tseng Information Systems, Inc. Manufactured in the United States of America. The paper in this book meets the guidelines for permanence and durability of the Committee on Production Guidelines for Book Longevity of the Council on Library Resources. The University of North Carolina Press has been a member of the Green Press Initiative since 2003.

Library of Congress Cataloging-in-Publication Data
Marten, James Alan.
Sing not war : the lives of Union and Confederate veterans in Gilded Age America / James Marten.
p. cm. — (Civil War America)
Includes bibliographical references and index.
ISBN 978-0-8078-3476-3 (cloth : alk. paper)
1. United States—History—Civil War, 1861–1865—Veterans. 2. United States—History—Civil War, 1861–1865—Social aspects. 3. Adaptability (Psychology) 4. Adjustment (Psychology) I. Title.
E491.M14 2011
973.7′1—dc22

2010043603

Portions of this book appeared previously as "Not a Veteran in the Poorhouse: Civil War Pensions and Soldiers' Homes," in *Wars within a War: Controversy and Conflict over the American Civil War*, ed. Gary Gallagher and Joan Waugh (Chapel Hill: University of North Carolina Press, 2009); "Exempt from the Ordinary Rules of Life: Sources on Maladjusted Union Civil War Veterans," *Civil War History* 47 (March 2001): 57–71; and "Nomads in Blue: Disabled Veterans and Alcohol at the National Home," in *Disabled Veterans in History*, ed. David A. Gerber (Ann Arbor: University of Michigan Press, 2000). Used with permission.

15 14 13 12 11   5 4 3 2 1

Contents   *Acknowledgments xi*

Illustrations

Acknowledgments

It is my happy responsibility to acknowledge the help and advice of the myriad friends and colleagues who aided me in large and small ways while I worked on this project on and off for the last dozen years. At Marquette, I benefitted from the help of several graduate students, including Kyle Bode, Charissa Keup, Stanford Lester, Chris Luedke, and Monica Witkowski. The notes and bibliography list the numerous libraries and repositories that I visited or with which I corresponded; I especially thank Scott Lambert of the Indiana State Library, Maureen Malloy at the library in the Clement J. Zablocki VA Medical Center in Milwaukee, Steve Nielsen of the Minnesota Historical Society, and Charles Scott of the State Historical Society of Iowa. Gerrit L. Blauvelt let me use his unpublished paper on the Soldiers' Colony in Fitzgerald, Rob Donnelly found a grim but telling story about a tragic Milwaukee veteran, Kristy Nielsen and Bill Lorber provided useful citations for articles on psychological issues facing contemporary veterans, Linda Lee Weiner provided a photocopy of her great-grandfather's soldiers' home journal, Johanna Weber of the National Building Museum in Washington, D.C., provided wonderful images of the old Pension Building, and Susan Stawicki helped out with images from the Marquette University archives. Bill Blair, Steve Engle, and Matt Gallman tolerated frequent conversations about this topic over beers, and David Gerber and George Rable gave me a chance to try out ideas on readers and students. I also thank the forty or so historians and enthusiasts who responded to queries posted on H-Net about various elements of this book—especially veterans' newspapers and veterans' in nineteenth-century fiction. At UNC Press, David Perry, Paul Betz, and Zachary Read were efficient and helpful. Ellen Goldlust-Gingrich did a heroic job of copyediting on behalf of both the author and the Press. Finally, I especially appreciate the comments on the manuscript provided by Gary Gallagher and Joan Waugh. Of course, any errors of fact or judgment are mine alone.

This book is dedicated to five veterans I have known, loved, and respected for much of my life: my father, Roy Marten; my father-in-law, Rod Gist; my uncle, Howard Schlobohm; my first employer and dear family friend, "Uncle" Myles Walter; and my undergraduate mentor at South Dakota State University, Chuck Woodard.

introduction **Toil On, Heroes**

Among the most stirring sights in Gilded Age America were the periodic as-
semblages of Civil War veterans. They gathered, often in uniform, to commemorate, to reminisce, to march before cheering, flag-waving countrymen
and -women. They celebrated Memorial Day and the Fourth of July; were
honored at college reunions and Robert E. Lee's birthday celebrations; were
featured at state fairs and at the Great Columbian Exposition of 1893. For
many Americans, these graying, dignified survivors of the war were the representative men of the Union and Confederate armies. And they were the
most common and most easily understood members of the nineteenth century's "Greatest Generation."[1]

This book is partly about those men, the scores of thousands of Billy
Yanks and Johnny Rebs who returned to their families and communities
with only temporary fanfare and who melted with apparent ease back into
civilian life.

- The former Confederate captain in a Thomas Nelson Page short story,
  working as a conductor on the long Christmas Eve rail journey from
  New York to New Orleans, entertaining travelers with gentle war
  stories, passing out eggnog, and managing the passengers as if they
  were his old company in Virginia.[2]
- Joe Elser, whom Carl Sandburg recalled from his boyhood with fondness and awe as using carpentry skills and a veteran's pension to make
  a quiet, apparently contented life, telling stream-of-consciousness war
  stories to Carl and his brother, haunted somewhat by the scenes he
  had witnessed and by a loneliness he embraced but never admitted.[3]
- Eccentric old soldiers such as Cornelius Baker, who filled a vacant lot
  on the south side of Chicago with a battery of wooden cannon and a
  brace of American flags and called it Fort Baker.[4]
- And men who became famous for being veterans, among them

"Colonel" Polk Miller, who served as a private in a Confederate artillery battery and built a successful business before becoming one of America's best-known performers of "plantation music" by the 1890s. Miller told stories, played the banjo, and sang spirituals and Confederate anthems, recording a rousing version of the "The Bonnie Blue Flag" early in the twentieth century.[5]

Those veterans dominate parts of *Sing Not War*, just as they tended to dominate the public's perception of Civil War veterans. They are the typical "old soldiers," the veterans who as individuals and members of veterans' organizations influenced the politics and patriotic impulses of the Gilded Age like no other group of men. But *Sing Not War* is also—perhaps mainly—about the other veterans, those who fit less easily back into their prewar lives, who suffered from disabilities and poverty, from mental handicaps and institutionalization.

- The down-on-their-luck tramps memorialized a few years after the war by a new game making the rounds in the Dakota Territory. In the Old Soldier, one player tries to get the others to say "no" to his pitiful begging.[6]
- The usually nameless subjects of the short, tragic reports tucked deep inside the *New York Times*: the "poor old man with only one arm" mugged by an opportunistic thief; the invalid on his way to a soldiers' home swindled by a hack driver; the desperate old soldier who, when refused admittance to a soldiers' home, failed in his attempt to shoot the secretary of the Board of Commissioners when his revolver misfired; the man deserting his wife and children for another woman after collecting six months' worth of pension payments; the victim of con men/kidnappers disguised as policemen who "arrested" their mark after he became suspicious of the agent he had hired to collect fourteen hundred dollars in pension money; the participants in a bloody St. Louis street fight between an old Rebel and old Yankee; the old man "Driven Crazy by Drink" who tried to shoot his wife, failed, and then fired a bullet into his own head, failing to kill himself as well; the "tall, soldiery looking old man" in jail for public intoxication, begging for a reduced fine because, as he wrote on a note, "Did good fighting at Cold Harbor."[7]
- And the decidedly unheroic and nearly unnoticed faces in the background, like the "Grand Army Man" in Willa Cather's "The Sculptor's Funeral," a story about bitter West Kansans receiving the body of a

noted prodigal son who had gone east to seek his fortune. A veteran in a faded blue "Grand Army suit" lurks on the edge of every scene. Deferential, curious, a little odd, he at one point remarks, "It's too bad he didn't belong to some lodge or other. I like an order funeral. They seem more appropriate for people of some reputation." After making this, his longest speech in the story, "the spare man with an ingratiating concession in his shrill voice," who "always carried the flag at the G.A.R. funerals," recedes into the background.[8]

These are simply isolated examples, of course, and as in any book drawn largely from qualitative sources, one needs to consider the extent to which the necessarily anecdotal evidence provides a representative sample of former soldiers. *Sing Not War* does not attempt to provide a cross-section of all veterans' experiences. This approach is partly a function of the project's evolution since its origins more than a dozen years ago: it was conceived as a general history of Civil War veterans, North and South, black and white. But as certain questions emerged, certain kinds of sources came to dominate the answers, and certain choices had to be made. As a result, the best-adjusted men at times fade from the narrative, and the less fortunate, marginalized men take center stage. At other times, former Confederates become more or less invisible as the book veers into issues and events that affected them less deeply.

One group left virtually entirely out of this particular narrative are the tens of thousands of African American soldiers who survived the war. Recent scholarship has begun to explore the ways in which they did and did not share white veterans' postwar experiences. Although some African Americans belonged to integrated Grand Army of the Republic (GAR) posts and a few were admitted to national and state soldiers' homes, African Americans barely appear in documents related to the homes, and aside from the *National Tribune*, they are rarely found in soldiers' newspapers, mainstream media, or advertisements featuring old soldiers. Moreover, the racial issues that complicated the lives of black veterans would have added to the book an unwieldy layer of analysis. Finally, while other historians have explored black veterans' experiences by focusing on individual communities, specific GAR chapters, and pension records, that approach was too narrow for the issues raised here.[9]

Thus, *Sing Not War* is not a comprehensive account of Civil War veterans. Yet it does describe the lives of hundreds of thousands of Americans during the two or three generations after the Civil War. Indeed, military service was the most common characteristic among northern and southern men living during the Gilded Age who had not yet reached the age of forty in 1861. Forty-one percent of all northern white men born between 1822 and 1845 served in the Union Army, while the percentages were 60 for those between 1837 and 1845 and a whopping 81 for those born in 1843—the boys who turned eighteen in the war's first year. Similarly, perhaps three-quarters of all white men of military age living in the Confederate states served in the Confederate Army, with just over 80 percent of them between the ages of eighteen and twenty-nine at the time of enlistment.[10]

Moreover, veterans were everywhere in Gilded Age society. Although the fast-growing industrial city of Milwaukee, Wisconsin, might not have been representative of all American communities, the remarkable presence of veterans in this community of about 225,000 speaks to the wide variety of places and circumstances in which veterans found themselves. The 1890 special census of Union veterans and their widows reported many neighborhoods crowded with old soldiers. On two-block stretches of two streets just east of downtown lived nearly two dozen Union veterans, including two lawyers, a carpenter, a dentist, a travel agent, a gardener, two business executives, an editor, a printer, a salesman, and a laborer. A few blocks south, a grouping of seven veterans and four widows took up much of the 100 block and spilled over into the 200 block of Detroit Street. A few blocks farther west, twenty veterans and at least two widows lived on a four-block section of Fifth Street. Their occupations included police officer and lawyer, laundry worker and paper hanger, grocer and baker, electrician and wire worker. The 100, 200, and 300 blocks of Jefferson Street and its alley were home to a rather hardscrabble group of at least a dozen veterans and half a dozen widows; several of those with jobs worked as laborers, while the others had low-paying employment as teamsters, porters, tanners, and clerks. Not far away, several boardinghouses provided homes for veterans and at least one widow. Two of the men had lost legs, another had lost an arm, and yet another had been incarcerated at Libby Prison; only four had jobs, three of them as laborers. Three consecutive blocks of Prospect Avenue—physically a five-minute stroll from Jefferson, but a world away in terms of social status—contained the homes of a dozen veterans (including a lieutenant colonel, three captains, three lieutenants, and a brigade surgeon) who held important jobs, including a general manager, the president of an iron company, a lawyer, and a publisher, George W. Peck, who was also the current governor of Wisconsin.

All of these men and women lived within a short walk of one another in the crowded streets of one of America's rising cities. Census takers found more than seven hundred veterans, about 60 percent of whom appeared in the city directory. Their occupations reveal that Union veterans were present in all walks of life, working in just over one hundred different fields: although the most common occupation was "laborer" (10 percent), the directory also listed eighteen clerks, seventeen carpenters, sixteen engineers, a dozen farmers, eleven businessmen, ten messengers or coachmen, nine teamsters, eight shoemakers, seven lawyers, a half dozen machinists, five bookkeepers, four travel agents, three telephone operators, two cooks, and one judge, one artist, one bartender, one billboard repairman, and one florist. Altogether, about 43 percent were skilled or semiskilled workers, 18 percent were unskilled, and another 18 percent were white-collar workers, and 7 percent owned their own businesses or worked as attorneys or medical professionals.[11]

Sing Not War seeks to look beyond those numbers to explore the ways in which white veterans of the Union and Confederate armies reentered Gilded Age society. The book shows how the nineteenth century's "Greatest Generation" blended — or failed to blend — back into their lives and communities and how their nonveteran countrymen and -women perceived these experiences. Put simply, the volume asks, "How did veterans live, and how were they seen to live?" The effects of traumatic homecomings, economic discrimination, and physical and mental disabilities complicate our perceptions of veterans. Separate chapters dissect the pensions and homes created for old soldiers, less to talk about them as systems and more to expose the conflicts that they sometimes created in politics and in communities.

Sing Not War argues that Civil War veterans were set apart, and the specific ways in which this process took place encompass subsets of the larger, distinct group of old soldiers. Although the sad stories of disaffected, ruined men that dominate parts of *Sing Not War* might represent only a small percentage of veterans, the issues faced by the most marginalized veterans and the anger that flared from time to time over issues such as veterans' pensions loom larger than the simple numbers of men directly involved. Although relatively few men were wholly disabled, increasing numbers came to believe that the war had contributed to minor or even major physical handicaps, and by the end of the century, sympathetic observers estimated that hundreds of thousands of men had eventually lost their vigor as a result of vague wartime maladies and that the life expectancies of tens of thousands had been reduced by a decade or more. Even fewer veterans lived in soldiers' homes, although those who did served as quite visible representatives, especially in the towns and cities in which the homes were located. Very few men resorted to begging on the streets or ended up in almshouses or on county farms, although many, many men seem to have lived on the edges of survival, getting by on paltry pension checks, odd jobs, and charity.

To understand the ways in which the experiences of a minority can become representative of a much larger group, at least to the public, one needs only to flash forward a hundred years, when physically disabled and mentally traumatized Vietnam veterans—a relatively small percentage of the total number of men who served in Southeast Asia, where only a tiny fraction of servicemen saw combat—came to dominate public perceptions of veterans in the 1970s and 1980s. The ways in which dramatic and tragic experiences covered by journalists, imagined by novelists and screenwriters, projected by veteran memoirists, and diagnosed by psychiatrists created shortcuts to categorizing all veterans as traumatized "baby killers" is instructive. In one example of the power of image to trump reality, the images of psychologically damaged veterans that rose to prominence in the late 1960s and early 1970s were used to discredit veterans who opposed the war. That one observer could refer to "the Vietnam War as mental illness" suggests that the experiences of a few indeed have the power to shape public understanding of the many.[12]

Although comparing veterans of the Vietnam War to any other group of veterans is a risky business—the nature of combat, the political and technological contexts, the processes for recruiting and organizing armies, and the expectations of the soldiers differed substantially—the much-studied and -discussed postwar lives of the men who served in Southeast Asia are nevertheless instructive. At the very least, the well-documented difficulties many Vietnam veterans encountered in resuming their civilian lives and the way that the problems of a minority came to represent an entire generation of soldiers in the public consciousness and popular culture can help us understand the ways in which marginalized Civil War veterans could have influenced public perceptions more than their numbers would suggest. Marginalized and traumatized veterans became parables of representative men along a spectrum of public perceptions of veterans that ranged from "There but for the grace of God go I" unfortunates to exemplars of manly citizenship.

As a result, the specific experiences of the disabled, institutionalized, and troubled veterans described in *Sing Not War* might not have reflected the postwar lives of most veterans, but they did complicate public perceptions, especially in the North. And as opponents of expanding pensions increasingly applied the characteristics of less stable and less admirable old soldiers to all veterans, the more disturbing consequences of the war for the men who fought it took on an importance beyond their quantifiable effects.

The specific stories of unfortunate men that dominate parts of the book are simply extreme versions of stories that thousands of other veterans could tell. And the conditions and situations that cast those men into the margins of Gilded Age society were quite public and shaped civilians' attitudes about veterans as deeply as did parades and monuments.

According to Susan-Mary Grant, the three million or so men who fought and died, marched and garrisoned, deserted and bushwhacked—the men who represented the Union and the Confederacy on the battlefields and prisons and encampments of the great war—quickly receded from the vision of many Americans. The returning soldiers were separated from the "reimagined community" created in response to the huge changes wrought by the war. And many acted as though fitting in was all they wanted to do. Robert Beecham had fought in the Iron Brigade at Chancellorsville and Gettysburg, where he was captured and later exchanged; had served as an officer in the 23rd U.S. Colored Regiment; had fought at the Crater, where he was wounded and captured again; and had endured nine months of prison before escaping just before the war ended. Yet he ended his memoir of his three years of fighting with the bland comment, "My days of war were over; before me were the paths and the vocations of peace."[13]

But when Joshua Lawrence Chamberlain described the "clouds of men on foot or horse, singly or in groups, making their earnest way . . . each for his own little home" after the fighting ended, he captured the rather sudden shift in the lives of men who had shared hardships with comrades, survived bullets and disease, and fought big fights for big issues. Now they were just men, trudging to their "little homes" without well-defined roles in their nation's purpose and without an identity beyond that of laborer, farmer, or clerk. As Chamberlain reflected many years later, the newly minted veterans were "left alone, and lonesome" when they returned to peaceful pursuits.[14]

Yet their communities seemed to expect more of them than of other men—indeed, the men's own rhetoric seems to have encouraged others to expect more. Their epic sacrifices and bravery, the scale of the conflict and its high stakes, and the agonizing and wonderful changes wrought by the war ensured that no one could simply return to "normal," even if "normal" was still available.

The Fight Begins Again

Many men had no idea what the rest of their lives had in store when they returned from the greatest adventures, the most wrenching experiences, the
most serious hardships most would ever know. Despite their anticipation,
the reunions of soldiers and their families were rarely recorded in diaries
or memoirs. When they were, the authors tended to focus on relief and joy.
There was a certain sense of hurrying back to normality. Yet these worn,
somber men could not just shrug off all they had seen in camp and on the
battlefield and resume interrupted lives.

The writer Hamlin Garland's recollections of the subtle changes the war
wrought in his father suggests that even men who seemed to have fit in—
the ones who did not end up in soldiers' homes or almshouses or who were
not critically injured—were still affected deeply by the war. Richard Garland
spent nearly two years fighting and marching with Sherman, leaving behind
a wife; a daughter, Hattie; five-year-old Hamlin; and two-year-old Frank.
Hamlin spent the first few pages of his autobiography describing Richard's
reappearance on their little farm in western Wisconsin at the end of the war;
he also penned a much longer fictional version, "The Return of a Private,"
from the point of view of the returning soldier. The short story begins with
the title character and a few comrades getting off a train. The townsfolk are
too used to soldiers coming home to pay much attention to these dusty, tired
veterans. The men sleep a little but are eager to get home, so they set out on
foot.

The scene turns to the private's family members, who are visiting a neighbor's house when they spot a gaunt stranger trudging wearily up to their
gate. Emma, the wife, suddenly recognizes her husband, Edward, gathers
her children (an older girl and two boys about the same age as Hamlin and
Frank would have been in 1865), and dashes for home. The veteran "was like
a man lost in a dream. His wide, hungry eyes devoured the scene. The rough
lawn, the little unpainted house, the field of clear yellow wheat behind it,
down across which streamed the sun."

Then his wife is upon him, breaking his reverie, embracing and kissing
him as the children stand in "a curious row," daughter sobbing, sons uncer-
tain. The veteran hugs his wife and daughter, then turns to the little boys.
Tommy, the older one, greets him, but little Teddy hangs back, peering at his
father from behind the fence. "Come here, my little man; don't you know
me?" Anticipation verges on tragic disappointment. The soldier finally pro-
duces an apple that tempts the little boy into his arms.

After the family goes inside the little house, the veteran relaxes, stretched out on the floor. He asks about neighbors and about the dog who died while he was away. It is a quiet moment, only slightly marred by the hard work looming ahead: "His farm was weedy and encumbered . . . his children needed clothing, the years were coming upon him, he was sick and emaciated, but his heroic soul did not quail. With the same courage with which he had faced his Southern march he entered upon a still more hazardous future." Garland enhances the ambiguity of the private's return with his last sentence: "The common soldier of the American volunteer army had returned. His war with the South was over, and his fight, his daily running fight with nature and against the injustice of his fellow-men, was begun again."[15]

Garland's autobiography helps to explain this ambiguous resignation. Despite his family's joy at Richard's return, "all was not the same as before." Belle Garland seemed bitter that Richard had, "like thousands of others[,] . . . deserted his wife and children for an abstraction, a mere sentiment." A harsh side of Richard Garland also emerged, "for my father brought back from his two years' campaigning . . . the temper and habit of a soldier." His return suddenly shifted the female-oriented dynamics of the family, a change of pace for the two little boys, who barely remembered Richard and had grown accustomed to their mother's lighter touch. "We soon learned . . . that the soldier's promise of punishment was swift and precise in its fulfillment." "We knew he loved us," Garland wrote, "for he often took us to his knees of an evening and told us stories of marches and battles, or chanted war-songs for us." But "the moments of his tenderness were few," and the slightest misbehavior was corrected harshly and immediately.[16]

The two versions of Richard Garland's homecoming as told by this middle son of the middle border provides a shift in perspective that illuminates the complexity of telling the stories of Civil War veterans. Similar homecomings occurred at thousands of doors and gateways, in untold numbers of yards and barns and streets. But the long lives that followed veterans' war making and peacekeeping have been too little explored by historians. Indeed, although returning soldiers spent decades nursing old wounds and the disillusionment spawned by their combat experiences, both were supplanted in the 1880s by the patriotic, even nostalgic gloss imparted to the war by the GAR, the United Confederate Veterans (UCV), and other organizations. Historians have closely examined those organizations as well as the roles that veterans played in the development of sectional and national memories of the war and the process of reconciliation between the sections. Although the literature on the experiences of soldiers is quite large, most historians who study soldiers have not followed them into peacetime. A few have examined the experience of men in soldiers' homes in the North and South as well as the war's long-term ramifications on the psychological and physical health of soldiers. With only a few exceptions, these excellent histories have used veterans to help explain the paramount historiographical issues of the sectional conflict: memory, reconciliation, the Lost Cause, Republican politics, and other important subjects in which veterans are not necessarily the central characters.[17]

Sing Not War seeks to understand the lives of Civil War soldiers *as veterans*. One reason that historians have rarely attempted to do so may be that the richest sources for studying combatants are their countless letters, diaries, and memoirs. As two of the most literate armies to have fought up to that time, Yanks and Rebs constantly wrote to their families and kept personal accounts of what they had witnessed. Yet they stopped writing when the war ended, and when thousands took up pens a decade or two after mustering out, they wrote almost entirely about battles and marches and comrades rather than their response to returning to civilian life. Given the absence of a critical mass of first-person accounts by old soldiers writing about their postwar lives, one may be tempted to accept Beecham's prediction of a sudden and satisfying transition to civilian life. Perhaps their thoughts were just that uninteresting, their lives that straightforward—perhaps it really was that easy to turn their swords into plowshares.

But that supposition is not reasonable. As Eric Dean has shown in his sample of Indiana soldiers, veterans of Civil War combat were clearly exposed to traumas resembling those of twentieth-century soldiers, and although the memoir literature is virtually silent on the issue, such psychological responses as nightmares, delusions, and other manifestations of the terrors of combat must have plagued many soldiers. Conjecture based on research into the lives of modern veterans is supported by anecdotal but compelling evidence that suggests that things *were* different for countless men scarred by war. Even a casual survey of newspapers in the months after the war reveals extraordinary suffering and unease among veterans and among the civilians observing them. Antoine Adrian, a veteran of the 13th New York Cavalry, spent more time than usual dressing and combing his hair just a few weeks after the war ended; then, after calmly announcing that he "should not again sleep in the house," he walked to the outhouse and shot himself in the forehead. The *Utica Telegraph* blamed the state of a "raving lunatic" brought to an asylum on his suffering at Andersonville: "The scenes of that death-pen . . . had been seared into his brain as with a red-hot iron, till all else is burned out but that one terrible thing which is now within a living horror." A one-legged ex-soldier in St. Louis, employed at the federal arsenal but suffering from delirium tremens, slashed his throat three times and soon thereafter died in a hospital. Next to a road crowded with paroled Confederates walking home near Salisbury, North Carolina, a Confederate officer sat on a pile of railroad ties, his shirt covered with blood. Passersby gradually realized that he had wounded himself. He calmly declined offers of help and asked someone to take his greatcoat, lying on the ground a few feet away, to his wife in Augusta, Georgia. As he talked, he smeared the blood from his wound all over his arms.[18]

A quartet of isolated deaths hardly proves a point, and the ghastly forces that push men and women to end their lives violently are far beyond historians' power to understand or even adequately describe. Yet we do know that all veterans of major wars—especially combat veterans—return to a different world than they left. Postwar society invariably differs from prewar or even wartime society, so veterans need to adjust to the changes that occurred while they were gone. But veterans have also changed: they are two or three or four years older, haunted by horrific images and dead friends, slowed at least temporarily by injuries or other weakening conditions, freed from routines and discipline that have become second nature. And of course, their friends and families and communities have changed, too.

The veterans on the margins of Gilded Age society, *Sing Not War* suggests, may not be statistically representative of all Civil War veterans. Nevertheless, their experiences, however far from the postwar lives of most men, remain relevant. This book initially took all veterans as its subject, and although at times its descriptions of desperation and poverty and institutional ennui seem to leave most of them out of the narrative, it is not unreasonable to assume that most veterans shared at least some of the disappointments and fears of the men most obviously trapped in postwar nightmares.

Those Who Have Borne the Battle

Although this volume provides neither a history of the era nor, strictly speaking, a history of old soldiers' institutions or organizations, brief introductions to veterans' associations, soldiers' homes, and pensions are in order.

Like millions of their fellow Americans, Civil War veterans were organizers and joiners. The first Union veterans' organization was apparently the 3rd Army Corps Union, which, although it started out as a kind of burial insurance program for officers, began holding reunions on May 5, 1865, the anniversary of its first action at the Battle of Williamsburg. The societies of the Army of the Tennessee, Army of the Cumberland, and Army of the Ohio, which had fought during the war's last year with Sherman, were organized within two or three years after the war ended, and by 1868 the Society of the Army of the Potomac had been formed. Confederate associations started a little later and tended to be smaller. The first was the club formed by officers of the 3rd North Carolina at an 1866 funeral, but many other organizations emerged in the coming decades, ranging from Maryland's Society of the Army and Navy of the Confederate States to the veterans of the "Old First Virginia Infantry" and Pegram's Battalion in Richmond.[19]

During the next two decades, survivors of hundreds of Union and Confederate brigades, regiments, and even companies held reunions and organized associations. Union veterans also organized on behalf of political causes such as Winfield Scott Hancock's 1880 presidential campaign and Kansas Populism in the 1890s, while military telegraphers, prisoners of war, and other specialized groups formed their own associations.[20]

A few elite groups on both sides sought to preserve the history of the war through publications and lectures. Such organizations included the Military Order of the Loyal Legion of the United States, the Survivors' Association of the State of South Carolina, and the better-known Southern Historical Society, organized and administered by Jubal Early and other generals and officers from Virginia.[21]

The GAR and the UCV became the largest and most influential of the associations. After a false start in the late 1860s, the GAR benefited from the renewal of interest in the war in the late 1870s and the expansion of the pension system, which covered only 60,000 men in 1880 but more than 400,000 a decade later. The Robert E. Lee Camp No. 1, Confederate Veterans, formed in Richmond in April 1883, promoted a philosophy of sectional reconciliation and took the lead in organizing the UCV in 1889. As many as 160,000 men—between a quarter and a third of all surviving Confederates— eventually joined the group's more than eighteen hundred local chapters.[22]

These organizations would become inextricably linked with the homes and pensions created for soldiers in both the North and the South. Most programs to care for Union veterans, widows, and orphans took their inspiration from a passage in the final paragraph of Abraham Lincoln's Second Inaugural Address: "With malice toward none, with charity for all, with firmness in the right as God gives us to see the right, let us strive on to finish the work we are in, to bind up the nation's wounds, to care for him who shall have borne the battle and for his widow and his orphan, to do all which may achieve and cherish a just and lasting peace among ourselves and with all nations." For many people, Lincoln's suggestion that the nation should care for the northern victims of war became an irrevocable pledge following his assassination and the victorious close of the war.[23]

Lincoln's promise did not cover former rebels, but a rough equivalent to Lincoln's vow appeared in a bill passed by the Confederate House of Representatives late in 1863 establishing the "Veteran Soldiers Home" for disabled Confederates. The bill offered "Confederate States and the citizens thereof . . . the opportunity of becoming identified with this philanthropic and patriotic enterprise, and of participating in the pleasing and grateful duty of contributing to the relief of those who have periled all, and have been disabled in the service of their country." Although the rhetoric did not quite match the Second Inaugural, the charitable and patriotic impulse was similar, and the former Confederate states ultimately honored the service of their disabled volunteer soldiers with homes and pensions, albeit on a much smaller scale than in the North. The soldiers' homes and pension programs no doubt transcended anything that either President Lincoln or the Confederate House of Representatives had in mind.[24]

Congress took the first step in the spring of 1865, when it established the National Asylum for Disabled Volunteer Soldiers. By the end of the decade, branches had been established in Milwaukee, Wisconsin (the Northwestern Branch); Dayton, Ohio (Central); Togus, Maine (Eastern); and Norfolk, Virginia (Southern); with five more subsequently added in Leavenworth, Kansas; Johnson City, Tennessee; Danville, Illinois; Santa Monica, California; and Marion, Indiana. The philosophy that shaped the homes grew out of the antebellum growth of a new notion of family that revolved around the idea of home as not simply a dwelling but a kind of support group from which parents and children drew comfort, strength, and stability. "Homes" rather than colder and less welcoming "asylums" were established for orphans, widows, former prostitutes, and other dependent groups. During the war, the U.S. Sanitary Commission and other voluntary, largely female organizations in the North and South established "soldiers' homes" to provide temporary care for the sick and temporary housing and meals for men traveling to and from the front. The National Asylum for Disabled Volunteer Soldiers was created in the contexts of these assumptions and preexisting institutions. Indeed, almost without fail, residents and neighbors referred to the new asylums as "soldiers' homes," and Congress changed the name to the National Home for Disabled Volunteer Soldiers (NHDVS) in 1873. Over the next several decades, the treatment and the behavior of the men in these homes would be held to a very high standard of domesticity. In 1884, Congress dropped the requirement that veterans have disabilities as a result of wartime injuries, and by late in the century, the National Homes had become havens for elderly veterans.[25]

In addition to the ever-expanding federal institutions, nearly thirty states also established homes for Union veterans, subsidized in part by federal funds. Some state homes were founded in reaction to specific policies and complaints regarding the NHDVS: men living in the states where the branches were located were not favored in placements, wives were unable to live with their husbands, and, as the veteran population aged and rules regarding admission were loosened to include men whose disabilities might not be related directly to service, overcrowding occurred. In most states, the state departments of the GAR and GAR members in state legislatures provided the necessary push to establish a separate system of state homes. A common complaint was the increasing number of veterans appearing in county poorhouses, insane asylums, and other facilities. The first annual report from the Massachusetts home, for example, claimed that 103 of the 248 men admitted during the institution's first year came from almshouses, while the Michigan GAR found 460 veterans living in poorhouses. In state after state during the 1880s and early 1890s, the GAR convinced legislatures to fund homes, many of which provided cottage-style housing for at least a few veterans and their wives.[26]

By the turn of the twentieth century, the differences between state and federal homes had narrowed, aside from their size and some states' practice of allowing wives and husbands to live together in individual cottages. Thirty homes existed in twenty-seven states, ranging in size from the Illinois Soldiers' and Sailors' Home in Quincy, which had more than nineteen hundred residents, to the North Dakota Soldiers' Home in Lisbon, with thirty-three. Most housed between two hundred and five hundred men, with fewer in small eastern states and recently settled western states. State homes submitted to biannual visits by inspectors from the Board of Managers of the NHDVS as a condition of the annual payment of one hundred dollars they received from Congress for each soldier in their care.[27]

A similar collection of motivations characterized the Confederate soldiers' home movement, which was propelled by the rise of the Lost Cause and, more important, by the South's worsening economic conditions in the 1870s and 1880s. The Panic of 1873, flat prices for southern cash crops, and the second depression in less than a generation in the early 1890s pushed already hard-pressed veterans to the edge, forcing them to rely increasingly on family members, local charities, and county poorhouses. In urban areas, homeless and often disabled veterans had become common enough sights to raise eyebrows and to inspire governments and individuals to do something about the problem. Like their northern counterparts, soldiers' home supporters' depicted asylums and poorhouses as unworthy refuges for disabled and poor heroes. It was demeaning for old soldiers and dishonorable for their luckier countrymen to allow these men to languish in tawdry county institutions. The *Richmond Dispatch* declared in 1892 that "it is disgraceful that any worthy veteran . . . should be forced to live like a pauper."[28]

As in the North, southern veterans' groups commonly made the initial investments to create homes and then appealed to the state legislatures for help. In Texas, the John B. Hood Camp of Confederate Veterans opened the Texas Confederate Home in 1884. By 1891, the home had been transferred to the state. The Confederate Home in Missouri followed a similar path despite objections from the United Daughters of the Confederacy, which had more or less managed the home from its founding in 1891 to its takeover by the state six years later. North Carolina's home had started as a tiny, private concern in 1890 after a fund-raising fair brought in enough money to rent a house for seven soldiers. Within a year, the legislature had taken over, doubling the number of men housed in the institution. Virginia held out longer than most states; the R. E. Lee Camp had established a home in 1890 to prevent "honorable and brave Confederate soldiers . . . from dying in the county almshouses." In 1892, the group began receiving thirty thousand dollars from the legislature each year, with an agreement that in twenty-two years, the property would revert to the state. But the hard times of the 1890s caused donations to plummet and admissions to soar by 25 percent; by 1896, the home was filled to overflowing, and thirty-five applications were awaiting decisions.[29]

In 1910, 31,830 veterans—about 5 percent of those still living—resided in federal or state homes. Just under 100,000 Union soldiers eventually entered federal or state facilities, and about 20,000 Confederate veterans were admitted to southern homes.[30]

The other programs devoted to those who had borne the battle were the pension systems for volunteer soldiers established by Congress and southern state governments. Precedents existed for these initiatives. Poor Revolutionary War veterans had received pensions early in the century, and disabled veterans of the War of 1812 and the war with Mexico had been pensioned prior to 1861; those systems were expanded during the Gilded Age to include most veterans of those wars.[31]

Although the pension system for Civil War volunteers was tweaked a number of times, three main laws shaped the government's responsibilities. The General Law, first passed in 1861 and amended several times, established pensions for soldiers' widows and orphans and for soldiers disabled as a direct result of military service. The law established a precise table of injuries and conditions and amounts covered by pensions based on rank and the extent to which the injuries prevented men from performing labor requiring physical exertion; a scale setting rates for "total disability" and fractions thereof was the basis for quarterly payments. Privates received eight dollars a month for total disability, while officers received as much as thirty dollars. Over the years, rates were changed, specific conditions were added, and the percentage of disability surgeons had to assign to applicants was changed from fractions of eight to eighteen. The major systemic revision of the General Law came with the Act of 1890, which extended pensions to any disabled man who had received an honorable discharge after serving at least ninety days. His disability need not have been incurred during his military service but could not be caused by "vicious habits." Early in the twentieth century, a presidential executive order and several laws made age a disability.[32]

Southern states, of course, paid for Confederate pensions, which, in several cases, grew out of artificial limb programs. South Carolina began distributing artificial legs in 1866, when the legislature appropriated twenty thousand dollars, obtained lists of amputees from tax collectors, and awarded a contract to supply artificial limbs to a Rochester, New York, firm. Radical Republicans interrupted the process, but after the state was "redeemed" in 1877, the program was reinstituted, this time including prosthetic arms. By the late 1880s, the artificial limb effort had been replaced by pensions. Similarly, Virginia's prosthetics program evolved into a pension plan in 1882, when the state began providing sixty dollars in cash for each missing limb or eye. Six years later, the legislature passed the first true pension law for Virginia Confederates. Dedicated only to the state's poorest disabled veterans—recipients had to have an annual income of less than three hundred dollars and no more than one thousand dollars in personal wealth—the first rate scale reached a maximum annual payment of sixty dollars. Although the acceptance rate was higher, it seems, than for Union pensions—in one Virginia county, about 80 percent of those who applied immediately after the law passed received pensions—the application process was fairly elaborate. As in most southern states, the rates gradually rose and the process was somewhat eased, until in 1900 disability due to old age was allowed and a full disability earned a pensioner one hundred dollars.[33]

Union pensions were much larger than Confederate pensions. By the 1890s, the average northern recipient was receiving $160 a year, while the average payment to Confederate veterans was $40. In 1885, a quarter of a million men—nearly 17 percent of all Union veterans—were receiving federal pensions, and the percentage continued to climb until 1915, when more than 93 percent of all living veterans—just under 400,000—received pensions. By 1893, pensions to Union veterans accounted for 43 percent of federal expenses; in contrast, a century later only 21 percent of the federal budget was taken up by social security. An 1893 report stated that the number of Confederate veterans receiving pensions or living in state soldiers' homes was just over 27,000, with a total annual cost of $1,126,736. At the same time, the number of Union veterans receiving pensions was 876,068, while 19,518 men were in federal or state soldiers' homes. The total appropriation for Union pensions for 1893 was $146,737,350, although a deficit of at least that much was projected. The article pointedly suggested that federal pension rolls contained over 300,000 more men than had served in the Confederate Army.[34]

Sentenced to Life

For civilians and soldiers alike, being a veteran came to mean something different than being a soldier. Ambrose Bierce was definitely not speaking for all veterans when he remarked that the war had left him "sentenced to life" or when he answered the question, "What has happened to Ambrose Bierce the youth, who fought at Chickamauga?" with the simple, "He is dead." Yet even veterans who did not share Bierce's bitter and macabre response to their wartime service were in a sense reborn as different men because of their experiences.[35]

One way of understanding more fully the lives of veterans is to study the margins of society—the least successful veterans. Of course, most veterans managed peaceful and more or less satisfying transitions back to civilian life, a phenomenon that says something important about the United States and about Americans' relationship to wars and to the men who fight them. But equally important issues can be raised by examining the ways in which society responded to and interacted with those veterans who did not pick up their lives where they left off, who ended up on the fringes of their communities.

As a result, as they do in virtually all histories, the men who left behind concrete evidence of their attitudes and experiences have to represent those who remain silent, at least to historians. *Sing Not War* relies on a number of traditional types of sources but also draws heavily on sources that historians have not utilized. These include hundreds of pages of testimony to both congressional and GAR investigators of soldiers' homes in the 1880s. They also include the dozen or more "soldiers' newspapers" published in the North as well as the better-known *Confederate Veteran* and rarely cited newsletters produced by the Arkansas and Kentucky state homes. And they include various accounts by inmates of veterans' homes, mainly in the North, who wrote with passion and despair and hopefulness about their lives. Most men did not publish reminiscences or letters in soldiers' newspapers—indeed, most of these men do not appear in any source useful to exploring their inner lives—but we must believe that those who do appear are somehow representative of the men who chose not to put pen to paper. Many old soldiers undoubtedly flinched when they read or heard the extreme rhetoric that sometimes spouted from pension advocates, yet most of the veterans probably sighed and agreed with at least some of the partisan language. And while many veterans probably deplored the resentment that fired some advocates' harsher public statements, it is quite likely that they deplored the public airing of those sentiments rather than the sentiments themselves.

A number of threads wind through the six chapters that follow. One is the clash between the rhetoric of patriotism and gratitude and the political, economic, and moral differences that grew between veterans and civilians, especially in the North. Although Memorial Day and GAR reunion parades reminded northerners of the excitement and gratitude that had welled up during the Grand Review in May 1865 and for months thereafter in more intimate homecoming celebrations throughout the country, a widening chasm characterized the relationship between Yankee veterans and non-veterans. Veterans—not all of them but enough to become stereotypes— came to be associated with addiction, failure, and fraud. Poor, disabled, wounded veterans reminded civilians of the fine line between success and failure, the catastrophe that a long-term illness or injury could wreak in the lives of Americans at a time with poor medical treatment, no health insurance, and virtually no disability insurance. Seeing failed veterans also reminded the more successful of the vulnerability of men's moral strength and character, reinforcing the idea that the building blocks to a thriving life in business had to be put in place early in life.

But the ambiguities of the relationship between those often aggressively patriotic and even defensive organizations and the larger public also reveals that while veterans may have become constructive citizens, even leaders, their identification with military service and the honors and privileges that it should have bestowed on them automatically put them on the margins of the larger society. Specific issues—especially pensions and the behavior of the men who failed to flourish in postwar society—led to a clash between the nation's natural gratitude and deep-seated notions about independence, charity, and the role of government. Americans were uneasy about "volunteers" claiming pensions or other rewards. And civilians' reluctance fully to appreciate veterans caused them to withdraw to their own organizations and issues.

Another thread that runs through this book is the startling differences in the way Union and Confederate veterans were perceived by the societies in which they lived. The heroic version of the veteran served as a common denominator in both sections, but although that image continued to dominate in the South, in the North it was joined by much more complicated images and attitudes. Union veterans came to be seen not only as symbols but also as social problems. Those same predicaments simply made the symbolism of defeated Confederates more poignant. They became relics, like so many of the war objects being collected by the Gilded Age Americans described in chapter 3. R. B. Rosenburg titled his book on Confederate soldiers' homes *Living Monuments*, and that term goes a long way in describing the peculiar position that Confederate veterans filled in postwar southern society. They were indeed frozen, made into living statues only a little more capable of animation than the thousands of stone sentinels guarding county courthouses and village squares throughout the South by the 1880s and 1890s. As a result, memory inevitably plays an important role in the story, but *Sing Not War* is almost equally about forgetting, as Americans put behind them much of what it meant to be a soldier and "remembered" a one-dimensional heroic version that many veterans could not realize.

Of course, families and communities in the North celebrated the return of their men and boys and continued to respect them throughout the remainder of their lives. And some Confederate veterans earned the contempt of their fellow southerners by behaving irresponsibly and by refusing to fit into civilian society.

But extraordinary differences existed. Confederate veterans were seen as central characters in southern society, honored and successful and valued simply because they were veterans. In the North, as veterans' papers came to argue, at least some veterans were ignored or even treated with contempt.

Despite the powerful symbol of the bloody shirt employed by many politicians who had served in the army, that reverence for military service did not extend to all veterans. Even the pity that fueled much of the public's reaction to veterans played out differently: for southerners, it often became a source of compassion and even honor; in the North, pity sometimes—and increasingly as the century progressed—could lead to scorn and criticism.

Hard luck followed some veterans in both sections, of course, but the ways in which society interpreted the men who succumbed to poverty, drink, or boredom tended to diverge. In the North, marginalized veterans were often seen as agents of their own decline, almost purposefully swimming against the stream of progress, economic growth, and opportunity. They may have served bravely in the war, but as the country moved deeper into peacetime, they were expected to get over their experiences and move on. Conversely, southern veterans who found themselves in the same situations could appear as victims of conditions outside their control.

Put simply, veterans in the North were seen through multiple lenses and exposed to critical commentary on their choices after leaving the army. In the South, veterans would always be those proud, ragged, honorable men who limped home with their heads held high. If they succeeded in their postwar lives, they would do so despite the hardships they had survived. If they failed, who could blame them? Although these differences can be exaggerated, the evidence suggests several conditions that led to significantly different relationships between civilians and veterans in the North and the South.

First, virtually all white men of military age had served in the Confederate Army, making it the main wartime experience for male southerners. In the North, although the percentage of men who served in the army was higher than in any other American war, a slight majority did not serve. In other words, many good, worthy men did not fight for the Union, ensuring that northerners could perceive multiple paths to fulfilling a citizen's duty.

Second, the economic explosion that made the United States the most powerful economy in the world during the Gilded Age obviously affected the sections differently. Many observers believed that anyone who could not make something of himself in the fast-paced and opportunity-rich North probably deserved to fail. But in the South, where sharecropping trapped white as well as black farmers and where the depressions of the 1870s and 1890s were particularly severe, needing help from family or communities did not necessarily bring shame to needy veterans.

Third, despite the fact that Republicans generally controlled the federal and many northern state governments, they held that power by fairly narrow margins. As a result, Democrats and Republicans alike did not hesitate to drag veterans' issues, especially federal pensions, into national politics, forcing veterans to choose between the parties and inevitably affecting the ways that Americans viewed pensions. In the South, as the one-party system established itself after Reconstruction, there was no reason to make any facet of veterans' lives into a political issue. Moreover, when the former Confederate states finally established pensions for needy veterans in the 1880s and 1890s, the amounts and number of people covered were tiny—and uncontroversial—compared to the federal pensions distributed by the U.S. government.

Because of the pension issue, the politicization of the GAR, and the occasional upsurge of interest in the large system of federal homes for disabled soldiers, Union veterans projected a much more complex set of images than did their Confederate counterparts. Southern veterans were not saddled with the complications created by national, taxpayer-financed programs; the aid that came their way was private, local, and eventually state-sponsored—sources of social welfare programs with which Americans had always been more comfortable. Union veterans were counted, individualized, remembered as people, and sometimes criticized, feared, and held in contempt. Individual Confederate veterans were rarely distinguished from this larger group of noble, painful symbols. Moreover, some issues—for example, pensions and soldiers' homes—that were vital to the lives of Union veterans and to civilians' perceptions of those veterans' lives were really nonissues for Confederates; as a result, southerners nearly disappear from parts of this book.

Finally, another thread that occasionally surfaces is the extent to which veterans matched society's expectations for them as men. According to some historians, Gilded Age males experienced a "crisis of manhood" in which the qualities of what it meant to be a man entered a time of flux and change. Emerging ideas about gender and race, the maturation of the industrial economy in the form of powerful corporations and bureaucracies, and the replacement of the geographic frontier with the more abstract and perhaps even more bruising frontiers of economic entrepreneurship and personal ambition cast men adrift in a gendered sea without a compass. Even if, as other historians suggest, the era's attitudes about manhood featured more continuity than crisis, many people nevertheless believed that such a crisis existed. Fewer chances for dramatic leadership were available; the work performed by most men shifted from straightforward, active labor in the fields or mines to more passive, less strenuous work in offices. More and more men in the classes that were the supposed victims of the crisis became doctors, lawyers, and other professionals, occupations that were lucrative but not traditionally manly. Men's responses were often conflicting—some developed an ethos of prudence, perseverance, and calm, while others modeled themselves after robber barons, adopted violent sports such as boxing and football and more cerebral sports such as golfing and baseball, took wilderness vacations and hunted game, joined a new generation of private militia companies, and joyfully marched off to war when it erupted with Spain in 1898.[36]

Issues related to masculinity had surfaced as the nation mobilized for war. Steven J. Ramold has recently suggested that men entering the Union Army encountered clashing versions of manhood. Most private soldiers came out of an American tradition of manhood that emphasized individualism and freedom, but the officers and policy makers creating the vast new armies were part of a more modern Victorian ethos of restraint and corporate goals. Moreover, the traditional American reliance on citizen-soldiers— called into service only in times of crisis, only barely controlled by their officers—ran headlong into the professionalism of the regular army, with its harsh discipline and separate legal system, and of the volunteer officers who adopted that regular army point of view. In a way, soldiers encountered a Catch-22: the extent to which they adapted to the Victorian restraint and military discipline was the extent to which they became lesser men according to antebellum standards. And the extent to which they failed to adjust to military expectations was the extent to which they failed to measure up to emerging postbellum standards of male behavior. Although states'-rights-loving Confederates were famously less "tamed" than Union soldiers, southern soldiers also found their previous notions of manhood challenged by military life.[37]

Most of the debate over whether American men faced a crisis has revolved around northern men. But military defeat, a ruined economy, and the sudden—and temporary—rise to political manhood of former slaves created a different set of challenges and opportunities for southerners' notions of manhood. They might not personally have felt their manhood threatened by the new order, but they most assuredly did not want anyone else to doubt their capacity to fulfill manly responsibilities. Some retreated to the comfortable antebellum paradigm of manhood shaped by honor, public piety, and self-control. Others sought a model that one historian calls the "masculine martial ideal." Holding up Confederate veterans as masculine archetypes, this version of manhood refigured the violence that lay just beneath the surface of prewar society as political and cultural necessities. Violent resistance to northern aggression provided a historic reference point and ensured that veterans in the South would never lose their archetypal symbolic luster. It also inspired violent insistence on protecting racial honor by unmanning freedmen through electoral aggression and by reasserting racial superiority in the reduction of African American men to savages threatening white society. Indeed, black men played a major role in establishing white manhood. As slaves, African American men had made all white men politically equal; in the post-Reconstruction era, as disfranchisement and Jim Crow metastasized, they provided a convenient if blunt definition of what "men" certainly were not. As a result, southern veterans and nonveterans alike could demonstrate and relish their manhood in the resubjugation of African Americans and shrug off any challenge to their masculinity by joining as actors or as audience in the rituals of racialized violence that ignited the South during and after the Gilded Age.[38]

Indeed, the aggressive foreign policy of the Gilded Age, the paths to war in Cuba and the Philippines, and the drive to establish an always-prepared citizen army through the National Guard embraced Civil War veterans. Most important, they served as inspirations and as models for the National Guard units that states began to organize during this time. Many of these units started off as private militia companies, but by early in the twentieth century, most states had established fairly coherent administrative structures and training. As one historian has pointed out, like Civil War veterans, National Guardsmen "explicitly linked" military service and manhood. Even if they never got into battle, offering themselves in service to their states and country fulfilled the voluntary, patriotic ideal that Civil War soldiers had so perfectly demonstrated. The connection was made real when, at veterans' encampments or National Guard gatherings, young and old soldiers drilled together or competed against one another in contests or even sham battles, providing a symbolic bridge from the bloody battlefields of the past to the possibility of future sacrifice. In the South, some Confederate veterans, still wearing their tattered uniforms, went straight into the ranks of the short-lived state militias. A number of the men who joined the burgeoning Illinois National Guard in the early 1870s were Civil War veterans, and several of the higher-ranking officers at the state level had commanded men during the conflict.[39]

Although few veterans were directly involved with the Guard, with or without their knowledge they formed part of the equation when the meaning of manhood reached the level of a crisis. The ways in which the general public perceived survivors of the war—especially those veterans who were physically or mentally disabled, who had fallen on hard economic times, or who had made their manliness an issue by demanding larger and broader pensions—were no doubt shaped by the ambiguity that came to surround manhood. As a result, the public discourse about veterans—the piteous commentary on the crippled, the nagging concerns about veteran tramps and beggars, the harsh criticism of "coffee-coolers" and "pension sharks"—can be fruitfully examined in the context of the era's ideas about men. Indeed, the conversation about manhood provided the language that helped critics articulate what was wrong with veterans. This discussion about manhood in the Gilded Age has many facets, many of which do not help explain attitudes about veterans. But several are useful in understanding those complicated perceptions.

Perhaps the most valuable concepts are those that came to be associated with males who failed to act like men. Gilded Age Americans could easily identify those character traits that inevitably contributed to a man's inability to thrive and lack of capacity to meet his responsibilities. Men and women of this era certainly did not invent these qualities, but they seem to have taken on a greater sense of urgency and to have acquired a secular tone during this crucial time in the evolution of American values. "Failure was a want of achievement where achievement measured manhood," writes E. Anthony Rotundo; "failure was a sign of poor character." Failed men's chief shortcomings included a lack of industry, or laziness; a shortage of moral fiber, or a weakness for "vice and debauchery"; and a general submission to habits that prevented men from overcoming the obstacles and bad luck that everyone encountered from time to time. All of these terms were applied to veterans at one time or another during the Gilded Age. And that public discourse gave editors and politicians the terms on which to challenge the more common stereotype of soldiers as worthy recipients of a nation's emotional and material gratitude.[40]

Ironically, even as selected veterans were held up as poor examples of manhood, the notion of "manliness and the military ideal," as Rotundo calls it, gained force throughout the period. However, with the Civil War as an increasingly distant inspiration for Gilded Age men, one did not have to actually experience war or even to want to experience war to demonstrate the courage and self-sacrifice and contempt for soft living that characterized so many modern lives. William James's "Moral Equivalent of War" suggested that hard work, discipline, and purposeful maturity could create virtual soldiers who would provide a stiff backbone for the nation. In some ways, although Americans could wax effusive in their praise of the aging Civil War veterans who marched past them in Memorial Day and Fourth of July parades, it was difficult for any veteran who did not fit the physical and moral mold of those dignified but graying old soldiers to match the idealistic version of manhood being created by James and other Americans. How could old men ravaged by disease or alcohol or battered by economic forces beyond their control compete with "virtual" veterans?[41]

At a different level, Civil War veterans—actual "heroes" whose actions had saved the Union or nobly represented the Confederacy—also could not compete with a generation of "heroes" built up by "the cult of the self-made man and the philosophy of laissez-faire," as David G. Pugh has written. Inspired by social Darwinism, these "heroes" "confiscated huge chunks of land, built great machines and factories, fixed prices via secret alliances, and formed their empires with oil, coal, and steel." Such "prophets of progress"—the Carnegies, the Rockefellers, the Morgans—were heroic simply because of their oversized success stories. They were individuals, not parts of giant armies; they were titans, not privates and corporals; they were famous for being bold, not for following orders. They exerted their excessive masculinity by creating their own rules and by celebrating the "gaining of wealth and prestige" rather than marching in step with faceless comrades in search of honor and gratitude. They viewed their businesses as armies and their markets as battlefields; they waged war, at least in their own minds, no less than the men who had been fighting at Gettysburg or the Wilderness while Carnegie and Rockefeller, both in their twenties, had started building their fortunes.[42]

Men who failed to live up to this capitalist ethos were, according to Scott A. Sandage, "born losers," either unable or unwilling to fulfill their roles in the incessant "moving forward" that shaped American ideas about success. Of course, more men failed than succeeded at getting rich, following a linear path to success, or avoiding the "stagnation that must be avoided at all costs." Inevitably, however, winners, not losers, became key cultural markers in the postwar United States. And all veterans who were observed begging on the street, lurking in a saloon, scheming for a bigger pension, or lounging idly in a soldiers' home exemplified failure, identifying themselves as the sort of men Sandage calls "misfits of capitalism." Expectations about men's personal behavior had also changed. Richard Stott's recent book on male culture shows that the drinking, gambling, and fighting that had characterized men's society in antebellum America had largely been squeezed out of the acceptable boundaries of manhood in most of the country by shortly after the Civil War. Not incidentally, some of the same qualities were applied to the least savory groups of veterans during the Gilded Age.[43]

Indeed, at the level of popular culture, Civil War veterans were trapped in a developing notion of manhood shaped by a raft of self-help books that taught eager young men how to succeed in a society characterized by both opportunity and intense competition. Even the causes for which veterans had fought, the issues that had animated prewar politics and inspired wartime enlistments, had been replaced. "Success and failure—not slavery and freedom—became the quintessential American axis," writes Sandage. One of the leading authors of Gilded Age advice books, Samuel Smiles, provided a nutshell description of what was expected of men in the subtitle to *Duty: With Illustrations of Courage, Patience, and Endurance*. Like most authors in the genre, Smiles, who also wrote books titled *Character* and *Thrift*, focused on creating long-term goals, accepting delayed gratification, and displaying courage in the face of adversity. Borrowing liberally and selectively from the lives of great men from all occupations and generations, Smiles included only a few chapters on prominent military men, but even they seemed to reflect the same qualities of perseverance and skilled management as did successful civilians. Military men's successes tended to come after their military service, although Smiles suggested that military service might even have helped poets, authors, and scientists become better men. "It may be that the obedience, drill, and discipline which are the soul of the soldier's life, possess some potent and formative influence upon the character, and develop that power of disciplined concentration which is so essential to the formation of true genius."[44]

But few other authors mention surviving combat or belonging to the closed military society as particular models for developing manly qualities. Some writers used military and battle metaphors and even illustrations of battle scenes, but only to impart color and dramatic effect. Military service was presented less as a career option or the experience of typical men and more as an example of manly accomplishment that most men would never enjoy. "The call to battle," argues one historian, "was a call for revitalization, to resist effeminacy and weakness bred by prosperity and to stave off the feared decline and fall of an overdeveloped civilization." It was a call not to actual battle but to symbolic battle against personal weakness, demoralizing passivity, socialistic labor unions, and a weak foreign policy. The meaning of Gilded Age manhood ultimately came to exclude martial abilities. If the end result of military service and combat was the loss of self-control, the adoption of poor moral habits, the decline of initiative, and the weakening of the work ethic—all characteristics perceived to plague returning soldiers in 1865 and in some instances veterans throughout the Gilded Age—then military service could hinder the development of manhood. In fact, the terror and tumult of combat, the subjection of most soldiers to orders they only partially understood, the degrading living conditions, and the bad habits and poor health that often came with military service seemed to contradict the sorts of experiences that could build up a country of men. One of the lone books to offer the Union soldier—the common soldier, rather than the generals—as a manly example was published just after the war and was written by Edwin Percy Whipple, a member of the circle of New England intellectuals led by Ralph Waldo Emerson and Nathaniel Hawthorne. Among the many qualities necessary to manhood were those demonstrated by Union soldiers, who passed through "the baptism of fire and blood" to save the Union from "the insolent domination of a perjured horde of slave-holders and libertines." But these men's martial defense of the country really represented just an extension of their patriotism and commitment, their political ideals and their reform-minded values. Military service, with its temporary setbacks, its challenges to good order and Christian ideals, simply constituted an exaggerated version of the sturdy, determined manhood expected of any northern man. In other words, serving in the military did not necessarily provide different challenges than did civilian life, just more extreme versions of the obstacles that all men had to surmount.[45]

For Gilded Age advice writers, success and manhood were virtually interchangeable and were really quite simple. "Young man," wrote H. A. Lewis in *Why Some Succeed while Others Fail*, "two ways are open before you in life. One points to degradation and want, the other, to usefulness and wealth." In the confident duality that echoed antebellum temperance reformers who illustrated good and evil with the "Tree of Life," advice writers created linear paths to success that entailed accepting responsibility, coming to deserve the trust and respect of others, and perhaps acquiring wealth. The stark simplicity of this all-or-nothing point of view did not mesh easily with the ambivalence of many veterans' lives.[46]

Although many individual veterans succeeded in their postwar lives by following just such a course, veterans as a class were not expected to be particularly successful. Indeed, it is not hard to read between the lines of the advice books—especially in the context of common stereotypes about the negative effects on a man's character of serving in the military—to see that veterans who succeeded did so despite rather than because of their military service. The notion that one either succeeds or fails, that fame and wealth come not in a flash of daring or inspiration but in a well-planned, calm campaign of steadfast competence, that only the constant application of genius and energy would lead to happiness and success suggests that demonstrating bravery and loyalty for a battle, a campaign, or even an entire war was not enough to prove one's manhood, which could really be verified only through perseverance and constancy and gradually increasing levels of success over a whole lifetime. The "lives of eminent men" that illustrated William D. Owen's *Success in Life, and How to Secure It*, featured business-men, politicians, professionals, and others who applied discipline to their lives, but this discipline was shaped by their decisions and values or by insti-tutions such as churches and universities rather than by discipline imposed by an autocratic government or especially the military.[47]

Simply put, many, perhaps most, old soldiers, did not fade tastefully away, become titans of industry, or become the kind of men described in the ad-vice books—men who, when the veterans' great-grandsons came of age, would wear gray flannel suits.

"Veteranizing"

Veterans realized that fame could be based on passing wealth or passing sensationalism rather than patriotic accomplishment, that material gain could outweigh duty fulfilled, and that the dramatically successful could overshadow the steadily obedient. Such knowledge led to an often-justified but nevertheless self-righteous attitude about wartime service. No one who had not been on a firing line; in a smoky, malodorous camp; on a bitterly cold picket outpost; in a wretched hospital—no one who had not heard the bul-lets clipping the branches above them, endured endless nights on guard, or known men whose bodies had been shredded by shrapnel—could begin to understand the meaning of being a veteran. The war became a centerpiece of veterans' lives that they could never have imagined as boys and could not imagine having missed as men. The qualities the war brought out or taught differed from civilian qualities.

A few veterans used those differences to rise in the world, waving "bloody shirts" to win votes and influence and to improve their lives. An exceedingly cynical version of such a man was Cyrus Trask, the father of one of the main characters in John Steinbeck's *East of Eden*. Cyrus spends a few months in the Union Army and half an hour on a battlefield, where a bullet shatters his leg. He comes home with one leg and a case of venereal disease that eventually kills his wife. He begins to exaggerate the number of battles in which he has fought, to write letters to soldiers' papers and magazines, and to become a self-taught "expert" in military affairs. He becomes active in the GAR and eventually accepts a sinecure as a general secretary in the organization, traveling the country and advising the secretary of war and president on military matters. "I wonder if you know how much influence I really have," he brags to his son, Adam, who holds his father in quiet contempt. "I can throw the Grand Army at any candidate like a sock. . . . I can get senators defeated and I can pick appointments like apples. I can make men and I can destroy men."[48]

Of course, most veterans had neither the inclination nor the cynicism to conduct themselves in such a way. Yet on a smaller scale, they too could become professional veterans, drawn by failures or limitations in other parts of their lives to focus more on the past than the present. Writer Sherwood Anderson's father, Irwin, had served in the Union Army and was enthusiastic in his "veteranizing," which included marching in GAR parades and telling usually fictional accounts of his own war service. In his memoirs, Anderson offered an unsparing and impatient portrait of this irresponsible father and irrepressible comrade. Yet the younger Anderson also wrote with some empathy of Irwin's realization that after leaving the army and starting a family, "he would never be a hero again" and that "all the rest of his life" would never measure up to those few years of his youth. The war, "that universal, passionate, death-spitting thing," would have to last a lifetime, and given the elder Anderson's profound inability to make a consistent living, that experience was the only thing elevating him above a semiemployed laborer.[49]

Despite his best efforts, Irwin Anderson could not force his view of himself into a reality. And in a sense, all veterans lost control of their legacies. They certainly remained relevant to most Americans during the two generations following the war, but that relevance applied to only a small portion of veterans' lives. And the extent to which they were remembered solely for what they did for a few years in their youth was the extent to which they became both more and less than real men.

Before the Civil War, most Americans did not know anyone who had served in the military, let alone in deadly combat. Only .2 percent of the U.S. population had served in the Mexican-American War or the War of 1812. But after Appomattox, virtually everyone had a relative or neighbor or friend who had served in the Union or Confederate army. Union veterans alone made up just under 6 percent of the population in 1865; twenty-five years later, they remained 2 percent of the population. And although Revolutionary War veterans had been honored, especially during the fiftieth anniversary of the Declaration of Independence, the decentralized and disjointed nature of military service during that war reduced the chances that anyone would be recognized mainly for his service to the new country.[50]

But being aware of Civil War veterans differed from understanding them. And doing so became more difficult as veterans grew older and began to withdraw from the larger community. "The 'old soldier' slowly eliminates himself from the mass," Charles Dudley Warner wrote in 1893, "and begins to take, and to make us take, a romantic view of his career. There was one event in his life, and his personality in it looms larger and larger as he recedes from it." In addition to their physical separation in veterans' organizations, soldiers' homes, and the pension system, veterans emotionally separated themselves from the rest of society, thus creating a specific set of images. "The past centres about him and his great achievement, and the whole of life is seen in the light of it." Although members of the veteran's generation have moved on, and although the current generation "looks upon the hero as an illustration in the story of the war, which it reads like history," the war remained very much alive and living in the veteran's memory and perceptions. Although Warner had been of military age during the war, he had worked instead as a Hartford newspaperman. Perhaps because he could have but did not serve, Warner clearly perceived the tension between veterans and nonveterans in Gilded Age America that lies at the center of this book.[51]

The central questions that explore that tension are simple: How did white veterans of the Union and Confederate armies reinsert themselves into civilian life? How did Americans perceive veterans—not as somewhat abstract heroes and representations of patriotic values but as men? Gilded Age Americans witnessed many versions of veterans and developed many ways of thinking about them. *Sing Not War* considers the old soldiers beyond the GAR and UCV halls and the holiday parades and sentimental songs, examining the public expectations of Civil War veterans and the ways in which veterans met or failed to meet those expectations. The last third of the nineteenth century was the first era in which veterans comprised a visible, assertive cohort in American culture. Exploring the ways in which veterans and the idea of veterans were most present in American life reveals that "veteran" is not a single concept but a social construction with multiple meanings and uses.

Sing Not War

The chapter titles for this book are borrowed from Walt Whitman's poem "A Carol of Harvest, for 1867," which was published in the *New York Galaxy* in September 1867. Whitman revised and renamed the poem "The Return of the Heroes" for the 1881–82 version of *Leaves of Grass*. The poem begins and ends with Whitmanesque celebrations of America's bounty—"Fecund America! Today . . . Thou grown'st with riches"—but a number of stanzas urge the "returning heroes" to leave war behind, to immerse themselves in hard work, to plow and plant and harvest so that they create rather than destroy. Yet Whitman recognized that not all of the men would march easily or successfully from the battlefield to wheat or cotton fields. Although the title change from celebrating America's capacity to absorb the wages of war to commemorating the returning soldiers might be part of the sentimentalization of Civil War soldiers that characterized the 1880s and 1890s, Whitman recognized the irony in the fact that many of those "heroes" would hardly have heroic lives.[52]

> When last I sang, sad was my voice;
> Sad were the shows around me, with deafening noises of hatred,
>   and smoke of conflict;
> In the midst of the armies, the Heroes, I stood,
> Or pass'd with slow step through the wounded and dying.
>
> But now I sing not War,
> Nor the measur'd march of soldiers, nor the tents of camps,
> Nor the regiments hastily coming up, deploying in line of battle.
>
> No more the dead and wounded;
> No more the sad, unnatural shows of War.
> .   .   .   .
> For an army heaves in sight—O another gathering army!
> Swarming, trailing on the rear—O you dread, accruing army!
> O you regiments so piteous, with your mortal diarrhoea! with your
>   fever!
> O my land's maimed darlings! with the plenteous bloody bandage
>   and the crutch!
> Lo! your pallid army follow'd!
> .   .   .   .

I saw the return of the Heroes;
(Yet the heroes never surpass'd, shall never return;
Them, that day, I saw not.)
. . . .

I saw the processions of armies,
Streaming northward, their work done, they paused awhile in
    clusters of mighty camps.

No holiday soldiers!—youthful, yet veterans;
Worn, swart, handsome, strong, of the stock of homestead and
    workshop,
Harden'd of many a long campaign and sweaty march,
Inured on many a hard-fought, bloody field.
. . . .

A pause—the armies wait;
A million flush'd, embattled conquerors wait;
The world, too, waits—then, soft as breaking night, and sure as dawn,
They melt—they disappear.
. . . .

Melt, melt away, ye armies! disperse, ye blue-clad soldiers!
Resolve ye back again—give up, for good, your deadly arms;
Other the arms, the fields henceforth for you, or South or North, or
    East or West,
With saner wars—sweet wars—life-giving wars.
. . . .

Toil on, Heroes! harvest the products!
Not alone on those warlike fields, the Mother of All,
With dilated form and lambent eyes, watch'd you.

Toil on, Heroes! toil well! Handle the weapons well!
The Mother of All—yet here, as ever, she watches you.

chapter one **Melt Away Ye Armies**

ENDINGS AND BEGINNINGS

The vagaries of nineteenth-century travel claimed the last victims of the Civil War. The explosion of the Mississippi riverboat *Sultana* near Memphis in April 1865 killed perhaps seventeen hundred returning Union veterans, most of them survivors of Confederate prison camps. Among the fourteen dead after an explosion in the Danville, Virginia, arsenal were a number of surrendered Confederate soldiers who, like the other victims, had entered the building after it was abandoned by its guards; a boy playing with a loaded pistol set off the gunpowder scattered on the floor.[1]

But smaller tragedies occurred throughout the diasporas of the Union and Confederate armies. Railroad accidents killed two members of the 103rd Ohio and maimed two more as well as a Wisconsin artilleryman and several members of the 51st Tennessee. A conscript in the 17th Maine collapsed and died during the regiment's last formal review near Washington, D.C., while the family of a Minnesota soldier found him dead on the steamer carrying his regiment back to St. Paul. A deceased cavalryman was discovered on a St. Louis street in June 1865; two months later, another veteran was found drowned in the Missouri River.[2]

These anecdotes drew notice for their sad ironies, but most men managed to survive demobilization. Terms of enlistment varied widely, and the volume of paperwork and logistics required to muster out and arrange transport for hundreds of thousands of men from battlefields and garrisons throughout the South to homes throughout the North meant that some regiments had to wait longer than others to get out of uniform and back home. Indeed, although the Grand Review in Washington, D.C., seemed like the end of the war for the participating soldiers, many remained in the army for weeks or even months after the fighting stopped. Union soldiers, who collected an average of about $250 in back pay and bounties when they were discharged, faced a gauntlet of con artists and thieves in major eastern cities. In St. Louis and elsewhere, "runners" and "hawkers" offered over-priced railway tickets and tracked recently discharged soldiers still wearing their uniforms and sought to convince them to patronize "certain clothing stores, where they have to pay exorbitant prices." If a booklet published by the U.S. Sanitary Commission (USSC) can be believed, a flourishing busi-ness of bilking and robbing soldiers sprang up in the towns and cities where men received their discharges. "The camps, and especially the cities, railway stations, cars and boats are full of *pretended friends* of soldiers, and there are hundreds of soldiers robbed every week by these imposters." The pamphlet urged soldiers to ignore the "hawkers" and simply to continue to wear their uniforms until arriving among friends; to avoid unsavory restaurants and saloons and "all liquor shops" (the USSC and other reputable organizations offered plenty of free food and beverages), where soldiers were "very often" drugged and robbed; never to turn their money or baggage over to comrades or strangers, trusting instead USSC agents; and to beware of men offering to take servicemen to claim agents unauthorized to intervene with the govern-ment on behalf of soldiers.[3]

Such sincere condescension permeated the advice soldiers received as they transitioned from military to civilian life. Indeed, in the eyes of many northerners, the saviors of the Union, once discharged, became helpless innocents, dependent on the help and advice of others as they began to re-negotiate civilian life. A list of some of the services provided by the USSC reflects this belief. In addition to medical care for wounded soldiers and temporary housing for soldiers in transit, the commission offered to help men process the paperwork for their discharges; collect the pay and boun-ties owed to discharged soldiers "too feeble, or too utterly disabled" to do so themselves; to provide transportation home for men who lacked the means to pay; to see that men were "not robbed or imposed upon by sharpers" when buying railroad tickets; to encourage men immediately to leave the cities in which they were discharged and paid off, before they were "induced by evil companions to remain behind"; to "rescue" those who succumbed to the temptations of the city and "see them started with through-tickets to their own towns"; and to help men who "are deficient in cleanliness and clothes" make themselves presentable before departing for home. In fact, most soldiers apparently ignored the USSC's presence as they received their discharges and headed home, although a few received meals and a chance to clean up at what seemed to be USSC facilities. But the attitudes expressed in the booklet would continue into the postwar period.[4]

An idealistic version of a veteran returning from war. *Home Again*, painting by Trevor McClurg, lithograph by Fabronius (Endicott, 1866). Prints and Photographs Division, Library of Congress.

If few soldiers remarked on predators, many veterans described in some detail their journeys home. The 6th Wisconsin Battery's trip was in some ways idyllic. A "special" train, made up primarily of cattle cars, carried the unit through the Midwest. Children gathered outside country schoolhouses to watch as the soldiers rattled through the Indiana countryside. "White handkerchiefs are waved enthusiastically from every house and hamlet, stars and stripes were thrown out triumphantly to the breeze as we passed along, each demonstration drawing forth ringing response from the joyous soldier boys." At one town, "an entire school of young ladies turned out to welcome" the men, with the schoolhouse draped with a huge flag. Residents of another town had erected an arch over the tracks that read "Welcome Home, Brave Soldiers."[5]

At the other end of the spectrum was the excruciating passage of the 17th Maine. After participating in the Grand Review, the men settled into camp for several days. They took part in a spontaneous nighttime review of the enlisted men of V Corps, who carried lighted candles stuck into rifle barrels. After mustering out on June 3, the men marched together one last time to the Baltimore Depot in Washington, D.C. There they began a five-day odyssey during which they marched across town to change trains four times and steamers twice; rode in coal cars and cattle cars and on the windy, wet deck of a tiny steamer; barely slept but managed to find liquor at Castle Garden in New York; threatened a ship captain at bayonet point when he tried to force them off the vessel before they received orders from their commander; and ate soggy hardtack and rancid meat—but also a welcome lunch of fresh bread, ham, cheese, coffee, and cake at the Cooper Shop Refreshment Saloon in Philadelphia. When the regiment finally arrived in Portland, they were feasted, welcomed, and marched to city hall, where they bedded down for the night on a floor one veteran called "too filthy for a dog to lie on." Similar conditions welcomed the 20th Illinois, which had marched to the sea with Sherman, when the men reached Chicago, where they were assigned to barracks at Camp Douglas, an infamous prison. "The boys did not stay at the camp much for it was a filthy place," wrote one veteran. Instead, the men "found accommodations in the different boarding houses in the locality, that our stay might be as agreeable as possible, and as some of them would say, to become accustomed to living in a house again."[6]

With so many units discharged as fast as overworked clerks and paymasters could sign the papers, some homecomings did not go as planned. In St. Paul, Minnesota, state and local officials were caught off guard by the sudden arrival late in May of released prisoners and convalescing hospital patients, weeks before regiments in the field began to reach home. Indeed, a minor scandal arose when members of the 9th Minnesota, just out of a Confederate prison, were found to have slept all night on the street after a supper of stale bread scavenged from a local bakery. A "soldiers' home" with kitchen and dormitory was quickly organized for returning men. The first full units to make it to St. Paul arrived quietly via steamer on June 18; no crowds greeted them, although the dock was crowded with opportunistic peddlers trying to sell the recently paid soldiers cheap clothes. Two hundred men of the 4th Minnesota came to town in civilian clothes and immediately went to their homes, uncheered and virtually unnoticed by St. Paul residents. Embarrassed by these desultory greetings, the governor, mayor, and commander of the District of Minnesota formed themselves into a reception committee and established a process for welcoming returning regiments that included telegraphs from the passenger lines carrying the soldiers, a standing military band, a brief parade through triumphal arches boasting each regiment's notable battles, welcoming speeches from local politicians and a response from the unit's commanding officer, and a meal served in the State Capitol. The unit subsequently would reboard its steamer and finish the short last leg of the journey to Fort Snelling, where the men would finally become civilians again. Between early July and early October, virtually all of Minnesota's volunteer regiments and artillery batteries enjoyed this brief but satisfying ritual.[7]

The city fathers of Cleveland established a similar organization that sent agents to all of the major railroad intersections with instructions to telegraph when Ohio regiments passed through. Nevertheless, the 98th Ohio slipped through the picket line and arrived before adequate plans could be made for a reception. The ladies of the Soldiers' Aid Society scrambled to put out a lunch and provide baths and then prepared "a bountiful cooked supper."[8]

The celebrations continued through the summer and into the early fall. Maine regiments paraded through the streets of Bangor on July 4, carrying banners bearing the names of the battles in which the men had fought. A "Festival of Peace" in Philadelphia honoring seven hundred veterans of the 28th and 29th Pennsylvania Regiments featured tableaux of union, disunion, war, and peace, with thirty-six "ladies" representing the states of the Union, now whole again. Musicians from several largely German New York regiments held a "drummers' day" late in August. More than a hundred "veteran" drummers "beat . . . the air with all sorts of concussion" throughout the afternoon. The celebration also featured speeches in English and German by the regiments' officers, shooting contests, dancing, a brass band, and endless toasts.[9]

The enthusiasm inevitably wilted, however. By the time the surviving members Company F, 57th Massachusetts, arrived in their hometown of Fitchburg, the civilian population had tired of the big, formal receptions that had greeted regiments mustered out earlier in the summer. Members of Company F were met by family and friends; no speeches were recorded as they broke ranks for the first time in a year and a half. Of the thirty-eight men who came home, nine had been wounded and six had been prisoners of war, but five had never fired their guns in battle.[10]

The 61st Illinois was not mustered out until September 1865, and although the regiment as a whole was well received during its trip north, a young lieutenant arrived in his hometown—a village with a handful of businesses and perhaps a dozen homes—at about sundown. He walked up the street, sheathed sword resting on his shoulder, "feeling happy and proud."

He looked around as he walked, "hoping to see some old friend," but roused only mild curiosity from a man peering from the door of the general store and from a "big dog" who barked "loudly and persistently." Earlier regiments had been received with parades and triumphal arches, bands and cheers, but the 61st was among the last to return home, and "the discharged soldiers were now numerous and common, and no longer a novelty." He was not bothered by the lack of fanfare, although he admitted that "I would have felt better to have met at least one person as I passed through the little village who would have given me a hearty hand-shake, and said he was glad to see me home, safe from the war." He walked the two miles to his parents' farm; they were expecting him and so were not surprised: "There was no 'scene' when we met, nor any effusive display, but we all had a feeling of profound contentment and satisfaction which was too deep to be expressed by mere words." The next day, he put on some of his father's work clothes and helped him shock corn.[11]

A Hazardous, Trying Time

Returning Confederates enjoyed few parades, although some were rather surprised to be formally welcomed home by their communities. A group of musicians returning to Memphis played "Dixie" from the deck of their riverboat as it approached the landing; one of them recalled "several thousand" civilians gathered along the bluff to witness their arrival. As members of the 17th Tennessee approached Winchester after surrendering at Appomattox, "great crowds met us as we neared home and welcomed us back though defeated." But most came home anonymously and quietly.[12]

In addition to coping with whatever feelings they experienced after being surrendered by their commanding generals, Confederates had to maneuver through a region in chaos. Many, especially those who trudged through war-ravaged Virginia or along the paths of Sherman's marches through Georgia and the Carolinas or recent cavalry raids in Alabama, found confirmation of the rumors they had heard about the Union Army's destruction of civilian property. Old camps and garrisons were strewn with the debris of war and polluted by the stench of dead horses.[13]

A sense of the state of the South through which Confederates passed can be gleaned from the journal kept by Confederate senator Williamson S. Oldham as he traveled with a small entourage from Richmond, Virginia, to Texas in April and May. He reported abandoned towns and Confederate offices and garrisons; suspicious planters, farmers, and ferry operators; demoralized civilians who refused to take Confederate money or to meet the usual standards of southern hospitality; and Confederate soldiers behaving badly. He heard of Texas soldiers who rather than waiting for formal discharges and paroles had simply left their units in Louisiana and headed home, many with their guns and remaining equipment. Along the way, they stole Confederate property, especially cotton, forced planters to transport it to river landings, and sold it to Yankee speculators. The U.S. currency they received, one of them told Oldham, would replace their now worthless Confederate money and finance their trip home. Thousands of Confederate deserters had come out of the bush when they learned of the surrender; they, too, preyed on civilians and Confederates alike. The Texan was chagrined to witness the "disorder, confusion, and anarchy [that] prevailed . . . throughout Texas," where troops had sacked supply depots. Oldham suspected that most of the culprits were deserters, stragglers, "detailed men," and other men who had never been soldiers; in Huntsville, Alabama, a motley mob trying to break into the state penitentiary was prevented from doing so by a unit of returned veterans. "The worst men in the army had banded themselves together in some instances, and in others, acting singly, were roaming through the country, stealing and robbing."[14]

Considering the chaos that Oldham described, some Confederate soldiers—especially those from southeastern states who surrendered in Virginia, North Carolina, or Alabama and those Texans and Louisianans serving west of the Mississippi—were fortunate to have shorter trips home than Yankees. Moreover, since the Confederate armies no longer existed, southerners could leave sooner, and most arrived home long before their northern counterparts. A group of Tennessee Confederates frequently passed companies of bluecoats who would shout out, "Where are you going boys?" When the Rebels replied "Home," the Yankees would shout back, "I would to God we were going there to[o]." The fraternization that had sometimes characterized relationships between enemy soldiers during the war also appeared during the first few weeks of peace. When the federal officers appointed to administer them the oath of allegiance came to the camp of the 9th Tennessee, they brought whiskey. "We became so intoxicated," one Confederate remembered, "that we ran home without taking the oath." Another Confederate recalled that he and his traveling companions were delayed for a day or two in Chattanooga while awaiting transportation. They "put up" at the city's Soldiers' Home, with "'Yank' and 'Confed' eating out of the same platter, and cracking jokes at each other; as though they had never met in many a mortal combat."[15]

But those fraternal moments only briefly obscured the challenges facing Confederates discharged far from home. The curt description offered by Edward Silas Doe no doubt fit the experiences of many returning Confederates: "It was a hazardous trying time when I think of it now I shuder." Benjamin Rogers's trip from a Virginia hospital to Wilson County, Tennessee, took more than six weeks, during which the crutch-slowed veteran walked, hitched a ride with an African American driving an ox team, rode on a salt train, spent a couple of days in a Chattanooga prison, caught a freight train, and finally took a buggy for the last few miles of the journey. At one point, he spent four weeks under the care of a woman named Alice Preston, who "kept me like a mother" and after whom Rogers named his firstborn daughter.[16]

Returning prisoners of war had the longest trips to make and probably had the widest set of experiences, partly because of their unique situation, partly because of the distance they had to travel, and partly because of the varying responses to them in the northern communities through which they passed. After John Benton Allen's release from Fort Delaware, he and a number of comrades were taken through Philadelphia, "where we received good treatment by the old soldiers & citizens." Similar experiences greeted them as they journeyed through Ohio, Indiana, and Kentucky to their homes in Tennessee. A prisoner at Johnson Island received a loan of twenty dollars from a Union officer prior to his departure; he may have been a Mason, because he also "made himself known," he recalled, to a gentlemen in Cincinnati, who spent ten minutes "cussing" Jefferson Davis before giving the former prisoner five dollars. Another Johnson's Island inmate made enough money selling abandoned clothes and blankets on the streets of Cleveland to get most of the way home. George W. Gosnell "walked and hoboed trains" for more than two weeks to travel from an Indiana prison to his Greer County, Tennessee, home, while Sam A. Grubb traveled from Point Lookout to Nashville but then "stole my way home" from there.[17]

Confederate Manhood

Among the flotsam and jetsam clogging the roads in the days after the Confederate surrenders were the "odd voyagers" described by Stephen Vincent Benét in *John Brown's Body*:

> Disbanded soldiers, tramping toward the West
> In faded army blouses, singing strange songs,

Heroes and chicken thieves, true men and liars,
Some with old wounds that galled them in the rains
And some who sold the wounds they never had
Seven times over in each new saloon.[18]

The motley Confederate armies turned into even more motley returning veterans whose stories of journeys home rivaled Benét's poetic version.
One of the best sources for understanding the conditions faced by Confederate veterans immediately after the war came out of the efforts by Dr. Gus
Dyer, the Tennessee state archivist, to capture those stories. Between 1914
and 1922, 1,650 Civil War veterans—mostly men who had served in Confederate units from Tennessee—completed two different but very similar versions of a survey prepared by Dyer and his successor, John Trotwood Moore.
The forty or so questions dealt mainly with prewar economic and wartime
military issues, but veterans were also urged to "tell something of your trip
home," to relate the work they took up after returning home, and to "give a
sketch of your life since the close of the Civil War." Although one veteran
warned that "the time has passed to get correct information for history" and
admitted, "I have forgotten a great deal my self," the old soldiers' answers
provide fascinating detail about the immediate postwar experiences of Confederate—and a few Union—veterans.[19]

Among the insights that can be gleaned from the questionnaires is the
extent to which Confederate veterans were determined to retain their dignity and manhood in the face of defeat and hardship. E. Anthony Rotundo
has suggested that the way a man dealt with failure was one measure of his
manhood. For Civil War veterans, "failure" had multiple meanings, sometimes unrelated to actual defeat on the battlefield, and efforts to overcome
any of these forms of defeat show a few of the ways in which the aftermath
of war intersected with constructions of manhood.[20]

Some Confederate veterans maintained their sense of themselves as
men by traveling with their companies or even regiments for at least part
of the trip home. Entire units of some of the western armies marched off
en masse, some with field guns and most with their small arms. As they
marched home, many maintained military discipline, even to the extent of
following the familiar bugle calls. In the journal he kept and later published
in several issues of the *Confederate Veteran*, B. L. Ridley described the extreme cohesion of his Tennessee cavalry unit on its march home from North
Carolina. Several officers maintained the command structure, and the group
sent scouts and foragers in advance of the main body. Deciding not to chal-

lenge the bushwhackers in East Tennessee, they detoured through north-western South Carolina and Georgia. Covering up to twenty-five miles a day, they nevertheless had time to visit relatives, call on ladies, and visit historic sites such as King's Mountain, scene of a famous Revolutionary War battle. Although they saw hundreds of Confederates—the road was "jammed with soldiers," towns were "full of soldiers"—the unit went two weeks without seeing a Yankee. The first northerners the men encountered were a squad of twelve assigned to take over a commissary store near Abbeville; outnum-bered and perhaps a little lost, they "looked scared." After a journey of nearly a month, the men began to break up in northwestern Georgia. They tarried "to drive off the storm cloud of defeat" in a village near Macon, where they flirted with girls, had plenty to eat, and enjoyed tasting the local applejack. A year after arriving home, Ridley received a kindly letter from his old com-manding general, who hoped "that you are making the best possible use of your time and opportunities. You have passed creditably through the scenes of the great struggle for constitutional liberty, and I hope will be prepared to pass with distinction through the still more stirring scenes which are be-fore you."[21]

Most discharged Confederates could not rely on such gratifying solidarity, and many had to run the gauntlet of lawless bands of deserters and outlaws operating in the Appalachians, Union troops guarding the mountain passes and river crossings into Tennessee, and hostile Unionists and returning Yankee soldiers living in the eastern part of the state. Jesse Shelton called his passage through mountains "infested with thieves and Bushwhackers" the "lonesomest trip of my life." Reports of Unionist retaliation against re-turning Confederates began just after the war and continued for several months. The worst violence occurred in East Tennessee, where dozens of Rebel privates, officers, and politicians were killed or beaten; hundreds of Confederates left the state at least temporarily. Some of the violence was perpetrated by Union veterans returning to Tennessee, one of whom de-clared that "Union men and Rebels cannot live together." Vigilante bands and criminal gangs alike preyed on returning Confederates and their fami-lies. Hours after a Confederate cavalryman was arrested for avenging his murdered father by gunning down his Unionist killer in Knoxville, a lynch mob hanged the former rebel.[22]

Although the men who formally surrendered at Appomattox, Virginia, or Durham Station, North Carolina, had been allowed to retain their horses and sidearms, Union commanders in Tennessee apparently refused to accept those terms, frequently requiring former Confederates entering the state to

give up their horses and guns and sometimes forcing them to remove buttons and military insignia from their uniforms. A number of former Rebels
reported having to surrender their weapons and horses at Strawberry Plains,
a hamlet near Knoxville, where a Union garrison protected a strategic railroad bridge over the Hosten River. Such treatment seemed like salt ground
into the wound of defeat. "Our terms were ignored," one veteran remembered years later, "we were insulted until we resented it, and were strip[p]
ed of every thing, then sent to Nashville on stock cars." Even worse was the
possibility of being deprived of their property by the African American soldiers garrisoning various towns and passes in Tennessee. George Donnell of
the 4th Tennessee had a "very pleasant trip home" until he reached Chattanooga, where a company "of negroes took my horse from me, and talked
very rough and commanding to us." Another group of Confederates entering Tennessee encountered a brigade of negro troops who heckled the defeated men with "their hatefull lingo 'hello Reb, you had to give it up, you
look hungry, come up and get some coffee, we know you haven't had any. . . .
Ha' Ha' Ha.'" Another black soldier ridiculed surrendered Confederates as
"Jef. Davis shin plaster. We had to endure it."[23]

Dishonor could come in a variety of guises. After surrendering in North
Carolina with the rest of the 16th Tennessee, J. B. King eventually made it to
his home in East Tennessee. He and his companions encountered a mixed
reception; some of the Unionists they had known "spoke to us kindly but
others cocked their hats up on the side of their heads and swore at us." Later,
a Captain Collins and his company of Tennessee Yankees rode up. Collins
"cocked his hat on one side and didn't speak to us," then led his men in singing "Rye Straw," a scatological ditty apparently meant to insult the Confederates. Although King did not record the lyrics, one version has survived:

> Dog shit a rye straw, dog shit a needle,
> Dog shit a little boy playing on a fiddle.
> Dog shit a rye straw, dog shit a minnow,
> Dog shit a catfish big enough for dinner.
> Dog shit a rye straw, dog shit a fiddle bow,
> Dog shit a little boy working with a grubbing hoe.[24]

It is no wonder, then, that one mark of honor for returning Rebels was to
deprive the Yankees of the pleasure of pouring scorn over defeat. One veteran bragged that he and ten comrades ignored orders by Union troops in
Chattanooga to turn over their horses, while three hundred members of the
4th Tennessee Cavalry, led by their major, swam across the Tennessee River

at night rather than give up their horses and arms. A battle-hardened trio from the 18th Tennessee surrendered in Alabama. Confronted by a band of "bushwhackers . . . robbers, deserters from both armies" as they crossed the Sand Mountains, they calmly displayed their six-shooters and said that "we were Confederates and if they were not, we were ready for them." The ex-soldiers were not bothered again.[25]

A similar confrontation developed when a large group from the 5th Tennessee Cavalry, apparently led by their commander, Colonel George W. McKenzie, traveled together from Durham Station to their homes in Rhea County. In the mountains of North Carolina, they encountered the infamous Colonel George W. Kirk and his force of perhaps three hundred mounted partisans, most of whom, like their commander, apparently had deserted from the Confederate Army and had terrorized civilians in the area. Kirk and his men demanded that the men from the 5th give up their guns and mounts. McKenzie called forward his fourteen remaining officers, the only men of the 5th with pistols, and ordered Kirk "to open the ranks and let us pass or somebody would be killed." A path was opened "through his robbing and murderous gang," and the regiment's survivors returned home safely. When yet another large band of Tennesseans got through the Blue Ridge unopposed by the "cowardly" guerrillas they had expected to meet, they paused at Asheville, North Carolina, broke out their flags, and for perhaps the last time "made the welkin ring" with the Rebel yell.[26]

Although many Confederates who spent days or weeks on the road no doubt appreciated their adventures—one veteran rather enigmatically wrote, "I seen wonders"—many were simply relieved that their wars were over. The memory of that relief led Solomon Brantley, who had served with Nathan Bedford Forrest, to write that his trip home was "a jolly good time wasent scared at all. Dident have to do picket duty or shoot at Yankees." Another Rebel who had been a farm laborer before the war relished the thirty-two dollars he had to spend, "more money than we had at one time in the last 4 years," and had "a pretty good time on our trip home."[27]

And yet a few were tormented by their personal and collective losses. A young officer in the Army of Northern Virginia visited relatives in Mississippi rather than return to the Old Dominion during the summer of 1865. "The war and its objects, its causes, & the causes of its failure, are not subjects of thought with me as are other things," he wrote in his diary a few months after Appomattox, "but are become thought itself, parts of my mind, burned into my heart as with a branding iron."[28]

Thankful Hearts

A Missouri Confederate recalled that once home, "with thankful heart and joyous greeting the soldier stood once more in his old home, and all those bright faces were around him." Reality sometimes was just that simple for returning veterans on both sides. Lucullus Atkins was gratified that his dog recognized him after four years' absence, and when two St. Louis brothers arrived home early on a Sunday morning in June 1865, their grateful and relieved parents found new clothes for them to wear and triumphantly marched them to church to show them off to the Unionist-dominated congregation. Other receptions were a little more complicated. Richard Abernathy arrived the day before his own funeral; he had been in a Confederate hospital for seven months before his discharge, and his mother had been mistakenly told of his death. A Tennessean returned home to find his entire family quarantined with smallpox and was forced to sleep for a week under a shade tree, although he could talk to his mother from a distance.[29]

As a consequence of time and hard living and the fact that many soldiers had grown from teenagers to adults while away, some soldiers' families did not recognize them. David Holt made the long journey from Virginia to his home near Woodville, Mississippi, arriving at his parents' house after dark on a warm spring night. Undetected, Holt peered through the open front door at a scene straight out of a popular wartime Currier and Ives print of a soldier's dream: "There sat my father, beside the table, with a Bible in his hand." His mother and nieces and nephews were "cuddling and cooing around," while his sisters were "busy with domestic work." After he knocked on the door, one of his sisters glanced toward him and remarked casually to her father, "There is a soldier at the door." The father, too, did not recognize his son. When Holt announced that he was a Confederate soldier and that he needed a room for the night, his father replied proudly, "I have sons in the Confederate service and have never turned a soldier away from my door." He invited the young man into the house and was about to introduce the "stranger," but "it was too much," Holt wrote many years later, "this affair of being introduced by my own father to my own mother, and so I laughed." One of the sisters cried "Davie!" and he was quickly "smothered in embraces of love," while the confused younger children cried. The family celebrated his safe arrival by reading the 103rd Psalm and praying together for the first time in years. "Thus I came home," Holt concluded.[30]

City homecomings differed from country homecomings. Savannah, observed journalist Whitelaw Reid during his tour of the South immediately after the war, "was full of returning soldiers." Many grizzled soldiers—especially those missing limbs—were surrounded by "a bevy of . . . fair friends," and it was "very pretty . . . to see the warmth of their welcome home; to watch little children clinging to the knees of papas they had almost forgotten; to observe wives promenading proudly with husbands they had not seen for years; to notice the delighted gathering of family groups." A chair was set up in the piazza and was occupied "by a crippled soldier, home from the wars, with only his wounds and his glory for his pay." In Savannah, at least, former Confederates were unlikely to wear their old uniforms and seemed to be making a concerted effort to show respect to occupying Union soldiers, including a drunken sergeant who made a display of cutting the buttons off the uniform of a gray-haired Confederate brigadier, "to bring no severer punishment upon the city than it had already received." A few weeks later, Reid witnessed soldiers crowding into the city blocks near the provost marshal's office on Carondelet Street in New Orleans. "It was a jolly, hand-shaking, noisy, chattering crowd," as men spotted old friends and the many women mingling with the soldiers found brothers or husbands.[31]

Another Yankee journalist, John Richard Dennett, witnessed similar scenes but took away somewhat different impressions. Traveling south in July 1865 in a train car still painted with Confederate flags and with a one-armed Rebel selling cigars, he passed through Lynchburg, Virginia, where he saw large numbers of "able-bodied" men "lounging in the streets and in the bar-rooms" and "listlessly sitting about the railway stations." Throughout rural Virginia, in fact, virtually no white men were at work. Postwar ennui had settled over returning Confederates. "At the store or tavern of every village just such a group of idlers is sure to be found," chewing tobacco and drinking the apple brandy made in stills on almost every farm. Most were wearing their faded gray Confederate uniforms, which were "so very common as to seem almost the universal male dress."[32]

Although Reid saw no evidence that the "warmth" of the welcomes accorded Confederate veterans was in any way "tempered by contempt for their lack of success," defeat burdened some southern homecomings. Family and friends were glad that the men had safely reached home, but many, at least for a moment, would have agreed with ardent Rebel Emma LeConte when she wrote in her diary that the return of her cousins was "pleasant" but "more sad than glad. We would have waited many years if only we could have received them back triumphant." She spent several lines mourning the homecoming that was not to be, of soldiers "exulting and victorious" returning to loved ones who had been sustained during the hard times of war by anticipation of that "day of wildest joy." A Georgian described what must have been a heartbreaking welcome from his father, who, "crushed at our defeat . . . asked if Lee and Johnson had really surrendered." When the son confirmed the news, the old man "said no more." Other soldiers, too, must have encountered similar disappointment and bitterness.[33]

In addition to projecting emotions onto veterans, family members studied returnees for evidence of physical or emotional changes. A Louisiana girl was only briefly fooled by the appearance of a strange soldier; he tried to hide his face while speaking from the other side of his horse, but she quickly saw through his queries about the family. Her brother had been gone only nine months, but the nineteen-year-old had "changed very much" during that time. He "had quite a visible mustache, was much taller, more sun burned and more slender." He had changed in other ways, too. One of the themes of their young lives had been their mother's outbursts of temper and physical abuse. The returned brother had learned "some sort of independence in the army." He disciplined his younger brothers and sisters when they misbehaved with the tutor and "seemed to fear Ma much less than before." He had also become more private, having "outgrown saying his prayers with us."[34]

When twenty-three-year-old Lieutenant Calhoun Clemson, one of John C. Calhoun's grandsons, returned to his home after nearly two years in the Union prison camp at Johnson's Island, his sister, Floride, found him unchanged "in character" but "graver." He had also become "very profane" and "roughened in his every day manners." The "loss of hope" while in prison had been his most trying experience; Floride believed the "two white hairs" she found on his otherwise brown head to be hints of his "sufferings."[35]

Sometimes men had changed for the better. A hard-pressed Georgia woman discovered that her returned brother was now "worth something . . . very sweet and lovely" and manly. He said he had "learned in this war what he might never have learnt out of it, to shift for himself, & not to dread going out into the world with nothing." His sister was delighted: "I feel as tho' we may now have a strong and willing arm to lean on."[36]

When Govan Williams returned to his Louisiana family, his daughter recalled, "he looked as if he would never laugh again." He "couldn't stay in one place but a little while," and the family was on the road to a new home within months. His mood brightened when they encountered a fellow traveler one night. The stranger called out, "Where've you been and where are you going?" Williams replied, "I'm just back from hell and I'm going to do the best I can." The stranger was also a veteran; his family joined the Williamses for an impromptu banquet followed by an evening of singing old war songs.[37]

Singing songs was not enough for most veterans. The death by disease of his only brother, who lay in an unmarked grave somewhere in North Carolina, haunted a young veteran from Arkansas. His younger sister reported that he "shrank from talk about the war, seemed to wish to forget the horrors and suffering of the past four years." Jimmy Stone, who had gone to war as a seventeen-year-old and returned to his Louisiana family a year later, was, according to his sister, Kate, "no longer a soldier but a poor discouraged boy." He recovered fairly quickly; a few days later, Kate took him to "see half of the girls in town," and he quickly arranged to escort one to church. Kate's oldest brother, Captain William Stone, returned a couple of weeks later. He had to sell his horse to pay for his trip home and had broken his sword over his knee rather than surrender it to "haughty Federal soldiers" on an Ohio River steamboat. William had much more difficulty than Jimmy did with the war's end. During the first few weeks after William's arrival, Kate noticed "how exceedingly quiet he is. Rarely talks at all." He had never said much, but "being in the army has intensified his silence and reserve, and he seems to take little interest in hearing others. . . . He feels the bitterness of defeat more than anyone we have met."[38]

Fewer northern families left comments on changes to returning Yankees, though dramatic changes must have occurred. Eliza Starbuck, a young girl who spent the war on Massachusetts's Nantucket Island, had only a single memory of her mother's nephew, "Cousin Seth." But she had been drawn to the photograph he had sent home from the army: the daring angle at which he wore his cap and his nonchalant, crossed-legs pose seemed to reveal a cocky, dashing, and devil-may-care attitude. But like so many other soldiers, Seth came home a changed man, scarred by long months in Libby Prison. Seth had been a fine physical specimen when he left for the war, but the man who returned was not the boy Eliza had come to know from the photograph. "In that quiet voice which had the curious hint of finality that I've always noticed in the returned soldier," he described his experiences in prison, where a close friend had died in his arms. Prison had ravaged his body and broken his spirit, and he died shortly after returning home. Eliza wondered if, had he lived, "the twinkle would ever have come back to those deep-set gray eyes! Or was everything 'different'?"[39]

Everything was different for these men and boys, of course, even for those who were not broken physically or mentally. They had been soldiers for a year or two or three but would be veterans for the rest of their lives. And the process of becoming a veteran, of being a civilian again, lasted longer and was much harder for many of them than anyone would have expected.

Beginning Anew

The hard part of demobilization for all soldiers, north and south, was re-acquainting themselves with the rhythms and demands of civilian life. Most returning Yankees seem to have been keenly aware that readjusting would take time. Moreover, they could hardly have failed to notice that the eyes of the nation were on them. In one of its first issues, published just before the surrender at Appomattox, the *Soldier's Friend* offered four "rules" that would ease discharged soldiers' transitions back to civilian life. "Preserve a soldierly bearing" to impress employers and show them that not all soldiers are dirty tramps. "Select quickly some fitting employment," leaving nothing "to luck or chance." "Fit yourself for such employments immediately" by learning a trade. And, especially for disabled soldiers, "What you have lost in body, try and make up in energy, decision, and mental rigor."[40]

A poem published in a soldiers' magazine a year after the end of the war celebrated exactly that transition to peaceful pursuits:

> The erstwhile soldiers, plough in hand,
> Of their own hard-won fields demand
> The earth's increase,
> Or ply their skill with sharper zest,
> Where shafts and wheels nor halt nor rest.

Truly, the poet believed, swords were beaten into plowshares as "our million soldiers melt" back into "common life." This triumphant account of the veterans' return to civilian life may eventually have reflected the lived experience of most soldiers. But all had to navigate some sort of decompression period. As a USSC report observed, soldiers had "lost the momentum of previous industrial enterprise, and must begin anew the task of settling themselves" into civilian life.[41]

For some, the transition was almost seamless. Charles Fields, a twenty-year-old Virginian, returned from an extended leave just in time for the death throes of the dwindling Army of Northern Virginia. By the time the army staggered toward Appomattox, he was "unwell compleatly Broken down," but the surrender was still "one of the mos paneful thing ever hapened." He quickly took his parole and reached home after a few days' journey. He spent the next three weeks at his grandmother's, burning logs, clearing brush, plowing, planting corn, digging stumps, and other "divers things"; he also had time to call on many friends and to join the "Bibel Class" at church. By May 5, he had almost completely resumed his normal life — nearly a week before the capture of Jefferson Davis and nearly a month before the surrender of Confederate forces in Texas and Louisiana.[42]

But Field's easy transition represented one end of the spectrum of readjustment. Other men had far more difficulty. A few had to reaccustom themselves to rather basic features of civilian life. One Arkansas private found himself unable to rest comfortably in a bed and slept in the yard for his first few nights at home until "mother could not stand that and I had to go back." Another returning Confederate expressed the pleasure of experiencing little things, especially his first meal back home. "Oh that Rio Coffee. I have been a coffee [fiend] since then but no cup tasted like that *one*."[43]

But the most commented-upon adjustment was to the pace and social expectations of peaceful lives. As Gerald Linderman has written, "The rules governing their daily lives changed so abruptly as to require almost overnight adjustments. Killing once again became homicide; foraging was again theft, and incendiarism arson. Even language was a problem: Camp talk had to be cleaned up." Philip Daingerfield Stephenson, a twenty-year-old who had survived seventeen battles during his four years in the service, wrestled with postwar boredom. His parents wanted him to return to school, "but to me that seemed absurd. What! *I* become a school boy again! *I*, who had been playing the man for four bloody years." Not only did Stephenson think himself too old and too mature to return to the classroom, but his "heart was sick unto death with crushed hopes," and he simply could not "have stood school life at that time." He "had lost all interest in life and faith in humanity and well nigh lost all faith in God." He looked to the future and saw only "a dreary sterile flat" that he "looked on . . . with loathing." For him, "all good and genuineness were crushed out of sight." He went to work for a tobacco broker but hated the job, at least at first. He wrote a memoir that would be published years later and endured "restlessness, restlessness, restlessness" and "disgust with the tame sordid life about me." He refused to enter a church for eighteen months.[44]

A similar restlessness roiled many men. One Confederate recalled many years after the war that he "tried to go to school but could not consetrate my mind on books." Many simply commented at the end of diaries and memoirs that they would find it, as one recalled, "hard to discard the habits acquired in the army, and to fall again into the humdrum customs of peaceful life." A Yankee diarist recorded his commitment to assuming "the position" of a citizen and his hope that once he returned home to Elkhart, Indiana, his "friends will help me to reclaim my position in society and throw off the habits of a soldier." Others refused to give up the vices that were commonly believed to accompany soldiering.[45]

The politicians and generals officially greeting the veterans frequently acknowledged such bad habits when referring to the challenges of the conversion back to civilian life. When Governor J. Gregory Smith welcomed the 9th Vermont, he felt compelled to mention the "problem as to what would become of our citizen soldiers, now that the war was ended." Although many civilians worried that "the long habit of the camp and battle-field" would prevent soldiers from returning "quickly to the walks of peace and industry," he had "no fears of the result." Smith challenged the men to prove the skeptics wrong, to "resume the habits of the citizen and lend your voice to the restoration of that national harmony, which, if not preserved and perpetuated, all we have secured by this war is lost." Three years after the war, the *Soldier's Friend* parodied the attitude that had seemed to prevail among the public: "Fears were entertained that the warlike spirit would have led the restless, the daring, and the ambitious into new organizations, that would have overrun Canada, or Mexico, or Central America, and thus have begun a wild career of conquest, and established the era of bloody warfare and military domination."[46]

Few returning soldiers proposed filibustering expeditions against neighboring countries—men generally found it easy to leave behind the bloodier facets of army life—but many commented on the difficulty of giving up what future president James A. Garfield called the "wild life of the army." That "wild life" included sexual adventures that would have seemed out of place in most Victorian communities. Although few soldiers wrote or talked about such escapades, as one early-twentieth-century historian has suggested, the many contemporary newspaper advertisements for cures for venereal disease provide hints that soldiers and others had transcended the civilian sexual mores of the period.[47]

Civilians and soldiers alike had fretted about the corrupting influence of military life. Long before the war ended, civilians had begun commenting on what life would be like when the men returned. An Iowa church newspaper announced less than two years into the war, "We look forward with dread to the restoration of peace and the disbanding of the army," while at about the same time a Yankee reformer declared that "the moralization of the soldier is the demoralization of the man." Some men worried that they had become poor fathers and husbands. Stephen M. Frank points out that most fathers associated their patriotic duty with their duty to their children, but some also believed that relationship might be ruined by army life. One man wrote to his wife that he had heard from other old soldiers that "it makes them cross, ugly to their wives & children & 9 cases out of ten if they are in the service 6 months they will go home the wickedest kind of men."[48]

Such fears led the USSC, which claimed to understand soldiers better than did most other civilians, to predict a tough transition for both veterans and civilians. Just after the Grand Review, the USSC set up a Bureau of Information and Employment, which took as its chief purpose "lessen-[ing] the pauperism and crime, necessarily more or less a consequence of war, which surely attend on large numbers of unoccupied men left to themselves without employment or means of subsistence." Another USSC document issued at about the same time explained that "many of these men will be not only physically but morally disabled, and will exhibit the injurious effects of camp life in a weakened power of self-guidance and self-restraint, inducing a certain kind of indolence, and, for the time, indisposition to take hold of hard work."[49]

Frank descriptions of the ways in which the men's morals had been compromised appeared in some unlikely places. A high school newspaper published in Newark, New Jersey, presented the corruption of soldiers as a commonplace. An editorial supporting the work of the U.S. Christian Commission explained that since that the typical soldier was "ready for every kind of fun and adventure" and in camp had the kind of "idle time" that is a "source of evil," it was not surprising that "surrounded as he is by temptation of nearly every description, he often returns from the battle-field ruined as to all that is virtuous and religious."[50]

In *Frank Manly, the Drummer Boy*, well-known children's author J. T. Trowbridge acknowledged the moral corruption that soldiers faced. The young hero's mother admits that "there is one danger I should dread for you worse than the chances of the battlefield. . . . That you might be led away by bad company." She worries about soldiers who were "not such persons as I would wish to have you on very intimate terms with." She "could endure any thing, even his death" better than knowing "that my boy was no longer the pure, truthful child he was; that he would blush to have his sisters know his habits and companions; to see him come home, if he ever does, reckless and dissipated." Frank, pained that his mother might think his resistance to corruption could be so weak, declares, "You shall hear of my death, before you hear of my drinking, or gambling, or swearing, or any thing of the kind." He seals his vow by writing his promise on a blank leaf of his New Testament. Nevertheless, not long after he arrives at his regiment, Frank succumbs to the soldierly temptations of drink and playing cards, before recovering to reform himself and other soldiers.[51]

Most situations like these were not so easily resolved. C. W. Bardeen, who entered the army at the age of fourteen, admitted to his diary on a drizzly New Year's Day 1864 that the preceding year had not had a positive effect on his character. "I bear witness to [the army's] contaminating effects. Many an evil habit has sprung up in me since Jan 1st, 1863. God grant that the year on which we have now entered be not so." Indeed, the career of this drummer turned fifer would have inspired most parents to keep their sons at home. Bardeen barely mentioned church—although he attended from time to time, he "was not much interested" in the only Bible class he attended—and although he professed to have signed the temperance pledge, he eventually came to enjoy his occasional ration of whiskey. He was arrested and very briefly confined to the guardhouse when he failed to obey orders. Bardeen was on his own much of the time after leaving his Boston home, and he had to make his own shelter in winter quarters. The vice he came to love best was gambling. He frequently played Bluff, a card game, and although Bardeen the reminiscing senior citizen knew the evils of the sporting life, the teenaged musician could not get enough of it. During the month following the Battle of Chancellorsville, Bardeen's brief diary entries mentioned playing Bluff ten times, sometimes "all day." He won a few times, but his losses mounted throughout the month, topping thirty dollars by early June. One day he lost a whopping twenty dollars: "No comment is needed," he wrote in his diary.[52]

There is no way to quantify the corruption of veteran soldiers, but the belief that they had been damaged by their service ran deep. A long, rather sad piece in the *Soldier's Friend* a year after the end of the war admitted that the reason there were "so many homeless, friendless wanderers of the blue coat" was that civilians "ARE AFRAID OF US." The general public, unfamiliar with war and unable to fathom the sacrifices made by veterans, believed the "many strange and bad stories about some of us while we were in the army," of soldiers camped near northern towns who "played cards, gambled, were fearfully profane . . . and habitually intemperate." Citizens knew that some soldiers visited "the dark places of resort which some of our companions—to their shame be it said—so often frequented." Civilians could not imagine bringing such men into their offices, homes, and families. The author, writing over the name "New Hampshire" but sounding very much like the army chaplain that the *Friend*'s editor, William Bourne, had been during the war, urged men who "have fallen into any of these soul-destroying evils, which ever beset the pathway of the unwary soldier" to "renounce them, and turn from them as from a poisonous serpent." The writer apologized for speaking so frankly but stressed his "earnest desire to see you looked up to as MEN, as I have seen you applauded as soldiers."[53]

A Terrible Waste of Time

The handicaps of long service in the military transcended drinking and whoring. Rice Bull recalled years later that he and his comrades were "unprepared . . . to meet the life conditions that faced us, not alone from wounds or broken health but from the greater reason that our long absence during the years of life when we would have fitted ourselves by education and experience for a successful effort were years gone." Soldiers generally entered the army in their late teens and early twenties, thereby missing out on the time in their lives when they were best prepared for schooling and training in specific trades. According to Bull, "Many faced the future" plagued not only by physical handicaps but also by "ignorance and lost opportunities." In a diary entry commemorating his fourth year in the service, an Illinois soldier frankly assessed his chances of surmounting his years in the army, which he described as a "terrible waste of time for me who have to make a start in life yet." He feared that his service had rendered him "unfit . . . for civil life" and dreaded "being a citizen, . . . trying to be sharp, and trying to make money." He believed that his fear came not from the work but from the fact that he would be operating outside a structure he had known for a significant portion of his young life and would be competing with men who had not been soldiers. "Citizens are not like soldiers," he wrote, "and I like soldier ways much the best."[54]

That sense of loss, of having missed a vital period in their young lives, became a key component of veterans' sense of themselves that for many would last the rest of their lives. Bitter comments from recently discharged members of the Iron Brigade described many veterans' state of mind. Complaining that he was "out of money and out of friends," one man wrote to a comrade, "I am well but have got the blews awful bad. I wish that I was in the army a gan." An officer biding his time waiting for a discharge wrote, "Action is what we wanted, action we had; but now that the last important act is passed, the drama closed—there's nothing in our present occupation but idleness and that is our bane."[55]

Soldiers grew restless almost as soon as the shooting stopped, partly because they had no firm sense of what the next phase of their lives would bring. Immediately after the war, a Wisconsin man noted the day of his mustering out with forebodings and hopefulness: "Three of the best years of my life have been lost . . . and the plans and hopes of my childhood have been ruthlessly toppled down, but the time has not been lost. I have no regrets for the way it has been spent. My prayer is that the remainder of my life may be as usefully spent."[56]

At least a few soldiers tried to get a head start on a useful life by collecting recommendations from their superior officers before leaving the service. When First Sergeant William Tucker left his engineering regiment in September 1865, he asked the officers and colleagues with whom he had served for three years to sign a recommendation "to a man of business, as a business man." A few captains and lieutenants, a couple of majors, another first sergeant, and several other officers asserted in writing that Tucker was "a thorough, practical business man, energetic, honest, and only known to be appreciated." Benjamin Smith, who by the end of the war was serving in the headquarters of General George H. Thomas, secured recommendations "as to habits, character and ability, and the kindly feeling of the donors" from Thomas as well as several staff officers. Allen Morgan Geer hit the ground running when he finally returned to Lexington, Illinois, after mustering out. He spent his first two days visiting with the family, "at home and in retirement," but soon began meeting with potential business associates. Over the next fortnight, he arranged "confidential" business plans with a partner, considered the possibility of taking over his uncle's farm, explored the prices of properties in Lexington and Alton, and discussed publishing a newspaper with yet another potential partner. He also found time to call on several female friends, take up the study of the German language, endure severe headaches, "attempt to establish a system of hygiene in our family," and evict a tenant.[57]

Yet as in most economies immediately following a war, soldiers could not control all the variables affecting their goals. Although many men returned to their homes and picked up careers and occupations where they left off, others found themselves facing at least temporary economic dislocation. A sample of five dozen veterans of the 103rd Ohio found that by 1870, these residents of the Cleveland area had improved their prewar economic standing by obtaining better jobs. A much larger sample of northern soldiers indicated that three- and four-year veterans were likely to return to their prewar jobs; less experienced, younger men were more likely to try something new or to take on their first serious work as adults.[58]

Whether or not the economic odds were stacked against them, soldiers believed that their prospects for prospering seemed grim, and many civilians agreed. In the larger cities, men still wearing their uniforms became common sights on the streets; some made a meager living on the change that passersby tossed into the boxes the veterans held or placed on the sidewalk. The governor of New York suggested that thousands of former soldiers would be homeless during the first winter after the war and complained that alleviating the crisis was beyond the state's power. A resident of Boston reported three years after the war that there were still many veterans grinding organs for a few cents a day; most people "pass coldly by . . . or quiet their consciences with dropping five or ten cents in the soldier's box."[59]

Recognizing the difficult job market after the war, a number of organizations created employment agencies for soldiers. New York City's Bureau of Employment for Disabled and Discharged Soldiers and Sailors was established by a committee of wartime philanthropists in January 1865. USSC branches and local organizations in other cities followed suit over the next several months, responding to the appearance, "day after day, hour after hour," of the "disabled begging not for bread, but for occupation." A flyer advertising the bureau's Philadelphia office asserted that its work would "prevent the necessity of costly charitable institutions" like those established for disabled veterans in Europe, which were "repulsive to the innate dignity of American soldiers and sailors," and would "lessen the pauperism and crime that follows war."[60]

During its first week of operation, the New York office received numerous applications from bookkeepers, clerks, salesmen, merchants, farmers, watchmakers, tailors, and cutters—in short, according to an approving *New York Times*, "representatives of every trade and occupation." By mid-1865, more than seven hundred men remained on the books, with a third of them reporting serious disabilities. Nineteenth-century technology meant that in many cases the occupations for which these men were qualified—generally their prewar jobs—were almost impossible for disabled men to perform: mechanic, coachman and teamster, farmer, and laborer (although about a fourth of the men signed up to be clerks, watchmen, and messengers, which were believed to be appropriate for men with permanent injuries). The *Independent* argued that the "claims of the soldier ought to be heeded" by the public with "the same benevolence which cared for him on the field of battle," but few employers were interested.[61]

Perhaps, wrote the *Times*, these employers had succumbed to the popular belief that soldiers accustomed to being fed, clothed, housed, and nursed back to health by the army were no longer "fitted to push their way as they did before" the war. The military had necessarily made men less independent and less able to work and think for themselves. However, the *Times* urged employers to consider another element of army life in their quest for reliable workers: the obedience instilled in the common soldier. "When a man comes from a well-disciplined regiment, there is an air of quickness, of neatness, promptitude and dispatch—a readiness to obey orders and perform what he is told—that is agreeable, to say the least, in an employee." Left unsaid was the idea that these characteristics were most important in workers placed in jobs requiring no imagination, decision making, or initiative; condescension and class assumptions fairly drip from the page.[62]

Employers also worried about veterans' trustworthiness. Prison officials in Massachusetts, Pennsylvania, Illinois, and Wisconsin reported that between 50 and 90 percent of all inmates were discharged soldiers. A warden in eastern Pennsylvania attributed the situation to the fact that so many men "had been more or less incapacitated and demoralized by an apprenticeship to the trade of war." Others were physically unfit to work and had turned to crime as a last resort. Contemporary accounts suggest that between five thousand and six thousand veterans ended up in prisons, with untold numbers of others in local jails. These figures seemed to support the frequent assertions that military service had rendered men unfit for peaceful pursuits.[63]

Perhaps because of the low interest manifested in a tough job market, a half year later, the Bureau of Employment established the Soldiers' Messenger Corps, which assigned soldiers to posts at prominent office buildings and intersections. Although this plan obviously contained a "charitable" element, only "deserving . . . men whose character for promptness and faithfulness has been perfectly tested" were hired, and the managers assured the public that the operation would be profitable and efficient. The *New York Times* endorsed the idea, based on the success of similar employment of mostly disabled old soldiers in Berlin and London. By November 1865, twenty-three one-armed men had obtained references assuring that they were "temperate, industrious, honest, and trustworthy" and were making from $1.00 to $1.50 a day. A few months later, the Wisconsin Soldiers' Aid

Society organized a similar bureau, and during the fall of 1865, a dozen and a half veterans worked as messengers in Boston's business district. The red-capped veterans sporting the badges of the Soldiers' Philadelphia City Messenger Company had been chosen only from the "best men of good character and with good references." Despite plans to build the force to as many as a thousand men, the New York bureau suspended its operations in February 1866, and other branches soon followed suit.[64]

Newspapers constantly ran ads offering supposedly lucrative jobs to soldiers. In particular, the *Soldier's Friend* specialized in advertising and in some cases creating employment opportunities for veterans. Published by William Oland Bourne, who had been chaplain of New York's Central Park Hospital during the war, the *Friend* not only provided sympathy for disabled Yankees but also celebrated their ambition and lack of self-pity. Although the *Friend* did not advertise itself as an employment agency, veterans of "every class and qualification" frequently requested information about jobs. The *Friend* urged employers to consider hiring disabled veterans, "who can well and faithfully fill situations as watchman, gatekeepers, porters, messengers, doorkeepers, etc., as well as mechanics of every kind." The paper employed veterans, too; its monthly advertisement for "Agents Wanted" specifically encouraged applications from "disabled Soldiers, ACTIVE INTELLIGENT, and HONEST." Personal ads occasionally appeared on behalf of individual soldiers. A member of the "left-armed corps" sought a position in an office and was "willing to commence with a small salary."[65]

Apparently operating under the belief that war-related items would be more attractive to consumers if they were peddled by former soldiers, firms guaranteed veterans the opportunity to make money "HONESTLY AND HONORABLY" by selling engravings, prints, albums, and personal photographs. Many ads included disabled veterans on a list of other worthy beneficiaries. One firm offered "*congenial and lucrative employment for ministers*, competent Christian men, and *worthy* disabled soldiers" selling a new artistic representation of the Lord's Prayer. The publishers of *De Witt's Campaign Life of General Grant* offered "special terms . . . to one-armed and other sailors and soldiers" and suggested that they could make between three and five dollars a day. In the same issue of the *Soldier's Friend*, a Cincinnati bookseller acknowledged the "HARD TIMES" still facing veterans three years after the war's end but promised "steady and remunerative" employment for "discharged SOLDIERS and all energetic and competent men" who went on the road selling the company's catalog of books. Bourne published a "lively and spirited" epic poem relating the entire history of the war—*The New Yankee*

Doodle: Being an Account of the Little Difficulty in the Family of Uncle Sam and advertised for agents in the *Soldier's Friend*. Only five dollars would set up "convalescent and disabled soldier[s]" from all parts of the country in the business of selling pictures and engravings issued by Sparks and Company, a New York publisher. Countless other employers recruited soldiers, and at least one town made it easier for disabled soldiers to make livings on the street by passing an ordnance specifying that only disabled soldiers were allowed to peddle without licenses.[66]

Hard times would highlight another issue fraught with future ramifications. Although the subject of pensions would come to dominate public discourse about Union veterans later in the century, hints of some of the topics that would shape the debate surfaced immediately after the war. The USSC specifically warned soldiers not to trust private claims agencies. Most of the claims filed during and immediately after the war were for disabilities suffered while in the service or for disputed pay and bounties. Submitting claims to the government, like any interaction with the government in the nineteenth—or the twenty-first—century, could be forbidding, and many soldiers employed agents. An enterprise that billed itself as the U.S. Army Agency apparently was not an official arm of either the government or the army. The USSC warned men and their survivors that a number of these agents at best charged exorbitant prices and at worst cheated soldiers and their widows. According to the commission, one client attempting to collect a hundred dollars with the help of an agent found that his itemized charges included five dollars each for crossing a river and for recrossing it, for filling out the form, for mailing it, for delivering the government's response, and so forth. When all was said and done, the widow received only fifteen dollars. Other victims netted only thirty-eight dollars out of two hundred and three dollars out of thirty-eight. Agents commonly collected five dollars to fill out a form and forward it to the Pension Office but then dropped the case, leaving claimants in the lurch. Other agents paid nurses or other hospital employees a dollar for information about deceased soldiers; agents would then write to the bereaved families, offering condolences and services. In some cases, family members had not yet been formally notified of their loved ones' deaths. The USSC offered to help soldiers and their families complete the documents at no charge, and by the spring of 1865, the commission had established claim offices in New York; New Orleans; Rochester, New York; Annapolis; Beaufort, South Carolina; several towns in Maine; and Philadelphia. A notice for the USSC "Army & Navy Claim Agency" was headed "Protection for Disabled Soldiers and Seamen." In this phase of the pension wars, claims agents were the only villains, but the situation changed with the rapid expansion of the system to previously unimaginable levels in the 1880s and 1890s.[67]

Less than a year after the end of the war, some soldiers were so desperate for quick cash that they sold their discharge papers, immediately disqualifying them from receiving benefits from state or federal governments and meaning that they could not prove their veteran status to employers. In an age before a system of reliable identification was available, discharge papers took great importance to hard-pressed veterans, disabled or not. Indeed, throughout the Gilded Age, soldiers' newspapers commented on the market in real discharge records and other proofs of service. The Soldiers' and Sailors' National Union League of Washington, D.C., an early veterans' association, expressed its "sorrow and chagrin" that anyone would consider selling this witness to his contribution. "It is the only evidence you possess of having served throughout your term with honor unhinged or unblotted by any disgraceful or cowardly act; it will ever be a pass to you for obtaining honest and honorable employment or positions in the walks of civil life; it is the only voucher which enables you to claim or receive from time to time such benefits and blessings as a free and grateful people . . . will unquestionably bestow upon its country's saviors, particularly in their old age."[68]

Despite the many, if disparate, efforts to find employment for veterans, northern observers realized that the transition from war to peace would not necessarily be easy. "An immense amount of suffering and privation is unavoidable," declared a Boston newspaper a few months after Appomattox. "Many brave men will find it hard to discover the opening in civil society for which their abilities are suited," and their "humble families" would find it difficult to make ends meet between the last month of army pay and the "first instalment of the mechanic's or laborer's wages." The army's rapid demobilization and the sudden disruption of the booming wartime economy made it "our nearest and imperative duty to find for as many of these gallant men as possible the paying employment which is the sole boon they ask." The alternative was "unhappy and demoralizing idleness," which nobody wanted. At the same time that the community had a responsibility to the returning soldiers, the soldiers had a responsibility to the community. They must be treated with respect but must also act respectfully. They must not assume that rejection by employers or insults from individuals represented true northern opinion. Most important, "they should bear themselves . . . with the dignity and manliness which are alike the noblest attributes of the American soldier and of the American citizen," avoiding surrender to the "outbreaks of ruffianism and brutality just now so common, and not seldom clothed in the disguise of veteran uniforms."[69]

The economic costs of the war would haunt many veterans, northern as well as southern, for the rest of the century. Their belief that participating in the war had held them back and forced them to fall behind their civilian peers would animate their insistence on a vast pension system and veterans' preference in government and other jobs. Less than three months after the Grand Review, the contours were developing of what civilians considered a responsible and reasonable patience toward soldiers' reentry into civilian life and the extent to which public gratitude would overlook veterans' peculiar needs and responses to peacetime. The clashing assertions of the public's duties to returning soldiers and of returning soldiers' duties to the public would continue throughout the Gilded Age.

Building Up What the Yankees Tore Down

A few returning southerners relieved their grief and in that most ancient of ways exerted their manhood immediately after reaching home. John W. Carpenter reported that he went to work, but only "after I visited all the gals and had a good time." Another veteran spent eight months "resting and rambling." Lucullus Atkins's father, a prosperous yeoman farmer before the war, gave him a horse and saddle "and told me get go until next Jan. 1866 before I went to work." Many returned men no doubt would have agreed with Stephen Harrison Hows, who recalled his main occupations after the war as "farming and going to see the girls, the latter however was not laborious."[70]

In a way, these men sound like the veterans described by historian Jason Phillips, who has argued that Confederates quickly recovered from whatever depression they experienced when they mustered out of or simply walked away from their armies. "Instead of doubting that God was on their side," he writes, "white southerners saw defeat as providential; they viewed their trials in biblical terms and looked forward to resurrection and redemption." This "culture of invincibility," as Phillips calls it, ultimately led to the rise of the Lost Cause.[71]

But the process was rarely that easy. The immediate aftermath of the war required former Confederates to call up whatever reserves of invincibility they had retained in the face of bruising defeat and crushing hardship. Many of the conditions southern men faced immediately after the war challenged their sense of themselves as men. Some were economic, others were familial, and still others were racial.

A crude snapshot of the economic effect of the war on southern families suggests that although most southerners were worth less in 1870 than in 1860, soldiers' families suffered even more. In Pittsylvania County, Virginia, families whose soldier/head-of-household returned home healthy were worth an average of $6,522 in 1860; that number had plummeted nearly 75 percent to $1,673 ten years later. Families whose veterans returned home sick or injured saw their wealth drop even more, from an average of $6,907 to $1,161 (83 percent).[72]

In the piney woods region of western Georgia, the disruption of the local economy by the logging industry and other economic changes during the Gilded Age provided a devastating continuation of the psychological blow caused by defeat in the war. Between them, those macroeconomic changes and microcosmic disturbances challenged prewar assumptions and postwar hopes, leading Confederate veterans to join with their civilian neighbors to threaten, harass, and murder local Unionists and African Americans. Unable to prevent dubious land grabs and political manipulation by northern corporations, southerners deflected their sense of defeat by fighting a battle they could believe they had won—at least in the short run. But this analysis is a meta version of the southern response to defeat. All over the South, men had to pull themselves together to get through the war's immediate aftermath. Soldiers often found their families and friends hard-pressed to put food on the table, depressed about the war's outcome, and not particularly interested in building up veterans' self-esteem. The cloud of defeat darkened the way home for many Confederates.[73]

Yet few could afford to give in to the hardships they faced. Many years later, when Tennessee veterans recalled their lives in 1865 and 1866, many proudly described the hard work and perseverance that helped them surmount difficult conditions. Zachary Taylor Crouch expressed "a pride in my life and what I have accomplished." He had come back from the war "without a change of clothes or a penny" and had begun working as a day laborer. As a farmer and livestock and grain merchant, he had subsequently "accumulated by honest effort about $30,000" and "reared a family of nine children, five girls and four boys, giving them all a good education; and feel that I have done my part in church relations and charitable work."[74]

As Crouch demonstrated, although Confederate soldiers had been vanquished on the battlefield, they would not accept defeat off it. "I reached home to find everything in a very much run down condition," one veteran remembered, "and tho the future was very dark, we pitched in and as the saying goes, rolled up our sleeves and went at it with head up and a determination to win or die in the conflict." One nineteen-year-old who had survived capture at both Fort Donelson and Vicksburg arrived home and the next day "went to cutting wheat" so he could buy new clothes. Another veteran arrived home on Saturday, May 19 and "hitched a mule to a plow and went to plowing" two days later. The overwhelming majority of Tennessee Confederates had been farmers or farmers' sons before the war, and most spent at least part of the first few months of peace asserting their manhood by trying to restore farms ravaged by neglect or by passing armies.[75]

Long after the war, a retrospective piece in the *Richmond Dispatch* painted a romanticized picture of the noble determination and spirit of sacrifice displayed by the "overwhelmed, not whipped" Confederate Virginians. Their only resources were the scrawny mounts salvaged from artillery and cavalry stock and a willingness to forget their stations in life and work harder than they had ever worked. Most toiled on farms; others went into towns and took jobs as watchmen, brakemen, streetcar drivers, factory foremen—"anything that would enable them to support themselves and those dependent on them, and would aid them in educating themselves." Although the article spoke mainly to the experiences of the sons of the state's first families—"It was a strange spectacle, the people commonly supposed to be the proudest in the land engaging in the work of laborers and losing no caste by it"—the analysis nevertheless seemed to include most veterans in its approving description of the men's transition to peacetime and their calm approach to defeating the poverty that accompanied loss. "A man who had hitched the horses to a gun under fire and brought it off under a storm of shot and shell could drive a street-car without chagrin."[76]

A number of recollections matched this brave version of the immediate aftermath of the war. "I took charge of my father's home," wrote one old soldier, further confirming the transition from dependent to man by cataloging the difficulties he faced on his family's home place, which before the war had employed more than a dozen slaves on 250 acres: "I did not find but one old broken leged mule" and "one old sore backed saddle mare." The place had been "strip[p]ed of stock, forage, poultry, and cattle" when a Confederate army had camped nearby. Another veteran boasted that he had raised a "pretty fair corn crop" despite having virtually no tools to work the ground. Gentry McGee left college to enlist in the Confederate Army; although he arrived home long after crops should have been planted, he proudly remembered that he still made more than four bales of cotton and three hundred bushels of corn during that first summer. Some men commented on the difficulty of having to make a living while still suffering from wounds or after having lost an arm or leg. All took pride, as did Solomon Brantley, in "building up what the Yankees tore down."[77]

Simply put, Confederate veterans would do whatever was necessary. A chatty middle-aged veteran of the Confederate Army reported that he had made a living for his family during the first months after the war by selling clothes found on battlefields in northern Virginia—some thrown away, some stripped from dead bodies. "Any number of families," he claimed, "jest lived on what they got from the Union armies in that way." This particular veteran also made a few extra dollars giving tours of the nearby battlefields, although he got many of the details about the Battle of Chancellorsville wrong.[78]

Veterans took special pride in taking responsibility for supporting family members. J. B. Gracey, who had been raised in comfort in Iredell County, North Carolina, keenly felt the loss of his youth, "the time so necessary for fitting myself for a useful life." Yet because his sister and her baby needed him—her husband had died during the war—he "went to work as a hireling on the farm." Lemuel Tyree, who had gone into the army at the age of seventeen, "came home as sad a boy as ever lived. I felt all was lost except our honor." After briefly considering going west with friends, he decided to stay at home and become a good citizen. After arriving home after dark, he rose at sunup the next day, hitched his cavalry horse to the plow, and began to "work . . . like the dickens to make a living for Mother and Sister."[79]

But some men could not rebuild the homes they had left. With no resources but the clothes they wore and no family to tie them down, some men moved on. J. C. McCarty of Hawkins County, Tennessee, recalled that "it had all been carried off and ruin stalked the land." He lived in Texas for a few years, returning to Tennessee in the early 1870s to serve as a city marshal and as a prison guard. "All who came through that," wrote a Confederate veteran fifty years after the end of the war, "will remember what conditions we had to meet in addition to our imposed manhood and nothing with which to make a start." After the welcome embrace of relieved family and friends, "the realities of the situation dawned upon me; what course to adopt in order that I might get a start in the world. This and other vexing problems became a very serious affair."[80]

Retrieving Manhood

Early in Reconstruction, federal authorities sought to keep Confederates from processing to Confederate memorial events and from wearing Confederate gray. (Anyone too poor to buy new clothes was supposed to cut off all Confederate States of America insignia and buttons.) These restrictions were intended to separate veterans from their military experience as much as possible and to discourage any thought of further rebellion. Nevertheless, former Confederates found ways of commemorating their service and honoring dead comrades. Veterans attended memorial services en masse at Shockoe and Hollywood Cemeteries in Richmond, Virginia, in the spring of 1866, wearing blue ribbons in their buttonholes as a hint of their banned uniforms. A few weeks later, at the city's first Memorial Day ceremony, many men (far more than those who could not afford other garb) showed up in gray uniforms, and at least two dozen separate military units marched through the streets.[81]

But a much deeper and less orderly response to peace and exertion of manhood paralleled this early sample of veterans' rituals. In a fictional exchange, the well-hated Congressional Joint Committee on Reconstruction asked Bill Arp, the alter ego of humorist and former Confederate Charles Henry Smith, if the "peepul of your sekshun" were "sufishently umbled and repentant to cum back into the Union." Arp replied, "Not much they aint. . . . They say the deel wasn't fair, and you hav markd the kards and stole the trumps, but at the same time they don't care a darn what you do. They hav bekum indifferent and don't care nuthin about your Guy Fawkes bisness. Our peepul ain't a notisin you, only out of kurosity. They don't xpkt anything direct, or onerable, from you, and they've gone to work, a diggin and plowin, and plantin, and raisin boy children."[82]

As this surprisingly bitter column from the usually affable Arp reveals, the hard slog of economic recovery that dominated the lives of virtually all Confederate veterans was at times overshadowed by another fight. Many southern white men saw an urgent challenge to their manhood that included a built-in opportunity to redeem that manhood: the sudden, confusing, and enraging existence of millions of freedmen and -women. Race had united white men before the war through economic superiority and political ideology. But even as African Americans' political rights were being implemented, the movement that George Rable has called a counterrevolution, frequently fought by former Confederate soldiers, began the process of undermining the extension of democracy. Ex-Confederates formed the most recognizable organization devoted to white supremacy, the Ku Klux Klan, and observers frequently commented on the high percentage of members who were former Confederate soldiers. Rebel officers spread the organization throughout the South and led local chapters. Klansmen declared that they were the ghosts of Confederate dead, displayed Confederate flags, and conducted raids and campaigns with something approaching military efficiency.[83]

This surge was described most famously in Thomas Dixon's Klan trilogy published early in the twentieth century, which provided a romanticized, whitewashed version of the violent retrieval of southern veterans' manhood. In many ways, the novels, written thirty years after the events they portray, offer a nonsectional view of a postwar world in which soldiers who served courageously and honorably during the war and remained uncorrupted by political or material greed—and who were, of course, white—could be admired as true men no matter what color uniform they wore. Indeed, when a clansman asserts that the watchwords of the "Invisible Empire" are "Chivalry, Humanity, Mercy, and Patriotism," he echoes many of the sentiments of the motto of the Grand Army of the Republic: "Fraternity, Charity and Loyalty." What veteran of either army could oppose the stated purposes of this fictional version of the Klan: to protect and aid soldiers' widows and orphans as well as the Constitution? And what old soldier could deny the power of the story of the Klan as it appeared in *The Leopard's Spots*?

> The origin of this Law and Order League . . . was a spontaneous and resistless racial uprising of clansmen of highland origin living along the Appalachian mountains and foothills of the South, and it appeared almost simultaneously in every Southern state, produced by the same terrible conditions.
>
> It was the answer to their foes of a proud and indomitable race of men driven to the wall. In the hour of their defeat they laid down their arms and accepted in good faith the results of the war. And then, when unarmed and defenceless, a group of pothouse politicians for political ends, renewed the war, and attempted to wipe out the civilisation of the South.
>
> This Invisible Empire of White Robed Anglo-Saxon Knights [rose up] to bring order out of chaos, protect the weak and defenceless, the widows and orphans of brave men who had died for their country, to drive from power the thieves who were robbing the people, redeem the commonwealth from infamy, and reëstablish civilization.[84]

Dixon suggested that the men who achieved the "recivilization" of the South were, for the most part, Confederate veterans, and in *The Clansman*, the hooded heroes ride in well-organized squadrons, deploy pickets, and conduct operations as effectively as any Rebel unit during the war. In this world, the Confederate veterans and their allies who form the Klan and redeem their country from carpetbaggers and freed slaves bring order out of chaos.[85]

A very different novelistic treatment of the era had appeared twenty years earlier. Boasting a less grandiose theme but dripping with contempt for the Klan—although it is not mentioned by name, the villains are described as hooded thugs making indifferent efforts to remain anonymous—*Bristling with Thorns: A Story of War and Reconstruction* launched a frontal attack on the kind of manhood described by Dixon. Written by O. T. Beard, an editor, Republican operative, and former officer in a black regiment, the novel featured a few of the conventions of Gilded Age novels showing reconciliation between the North and South, but it is notable for two reasons. First, Beard separated those honorable Confederates who laid down their arms and committed themselves to peaceful lives from the deserters and cowards who had been Confederates in name only. The latter hid behind ragged hoods and white man's rhetoric to conduct a reign of terror in the South. Second, the plot is propelled by almost pornographic violence, from blood-soaked whippings and the apparent rape of an old black woman to the use of a powder horn literally to blow off a black preacher's head and the murder of a white mother and maiming of her child in a crowded jail cell. In *Bristling with Thorns*, Dixon's "knights" protecting the South's women and children are depicted as cold-blooded, sadistic murderers.[86]

Although historians have frequently connected Confederate veterans to the early organization of the Klan, former Rebels did not need to don hoods to use racialized violence in making their claims to manhood. Over and above the political ramifications of emancipation that lie at the center of these very disparate books, Confederate veterans instinctively sought to hang onto the shreds of their manhood by reimposing the racial hierarchy that had been central to their purpose in fighting. Aaron Sheehan-Dean suggests that the internalization of violence and the belief that southern men had been fighting to protect their families during the war combined to transform southern white masculinity. Men became even more devoted to protecting their families and were more willing to use violence against perceived enemies to do so. As a result, they sought to intimidate and threaten or at the very least refused to back down before Union officials and African Americans.[87]

Much of the evidence for this argument comes from the writings (though obviously biased) of northern travelers, who were constantly reminded that they were in a region that only a few months earlier considered itself a separate nation. Brigadier General Charles H. Howard, brother of Major General O. O. Howard and an inspector for the Freedmen's Bureau, told the Joint Committee on Reconstruction that in the summer of 1865, Rebel officers were still wearing their uniforms "and seemed rather disposed to make a display of them." Faded paintings of Confederate flags and battle scenes of Confederate soldiers pursuing Union soldiers still appeared on the sides of railroad cars. Inside the cars, Yankees would often be serenaded by children singing "songs that would be very obnoxious to United States soldiers — songs containing reproaches upon the flag and upon everything we hold sacred."[88]

One Freedmen's Bureau officer believed that Texans were the most obstinate Rebels. Many officers and men continued to wear their uniforms and insignia of rank, and most were armed with shotguns, pistols, and knives. The former soldiers tended to congregate on the verandas of hotels and in other public places and to "talk, in a tone particularly intended for our ears, of the deeds they had performed, and the number of Yankees they had slain, and [to say] that if an opportunity ever occurred they were ready and anxious to fight against the United States." The commander of the 4th Corps in Texas, Major General David S. Stanley, distinguished between Texas Confederates who had served in the East — who had submitted to defeat "without any opposition or grumbling" — and those who had remained in Texas. The latter, who he believed were a majority of Texas veterans, "were insolent and overbearing where they dared to be, and were not afraid of military punishment, cursing the government and the Yankees." Less than a year after the war, Texans in Lamar County apparently murdered three Union men who had fled the state during the war and served in the 2nd Kansas Cavalry before returning home: a Topeka newspaper reported that "the rebels in Texas declare that no Yankee, or federal soldier shall reside there." One historian has called the violence that raged in Texas during this time the War of Reconstruction, blaming the family feuds and lawlessness of the infamous Four Corners district of northeastern Texas on political disagreements between Unionists and former Confederate soldiers. Ex-Rebels and guerrillas killed perhaps two hundred African Americans, federal soldiers, and Unionists in the years following the war.[89]

Some and maybe even most Confederates demonstrated their manhood by simply refusing to admit the possibility that they had been wrong. A former Union soldier living in Alexandria, Virginia, lamented the fact that none of the returned Rebels regretted their actions and that most citizens supported these beliefs: "They claim that they acted honorably and well" and base their behavior "upon the principle that those who took the most active part in the rebellion should be first cared for in the way of civil offices, or anything of that kind." Another witness complained that all of the successful candidates for local offices in a recent election had "boast[ed] they have been positive rebels, and that they fought this thing out . . . until the surrender."[90]

Observers often distinguished between the officer class of the Confederate gentry and the common soldier. The former tended to project their sense of manly nondefeat through expressions of pride and stiff-upper-lip disdain. The latter were insolent and threatening in a street-fighter sort of way. A Yankee lieutenant had been "insulted" on two occasions. The first person, apparently of the upper crust, later apologized. The second was a man "of such a low character that I paid no attention to it." The northerner reported the presence of a "class of young men, returned from the army, and who have been with Mosby" but were now "lying around bar-rooms" in Culpeper County. They "are very bitter against the government."[91]

Another traveler through the postwar South reported that the "men who did the fighting," officers and enlisted alike, had adjusted fairly well to their situation. "They mourn over the defeat of their armies, and are very fond of showing that but for this little mistake, or that little accident, or that other little blunder, the Confederacy would now be a great nation." But few were disposed to further resistance; rather, they "accept the issue of the war in good faith and with a determination to do their duties hereafter as orderly citizens." He encountered at least one pretty boisterous Rebel, however, who blustered, "I can whip any three Yankees in this town," although he had never seen combat. Another one of "the most malignant men" in southwestern Georgia had served only in a home guard company and as commandant of a prison.[92]

Those without the personal self-confidence, economic resources, or moral strength to sustain themselves with pride in their political manhood had to find other ways to overcome defeat. Many fell back on their presumed racial superiority to restore their sense of themselves as men in the face of unmanly defeat and economic dislocation. Although some observers testified to the Joint Committee that returned Confederates simply wanted to live in peace and that they basically ignored the freedpeople, a number of other witnesses asserted the opposite. According to a federal judge in Virginia, the "vulgar and uneducated" Confederate soldiers "would kill a nigger as soon as [they] could see him." A former officer in a black regiment who was hoping to settle permanently in North Carolina believed that "the confederate soldiers, in fact all of the poorer classes . . . seem to feel bitter toward the free class on account of their being raised to an equality with them."[93]

The brazenness with which former Rebels committed acts of violence against both black and white enemies must have resulted in a powerful if fleeting sense of mastery that belied the veterans' status as members of a defeated army. At the same time that they detailed the ways in which such men posed a danger to society, witnesses before the Joint Committee on Reconstruction referred to these men in rather dismissive terms, as though they were juvenile delinquents. A northerner trying to make a living publishing a newspaper in Wilmington, North Carolina, called them "young boys around the street; ex-Rebel officers who have not had their blood cooled down." A little later in his testimony he referred to these "hot-heads" as "an unimportant class of the community. They are boys and young men thrown upon the world and living upon the street corners."[94]

An assistant commissioner for the Freedmen's Bureau in North Carolina told of a gang of four young men, at least some of them veterans of the Confederate Army, who went on a rampage just after the war ended. Encountering a black man who had formerly been a slave to one of their families, the quartet beat him senseless and left him to die on the road. They stormed into the town of Washington, firing at a white citizen with whom they had quarreled; they missed him but hit a different man and then attacked another black man before moving on. "In short," reported the frustrated colonel, the gang "took possession of the town." When he tried to track the men down, the people refused to help. The same gang, reinforced by more than twenty other former Confederates, apparently later captured, disarmed, and then murdered a former scout for the Union Army.[95]

Inevitably, men without work, without money, and without much in the way of leadership congregated in idle groups, eager for the next bit of excitement. A crowd of perhaps two hundred men, most of them returned soldiers and many still wearing gray coats, cheered as a New Orleans policeman "went up and down the street knocking in the head every negro man, woman, and child that he met, tumbling some of them into the gutter, and knocking others upon the sidewalks." Police work also became an outlet for racial violence in Wilmington, North Carolina, where a number of veterans found a method for redeeming their manhood. The local marshal hired only former Confederate soldiers, whom a former Freedmen's Bureau officer described as "the hardest and most brutal looking and acting set of civil or municipal officers I ever saw." They were a "terror to everybody," especially black men and Unionists. Aided at times by other Confederate veterans, the deputies ransacked the houses and seized the arms and livestock of African Americans, frightening them and making them less likely to work. According to a Union general, Mississippi veterans traveled through the countryside, making sure that former slaves were working. Brevet Major General Edward Hatch appreciated this extralegal but apparently fairly nonviolent work, testifying that "the rebel soldier who has fought through the war is by far the best man in the country, and the most willing to accept the state of affairs as they are, and the most ready to go to work. The worst class of people there are those who have been in the bands of guerrillas—the irregular bands of rebels."[96]

A striking example of a former Confederate lashing out in the months after the war occurred on a train in Georgia in the fall of 1865. An official of the U.S. Interior Department found himself traveling on an open baggage car with a "boisterously drunk" planter who had lost his arm as a Confederate officer. About thirty years of age, the planter was "one of those resolute, daring, desperate looking men." As the train crept along, the former Rebel drew a pistol and started shooting at random targets along the tracks. He later snatched a live chicken from a black passenger and swung it by the neck until its head popped off; he grabbed the hat off another African American and cuffed him in the head. At one point, directing his ire toward the official, the Confederate declared, "I can whip any damned Yankee aboard of this train." Such anecdotal reports from northern observers support Anne Sarah Rubin's assertion that the aftermath of war convinced former Confederates that reason and conciliation would not accomplish their goals of a speedy return to normality, leading many to seek to restore their manhood more violently. This decision, writes Rubin, unleashed "a veritable orgy of racial-political violence."[97]

But extreme demonstrations of pride and racism may have been less common than relatively peaceful returns to what passed for normal lives. Most former Confederate soldiers had not owned slaves before the war and would not have to have direct contact with African Americans afterward. As one Augusta County, Virginia, Unionist told the Joint Committee on Reconstruction,

> People are thinking about their private business; they want to go to work to repair their losses; they do not wish any more war, domestic or foreign . . . if it can be avoided. They are tired of war. They knew nothing of what war was before the rebellion; they had no idea at all of the kind of war they were engaging in; they are heartily sick of war. They

are an afflicted people, terribly afflicted; almost all of them have lost sons or brothers; the country is full of widows and orphans and destitute people. . . . If politicians would let them alone, I think there would be no trouble whatever.[98]

Turning Backs on the Past

More men than will ever be known tried to forget the war. The son of one Confederate colonel reported that his father returned from the war "bitter and broken in health and spirit and estate. He destroyed all evidence of service, all photographs in uniform and wanted to forget it all." The ex-officer sold most of his family's possessions, including a rare edition of John James Audubon's portfolio of bird paintings, and scrambled to support his loved ones on a series of rented farms. A few years after the war, the old colonel died at the age of sixty-three, still bitter and ravaged by rheumatism contracted during his service. His son described him simply as "a wreck of the Civil War."[99]

Although dramatic expressions of Confederate manhood through racial violence were an important feature in the postwar South, most returned veterans simply kept their heads down and went to work, leaving the war and their wounded pride behind them. W. B. Drake of the 1st Virginia Artillery made the sixty-mile hike home from Appomattox to Powhatan County in two days with virtually no food and with feet worn out from the retreat from Richmond. He recalled his comrades' reactions to the surrender: "Some men cried[;] other[s] curse[d] and swore." But Drake "took a different view[.] I had done my duty as best I could[,] had followed Lee until he said it was enough[,] he could do no more[. M]y life was spared to go home to mother and friends and I was satisfied." David Bodenhamer also rejected a rose-colored memory of his Confederate boyhood. He had grown up on a five-hundred-acre farm with a dozen slaves before enlisting as a teenager. Following the war, he earned a doctorate and became a professor at Trinity University in Texas. "When the Confederate armies surrendered and the war was over," he declared, "I turned my back upon the past and set my face like a flint toward the goal of my ambition."[100]

We can catch only glimpses of the ways in which veterans and their families experienced the immediate aftermath of the war. Two respondents to the Tennessee Civil War Veterans Questionnaire early in the twentieth century covered the gamut of attitudes of returning Civil War veterans. Noah J. Love of North Carolina no doubt spoke for virtually all surviving soldiers, north and south, when he recalled how he felt when the shooting stopped: "I was so glad the war was over I felt like a new man." Another remembered the dispirited Confederate veterans who "went in sorrow and poverty to our homes."[101]

Homecomings were rarely recorded in diaries or memoirs, and authors who did so tended merely to note briefly their relief and joy. Yet Civil War soldiers could not just shrug off all they had seen in camp and on the battlefield and resume interrupted lives. Many would begin writing about their experiences in the 1870s and 1880s, when a deluge of personal narratives would offer extraordinary accounts of what it meant to be a soldier. But few men would write about what it meant to be a veteran. Yet if we know little about the interior lives of veterans, we can learn much about the attitudes that developed among Union and Confederate veterans and civilians during the several decades after those homecomings. Many of the conditions and responses, the rhetoric and reality, the contempt and contentiousness that characterized the demobilization of the great armies of the rebellion would animate politics and society for the rest of the century. The public discourse might change, but disabled and poor veterans would never disappear, their uneasy reentry into civilian society would continue to shape the lives of veterans, and the gulf between those who served and those who did not serve would grow. The following chapters will unravel the threads of those experiences sewn into the fabric of Gilded Age society.

chapter two

Maimed Darlings

LIVING WITH DISABILITY

Disabled Civil War veterans projected and elicited a number of contradictory responses:

Resigned pity: "The Last Review," a poem published in a children's magazine, the *Little Corporal*, just months after the end of the war, urged readers to

> Think of the maimed, and wasted band,
> Seeking the homes of this stricken land,
> For whom the brightness of life is o'er,
> Whose feet are nearing the other shore,
> *Remnants* of manhood *once so* strong,
> These cannot march in the gala throng.[1]

Wry humor: "John, you had one leg shot off in the war," commented an old Rebel's wife in a short piece in the *Confederate Veteran*. "Yes," he replied. "An' you gits er right smart pension fer it." "Yes," he said again, "but what set you to thinkin' 'bout it?" "I was thinkin'," explained the old lady, "that ef yer had jes' lost two legs, we could paint the house, pay off the mortgage, an' buy Mary a pianner. Ole Brown lost two, an' his wife holds her head high, dresses fit to kill, an' goes in the best society."[2]

Chipper perseverance: A short poem published by Charles Edgeworth Jones somehow found humor in an old Confederate veteran whose jaw had been torn off by a shell at Chickamauga. The lighthearted "A Family Reunion" described the horribly disfigured man's tramping about the battlefield many years later until he found an old jawbone and several teeth on the spot where he had been wounded. The poem suggests that the reunion somehow makes up for a life forever altered by violence: "Then rest in peace, for they are found, and once again you view / The grateful sight of *self-reclaimed*, although you cannot chew."[3]

Angry despair: "I would like to say a good deal about the men here," testified a veteran to a congressional committee investigating the National Home for Disabled Volunteer Soldiers (NHDVS). "They are all dissatisfied, every one of them. . . . We are not comfortable. We are unhappy. I would venture to say—in fact, I know it to be the case—that this petty persecution has caused men to commit suicide. I know this to be a fact, because I know my own feelings, and I can judge others by those. Often I wish I was in the penitentiary; that I was hanged or dead, or in some other place."[4]

Perception as public nuisances: The *Soldier's Friend* suggested a few years after the war that the sight of one-armed veterans making a meager living by playing hand organs on the streets of New York was so common that when a child asked about the source of the music being played down the block, an adult could say, "Only a soldier grinding an organ."[5]

Admiration at determined manhood: A short story published in *Harper's Weekly* just after the war features Captain Harry Ash, a well-to-do New Englander who has lost his left arm during the war. He reluctantly agrees to summer in Newport and immediately feels left out and behind the times; the women talk loudly and boldly and race buggies up and down the beach. He is crushed when he spies an old flame, Edna Ackland, joining in. Before the war, she rode demurely next to him, but he fears those days have ended. Harry avoids her and the young men who did not go off to war; when he finally speaks to her, he laments that he is "sadly altered—neither useful nor ornamental to the world." To his astonishment, Edna has neither rejected Harry nor she turned into a "fast" girl. Rather, she has learned to drive because she hopes to resume their courtship and their drives along the beach, with her at the reins. They marry, and the story ends with a drive along the beach on a sunny summer day.[6]

Many thousands of Union and Confederate veterans lived with their disabilities for decades after the war. Over and above its physical challenges, disability could deepen defeat and make victory ring hollow. Even less than other veterans—much less, in most cases—physically disabled men could not simply step back into their peacetime lives. In particular, one-armed or one-legged veterans almost immediately became a stereotype of noble sacrifice and deserving pity. Although the war had ended only a few months earlier, an 1865 broadside that sought support for a fair to aid disabled soldiers in Philadelphia suggested that northerners had already forgotten about the "hopelessly crippled" men who had returned home after "rush-

[ing] to the battle-front and driv[ing] back the invading host." City residents were asked to remember a little more than two years earlier when Lee's army had threatened the city during the Gettysburg campaign: "How gladly would all have contributed *then*, to enable our brave army to drive the invader from our noble State, and save our beloved homes from wreck and ruin." The poster contrasted the city's flourishing businesses with the poor conditions in which the veterans found themselves, showing a woodcut of a one-legged veteran and a one-armed veteran who had also lost an eye still wearing their tattered uniforms and standing idly and woefully on the street. As this broadside suggests, the public conversation about disabled soldiers rarely dwelt on pain or suffering, just as it rarely confronted disabilities caused by chronic disease. Rather, observers tended to focus on the veterans' helplessness and dependence. As the Philadelphia philanthropists asked, "Are you prepared to see them beg from door to door, or seek an asylum in the Almshouse, as common paupers?"[7]

For all the sympathy and kindness bestowed on individual men, civilians often had difficulty establishing a workable philosophy about how society should deal with men crippled by war. A correspondent to a veterans' newspaper recognized the irony that Americans, especially in the North, could express their gratitude so easily and publicly to the dead with speeches and ceremonies and by strewing their graves with flowers. Such remembrances were well and good—the dead must be noted for giving their all for the Union—but "let us also remember him who shared in the soldier's toils, and lived, perhaps to eke out a life of hardship bereft of limb, perhaps of sight, and, maybe, reason. . . . [I]n heaven's name, while we remember the dead let us not forget the living."[8]

The scale of the problem challenged Americans in a number of ways. The men with pinned sleeves and wooden legs were easy to identify and to admire. But civilians found it difficult to know how to react to veterans whose vague disabilities—constant illness, a lack of energy, intimate maladies such as chronic dysentery, hernias, and the like—seemed unrelated to the war. These sorts of misfortunes could befall anyone. And when the disabilities were psychological and, in the case of alcohol abuse, violated community standards, understanding became even more difficult. The number of handicapped men forced society to confront the meaning of disability. But without adequate terminology or institutional supports (aside from soldiers' homes), Americans tended to apply to this new situation traditional notions about dependence and manhood.

"It was all over but the empty sleeves and wooden legs," wrote a Georgian at the end of the war, and missing limbs were the most noticeable and remarked-on disability among Civil War veterans. Perhaps sixty thousand amputations were performed during the war, and about forty-five thousand men survived the procedure. About a quarter of the amputations performed on Union soldiers removed a finger or hand, while a slightly larger percentage of amputees lost all or part of an arm and well over a third lost a leg, a thigh bone, or knee or hip joint. (More than four hundred men lost joints without losing limbs.)[9]

About two hundred thousand Confederates came out of the war still suffering from wounds or disease. R. B. Rosenberg suggests that during the first few years or even decade after the war, these men would have been common sights on country roads and especially in towns and cities, where they begged for food at private homes, sought out odd jobs, or simply waited. Some managed to eke out livings: Billy Beasley was shot through the hips at the Wilderness and never walked upright again, suffering for thirty years from pain and abdominal and kidney infections and for part of that time from an addiction to alcohol. Yet he found low-paying but steady work as a typesetter and drifted from town to town until he sobered up, married, and with help from veteran comrades in Louisville, Kentucky, opened a popular newsstand. Although Confederate veterans might have been somewhat less noticeable than northerners simply because of the more rural nature of the South as well as less surprising given the South's defeat and economic distress for decades after the war, out-of-work and even homeless veterans were part of the southern landscape throughout the Gilded Age.[10]

Both northerners and southerners might have become accustomed to the sight of disabled soldiers, but most would no doubt have been distressed if they had known about a research project begun early in the war by the U.S. Army Medical Department, which had made the most of the unprecedented opportunity to study in a scientific fashion the impact of war on the human body. Doctors created the Army Medical Museum and filled it with hundreds of amputated limbs, photographed amputees, and compiled the six-thousand-page *Medical and Surgical History of the War of the Rebellion*, which remained a standard reference for army doctors during World War I. This rather cool, professional approach to the most severely wounded veterans no doubt paid dividends for future soldiers but also seems to indicate a certain detachment from the plight of the men themselves. The

SHOE-LACE MAN.

THE LOST ARM.—"I GAVE MY RIGHT ARM GLADLY."—[SEE POEM, PAGE 151.]

Disabled veterans on city streets.
Harper's Weekly, March 7, 1868,
September 19, 1868.

photographs of maimed men displaying their stumps and other injuries in a variety of poses almost seemed to mock Victorian parlor settings or the *carte-de-visite* photographs taken of tens of thousands of recruits early in the war. Everything was normal—except for the egregious wound or the missing limb, which would be exposed in sometimes artistic ways. Other disabled men posed nearly naked, with only sheets or towels allowing them to retain a basic modesty. The veterans' exhibitionism, as one scholar calls it, must have shocked anyone who viewed the photographs. Few Americans visited the museum, of course, and while a larger percentage of the public may have seen versions of the photographs, for most civilians the primary evidence of the war's personal tragedies came in the form of neighbors and relatives who came back from the front less than whole. For northerners, the presence of maimed veterans provided a sobering disjunction between victory and tragedy, while for southerners, the disabled offered constant evidence of defeat and of valor.[11]

Although individual veterans found life as one-armed or one-legged men frustrating and economically challenging, the absence of a limb also became an obvious symbol of sacrifice. Although later in life a man might wear an empty sleeve pinned to his Grand Army of the Republic (GAR) uniform like a kind of medal, most tried to conceal their disability by buying or accepting from the government artificial limbs whose primary purpose was to conceal differentness. The federal government granted 133 patents for artificial limbs and other prosthetic devices between 1861 and 1873, and the evolving technology included hinges and natural-looking "skin" intended to help the disabled blend more easily into society. Prosthetics were hardly an absolute solution to these men's problems, however. Even those lucky enough to receive a prosthetic limb complained about the discomfort as well as the noise, awkwardness, and weight.[12]

But different men responded differently to their losses. A story about a Union colonel who refused to have his arm amputated included this jaunty parody of *Hamlet*:

> To amputate or not to amputate that
> Is the question.
> Whether tis nobler
> In the mind to suffer
> The unsymmetry of one armed men and draw
> A pension thereby shuffling off a part
> Of mortal coil or trusting unhinged nature
> Take arms against a cruel surgeon's knife
> And by opposing rusty theories
> Risk a return to dust in the full shape
> Of man.[13]

Yet that rather cavalier attitude was for public consumption and probably did not characterize the feelings of most amputees until years after their loss, if ever. Although exaggerated, a disturbing account of an officer's loss of all four limbs that appeared in the *Atlantic Monthly* just after the war provides real insight into the psychological scars of amputation. In fact, it seemed so realistic to at least a few readers that they offered donations or tried to visit the U.S. Army Hospital for Injuries and Diseases of the Nervous System in Philadelphia, where much of the action takes place. The hospital was real; the story was fictional. Told in a rather clinical first-person style from the point of view of a medical student and assistant surgeon who had transferred to the infantry early in the war, the story horrified readers with its realistic — and, more to the point, believable — description of the pain of the injuries and treatment, the weird effects on the victim's mind and body, and the accounts of the symptoms displayed by other men who suffered from some sort of nervous disability. A few had lost their sense of smell, while one could walk only sideways and others suffered from scores of seizures every day or were subject to bouts of palsy that bent their limbs into unnatural poses. Still others had become hysterical from pain and needed regular doses of morphine. Although the story climaxes with a séance in which the narrator is temporarily and only spiritually reunited with his legs, the haunting last paragraph describes the victim as "not a happy fraction of a man," despite his pension and the tender care provided by friends and relatives. He is simply an immobile shell, waiting to die. The calm tone of the story must have caused more than a little dissonance in readers, who would have expected panic and overwhelming sadness to dominate the narrator's account; indeed, the matter-of-fact chronicle might have suggested, at least subconsciously, that such tragedies were not uncommon among survivors of the war.[14]

In addition to the initial pain and immediate adjustment, most amputees had to endure frequent treatments for the side effects of their wounds. In the blood and bustle of a field hospital, surgeons' hurried procedures often led to complications—poorly executed sutures, the retention of too little flesh between the bone and skin—that could be painful, especially for men trying to manage on artificial legs. Wounds often reopened or required additional surgery. James Tanner, who would become a force in the GAR and head of the Pension Bureau despite being a double amputee, put up with pain and bleeding for thirty years before having additional portions of both legs removed.[15]

Amputations may have been the most shocking and most publicized condition, but a staggering variety of disabilities plagued veterans for the remainder of their days. A long poem published at the turn of the century by an inmate at the Ex-Confederate Soldiers' Home in Richmond, Virginia, cataloged residents' disabilities in a vaguely humorous tone that soldiers would likely have resented coming from an outsider. "There are cripples here of all the kinds that you will ever meet," with corporals, sergeants, majors, and even a general "with no command to see to." The men,

though owning few earthly possessions,
have followed almost all of the different well-known professions.
The one-legged are ready for a race, and the one-armed for a fight,
Or to take a game of base-ball, and to see them is a sight;
They put rights and lefts together, and this makes a man.

A similar epic was written by a North Carolina veteran living at the Soldiers' Home in Raleigh, where there were few enough residents that each man received a pair or trio of couplets describing his character and physical condition and some sort of reference to his wartime exploits. Although some of the verses were meant to be funny or heroic, others unblinkingly provided truthful glimpses of ravaged veterans. One was "sick and despondent, and seems without joy." Of another man, the poet wrote,

> With a shattered leg, and a shivered arm,
> The loss of an eye, and other great harm,
> He sits all day now and knits fishing-nets,
> In useful employment his suffering forgets.

Still another veteran warranted a plea to God:

> When we think of his suffering how sadly we feel:
> His form all wasted with wounds and disease—
> O! Father in Heaven, remember him, please!"[16]

Applications recorded by the U.S. government indicate that about 25 percent of the men awarded pensions through June 1888 had been disabled by gunshot or shell wounds. Chronic diarrhea, cuts and bruises, and rheumatism accounted for 11.8, 8.8, and 8.7 percent of the applications, respectively. Diseases of the heart and lungs and "of the rectum" totaled around 5 percent, while literally dozens of other conditions—diseases of the mouth and diseases of the scrotum and testes, nervous prostration and neuralgia and "disease of the brain," and chronic bronchitis and nasal catarrh—plagued at least a thousand men each.[17]

Additional information about the kinds of disabilities suffered by veterans can be found in the admission records from the Northwestern Branch of the NHDVS, which show the variety and severity of the wounds of disabled soldiers. A few reported disabilities stemmed from disease or accidents such as falling into latrines, getting kicked by mules, or being poked in the eye during night marches. But nearly every page of the hospital ledger offers violent echoes of the great battlefields of the Civil War. During a single week in October 1867, for example, applicants included a soldier who had lost an arm at Chancellorsville; one who had lost a lower leg at Cold Harbor; a man who lost an arm at Pleasant Hill; and a man partially paralyzed at Chickamauga. Just under 44 percent of the applicants listed injuries related to combat; nearly 14 percent listed "accident," nearly 35 percent listed "illness," and just over 6 percent listed "exposure" as the causes of their disabilities. Another 1.3 percent blamed "prison," while one applicant had been injured during a "mob action." Nearly 80 percent of the 964 men who reported injuries had been hurt in the arms, hands, legs, or feet; about three-quarters of the 339 who had endured amputations had lost all or parts of their arms or legs. Although 97 percent of the wounded men were hit by gunshot, shell, grapeshot, or canister, accidents came in a number of forms. Nineteen percent happened in camp, 18 percent involved riding a horse, and 12 and 11 percent occurred while riding trains and wagons, respectively. Horses fell on six soldiers, while horses or mules kicked another nine. Only one soldier sustained his injuries by falling out of a tree, but three were hurt when trees fell on them, and another claimed that his disability was caused by a collapsing barn. Applicants listed nearly eighty separate disabling illnesses, and some men claimed multiple maladies. Rheumatism was the leading complaint, appearing in 14.7 percent of the applications, and blindness or conjunctivitis was listed in 11 percent, but no other illness or condition appeared in more than 10 percent of the cases. Some of the ailments seem rather minor by modern standards: 9 percent of the men complained of "lameness," 3 percent had varicose veins, and just over 4 percent suffered from asthma or bronchitis. Other common problems included consumption or other lung problems (8.1 percent), "paralysis" (6.45), "general debility" (6.2), diarrhea/dysentery (4.2), and heart disease (3.0). Only one veteran listed "shellshock" as his main problem, the same number as had cholera, frostbite, gangrene, gonorrhea, jaundice, kidney stones, laryngitis, "sores," a speech impediment, swollen glands, and syphilis. Although the public would later come to associate substance abuse with soldiers, only one man mentioned "drug addiction," and neither "alcohol" nor "alcoholism" appeared on any applications.[18]

One veterans' newspaper, the *Neighbor's Home Mail*, periodically offered examples of the kind of disabilities suffered by soldiers as part of its campaign to inform veterans of pension opportunities while at the same time trying to convince the government to increase pensions. In the late 1870s, the men who had recently received increased pensions included a Vermont veteran discharged with heart disease who subsequently suffered from pain in his left arm and shoulder, shortness of breath, and "a violent beating of the heart" whenever he exerted himself, symptoms that prevented him from doing his normal work as a farm laborer; a cavalryman who was shot by a bullet that broke his arm near the shoulder, then traveled downward and lodged near his spine, resulting in a wound that remained unhealed; a New Yorker who drew a pension for chronic diarrhea that had left him too weak to work a regular job; another New Yorker whose face had been severely damaged by a bullet that tore through his lip, jaw, and tongue, breaking the upper and lower jaw, knocking out two teeth and loosening the rest, and resulting in constant swelling, dizziness, a severe speech impediment, and the inability to eat any but soft food; a veteran of the 52nd Ohio whose shoulder wound had caused ulcers, stiffness in the joint, and a shrunken arm and hand; a survivor of the 111th New York who suffered a bullet wound that fractured his femur and damaged the tendons behind his knee, rendering him unfit for his previous occupations, carpentry and farming; an artilleryman whose ankles were broken by a shell fragment, leaving them weak and prone to swelling and breaking out in sores, especially in warm weather; and a New York infantryman who was shot in the left side and suffered from pain and weakness in his left arm and from frequent respiratory problems in the left lung that kept him from working more than one out of every two or three days. An Indiana lieutenant had required more than ninety surgical procedures on his wounded arm in the decade after the war. When he died, according to the *Ohio Soldier*, the fact that his doctor had prescribed morphine to relieve the constant pain caused President Grover Cleveland to veto a private pension bill for the man's widow and to make disparaging remarks about his drug use.[19]

In the mid-1880s, the *Ohio Soldier* also reported the "remarkable" case of a man who, as a sixteen-year-old boy, had left his widowed mother and entered the Union Army. He had served through a number of battles with the Army of the Potomac, but on the first day at Gettysburg, three balls had slammed into his hip, thigh, and groin, leaving six wounds and fracturing his spine; shrapnel later tore off part of his right buttock. He lay unattended on the battlefield for four days, then received indifferent treatment from numerous doctors until he was finally admitted to a Philadelphia hospital. He was discharged from the hospital and the army a year later. He could hobble about on two canes but spent a quarter century changing the dressings on his still suppurating wounds two to four times a day, a process that entailed washing the wounds and replacing an eight-yard-long bandage. His digestive system had been virtually destroyed, and an opening had to be made to allow gases to escape from his stomach. He remained more or less constantly under a physician's supervision and was frequently confined to his bed for months at a time.[20]

Tales of disabilities provided hundreds of odd stories that also revealed the pain with which many veterans lived. In 1864, at Brandy Station, a Virginia captain was struck below the right eye by a pistol bullet. Surgeons could not find the bullet, and for many years, the wound caused the man violent pain "in the face and head" and discharges of pus and water through his eye and nose; he gradually lost sight in the eye. The pain led him to take morphine, which usually made him sick. In 1897, while the man was vomiting after a dose of the painkiller, the bullet dropped out of his mouth. His health improved, although he lost the eye entirely, and family members had the bullet mounted in gold to be used as a watch fob.[21]

Such dramatic and gruesome stories, usually told as parables of perseverance, were the easiest disabilities for civilians to understand. But some veterans were simply worn down by their service. The *Milwaukee Sunday Telegraph* acknowledged in 1882 that after the war ended, even those soldiers suffering from nagging wounds or illnesses had "thought themselves strong and patriotic, and said, 'while I can move, I won't ask for a pension.'" But a few years of toil "did its work, and young men are prematurely old." Nonsoldiers perceived such individuals, found in every community, as not having "amounted to anything since the war," as having become "men who have large intentions, but small executive ability; who are scolded rather than helped and pitied; young old men, whose best friend and most frequent counselor is the doctor." The medical profession in particular and society in general lacked the terminology to describe the condition of such men, a lacuna that became a problem when, after years of discomfort and weariness, they applied for pensions based on rather vague disabilities. According to the medical director of the Missouri GAR, the deaths of one-third of the former Union soldiers who expired in his department in 1887 were "directly traceable to exposure during the war." In 1888, the *Ohio Soldier* argued that the time lag between the hardships that caused many veterans' disabilities and their cumulative but gradual effects proved the necessity of the pension law under debate, which would pass two years later as the Dependent Pension Bill. The new policy would "furnish relief to men who by reason of loss of health through such exposure . . . are incapacitated for earning a living for themselves and their families." An 1890 petition to Congress by the "Maimed Soldiers of the United States," in which the disabled soldiers demanded that the government "should not now stop to measure the value of arms, legs and sight," traced many current problems to old disabilities. Amputees' stumps required constant treatment; worse, maimed men frequently suffered from heart problems. Painkillers and other medicines affected eyesight, and even veterans who could afford the health insurance plans beginning to appear on the market were virtually uninsurable because of the inevitable complications from injuries and disease that dated from the men's army days.[22]

The truly pathetic injuries that grabbed the attention of writers of newspaper human interest stories did not reflect the reality for most veterans. A poem that appeared in the newsletter of the NHDVS branch in Hampton, Virginia, offered a first-person account of the physical weariness and psychological ennui of which many old soldiers complained. Simply titled "Bob Ridley," the poem told the story of a man who had served for three years and had fought in twenty battles but had never been wounded.

> That was luck, but as soon as they mustered us out,
> I lost the old vigor, and wandered about;
> Somehow I'm a failure and scarcely know why.
> Doomed to live when it's harder to live than to die.

Despite being "unable to labor, too weary to roam," Ridley suffered from a vague disability that was not enough to get him a pension.[23]

As the medical profession developed more accurate diagnoses late in the Gilded Age, doctors found more plausible explanations for the complaints of real-life Bob Ridleys. In 1890, the surgeon at the NHDVS Central Branch in Dayton, Ohio, claimed that 80 percent of the five thousand men there suffered from heart disease brought on by the "forced physical exertion of the campaigns" they had fought a quarter century earlier. Although the diagnosis of such problems was in its infancy and the numbers were rather suspect, tens of thousands of men clearly were victimized by heart problems related to their wartime service. In the early 1890s, John Shaw Billings, a former army surgeon, published a study with similar results. Billings, whose findings were frequently cited in other sources, concluded that the average veteran "suffers more from illness and has a somewhat less expectation of life."[24]

These logical conclusions have been supported by modern researchers, who have found evidence to support the contention that even men who did not suffer from physical disabilities could develop disabling conditions related directly to their service. Pension and military records have provided evidence that veterans were much more likely to suffer from tuberculosis, heart disease, and rheumatism and were fifty-six times more likely to suffer from chronic diarrhea and dysentery. Those who survived "intimate violence"—who served in units with high casualty rates—were 51 percent more likely to develop cardiac, gastrointestinal, and nervous problems later in life. One team of researchers suggests that Civil War soldiers were more vulnerable than soldiers in later wars because they served in units with friends and family members, so the dead and maimed were not simply comrades but lifelong acquaintances. Moreover, many units received few or no replacements, so men were reminded of the results of the violence to which they were exposed every time their ever-dwindling companies and regiments lined up for roll call. One of the strongest variables in the development of long-term illnesses and conditions after the war was the percentage of men killed in any given company. The higher the casualty rate, the higher the rate of illness among survivors. Even more striking is the fact that 93 percent of the men who were younger than eighteen when they enlisted developed symptoms of diseases that have been linked to battlefield trauma.[25]

There is no reason to think that men like these victims of disabling and discouraging wounds did not succumb to the same dysfunction that plagued wounded and disabled veterans returning from World War II. The complex feelings of those men and the often debilitating fear, loathing, and shame of their wounds, both physical and mental, were a staple of postwar popular culture, and although many of the fictional versions of these veterans' lives also turned out more or less for the best, the psychological and sexual effects of their experiences were presented far more explicitly than such matters were discussed after the Civil War. Yet wounded and disabled Civil War veterans likely would have experienced the same resentment of their limitations.[26]

Army doctors had diagnosed some of these problems during the Civil War. The condition called "shell shock" in the 1920s and "posttraumatic stress syndrome" in the 1980s was labeled during the Civil War as "irritable heart" (the physiological version) and "nostalgia" (the psychological version). Both led to the discharge of thousands of men from the Confederate and Union armies. Doctors believed that certain types of young men were particularly likely to develop nostalgia—married men leaving their families for the first time as well as men with what one expert described as "feeble will, highly developed imaginative faculties, and strong sexual desires"—and assumed that the conditions were temporary. But side effects such as depression, poor appetite, lack of responsiveness to outside stimuli, headaches, and irregularity plagued many men for years after they left the military.[27]

State institutions for the insane came to blame certain pathologies on the war. In the year or two immediately after the conflict ended, a number of patients admitted to Wisconsin's state mental institution were diagnosed with problems suggesting wartime causes. George Pope entered the facility after a long bout with illness and an injury sustained while in a Confederate prison left him delusional, excitable, noisy, and violent. August Myers left his regiment's camp just before mustering out in the summer of 1865 and turned up at his Wisconsin home calling himself Louis Napoleon. He tried to burn down his house and was "sulky, morose, and irritable." Apparently affected by his experiences at the Battle of Perryville, James Orr began having delusions and worrying about some sort of evil influence threatening him and his family. His gun was taken away from him, and he spent time in a hospital; when he returned, his comrades' rather indelicate teasing about shooting him for desertion sent him over the edge, and he started talking about killing friends and comrades. Another veteran came to the institution "stupid, morose, obstinate"; yet another man was subject to violent attacks of epilepsy as a result of an intermittent fever that began while he was stationed at Vicksburg; and a third developed "ideas of his own sinfulness and unworthiness." A former captain, beset by sunstroke and overindulgence in alcohol, imagined himself second in command to U. S. Grant, refused to clean himself or his uniform, and tended to spit tobacco juice inside or directly out of windows. A musician with the 4th Wisconsin Cavalry was sent to the government asylum in Washington, D.C., during the war for "irrational thoughts of home," but when he was released and returned to Wisconsin, his wife refused to live with him. He started obsessing about her and the "colored race" and was frequently "incoherent, full of odd fancies and absurd ideas." Whether these men were victims of some sort of posttraumatic stress is unclear, but thousands of men returned to civilian life with hidden disabilities that to a greater or lesser degree shaped the rest of their lives.[28]

Virginia's Western Lunatic Asylum admitted fifty-seven people (including eighteen women) whose symptoms were officially blamed on the war. Some were parents or wives of soldiers consumed with fear about the plight of their absent loved ones or about their own situations. Many were men who had been made at least temporarily mentally ill by conscription, combat, or imprisonment. A few suffered from head wounds or other traumas from which they never recovered. Some became irrationally angry, while others displayed melancholy or other nervous habits.[29]

Anecdotes of war-related mental trauma provided a minor thread in Gilded Age thinking about veterans. According to the *Ohio Soldier*, "The once gallant soldier, Henry Lubker," a survivor of Andersonville, now spent his days pacing the streets of Quincy, Illinois. Physically healthy, "the cloud that darkened his mind while in that hell hole" made him constantly mark off possible places to dig escape tunnels. "While thus engaged he will eagerly grab up any stray bone he may notice in the gutter and desperately cling to it."[30]

Another victim of Andersonville, Boston Corbett, better known as the soldier who shot and killed John Wilkes Booth, suffered greatly not only from his incarceration but equally from the embarrassment of his ill-considered marksmanship, his brief arrest, and the government's decision not to give him the five-thousand-dollar reward he expected. He left the service and apparently disappeared for some time before surfacing on a homestead near Concordia, Kansas, in the late 1870s, where he earned a reputation as a flinty hermit whose main hobby was lying flat on his back and shooting crows out of the sky. He was fierce, confrontational, and a little odd; when a local church invited him to give a lecture about his experiences, he offered a vague rant about his religious beliefs. When a group of boys played baseball on his claim, he frightened them away by shooting over their heads. Arrested for assault, he acted as his own lawyer and pulled a pistol in the courtroom, backing out the door like a bank robber. He somehow arranged an appointment as assistant doorkeeper at the state legislature, a common sinecure for veterans, where he wore his old army cap and a pair of pistols; when legislators began acting in ways he did not approve, he pulled out his guns and called the lawmakers "blasphemers," resulting in his arrest, a trial, and a declaration of insanity. He lived in the state asylum in Topeka for a short time, and then escaped on a stolen horse and rode into obscurity.[31]

James Fraser, a Confederate who had lost his right leg below the knee during the Seven Days' Battles, turned to teaching when his injury rendered him unable to make a living at farming. In the many court documents that traced his postwar life, family members and neighbors described him as an angry, violent man who seemed to believe that his disability entitled him to special treatment. He married a widow with children, but when she died, the children were taken away from him amid reports of abuse. He was later charged with murder. It is striking that people who knew Fraser blamed his behavior on the disability incurred fighting for the Confederacy. Without honor and particularly without a way to make a decent living, men such as Fraser were scarred as deeply in their minds as in their bodies.[32]

A lurid early 1880 *Milwaukee Sentinel* report highlighted the connection, at least in the public mind, between disability and disaffection. Popular National Home bandmaster William Wilkinson and his wife, Maggie, died in a murder-suicide, the *Sentinel* suggested, at least partly because of the physical and psychological pain caused by the absence of one of his legs, which had been amputated during the war after he contracted a severe form of rheumatism. William's drinking had been an issue in the troubled marriage for years; Maggie had left him three times before but had returned; she was now threatening to leave again. The couple had three daughters between the ages of four years and four months, but William spent many evenings in saloons with fellow veterans. On the night of January 12, William had complained to his friends that Maggie had slapped him and threatened to hide his wooden leg so he could no longer go out drinking. As the evening wore on and William sank deeper into drunkenness, he tried unsuccessfully to get someone to buy his pistol. After driving a number of drunken soldiers back to the NHDVS in his wagon, he returned to his home, where he apparently discovered his wife writing a good-bye note, which ended, "I can[not] live this life an[y] longer, four it gets wours in[stead] of beter." William, "charged with all the electricity of the pent-up bitterness of the few years," "braced with liquor," and "whipped by the scorpion sting of an angry woman's tongue," then shot her in the head before ending his own "life of discomfort, guilt, and drunkenness." The three children were unharmed.[33]

These examples only scratch the surface. No one conducted longitudinal surveys of the psychological traumas of Civil War veterans, but researchers have found that more than 40 percent of Vietnam veterans have suffered from full or partial posttraumatic stress disorder (PTSD), with the likelihood of being so afflicted increased among men exposed to combat. Despite the vast differences in the nature of the Civil War and Vietnam War, similar findings may well hold true for veterans of the earlier conflict.[34]

Tens of thousands of veterans of both armies suffered from countless visible and invisible disabilities and maladies. The number of disabled men living in Gilded Age America created a kind of subculture, with such men appearing as minor characters in popular literature, as examples of the deserving poor, as symbols of the costs of war. As such, they were somewhat differently perceived and perceived themselves somewhat differently than other disabled men living during this era. The status of disabled railroad men has some relevance to the struggles of disabled soldiers. As very visible members of society and as laborers in one of Gilded Age America's more dangerous occupations, engineers, brakemen, and other railroaders who lost fingers, hands, and even limbs on the job were fraught with symbolism. They wanted to stay on the job if possible, to remain independent rather than scraping by on tiny pensions or depending on family members. Simply put, they wanted to retain their manhood. And their employers and society in general tended to hold them up as heroes even as they became less useful. Conversely, the railroaders' "brotherhoods," or labor unions, used disabled fellow workers as examples of the unfairness of corporate policies that pushed men to work harder and faster no matter the cost. Unions tended to marginalize the disabled men by pushing for institutions, insurance, and other programs designed to care for such men. The tension between a community caring for the men to whom it owed a great deal and the preference by those men to remain independent and manly was an important feature of labor relations in the late nineteenth century.[35]

Although these tensions help clarify some of the complexities of the relationship between the larger society and disabled soldiers, the fact that the latter had suffered their wounds in the service of their country complicated matters. Most Americans wanted to be fair to disabled veterans but were unsure about how best to do so.

A Spirit above Dependence

Of course, the rather stern beneficence of the Gilded Age awarded its greatest sympathy to unfortunates who tried to help themselves. The *Soldier's Friend* acknowledged that many disabled men—farmers, mechanics, men who worked on their feet or with both hands—could not return to their prewar occupations. But, it asked readers, "Are you to sit down at the street corners, as you have seen some of our number in the metropolis, and depend upon the charities of the people for a support? Are you to entertain the idea that, because you have suffered so much in your country's service, the world owes you a living, and you have a right to sit idle and demand it? No!" Men who denied that the world owed them anything and made their own way earned the admiration of veterans and civilians alike.[36]

Confederate amputee James E. Hanger exemplified the veteran who transcended his disability, building an artificial limb business with factories in Richmond, Atlanta, and St. Louis. His prosthetic legs were cheap and comfortable and won awards at national exhibitions. On the Union side, Jacob Gantz represented the ideal self-reliant handicapped veteran. His life was changed forever when a bullet broke both bones in his upper right arm, necessitating an amputation of the arm halfway between his elbow and shoulder. The veteran of the 4th Iowa could not return to farming, the only vocation he had ever known, but his drive and adaptability made him the model of the successful disabled veteran. He opened a boardinghouse and livery stable in Fairfield, Iowa, rented out his 160-acre farm, and served several terms as sheriff and tax assessor. He became a pillar of the community, taking leadership roles in his church, the local Odd Fellows chapter, and the GAR. When he died sixty years after he was wounded, the flag on the courthouse lawn flew at half mast, as it did whenever a Union veteran died.[37]

A few veterans answered the challenge to remain self-sufficient by calling attention to their disabilities as a means of making a living. Indeed, Frances Clarke has drawn on Victorian sensibilities unaffected by postmodern attitudes to show that Union amputees felt more rather than less like men despite the loss of limbs that prevented them from meeting many of the antebellum requirements of manhood. They offered as examples of their continuing manhood their obvious sacrifice and ability to withstand pain and suffering, the devotion to duty and patriotism that that sacrifice seemed to prove, and a work ethic that transcended mere handicaps.[38]

Unembarrassed and ambitious, such men sought to use their condition to elicit sympathy and business. An 1866 advertisement in the *Saturday Evening Post* offering a vague collection of "four new and valuable articles, for the preservation and promotion of health," demonstrated exactly that quality. The notice went into far more detail about the advertiser's personal life than most. He was a "crippled and helpless soldier" with an infirm mother and no other way to support himself. He was an honorably discharged soldier who had been robbed of several hundred dollars. Customers "shall have, (to say the least,) more real value and satisfaction for their money than they ever have got, or will ever get." The ad included the names of a number of references and added one final plea: "I need your patronage very much, and would be most humbly grateful to you for it."[39]

Not quite as obvious but also highlighting their sellers' disabilities were several songs and poems, ostensibly written by disabled soldiers and intended to be sold by disabled soldiers. *The One Arm and One Leg Soldier, Wounded at the Battle of Shiloh, Sunday Morning, April 6th, 1862*, appeared as a broadside in 1865. It painted a graphic picture of the bloody battlefield, but the main purpose of the six-verse, twenty-four-line poem was to raise money: it ended, "Stranger, pardon if I ask you, / Buy a crippled soldier's song."[40] The title of a memoir of service with Stonewall Jackson highlighted the author's disability: *How a One-Legged Rebel Lives: Reminiscences of the Civil War*. The author, who had lost his leg as a teenaged volunteer in the 52nd Virginia, made it clear that the "chief object in this work is to get something to support myself with—in fact, it is a scheme founded on food, raiment and shelter, which I find hard to come at by one in my situation, there being so few positions open to a man maimed as I am, with no more education and business training than I possess." Yet he proudly declared, "I am no applicant for charity."[41]

The most striking example of a disabled soldier highlighting rather than trying to hide a disability was the postwar career of J. F. Chase, an artillery-man in the 5th Maine Battery who was grievously wounded at Gettysburg when a shell landed three feet from his artillery piece during the bombard-ment of Cemetery Ridge. The shell tore off his right arm and knocked his left eye out of its socket; the shrapnel left six wounds in his neck and torso. He was believed dead, but just before he was to be buried, he groaned, catch-ing the attention of an attendant. When he recovered consciousness, his first words, according to witnesses, were, "Did we win the battle?" A poet named Frost from Chase's hometown penned an ode in his honor that bor-rowed those words and described his wounds to demonstrate his extraordi-nary patriotism. After the war, Chase received the Medal of Honor for dis-tinguished bravery at Chancellorsville, worked as an inventor (receiving patents for an improved hoopskirt and a bustle, among other things), and traveled the Northeast, giving lectures about his injuries and the temper-ance cause. The pamphlet he distributed advertised the "Battle Scarred John F. Chase" and featured a woodcut showing his stump and the thicket of scars on his chest and shoulder as well as the poem by Frost and a brief account of Chase's wounding that appeared in a number of newspapers in New England and New York in the mid-1880s. After working as a messen-ger in the Maine House of Representatives for several years, he moved to St. Petersburg, Florida, in the 1890s; just after the turn of the century, he tried to form Veteran City, a colony for old Union soldiers. Although the venture did not succeed, it did form the basis of the modern city of Gulfport, where a city park still carries his name. Chase clearly made his disability work for him. His famous, terribly scarred likeness appeared on temperance publica-tions; he lectured on temperance at the Gettysburg Cyclorama and accom-panied the giant painting when it went on tour. The etching of his wounds also appeared on promotional material for his patented wringer and water still.[42]

A well-publicized experiment in retraining—and in public relations—was announced in the summer of 1865, when William O. Bourne organized a "left-handed penmanship" contest for the men that the *Soldier's Friend* called the Left-Armed Corps. Offering five hundred dollars for the four "best specimens" of penmanship by right-handed men who had lost their dominant limbs, Bourne asked soldiers to write up to four pages on patriotic themes, particularly their personal experiences during the war. He planned an exhibition and a memorial volume of some of the entries. *Harper's Weekly* reported at least twice on the contest, approvingly suggesting that Bourne's "generous proposition . . . has undoubtedly stimulated many a man to accomplish himself for clerkly occupation"—as Bourne intended. The call for entries described the contest as "an inducement to the class of wounded and disabled soldiers . . . to make every effort to fit themselves for lucrative and honorable positions." The contest was also designed to inspire civilians' patriotism and enhance their appreciation of soldiers' sacrifices.[43]

The exhibition of left-handed writing took place over several evenings in May 1866 at Seaton Hall, on the corner of 9th and D Streets in Washington, D.C. The hall was decorated with flags and banners, portraits of generals, and paintings of battle scenes. Along the walls were patriotic and inspirational mottoes prepared by the ladies of the Union Relief Association, including, "The empty sleeve should not be the badge of an empty purse," "Our disabled soldiers have kept the Union from being disabled," and "The empty sleeve, Disabled but not disheartened." A number of prominent politicians and several generals spoke first; the highlight was the talk by General O. O. Howard, himself a member of the Left-Handed Corps. General U. S. Grant attended the display later in the week.[44]

Many of the essays asserted the masculinity of their writers in the face of the unmanning connoted by the loss of their most valuable limb by describing their wartime contributions, their resolution to persevere and adapt to their condition, and their ability to continue to perform the duties required of heads of households. But some also reflected soldiers' resentment toward the cold reception they received after returning home and toward most civilians' failure to understand—or to try to understand—the difficulties of being disabled. In a sense they wore their hearts on their empty sleeves, carefully articulating the differences between "heroes" and "cripples." But many Americans failed to make this distinction, especially with regard to veterans without disabilities that were easy to identify or understand.[45]

The left-handed writing contest garnered publicity but had little effect on the public's perceptions of veterans. The spectrum of responses ranged from sympathy to pity to contempt. Veterans could not have escaped the prevailing Gilded Age expectations that men should support themselves as well as their dependents and that aged males who had failed to save money for their retirement deserved whatever degraded and hopeless situation in which they found themselves. Even disabled men who were clearly unable to support themselves could not escape the burden of pity and blame. One historian has suggested that "the history of begging is virtually synonymous with the history of disability," and many Americans seem to have naturally associated disabled men with crushing poverty and dependence after the war.[46]

Working against veterans with major or even minor disabilities was the attitude that Americans would naturally resist the temptation to become dependent or to accept charity. Moreover, most citizens assumed that even men who were unable to perform labor or any other kind of work would avoid at all costs becoming dependent on others. Henry Bellows, president of the U.S. Sanitary Commission (ussc), had captured the attitudes of most Victorians when he stated in a postwar report that one of the reasons that Union veterans would not require permanent care was that Americans shared "a spirit above dependence."[47]

What Will You Do with the Disabled Soldiers?

An 1869 story underscores the challenges facing veterans without charitable assistance. Although it was intended to embarrass Republicans by exposing their hypocrisy in courting the "soldier vote," "The Story of a Crutch" offers a dreary picture of a crippled veteran who clomps around on his clumsy wooden leg collecting rags to sell for a few pennies. Some days he makes no money. He manages to pay for a fourth-floor garret with no windows and a straw pallet, where he lies every night, forgotten by the nation for which he fought. When he was "young," just seven years earlier, grand speeches had convinced him that his duty was to the Union and that his sacrifice would be appreciated. But just four years after the war, he had already been forgotten.[48]

The debate over how best to care for men like this fictional victim of the war led to a lively public discourse about disabled men in particular and veterans in general. Although veterans also entered the conversation—with a vengeance, in the case of soldiers' papers supporting pensions and hiring preferences in the 1880s and 1890s—the most vocal contributors to the dialogue immediately after the war were civilians. And for the most part, they urged the nation not to fall into the trap of providing excessive aid to disabled veterans out of a misplaced sense of gratitude or pity.

The ussc's Bellows had anticipated long before the war was over that many men would return to civilian life less than whole and knew that a decision would have to be made about how to deal with them. He urged that every effort be made to avoid long-term institutionalization of crippled and otherwise disabled veterans. Their treatment should incur "as little outside interference with natural laws and self-help as possible." Most of the "invalid class" should be absorbed "into the homes, and into the ordinary industry of the country." He feared that the governments of northern states, which raised enlistment bounties "to an excessive and injurious height," would also "attempt to make political capital out of the sympathy of the public with the invalids of the war . . . with much bad and demoralizing sentimentality." To do so would create a "class" of men "with a right to be idle, or to beg, or to claim exemption from the ordinary rules of life."[49]

In fact, a number of postwar commentators warned against allowing sentimental patriotism and gratitude to overrule common sense and traditional American strictures against saddling the community with the costs of supporting its undeserving members. Fred N. Knapp, another ussc official, wrote of the "feeling in the community that too much cannot . . . be done for the men who have become disabled in the war; that do all we may for their comfort, we shall never half repay them for the sacrifice they have made." That said, the programs created for them had to rise above the natural tendency to "seize upon them as the objects upon which we may *mark off* this nervous philanthropic excitability, and count the benefit rendered by the numbers we get into asylums." Knapp went on to provide a set of detailed suggestions for developing "sanitaria" for veterans with the most severe disabilities. His most crucial recommendation was that any institution caring for these men "be not merely an 'asylum,' but also a workshop, and a school, and a home."[50]

The ussc had begun studying how to deal with disabled soldiers as early as 1862. Based partly on an extensive examination of European institutions as well as on ussc leaders' very typical attitudes about work, class, and government, the commission discouraged efforts to establish homes for crippled soldiers except for the very small number of truly disabled survivors without home, family, or prospects. In their correspondence and their official reports, ussc officials argued that whenever possible, veterans should be "reabsorbed" into their own communities and assigned to light labor (or even be mustered as a permanent "invalid corps" in the army). They should never be put into a situation that "renders them . . . independent of public opinion, or segregate them from friends, kindred, or fellow-citizens"; nor should they be granted such large pensions that they could "live in absolute idleness." Stephen H. Perkins, who toured the leading European soldiers' homes, including the well-known, even to Americans, Hôtel des Invalides in Paris, concluded in his forty-page report that purposelessness and drunkenness characterized many inmates. In his final recommendations on the

One of the short-lived messenger services staffed by former soldiers. *Harper's Weekly*, March 7, 1868.

issue, Bellows declared that European homes were "costly failures," urged pensions over institutionalization for the overwhelming majority of veterans, and estimated that only two thousand men would be "so homeless, so helpless, so utterly disabled by sickness or wounds" that they would require permanent care.[51]

Simply being disabled did not justify, as Bellows put it, "an exemption from the ordinary rules of life." Soldiers bore responsibility for making the necessary changes in their lives. Many had been skilled laborers and farmers before the war; with those occupations closed to them, they needed to fit themselves for less physical labor. Indeed, a former Union chaplain assured readers of a New York newspaper that disabled veterans wanted to work and that "most disabled men can still do something." Employing disabled soldiers would save them "from all the miseries and evils of idleness." One crippled veteran demanded in a letter to the *Soldier's Friend*, "Give us employment! Give us your patronage and encouragement, and you will not be troubled with the pitiful sight of maimed paupers coming to your doors for bread." Even before the war ended, advocates for disabled veterans had urged the government to substitute disabled but functional veterans for able-bodied men working as clerks, bookkeepers, messengers, letter carriers, and watchmen in government offices, navy yards, and customhouses. "We cannot consent to make paupers of our soldiers," declared one editorialist. "Of all others they are the first who deserve well of the country." And less physically demanding jobs absorbed some of the disabled. Prefiguring a shift in occupation that would begin for all workers later in the Gilded Age, about 25 percent of disabled veterans moved from manual occupations to clerical work.[52]

Several branches of the NHDVS conducted schools for disabled veterans, and a number of men learned trades as clerks, bookkeepers, and telegraph operators. Others learned reading, writing, and arithmetic. By 1871, just over four hundred men were receiving some sort of training through the NHDVS, but the number quickly dwindled, and most of the schools closed by the mid-1870s. Although the 1881 guide to the Dayton branch of the NHDVS still promoted its school, the paragraph describing the many trades that could be learned by one-armed veterans and others was copied verbatim from a *Harper's Weekly* article published a decade earlier, when the home really did operate a school.[53]

Other sources suggest that at least some kind of education continued past the closing of the trade schools. One of the officers of the Central Branch recalled in 1884 that in the 1870s, men would occasionally "prepare themselves" to go out and teach. A normal school apparently trained a number of soldiers to be teachers, but the school closed, and by the mid-1880s, men were much less likely to learn anything in the home that would help them support themselves outside. The chaplain recalled that a woman from New England had run a school for a time; it served only about forty men per year, but "the effect was good" on those men. The school was closed by the early 1880s as the "old" soldiers entered middle age.[54]

Foreshadowing in a very small way the massive G.I. Bill of the 1940s, a number of educational institutions offered to help disabled veterans adapt to their new situations in the year or two after the close of the war. Northwestern Business College in Aurora, Illinois, offered full scholarships to the "western men" who were among the top finishers in Bourne's left-handed writing contest as well as to disabled men selected as most deserving by county judges around the state. Other disabled soldiers (and the children of clergymen) could receive discounts. St. Louis's Bryant, Stratton, and Carpenter Business College also offered discounts to disabled soldiers who "wish to qualify themselves thoroughly for the duties of a business life." Illinois College offered free tuition to the sons of deceased or disabled soldiers, while a dozen disabled soldiers received scholarships at Chicago's School of Trade beginning in the summer of 1865.[55]

Maimed Confederates could attend the University of Virginia free of charge during the last year of the war and for a year or two thereafter; in 1865, twenty-one of the school's fifty-five students were disabled veterans, while another dozen paying full tuition had lost arms, legs, or feet. The State' of Georgia offered up to three hundred dollars in grants, and several Georgia universities offered free tuition to veterans unable to work after the war; veterans taking advantage of these programs had only to teach in a public school while taking classes.[56]

The most extensive effort to educate disabled soldiers was the Illinois Soldiers' College in Fulton, which opened in 1866. The college took the place of a short-lived military academy. Its prospectus promised a nondenominational Christian education for disabled soldiers and their sons and a curriculum that included "preparatory" (high school), commercial, normal, scientific, and classical departments. Students would be held to a modified version of military discipline, although former soldiers would be exempt from drills. The rhetoric in the prospectus exactly matched the concerns and hopes articulated by Bellows and other USSC officials. "What will you do with the disabled soldiers?" asked the school's founders, answering, "There is no cheaper and certainly no better way, than to *help these men to help themselves*." Although the college would provide the students with a home and would provide "for the physical care of its inmates," the school also "educates and elevates them. Many will be rendered useful and self-supporting that would otherwise remain burdens upon public or private charity." As the college catalog suggested four years later, army service had molded the men into likely students. The "habits of order, regularity and discipline, had been formed, a wide acquaintance with human nature had been acquired, a laudable ambition had been fostered, and generous and unselfish impulses had been cultivated. Toil, privation and danger, anguish and joy, educate men."[57]

These beliefs—which, ironically, ran in almost direct opposition to how most observers interpreted the effects of military service on soldiers—failed to ensure success. The school got off to a promising start, engendering high hopes: the *Soldier's Friend* reported in 1868 that the institution was in a "flourishing condition," with three hundred disabled soldiers in the student body, and the catalog for 1870 listed nearly two hundred men and boys representing more than one hundred different Illinois regiments. The school had encountered difficulty, however, as a consequence of a series of unsatisfactory presidents and the failure in the midst of the 1870s depression to create the endowment that was supposed to have supported the school in perpetuity. In 1873, the school became Northern Illinois College; it later operated as a military academy for a decade and then closed just before World War I.[58]

Although not all disabled veterans became self-sufficient, one particularly notable stereotype of those permanently crippled by war wounds was of the man who had lost a leg or arm but persevered and contributed in meaningful ways to society. Such a self-reliant, productive disabled veteran even appeared in a series of children's books and comics published beginning in the 1910s. The *Teenie Weenies*, drawn by William Donahey, featured, among other almost entirely positive American archetypes, the "Old Soldier," who limps importantly through many adventures. Sporting a long white beard and kepi and wearing an outfit that could have passed for the uniform worn in soldiers' homes or by the GAR, the one-legged veteran supervises construction projects or watches as the other members of his tiny community skate, run rapids, and wage war against aggressors. He neither asks for nor receives special help from any of his comrades.[59]

After World War I produced its own disabled veterans, a book by a Red Cross official advocated occupational therapy for most disabled veterans and pensions and institutional care only for those who were truly unable to survive without help. *Your Duty to the War Cripple* acknowledged that "in the past we have done everything possible to make the cripple a failure." Simply pouring "sympathy and charity" on the disabled was not enough; Americans had to be committed to making sure that the maimed survivors of the Great War were retrained for useful lives. "Idleness is a calamity too great to be borne." It was, the Red Cross argued, "no kindness to reduce" men "to the ignominy of dependence on others, for that makes them 'crippled' indeed."[60]

That Great Resource of Veterans

Because drinking, as novelist Elizabeth Corbett recalled many years after her girlhood at the Northwestern Branch of the NHDVS in Milwaukee, was "that great resource of veterans," old soldiers were part of the Gilded Age effort to shape Americans' morals. Although former soldiers were hardly the only Americans to drink or drink to excess, they became one of the groups most closely identified with drinking in the United States. A recent book suggests that "Union troops took no stronger perception of themselves into the army than their right to drink" and that soldiers did not engage in mere "social drinking" but drank for the purpose of getting drunk. If soldiers saw drinking to excess as a way of "demonstrating their masculine control of alcohol," it is not surprising that their reputation as drinkers survived the war. And that reputation no doubt affected the ways that civilians viewed former soldiers who drank. The fact that residents of the NHDVS were examined, disciplined, and watched so closely makes them a useful source of information about soldiers' drinking habits and their effects on the men's health and well-being. Of course, institutionalized men cannot represent all veterans; these men had reasons for submitting to life in soldiers' homes. And, in fact, living in the homes was widely believed to encourage drinking. Nevertheless, the causes and effects of residents' drinking likely paralleled to a certain extent the alcohol use of many nonresident veterans.[61]

Drinking alcohol was a way of life at soldiers' homes. Only a couple of years after its opening, officials at the Northwestern Branch named inmates' spending their pensions on alcohol the number one problem at the home. "The soldier inmate," asserted the *Milwaukee Sentinel* in its report on a recent meeting of the home's Board of Managers, "is never easy so long as he is in possession of a dime." After receiving their pensions, which were distributed every three or six months, many soldiers applied to be discharged from the home and then went off to spend their money "in riotous living." After a month or two, "finding himself in the position of the prodigal son," a soldier would reapply for admission and be accepted, and the cycle would start over.[62]

A sergeant at in the NHDVS branch at Togus, Maine, testified to the desperation of the men, many of whom "you could not content" without some form of alcohol. The cheap, potent "kerosene article" they obtained from shady liquor dealers "makes them crazy"; another witness claimed that addiction led veterans to sell their uniforms for alcohol. Indeed, veterans gained a national reputation for drinking. The *National Police Gazette*, hardly a temperance publication, ran an illustration of veterans pushing and shoving, crutches flying and eyes wide with desperation, in their rush for free beer on Thanksgiving. "The soldier's Home at Dayton, Ohio, is badly demoralized by the Thanksgiving present of a generous brewery," read the caption.[63]

Although their relatively small size made them easier to manage, homes for Confederate veterans were also plagued by alcohol-related problems. In reports of the regular board meetings of the Confederate Home in Kentucky, the *Confederate Home Messenger* often acknowledged that some men drank to excess. In late 1910, an unspecified number of residents were "administered . . . reproofs" for "the use of intoxicants" and were warned that they could be expelled if they were caught again. A few months later, several men were suspended and one was discharged for similar conduct.[64]

The 1910 annual report of the Confederate Soldiers' Home of Georgia stated that 2 of the roughly 120 residents had been expelled in the previous year. Although the report did not specify the nature of their "gross misconduct" and rather primly admitted that "these cases of discipline are distressing and distasteful to the Board," the language used—expulsion was considered "only in very aggravated cases, and when it becomes absolutely necessary for the peace and good order of the Institution, and protection to the Inmates"—resembled the terminology used in alcohol-related incidents in almost all soldiers' homes.[65]

The National Home's policy of firm lenience and understanding regarding alcohol abuse matched the attitudes held by many Americans late in the nineteenth century. Even absolute temperance advocates such as the Women's Christian Temperance Union favored rehabilitation and sympathy for victims of alcohol. This approach was also reflected in physicians' growing acceptance of alcoholism as a disease. Heredity, a weak moral backbone, and the social and psychological pressures arising from the rapid modernization of the United States continued to receive blame for the apparently growing number of drug and alcohol addicts, which sensationalistic and unconfirmed estimates put at a million by 1900. Yet the medical community instinctively turned to the idea that addiction—to opium, to heroin, to alcohol, to sex, to tobacco—was a curable pathology.[66]

Yet not every man with a drinking problem suffered from daily physical pain, and not every painfully crippled veteran became an alcoholic. But a different kind of pain may well have been involved. Disabled or chronically ill people sometimes turn to alcohol or other addictive substances as a result of the depression growing out of their isolated lives, the frustration resulting from their helplessness, or from simple boredom. Alcohol abuse was one of the most frequent behaviors exhibited by psychologically troubled Vietnam veterans. Elizabeth Corbett maintained that the monotony of life at the home caused some of her beloved veterans to seek release in the bottle, and her amateur diagnosis certainly covered at least part of the problem. The men may have been well cared for—they were surrounded by beautiful grounds and had plenty to eat, clean beds in which to sleep, all the clothes they needed, a little spending money, and the grateful respect of the community in which they lived—but their lives had climaxed decades earlier. Their curse was to live for many years as wards of the nation. In the late nineteenth century, the vast majority of male Americans over the age of sixty-five were still gainfully employed; indeed, the 1890 veterans' census found that as Union veterans moved into and past middle age, 93 percent reported occupations, compared to 90 percent of all men over the age of forty-five. Yet few of the thousands of veterans living in the National Homes held steady jobs. To be sure, veterans earned a few dollars a month in return for providing much of the menial and some of the skilled labor at the homes, but even in the 1870s, only about a third of all inmates were employed. Their inability—some critics would call it their failure—to support themselves no doubt contributed to the malaise that early-twentieth-century experts blamed for veterans' readjustment problems.[67]

Somewhat more speculative as a possible cause of veterans' alcoholism is the notion that many of the veterans who lived out their years at the National Homes suffered from PTSD. Thousands of Vietnam veterans have been diagnosed with this illness, and their experiences and responses are instructive in piecing together the nature of Civil War veterans' postwar lives. Eric T. Dean was one of the first historians to explore the effects of combat on Civil War soldiers. He found a number of symptoms familiar in modern combat veterans: boredom with peacetime lives, a propensity for violence, and serious, long-term psychiatric problems ranging from depression and anxiety to "social numbing," irrational fears, and cognitive disorders. Many veterans fought with family members and old friends, slept poorly, and experienced flashbacks, while others turned into loners ill at ease with other men and women. Family members in Dean's sample of Indiana veterans admitted to the state asylum for the insane reported that their loved ones had lost ambition, had become irritable, and could no longer concentrate or think clearly, and nearly 30 percent turned to alcohol or narcotics. Moreover, substance abuse remains a frequent problem among veterans suffering from PTSD. One recent study suggests that the most important psychiatric distinction between Vietnam veterans suffering from PTSD and the general population is the former's dependence on alcohol or drugs, while another study argues that drug and alcohol abuse is a key "coping behavior" of PTSD victims, who also tend to withdraw from people who have not experienced combat. Of the more than one hundred veterans with PTSD examined by Herbert Hendin and Ann Pollinger Hass, three-quarters abused alcohol at one time or another after their return from Vietnam. Jim Goodwin suggests that Vietnam veterans' unique experiences—the rotation system, the ideological ambivalence of the war, their youth—made them peculiarly vulnerable to PTSD. Disability worsens the effects. Evidence suggests that disabled persons who "misuse" alcohol, prescription drugs, or illicit drugs are those who are "less accepting" of their disabilities and more likely to be depressed about their condition.[68]

During the Gilded Age and the first decades of the twentieth century, doctors, scientists, and members of the fledgling psychological profession sought an adequate terminology for the medicalization of addiction to alcohol. Although "alcoholism" did not became the standard term until the 1930s or 1940s, other words—"inebriety," "dipsomania," or more colloquial names such as "drunkard"—indicated a growing acceptance of the idea of addiction as a disease rather than a simple choice.[69]

Yet many Americans still held tightly to their moralistic disgust regarding drunkenness. Officials of the state veterans' homes who convened in Milwaukee late in 1894 believed that the issue of "habitual drunkards" was the biggest problem facing administrators of veterans' homes. The convention resolved that the National Homes should accept "such persons" who had been discharged from state homes immediately, rather than requiring a six-month wait, as was current practice, and that Congress should build a special asylum just for drunken veterans. "I have come to believe," thundered a delegate from Michigan, "that there is such a thing as the old soldier who has forfeited every right he had to the protection of the state. . . . [W]hen he goes so far as to lose all manhood, punish him just as you would a criminal." Perhaps, he suggested, the new institution should bear a sign reading, "This is the Drunkards' Home."[70]

At the same time that professionals and even a portion of the general public were accepting the concept of alcoholism as a disease, its role as evidence of moral degeneration and loss of control remained strong. Writers often presented "drunkards" as having lost their capacity for manhood, according to Elaine Frantz Parsons. They became less human, more animalistic, and less in control of themselves and became less like "men," having lost or failed to hang on to such typical male attributes as "strength, intelligence, ability, [and] prudence." The Gilded Age saw a complicating of the ancient contempt for drinkers; even though they were seen as weak and lacking in "free will and moral responsibility," to a certain extent they could not avoid their situation. Whether the failure to exert willpower over drink was inherently a matter of biology or only a condition that developed as the man sunk deeper and deeper into his cups was unclear. Whatever mitigating factors health professionals or sympathetic laymen and -women might have noted, men who succumbed regularly to drink clearly were seen as less deserving of sympathy than those suffering from disabilities or illnesses that could not be blamed on their lack of responsibility.[71]

A fictionalized version of the way that drink could seize control of a veteran appeared in a Thomas Nelson Page story published in the *Century* magazine in 1892. "The Gray Jacket" offered a gentle, sympathetic portrait of an old Confederate about whom the narrator says, "I never saw such absolute dominion as the love of liquor had over him. He was like a man in chains. . . . He said he had a disease . . . and he was in absolute slavery to it." The man had been raised to abhor alcohol and had fought bravely, nearly dying from bayonet wounds to his chest. But he had started drinking while in the army, driven by hardship and danger and convivial comrades. Obsessed with the effects of alcohol, he firmly believed that he would commit murder if necessary to obtain it. He had lost his fiancée and sold his mother's plantation; after losing that money, he was forced to survive on odd jobs when he was not in jail for drunkenness and resisting arrest. To buy alcohol, he said, "I have sold everything in the world I had, or could lay my hands on" except for his old uniform coat. "I have never got quite so low as to sell my old gray jacket that I used to wear," the former cavalryman declares. The narrator gives the man little loans, and from time to time the old man is sober for months or even a year. But he eventually falls back to his old ways, spending more than half his time behind bars. "He became a perfect vagabond, and with his clothes ragged and dirty might be seen reeling about, or standing around the street corners near disreputable bars, waiting for a chance drink, or sitting asleep in doorways of untenanted buildings." The veteran pulls himself together, sobers up, and somehow obtains a presentable set of clothes to attend the unveiling of a monument in Richmond, an occasion that would include reunions, speeches, and other reminders of his noble service during the war. The narrator encounters him at the ceremony and marvels at his fine, even youthful appearance in the old gray jacket he wears under the new set of clothes. But the man gets drunk, and the narrator is called to the jail, helping talk the judge into releasing the man for the next day's parade. The man is asked to carry the colors for his old regiment, and he has a proud moment in the parade. The reunion seems to restore the veteran, who seems cured of his disease. But the reprieve is short-lived, and within a few months, he is worse than ever. The next time the narrator sees him, he is in jail, "half-naked and little better than a madman. . . . Body and brain were both gone." He soon dies, and as the narrator walks down the street, he comes across a secondhand store with a torn and dirty Confederate uniform jacket hanging in the window. The shop owner had bought the jacket from a pawnbroker, "who had gotten it from some drunkard." It was the old veteran's jacket; he had finally broken his thirty-year vow not to sell the only possession that meant more to him than alcohol. The narrator buys the jacket, puts it on the dead old soldier, and ensures that he has a "soldier's burial" rather than a pauper's grave.[72]

Testimony during investigations of soldiers' homes speaks to the reputations that old soldiers had earned for their drinking and offers disturbing evidence that alcoholism and alcohol abuse were among the major disabilities suffered by veterans. A former manager of the Dayton home called the saloons along the city's West End "the constant enemies of the men," at least partly because of the reputation gained by all old soldiers because a few of their comrades drank to excess. The presence of these bars contributed to the scenes described by earlier witnesses: men lying in fence corners, misbehavior on streetcars, and frequent arrests (five to ten a day in earlier years). The administrator also believed that civilian citizens were treated differently than the old soldiers. "First, the mistake is made by almost everybody that one, two, or three hundred men among the inmates of this Home are a sample of the other inmates. They judge of the men of the Home from these few. A person sees three soldiers on different streets in the city drunk during a day, and he says, 'The soldiers are all drunk.' If a person were to see three ordinary citizens in that condition he would not conclude that the whole community was drunk. When he sees the three soldiers drunk on the streets he forgets that there are 3,997 sober members in the Home. There is no greater proportion of the intemperate men from the Home in the station-house than there is of the daily proportion of the citizens of Dayton." If a "citizen of prominence and wealth" were found drunk, the police would take him home, but "if he be a soldier, he would be taken up on the slightest provocation and put in the station-house."[73]

Temperance advocates attacked the "gaping mouth[s] of hell" that beckoned soldiers outside the gates of every soldiers' home. Residents of the Hampton branch of the NHDVS could visit more than a hundred saloons in nearby Phoebus or in Hampton itself. "The dives of Phoebus are appalling. . . . The porches and sidewalks in front of the saloons are occupied by pensioners in blue, sitting upon chairs furnished by the management. The passer-by can easily hear the ribald song within, the patter of dancing feet, the loud laughter in which the voices of women blend." The governor of the branch experimented with a quarantine of the outside saloons, allowing inmates to drink only in the home's canteen. Home police made only two arrests during that time, and according to one resident, "the camp has never been so quiet." Closing the canteen would leave veterans with no other option than to drink outside the gates. "This case does not indicate that the saloon is good, only that the lawless saloon is worse than the one which is controlled."[74]

More than a decade earlier, the *Home Bulletin* had described exactly the same scene outside the Southern Branch on pension day, but with a humorous rather than judgmental gloss. When the old soldiers received their money, the "traffickers outside" lay in ambush—figuratively as well as literally—near the home. The "Battle of the Kegs" began at Mill Creek, then pushed into Hampton itself, where "the fighting was brisk and the shots flew thick and fast." Reinforcements for the kegs arrived in the form of demijohns (glass containers used in the brewing process). Overwhelmed by temptation, "the old Vets showed their weakness and as the shades of night fell upon the scene they found themselves vanquished." Casualties resulted: the article ended with a list of several men who had broken bones and reported that an ambulance from the home had been kept busy throughout the "skirmish."[75]

J. U. Kriedler, the former director of the Third Street Railroad, which connected the Central Branch and the city of Dayton, testified that prior to the advent of Governor Marsena Patrick's stricter administration, the railroad received numerous complaints from citizens riding on the cars with the old soldiers. "They would use dirty language, come into the cars in a filthy condition, and with their persons exposed, and get into a wrangle with passengers; sometimes with the drivers; so much so that there was scarcely a week that passed without our having something of that kind going on." The situation seemed to represent a continuation of the disorder in the warren of saloons west of the city and east of the home, where "sometimes from ten to twenty soldiers would congregate, fighting in the street, and using the most filthy, foul language that can be used by anybody." The justice of the peace, who owed his office to the votes of the saloon keepers, was useless. When Kriedler tried to break up a fight outside one of the saloons, a local constable arrived, but rather than arresting the three veterans who had been beating up a fourth, he threatened to arrest Kriedler.[76]

Although the reputations of all old soldiers were tarnished by the actions of a few, alcohol-related lapses were clearly a major disciplinary problem. At the Northwestern Branch, being "drunk" and "under the influence of liquor" (two separate violations of home regulations) were among the most commonly broken rules. In 1881, for example, these two infractions accounted for more than 800 of the 1,840 offenses committed (trailing only being absent without leave, of which there were 858 incidents); in 1887–88, the two categories accounted for more than one-quarter of the total of 3,195 arrests. In addition, many other offenses were committed while the inmates were imbibing, bringing the overall percentage of drinking-related arrests to more than half the total. Some violators were "brought in from outside drunk in a wagon," apparently a worse violation than "coming from outside drunk" under one's own power.[77]

A wide array of additional offenses could be attributed to drinking. A number of veterans seemed deliberately to commit offenses that insulted their fellow inmates and violated one of the home's most important rules, maintaining personal cleanliness. In addition to being absent without leave nine times and to being charged with drinking offenses eleven times in a little over two years, William Crawford was charged with refusing to take a bath and was once "drunk and filthy in his bed." Michael Butler, a salty old sailor, was accused of being "drunk & disorderly" in his quarters and of calling another inmate a "son of a bitch & other vile names." Paul Cassidy had "befoul[ed] his bed" and gone "away & leaving it in a filthy condition"; Conrad Kellner "deliberately" urinated on the floor of the barracks and later "committ[ed] a filthy nuisance on Carl Younger." J. W. Adee was on occasion punished for drunkenness but was also an extremely violent man, committing "assault with intent to murder" and resisting being searched; prior to his dishonorable discharge from the home, he was "put in a cell for his violence" and was heard "howling & cursing all night." Others were charged with urinating on public property.[78]

Although Victorians were famously reluctant to talk about sexual matters, evidence of sexual frustration and maladjustment also crept into the hospital and disciplinary records. Several inmates were charged with "exposing" their "persons" in quarters, on National Avenue, at a nearby train depot, or in the presence of visiting women. In addition to swearing at guards or other inmates, veterans sometimes "insulted . . . ladies on Home grounds" or used "indecent language in presence of ladies [at the] depot." Rollin Black was charged with "repeatedly insulting schoolgirls & following them on Home grounds while they were going to and from school" and with "insulting a young girl & putting his hand under her clothes." Thomas Rauschm was admitted to the home in July 1879 and to the hospital nearly a decade later due to age and paralysis. Yet he was neither too old nor too paralyzed to be arrested by the civil authorities and taken away ("at the request of Governor [Kilbourn] Knox," the home commandant) after he was "accused of attempting to have connection with cattle."[79]

The most severe sanctions imposed by home officials punished behavior committed while under the influence of alcohol. Although most offenders ended up in the guardhouse, performed thirty or sixty days' labor without pay, or had their passes to leave the grounds revoked, a few were discharged from the home. Each year, between 1 and 2 percent of the system's inmates were expelled for drunkenness. The NHDVS's relatively high profile meant that civilians often saw residents as representing all veterans. The public wrestling with issues related to alcohol at the homes, then, helped create the reputation of veterans as hard drinkers.[80]

In addition to the direct effects of alcohol consumption, continued use and abuse created a wide range of health issues, especially as the veterans aged. Atypical because of how well it was documented but fairly typical in terms of its demonstration of the potential effects of alcohol on a veteran was the case of Henry Ives, who died on a Saturday evening in late March 1878 at the Northwestern Branch. Ives had spent all of Friday afternoon and most of the night drinking at Brady's, a nearby saloon. By Saturday morning, he was in the guardhouse, sleeping off what the home surgeon would later call a "recent debauch," and was charged with being absent without leave from his post as a home police officer. During the day, the surgeon prescribed several doses of chloral hydrate to steady Ives's nerves, and by suppertime he was well enough to eat a hearty meal. Shortly thereafter, however, he collapsed and died.

The surgeon's postmortem discovered that Ives had a damaged heart, liver, and spleen; an inflamed stomach; and "very much congested" kidneys, leading the doctor to conclude that Ives had died of the "muscular exhaustion of the heart" brought on by "chronic Alcoholism." The brief investigation that followed, which included testimony from doctors, the keeper of the guardhouse, and fellow veterans, came to the same conclusion. Two of the witnesses were also being held for drunkenness. One admitted that he had "been in the Guard-House, with Ives, several times before"—once for more than two weeks—for drinking offenses; in addition, the witness had been with Ives at Brady's on the fateful night. The other witness reported that he had still been drunk when Ives died: the preceding night, the witness "met some old friends; and drank too much; and, then, left the Home, without permission; and, then, got drunk again."[81]

Alcoholism became one of the most serious health problems at the National Home, one of the chief progressive disabilities afflicting members of an already disabled population. Drinking exacerbated existing conditions such as heart disease, asthma, insomnia, and digestive problems; resulted in falls down stairways, on sidewalks, and in quarters; caused sudden blackouts that led to frostbite during bitter Milwaukee winters; and caused psychological problems so severe that some men, suffering perhaps from what the home surgeon called "softening of the brain," had to be put in restraints, placed in the "insane ward," or transferred to the asylum for insane veterans in Washington, D.C. Other injuries were sustained when intoxicated veterans fell out of windows, tripped over sidewalks, or lurched into barroom brawls.[82]

The situation forced officials to develop policies for treating these sad men. Although such efforts failed to eradicate alcohol abuse at the home, these sometimes hesitant attempts to treat alcoholism as a disease rather than a moral failing foreshadowed the more humane assumptions about veterans and about the disabled that would be more fully realized in the twentieth century.[83]

Hospital records from the 1880s suggest that at least 14 percent of all cases of disease or injury were related to drinking. Attending physicians sometimes merely wrote "alcoholism" to describe a patient's condition, but most cases were more complicated. Patrick King came into the hospital with double pneumonia on November 3, 1883, after a "protracted debauch of 7 days" and died less than three days later. The surgeon blamed King's death on "long continued periodic sprees."[84]

Some men had obviously been alcoholics long before they entered the home. Leopold Knoll was accepted in May 1883 and was transferred from the guardhouse to the hospital in November of that year, "partially stupefied." In addition to an injured elbow from a hard fall, he had "been on a spree." He suffered from constipation, bedsores, and partial paralysis of his left side; by mid-December, he was "rapidly emaciating and becoming entirely demented." Despite turpentine enemas and strychnine pills, he died six weeks after going into the hospital and less than a year after entering the home. Charles Redburg had been in the home for only six months when he was admitted to the hospital with rheumatism and frostbitten ears. He, too, came straight from the guardhouse, "where he had been serving out a sentence for [a] debauch." The surgeon described Redburg as "an incorrigible Drunkard although a well educated man." Mathias Bauer transferred from the Central Branch in Dayton to Milwaukee on April 13, 1884; he went straight to the guardhouse and then, two days later, to the hospital. The surgeon reported that on the trip from Ohio, Bauer had drunk "considerable bad whiskey." His demeanor was by turns violent and morose; he returned for a time to the guardhouse but came back to the hospital, where he was kept until he could be sent to the veterans' insane asylum in Washington. Edward Simpson was "brought in from a low dive" twice in less than a year and was once transferred from the jail. The surgeon reported that Simpson "did not know how he got into jail, but was there 3 days" and "realizes that he is not of much account." The home surgeon also reported that seven years after his 1877 admission to the home, Joshua Quinn was suffering from "Premature Olde Age"; he was "also an Olde Inebriate."[85]

Although drug use among Civil War veterans was never the media sensation that drug use among soldiers in Vietnam in the 1960s would become, at least some turn-of-the-century Americans assumed that many former soldiers had become addicted to opium, with the result that it was frequently referred to as the "soldier's problem" or "disease." That stereotype oversimplified the issue, since only a minority of opium users were veterans. But thousands of severely wounded men as well as those suffering from chronic diseases such as diarrhea and malaria, which were also treated with opiates, became abusers and addicts. Such veterans became part of an extraordinarily negative stereotype, as suggested by a brief article on "Temperance" in *The Independent* magazine, which confidently stated that the eighty thousand to one hundred thousand opium eaters in the United States were "found chiefly" among "persons suffering from nervous disorders, overworked females, and the victims of exhausted vice, disabled soldiers, and hopeless wives and widows." That disabled soldiers appeared on this list of dependent or even hopeless classes of people indicates the depths to which the public believed these men could sink.[86]

Attacking the Drink Habit

Despite the obvious problems caused by alcohol, the Board of Managers virtually ignored the issue of alcohol use at the National Homes. Indeed, in Milwaukee, as in other soldiers' homes, doctors frequently prescribed quinine, whiskey, brandy, and other narcotics—usually classified under the misnomer "stimulants"—to treat any number of conditions, diseases, and problems, among them restlessness, sleeplessness, and rebelliousness. The surgeon at the Minnesota State Soldiers' Home argued late in the century that alcohol should never be prescribed as a therapeutic agent. Comparing such prescriptions to the use of "calomel, bleeding and starving" forty years earlier, Dr. D. R. Greenlee argued that alcohol damaged internal organs while providing only slight and impermanent relief. He blamed much of the alcoholism of the day on physicians who relied on whiskey or brandy to get old soldiers through immediate crises of laziness: "It is so much easier, no doubt, than writing a prescription, and probably will suit the old soldier as well as the most elaborate Latin one, and his bones will stop aching until the next morning." To those who said with misplaced sympathy that "the old soldiers have always been used to whiskey; why not give it to them now, and let them die happy," he declared, "Why let them die at all?" The "happiness experienced in dying full of whiskey," he suggested scornfully, was "very slight, and at all times open to doubt." Greenlee's account was substantiated by "An Old Soldier's Experience," a brief memoir of a veteran complaining about the use of drugs and alcohol in soldiers' homes. "If you would care to see the sad effects of calomel and whiskey," he wrote, "come with me to the Soldier's Home; there you can see men who are, if possible, greater wrecks than I am; men whom the doctors think *must* have alcohol, calomel, and opium to keep them alive."[87]

One commonsense approach to the problem was to try to manage the veterans' drinking. A practice that turned a potential evil into a positive good, at least from the points of view of home managers, was the policy of selling relatively cheap beer to residents. Profits went into the post fund, which paid for the home bands, the library and newspaper subscriptions, and the wide variety of entertainments that passed through all of the branches. The beer hall at the Central Branch cleared fifty thousand dollars a year, according to the *New York Times*. Located in a well-lit, well-heated brick building with twin oak bars, the establishment also gave out free pretzels with mustard and sold cheese sandwiches at lunch and cheap cigars throughout the day. Sometimes as many as five hundred inmates mobbed the building. Eight guards kept order, political discussions were prohibited, and although there were tables and chairs set along the walls, most veterans preferred to mill about. At Leavenworth, the post fund also paid for bowling. "We might go to Congress until we were gray," Colonel Andrew J. Smith, the branch governor, declared, "and ask for an appropriation for a bowling alley, and we would never get it; because we are petitioning, praying, and begging for barracks to take in 316 men that are awaiting admittance here, and we can't get it." When asked how the bowling alley benefited the men, he replied, "It keeps them away from badness."[88]

Indeed, the homes tried to prevent the men from abusing the beer privilege. The Pacific Branch limited its members to two glasses of beer a day, a policy followed more or less by other branches. Moreover, the beer sold at the homes was about 3–4 percent alcohol, less than most beers then on the market.[89]

Administrators argued that selling beer at the home prevented men from resorting to stronger drink. Officials carefully distinguished between the beer they wanted to sell and "intoxicating liquors" such as whiskey and the rotgut sold at neighborhood saloons. The home "is surrounded by a hundred groggeries, and it has been of great benefit to sell beer," argued General A. J. Sewell, governor of the Southern Branch in Hampton. "If we do not sell beer there, those men would go outside and be waylaid immediately by whisky shops and drink whisky and come home on a wheelbarrow very often." The Central Branch's General Patrick, a temperance man, believed that offering beer to the old soldiers was better than the alternative. The government could "either . . . furnish them with the best article of beer that can be purchased in the home at a cheap rate, and retain our men under our control, or suffer them to go outside, get drunk on the vilest drinks of every kind, get robbed of their money and kicked into the street, or secreted in the infamous dives that surround us until their money is exhausted and they are turned out penniless."[90]

The managers of soldiers' homes almost unanimously defended the practice of selling beer even if they personally opposed even that form of alcohol. However, an eyewitness account of the canteens in soldiers' homes by a temperance advocate published in 1902, though biased, suggested that although the sale of beer might have mitigated some of the worst excesses of inmates' drinking, the practice was hardly without consequences. At the NHDVS's Central Branch in Dayton, the beer hall was open from 7:00 A.M. to 5:00 P.M. Perhaps two hundred veterans at a time kept four bartenders busy throughout the day. "So long as a man was not disorderly, and gave no visible token of being intoxicated," he could drink until he ran out of money. One officer reported that many old soldiers drank eight to twelve glasses of beer a day. Intoxication among the beer-drinking veterans was more the rule than the exception, and spending pension money on beer deprived veterans' families of money. The branch governors eventually lost their case, and states began passing laws outlawing the sale of any kind of alcohol within a few miles of home grounds. In 1906, Congress abolished the sale of beer at the NHDVS.[91]

A hint of a treatment policy emerged along with the defense of the beer gardens. Temperance was to be encouraged but not required among inmates, and in 1872, the NHDVS board announced that furloughs would be "refused to inmates addicted to intemperance." The board also allowed physicians in the homes to "use such remedies as they, in their professional opinion, may deem proper." In the sometimes terse notes made whenever a veteran was admitted to the hospital, surgeons at the Northwestern Branch seemed to refer to "alcoholism" as a kind of temporary state, a short-term ailment that was gone once its effects wore off. By 1903, surgeons listed "alcoholism" as a distinct condition, with subcategories of "acute" and "chronic," and ascribed the illness to 62 men. Four years later, that number had grown to 284. Withdrawal symptoms were treated with small doses of whiskey, bromide solutions, morphine injections, and, as in Ives's case, chloral. Surgeons also prescribed special diets for a few men.[92]

But these treatments merely coaxed addicts through isolated crises. Physicians and entrepreneurs around the United States, building on the developing theory of addiction as a disease, sought permanent cures to the scourges of alcohol and opium. Doctors hoped to instill discipline and order in the lives of their patients, to eliminate the craving for consciousness-altering stimulation, to cure the muscular, respiratory, and digestive side-effects of long-term drug use. Most of the best-known "cures," however, focused on relieving patients of the pain and exhaustion of withdrawal. Cold-turkey remedies, while briefly popular in the 1870s and early 1880s, expected too much of patients. As a result, a number of self-proclaimed experts designed treatments that substituted different substances—codeine or heroin, for example—or gradually weaned patients from narcotics or alcohol with slowly decreasing doses of comforting drugs. Less respectable entrepreneurs offered "plant specifics" refined from oats or flowers. Most of these supposed cures, like their patent medicine cousins, did more harm than good in that they contained high concentrations of morphine or other narcotics. The nerve-steadying, sleep-inducing chloral hydrate administered during the 1880s and 1890s to many of the men consigned to the guardhouse at the Northwestern Branch, among other places, was highly addictive in its own right. Many products, such as those widely advertised in popular magazines and newspapers, were allegedly effective for home use, but the most respectable—and expensive—cures were designed to be administered over a several weeks in private sanitariums, which were all the rage by 1900.[93]

Institutionalized veterans were at the forefront of these experiments, and in its most comprehensive effort to treat alcoholism, the Northwestern Branch, along with most of the other NHDVS branches, a few state homes, and several prisons—tried out the well-known "Keeley Cure" in the mid-1890s. In 1894, the branch's governor, Cornelius Wheeler, devoted a full page of his brief report to the Board of Managers to "Temperance." By that time, the Keeley system had been available to his men for about a year, and he boasted that "the Home seems almost a model community when compared, or rather contrasted, with its character" three years earlier. Wheeler had reason to be happy, for the number of disciplinary cases at the home had plummeted from more than five thousand in 1890–91 to fewer than sixteen hundred for 1893–94. He obviously believed that at least part of the reduction resulted from the establishment of a "Veteran Keeley League" and of a "Keeley Institute" at the home: nearly four hundred residents were enrolled.[94]

The Keeley Institute at the Milwaukee home was only one of dozens of franchises established around the country. Leslie Keeley had spent years developing his formula. His service as an army surgeon at Jefferson Barracks during the Civil War exposed him to the effects of drink on the men under his care. Promotional pamphlets for his institute declared that Keeley had eventually come to believe that drunkenness was a disease rather than a sin and that he could find a way to cure it. He seems to have been willing to try anything, and in the 1870s he came up with the "Double Chloride of Gold," a medicine injected into and swallowed by thousands of patients all over the country. He never divulged the exact nature of the cure, other than to affirm that gold was the key component. Between 1880 and 1920, perhaps half a million people took the cure at clinics or at home, enabling Keeley to rake in at least $2.7 million during the 1890s alone.[95]

First marketed as a home remedy, the Keeley Cure became part of a much more comprehensive several-week-long course of therapy and the inspiration for a nationwide Keeley League, which held annual conventions and sponsored a Keeley Day at the Columbian Exposition in Chicago in 1893. Thousands of people from all walks of life—although primarily members of the middle and upper classes—flocked every year to Dwight, Illinois, where they submitted to injections of the secret compound four times a day and took less powerful doses of medicine every two hours. In addition, treatment consisted of kind words, sympathy, and freedom; the patients could stroll around the grounds and the streets of Dwight. Like members of the modern Alcoholics Anonymous, customers were encouraged to confront their addiction in front of their peers, face up to their shortcomings, and commit themselves to self-control. Neither their manhood nor their dignity was threatened. Ultimately, their addictions would be broken, their self-respect restored, and their lives put back on track. Keeley claimed that his "simple and mild, but thoroughly effective" treatment had proven "uniformly and almost miraculously successful," with only 5 percent of his patients backsliding into addiction.[96]

During an especially intense period of Keeley organizing at the NHDVS in 1892 and 1893, perhaps fifteen hundred men encountered the Keeley plan. Some simply took the cure; others joined local chapters of the league. At the Central Branch, the old beer hall became the Keeley League's headquarters, while at Togus, a spacious two-and-a-half story frame structure with a wrap-around porch housed the group. Although no evidence suggests that state homes in the South adopted the Keeley system, the *Confederate Veteran* also jumped on the Keeley bandwagon, targeting local camps of the United Confederate Veterans.[97]

The Northwestern Branch established a Keeley Institute in 1892. One of Keeley's biggest supporters was Milwaukee newspaperman Charles S. Clark, who wrote a memoir of his addiction to alcohol and the lasting cure he found at Dwight. The *Milwaukee Sunday Telegraph* credited Clark with facilitating the founding of the Milwaukee franchise in 1892. Clark alluded to the connection between old soldiers and drinking in dedicating his volume to, among others, the "Grand Army of American Inebriates"—a sly play on the "Grand Army of the Republic." Keeley's promotional literature touted the adoption of his program at the national and state homes for disabled soldiers. Milwaukee's Keeley Institute gained a measure of notoriety when attendees at a meeting of the Northwestern Soldiers' Association toured the National Home grounds and listened enthusiastically to Governor Wheeler's speech on a number of administrative issues, including "the drink habit and the Keeley cure."[98]

But the cure's apparent success did not go unchallenged. Even before Keeley died in 1900, his methods were controversial. Critics blasted his secrecy and his assertion that he had found the single, "perfect" cure for a wide variety of addictions. The simple fact that Keeley's business was extremely profitable and flourished outside the established medical community was enough to draw criticism from many circles. The significant number of relapses among his patients—even Governor Wheeler admitted that nearly 30 percent of the men who had taken the cure in Milwaukee had returned to drinking—called Keeley's credibility into question, and his far-flung empire eventually crumbled. Although the original institute in Dwight remained profitable well into the twentieth century, the cure had been thoroughly discredited long before. A backhanded compliment showing how far the Keeley Cure's fortunes had deteriorated appeared in a 1907 exposé of the patent drug industry in which muckraker Samuel Hopkins Adams said that since the former "extravagant claims" of the institutes had been modified, he could not now "include them in the swindling category." A hint that the Board of Managers may have had some doubts about the use of the cure at the National Homes appeared in the board's minutes late in 1894, when members passed a motion to "strike out certain lines touching the cure of drunkenness in the various Branches."[99]

Even worse, the cure drove wedges between inmates and between inmates and administrators. When Michael Butler, an old sailor at the Northwestern Branch, was brought into the guardhouse for being "drunk & disorderly," he called the attendant "a Keely Son of a Bitch & other vile names." At Togus, it was common knowledge that to obtain any job at the home, "from a clerkship down to a coal heaver," a man needed to take the Keeley Cure. Virtually every man arrested for drunkenness, regardless of his previous record, could have his thirty or sixty days of punishment dropped if he took the cure. He would pay $20.00 and endure the cure before beginning the cycle all over again. In addition, contrary to NHDVS rules, the governor admitted men temporarily so they could take the cure; they were charged $32.50. Although it was not clear if the governor was profiting from the scheme, the home made a pretty penny from the scores if not hundreds of men who paid for the cure. The practice was "a humbug pure and simple, and was inaugurated for the sole purpose of fleecing these poor old veterans," according to the anonymous author of a pamphlet that noted on its title page, "Rascality is the rule! No justice for the old Veterans!"[100]

The most extensive examination of the tensions caused by the application of the cure within the NHDVS occurred during an investigation of the Western Branch at Leavenworth in the mid-1890s. Colonel Andrew J. Smith, the home's governor, had been charged with more than twenty counts of seven different violations that included disobeying direct orders, using his position for personal profit, conduct unbecoming an officer and a gentleman, using his office to punish and vilify other officers, and general unfitness. A congressional investigating committee took evidence for more than a week in Kansas late in 1896 and on and off in Washington during the first few weeks of 1897. Although the committee's report did not reach conclusions on all of the charges and specifications, the seven-hundred-plus pages of testimony convinced investigators that Smith and all of the officers at Leavenworth should be removed. The committee was somewhat divided on the proper course of action, but the congressmen seemed to agree that lax accounting that failed to fully separate personal from public benefits, personal animosities among the officers and staff, and Smith's abrupt and autocratic management style were serious enough to warrant wholesale changes in the home's administration. "In short, your committee think most of the friction and disorder which they find in this branch is due to the way the governor has of doing things, and to the doubtful and indiscreet things he has done." He should be replaced by "some even-tempered, steady-going, practical man."[101]

Although dozens of inmates of the Western Branch lodged typical old soldiers' complaints about the administration with the committee, the testimony that seemed to carry the most weight dealt with the famous cure. Although he did not consider himself a recovering alcoholic, Smith believed that some years earlier, he had been in danger of becoming an abuser of liquor. He had stopped drinking cold turkey and eventually submitted to the Keeley regimen. As a result, although he made no effort to end the sale of beer at the home, he mounted a vigorous campaign against drink, drunkenness, and drunks. Many of the complaints against him revolved around his ardent support for the cure: despite his denials, he seemed to have profited from the exclusive contract he signed with the Keeley company. He favored staff members who approved of the cure and warned those who did not against speaking out against it. He treated harshly inmates who had taken the cure but lapsed back into old habits, even discharging them from the home. And on at least a few occasions, he forced inmates to submit to the cure despite their adamant protests.

The home's Keeley League functioned as a more or less independent entity. Chartered by the State of Kansas, the league could own property, sue and be sued, and elect officers. In addition to Smith, two other staff members served on the executive board, which made all decisions on behalf of the league. The organization made a profit of about five dollars on each case. At the time, Smith also served as president of the National Keeley League.[102]

Smith had been inspired to institute the Keeley Cure when "the men came before me one after another, some of them twenty or thirty times, for drunkenness. They had never been dismissed from the Home, for it had grown upon me that if I could not stop it these men could not stop it." He talked to the veterans about the Keeley Cure, telling them that they "were not talking to the governor, now; you are talking to Andrew Smith, who took the Keeley cure." More than twelve hundred men eventually took the cure at a cost of more than $22.30 each (which included the injections; a syringe; other medicines, among them a laxative; and the league's initiation fee, dues, and membership badge). Administrators had decided to charge the soldiers for the cure because "a man appreciates a thing at what it costs him." Smith claimed that the home's treasurer, not the governor, handled the money and denied accusations that he favored inmates who had taken the cure for jobs at the home, saying, "God knows [I] would like to, but all men are equal in the Home." He continued, "If a man is a drunkard, I will not furnish him the money to get drunk; I will furnish him the whisky to relieve him every time, but not go and debauch himself."[103]

According to the committee, Smith was "a man of moods, whole-souled and impulsive, and promptly responsive in word and gesture to the passing provocation. . . . His mind works rapidly, he speaks easily, his manner is emphatic, his temperament excitable." His ease of speech clearly emerged as he forcefully told the committee, "I want you to know what this Keeley Institute has done for the unfortunate men of this Home. I want you to talk with them personally whether the governor be present or not. I want you to see them collectively. I want you to see these ex-drunkards, horrible-looking old fellows a little while ago, but now just as clean and manly looking men as the sun shines upon. . . . I want you to see the great good that has come to these men, notwithstanding the assertions and accusations made against the governor, in which there is not one particle of truth."[104]

Smith's policies certainly generated success stories. Joseph B. Sitley had entered the Central Branch in 1877; sixteen years later, he had come to Leavenworth specifically to take the Keeley Cure. "I was drinking a little too much for my own good; in fact, I was drinking so much that it unfitted me for my occupation—that of clerk," he recalled. "I had heard a great deal of the treatment here at the Home . . . and after being here . . . for a few hours I became satisfied that it was all right." He applied directly to the governor and began the treatment the next day. "I became cured, and I am glad of it, and I am very thankful to him, too." The home's Roman Catholic chaplain claimed that the Keeley League had "done great things at the Home"; indeed, he gushed, "I am very much enamored of the Keeley league, on account of its moral influence at the Home." He also denied that the governor forced men to take the cure. Rather, when men plagued by alcoholism came before him, Smith "would first appeal to their present condition, and ask them to look at themselves, to consider the uniform they wore, the grand record they had made, and now to consider their present condition." Although men would often be "forgiven," to use the priest's words, for being drunk three or four times, his language with them was "very pointed." "Can you not straighten up; can you not do something for yourself? You are disgracing the Home."[105]

But several veterans painted a different picture of the process by which they "applied" for the cure. Richard Wall was threatened with a discharge when he refused. He finally gave in but then relapsed by drinking a few beers after a Memorial Day celebration with his GAR post. He was promptly dismissed. The GAR intervened to get him reinstated, but when he tried to enter the Illinois state home in Quincy, he claimed, Smith had written a letter preventing his admission out of "spite . . . against me on account of breaking the Keeley." The committee pressed Wall, suggesting that perhaps he had drunk more beer than he remembered that day and intimating that as an Irishman, he was used to drinking. Wall admitted that he had been arrested for drunkenness about thirty times but held that pledging sobriety with the Catholic chaplain, an approach he requested but was denied, would have been more binding on him. Finally, the seventy-one-year-old Wall, who had fought at Vicksburg, blamed the cure for his worsening deafness: "I cannot hear well since I took the Keeley."[106]

Smith's own words indicated the extent to which the men had been pressured into taking the cure. One man came into Smith's office after being arrested for drunkenness. Because of his "terrible physical condition"—apparently a head-splitting hangover—he received a glass of whiskey and was sent to the guardhouse. According to Smith, the man had "applied for the Keeley cure," which would begin after he was sobered up and given some beef tea. "We can straighten him up. These things that used to be such a fearful trial are as easy as that," Smith declared, "snapping his fingers, to the men who sincerely wish to get cured."[107]

The alcohol issue was part and parcel of the notion of "worthy" old soldiers. Indeed, the committee's report exposed the limits of Americans' largesse toward their veterans. Although it was not the purpose of the investigation, the committee recommended reducing the pensions paid to inmates of the NHDVS to four dollars per month for the sole reason that the decrease would reduce their ability to "waste [money] in drink and debauchery." As noted by witness after witness, "drunkenness came with pay day." The committee pointed out the redundancy of paying pensions to men who were fully supported in every way at the home. "Why should he still draw his pension" when "the Government takes him in and assumes his entire support?" Because so many veterans spent so much of their pension money on alcohol, "it would be an act of mercy to take from the inebriate his pension while in the Home. It would be equally an act of justice and fairness between the Government and such pensioner."[108]

As the nineteenth century faded into the twentieth, the old soldiers were finally truly old, and the disabilities that might have been simple aggravations or manageable aches or pains worsened and were joined by other age-induced ailments. Charles Morehouse's diary of the last year of his life, which he spent in the Minnesota State Soldiers' Home, painfully articulates the frustration, sadness, and weariness that must have crept into the lives of many veterans. Morehouse spent most of 1912 in the home in St. Paul while dying of a bladder ailment, for which he received excruciating treatments every few weeks. He also suffered from extreme loneliness and exhibited an absolute distaste for all elements of life at the home. The New York native and veteran of three years' service in two different Ohio regiments stayed in a Minneapolis boardinghouse for several weeks after submitting his application to the home in early February; soon after moving into the home, he wrote in his diary, "God only knows the sad and sorry memory of the following days and nights. Oh the pain and the hunger for the touch of a home hand and the sound of a home voice." Morehouse's conflict was almost entirely internal: the home was not a home, and he mourned for the life he could no longer have.[109]

Morehouse occasionally gave himself completely over to despair, wondering if he would ever again see a friendly face. When loved ones came to visit, as they did every two or three weeks, he generally met them in downtown St. Paul or Minneapolis, where they would have lunch at a hotel and do a little shopping. Although his visitors from time to time came to the home, Morehouse usually took them to a nearby park; he apparently did not want them to see him in his dreary new residence. Even when his son and daughter visited during his second week in the home, he remained unhappy. Their departure left him "sad because it all seemed so *different* from *what* I *expected*—almost as [though] they do not care for me and my broken heart."[110]

Morehouse refused to allow himself to settle into his new life. He referred by name to fellow veterans on only two or three occasions; he constantly tried to escape the confines of the home grounds; he hated the surgeon, only barely tolerated the chaplain, and found the quartermaster "not congenial." He described the institution in terms of what it was not: his own home. He described pitiful meals of weak soup and poor meat and regularly referred to the "vile suppers" served to the old men. He was grateful when a friend sent him a potted hyacinth, which reminded him of Easter, but thought it "out of place" in our "barn like room."[111]

Morehouse rarely mentioned other soldiers except to complain about their drunkenness and incessant playing of the "music box." Early in the spring, he and some other residents ventured to nearby Minnehaha Falls but complained that on the outing, the "usual amount of booze was consumed which just makes me sick." Morehouse objected when other old soldiers tried to be friendly: when "Old Andy" and "Bill" "jogged up" one evening, "they with others made the night hideous." He complained on another occasion that the "gang are keeping up the jamboree" but noted on another day, "The gang are tapering off on their orgies a trifle." A nice Sunday afternoon in June was ruined when "in the park there was a perfect mob which set me wild."[112]

By mid-April Morehouse's entries were dominated by day-by-day reports of the "exquisite" pain caused by his worsening bladder ailment and the excruciating and invasive treatments—the "washing out process"—conducted every week or two by the home surgeon or by a slightly gentler St. Paul doctor (Morehouse preferred the latter because of the pretty receptionist with whom he liked to chat). The pain kept him awake virtually every night, but the treatments were so frightful that he frequently lacked the nerve to go to them.[113]

Months before he reached the final medical crisis that eventually took his life, Morehouse wrote, "All of this isn't life—it is just agony." Three days later, he complained that he was "too despondent" to leave the barracks. He was accustomed to calling on his religious beliefs at such times: "I try hard to get the Christ Spirit into my mind and actions every day—but there is but little encouragement in this place. God help us all." He spent one long, cold weekend indoors, where he "roosted on the ragged edge of despair and pain." During the last half of 1912, his nearly daily entries dwindled to roughly once a week and then to even less, with a gap from midsummer to late October. His last dated entry recorded a light snow on November 23; he died less than two months later.[114]

Morehouse's self-pity was rooted in a very real despair. Like thousands of other disabled veterans, he felt isolated and neglected. Although some veterans lived for years with such disabilities, many passed in and out of various stages of dependence and pain. Morehouse's infected bladder was apparently unrelated to his military service, but its banality hardly provided the same honor and status as an arm lost defending Cemetery Ridge. Nevertheless, his painful words ring true. His physical suffering and frustration eliminated his capacity to fulfill his role as a man, forcing him into a soldiers' home to live with annoying men who were apparently less reflective but no less dependent. Suspected by the public of being slackers, dependent to a greater or lesser extent on their families, and subjected to discomfort and pain that went virtually untreated by Gilded Age doctors, disabled veterans occupied a unique and lonely place in society.

A DECADE BEFORE Charles Morehouse's agonizing death, a bitter old Texan published a memoir of his spotted wartime career, which apparently included participation in a number of atrocities against surrendered Union soldiers and African Americans as well as deserter hunting and other unsavory activities. Nearly forty years after the war, he chronicled his experiences in the form of a cautionary tale that warned against becoming a soldier and worried that his sins would never be forgiven. Soldiering "may be the cause of losing some of your limbs, a leg, an arm or perhaps an eye. Many old soldiers"—including him—"are carrying leaden balls in their bodies for life. Hundreds of crippled veterans are hopping around trying to make a living." In addition to the physical danger, soldiers lost all honor and standing in the community. "While you are able to fight for your state it is all right, but when you get old there appears to be no more use for you." And soldiers' victims would haunt them: killing fellow men "will bring you to ruin and distress the balance of your life." He also had harsh words for the Confederate home in Austin, where he lived for at least a year. Although the public saw it "as a place of peace," it was "far from that." The men "play cards, curse and swear, and [are] like the little boy learning to chew and spit big." Tensions ran high; he got into a fight in a nearby saloon when a fellow resident stole his hat. "There would be a good many leave if they could draw a pension of $8.00." The title of his self-published book said all that needed to be said about his life as a soldier and especially as a veteran: *Harder Than Death*.[115]

chapter three **Saner Wars**

Robert W. Douthat, the only captain in the 11th Virginia to survive Pickett's Charge, became a professor at the West Virginia University in Morgantown after the war. He published a number of articles and books on Latin and on the philosophy of pragmatism. But he also became well known as a lecturer on that bloody afternoon when fate had spared him. Testimonials published in his elaborate promotional brochure applauded his dramatic presentation for its "loftiness of statement, clear presentation, [and] manliness of spirit toward all parties." His testimony gained verisimilitude because he was "a participant in the great struggle." Douthat was still making the rounds with his two-hour talk at the turn of the century; the lecture was published in 1905 by a major New York publisher as *Gettysburg: A Battle Ode Descriptive of the Grand Charge of the Third Day, July 3, 1863.* In the spirit of the times— and no doubt with an eye toward book sales in the still-lucrative northern market for Civil War narratives—he refused to paint one side or the other as more deserving of victory.[1]

Some of the veterans of the hard-fighting Army of the Cumberland, whose men had fought at Shiloh, at Stones River, and more famously at Chickamauga, Lookout Mountain, and Franklin, insisted on getting their story onto the big screen, Victorian style, by paying an artist four thousand dollars to paint a panorama chronicling the army's exploits. Consisting of thirty-two separate "thrilling and amusing scenes," according to its advertising broadside, it covered a canvas eight feet high and five hundred feet long. The panorama followed the Army of the Cumberland from mustering in to mustering out. In addition to battle scenes, the giant paintings portrayed the army in camp, on the march, emancipating slaves, and foraging for food. The artist spent years touring with the panorama through the Midwest, where most soldiers in the army lived.[2]

These examples show just two of the ways in which veterans entered the world of commerce following the war. Entrepreneurial veterans and others seeking to memorialize the war while making a profit were part of the emerging consumer economy that became one of the hallmarks of the Gilded Age. Their efforts were only a tiny sliver of the explosion of Victorian commercialism displayed in department stores, over-the-top exhibits at world's fairs and other exhibitions, and crowded Victorian parlors. Businessmen, including a sprinkling of veterans, took advantage of innovations in print and other media, the ability to mass produce all kinds of ephemeral consumer goods, and a growing economy to introduce American customers to the ways in which patriotism and consumerism would be closely linked from the 1880s well into the twentieth century and beyond.[3]

Throughout this period, veterans and civilians encountered one another in the free market, where entrepreneurs sought to cash in on the demand for souvenirs and collectibles related to the war and to veterans' organizations. These businessmen opened museums and offered other forms of entertainment and mobilized to take advantage of the tourists crowding onto the newly opened national battlefields. Veterans were deeply involved in all of these forms of commerce, both as businessmen and as consumers — and in some cases as obstacles. On the surface, the commodification of the war in general and of the sacrifices and patriotism of veterans in particular seemed harmless enough. But like almost every other aspect of the veterans' experience in Gilded Age America, it held the potential to raise significant tensions between civilians and old soldiers.

War, Remembrance, and Profit

The most recognizable outlet for veteran identity was also one of the most lucrative forms of commercialization. Regional, state, and national encampments of veterans' organizations provided opportunities for veterans to renew old attachments and for communities to honor the old soldiers. But these occasions also reflected major commitments of time and effort by local officials and volunteers and provided huge opportunities for profit. The industrialists and manufacturers against whom some veterans railed made possible the huge, lavish encampments that other veterans relished. Railroad companies offered steep discounts on fares to veterans traveling to reunions, cities competed to host the gatherings, and merchants funded hospitality in the form of lodging, meals, and entertainment.[4]

The Grand Army of the Republic (GAR) held its national and state en-

campments in different locations every year to distribute commercial opportunities around the country. Major as well as midsized cities bid to host
the national encampments, while smaller cities and towns in the states and
territories took turns hosting the state encampments, and county seats and
villages served as sites for reunions of companies, regiments, and brigades.
Hosting a major encampment required extraordinary effort and resources
on the part of local veterans, businessmen, and volunteers. Preparations
for the September 1888 national encampment in Columbus, Ohio, began
months earlier. At a meeting of the several committees in March, the decoration committee estimated that it would spend thirteen thousand dollars
on review stands, interior and exterior decorations in public halls, and street
designs. The committee of music planned to spend fifty-five hundred dollars, the committee on badges thirty-five hundred dollars, and the regis-
tration committee one thousand dollars. By July, planners were estimating
that 250,000 people would be in Columbus for the encampment and had
set aside fourteen thousand dollars to build huge dining halls. An August
announcement that went out to all Grand Army posts promised that hotels
would not raise their usual rates and informed attendees that thousands of
rooms in private homes had been arranged for fixed fees (fifty cents per day
for lodging and twenty-five, thirty-five, and fifty cents per day for meals).
And 50,000 men could stay in the camps being laid out in lots throughout the city. Altogether, accommodations for 100,000 veterans had been arranged. The organizers had also assigned schools, government offices, a local
medical college, hotels, warehouses, and other facilities to act as headquarters and reunion spots for the hundreds of units and organizations holding
meetings.[5]

Although the *Ohio Soldier* claimed that "citizens, as an almost universal
rule, are not after money, but are bent only upon well receiving and taking
good care of the Grand Army," a lot of money was clearly to be made by hosting a national encampment during the GAR's heyday in the 1880s and 1890s.
When Indianapolis hosted the 1893 GAR national encampment, a local pharmaceutical magnate and veteran, Colonel Eli Lilly, headed up the committee of the Commercial Club that organized the city's response. Businesses
celebrated the veterans even as they celebrated themselves; virtually every
downtown building was covered in bunting or other decorations. Merchants
competed to have the biggest and brightest displays; one hung a twenty-nine-
by-thirty-one-foot flag from the side of a store, while English's Hotel boasted
electrical displays in the shapes of old Union Army corps badges. Weeks before the encampment, the owner of the local gas company had sown beds of

flowers that bloomed just in time for the veterans' arrival, revealing patriotic designs and GAR logos. Five thousand electric lights lit up the new Soldiers' and Sailors' Monument. Three thousand members of thirty committees spent countless hours preparing for the arrival of more than forty thousand veterans and their families, building temporary housing, lining up boarding-houses, installing electric lights and trolleys, and establishing a process for serving forty-eight thousand meals a day. Railroads sold 217,000 fares into Indianapolis during the course of the encampment. In addition to veteran pilgrims and their families, the horde included peddlers selling souvenirs and GAR paraphernalia, pickpockets, and, in Lilly's words, "a small army of Chicago fakirs and card sharks." More than twenty thousand veterans took part in the parade, and dozens of regiments, batteries, and brigades held re-unions.[6]

The 1880 reunion in Milwaukee inspired local merchants to fill the *Sunday Telegraph* with advertisements that borrowed veterans' phraseology and rituals. The Golden Eagle clothing store invited "bold soldiers, with their families" to its "Camp Fire," where they could listen to "our Tales of Valor" and "inspect the grandest and most elaborate display of stylish and well made clothing." Veterans' "wives, mothers and Sisters" were invited to at-tend receptions held every day at White and Van Peltto's Dry Goods Empo-rium, while two other department stores simply headlined their large ads "Soldiers" and "Attention Soldiers." When the GAR met again in Milwau-kee nine years later, the mayor declared August 27 a general holiday. About seventy-five thousand veterans and guests came to the city, which, accord-ing to one observer, was "profusely and tastefully decorated for the occa-sion." One of the leading sponsors of the event was the Pabst Brewing Com-pany, on its way to becoming one of the country's largest breweries; Captain Frederick Pabst published a full-color brochure for the GAR.[7]

Stories and ads for entertainment, official memorabilia, and other items of interest to men attending the GAR's 1886 convention in San Francisco filled the "National Encampment Issue" of the *Pacific Veteran*. A Battle of Gettysburg cyclorama ran shows from early in the morning to 11:00 at night, while the Tivoli Opera House offered a play, *At the Front*. Local GAR posts hosted open houses, while the Veteran Legion held a picnic at Sea-side Gardens. In addition to the customary ads for pension agents and arti-ficial limbs, local businesses promoted their connections to the veterans by highlighting operators' veteran status or by getting veterans to provide a sort of endorsement, as members of one regimental veteran organization did when they gave billiard instruction at an "Encampment Salon." A local

Grand Army post established a "GAR STORE" for the duration of the encampment. "The Bivouac" offered imported wines and liquor, while "The Campfire" apparently offered only domestic spirits. Several merchants advertised GAR visiting cards and official encampment badges. Some dishonest entrepreneurs cashed in by selling fake identification cards, forcing organizers to refuse admission to the formal exercises of the encampment to people without tickets, which could be obtained only from GAR department and post commanders. The *G.A.R. Gazette* reported that the city was "full of G.A.R. Any one can purchase G.A.R. cigars, G.A.R. tobacco, G.A.R. rum, G.A.R. beer, G.A.R. shine, G.A.R. fruit and G.A.R. bread. In fact, the boys will find everything G.A.R. there, except G.A.R. prices."[8]

The national reunions held by the United Confederate Veterans (UCV) were similarly driven at least partly by commerce. Southern cities competed to host the thousands of veterans, families, and other interested parties who came to the reunions—100,000 in Richmond in 1896, 60,000 in Atlanta in 1898. Of the 140,000 reported attendees at the 1902 reunion in Dallas, however, only 12,000 were veterans. Cities spent as much as one hundred thousand dollars on the various facets of a reunion, including the free room and board provided to poor veterans, decorations (including hundreds of Confederate flags of all sizes as well as a few U.S. flags), parades, and receptions. But the economic benefits far outweighed the costs.[9]

The description of the 1900 Confederate veterans' reunion in Louisville indicated the extent to which communities believed that hosting a reunion was good business. City fathers and private donors contributed fifty thousand dollars and built a ten-thousand-seat hall on the banks of the Ohio River just for the encampment. The city provided free barracks-style housing and meal tickets for budget-conscious veterans, offered free concerts and "spectacular amusements" at three different halls, and sponsored free excursions, complete with bands and refreshments, on the Ohio River. Each state headquarters received its own band, and the business district was decorated with arches and red and white electric lamps, and "suspended in colors [on each arch was] the name of some distinguished hero of our sacred cause." The gathering's crowning accomplishment, a fireworks display, featured fifteen thousand separate shots, twenty-five hundred colored rockets launched at the rate of more than four per second, and spectacular thirty-two-by-twenty-foot pictures of Robert E. Lee and other heroes.[10]

Even a county-sized reunion could become big business. By the turn of the century, the annual Ex-Union Soldiers' Inter-State Reunion in Baxter Springs, Kansas, attracted fifty thousand veterans and nonveterans for a week each summer. Baxter Springs had a permanent "camp" of more than one hundred acres that featured buildings, a large amphitheater, running water, electricity, excursions on the Spring River, and convenient railroad connections. The stock company that ran the reunion offered free tents, wood, straw, and fire to veterans and their widows. In addition, "to attract and entertain this vast crowd of visitors," local musical groups performed, nationally known orators spoke, and "half a mile of sideshows, restaurants, fakers [sic], peanut roasters, juice racks, hot tamales, cider mills, lunch joints, Jew stores, cigar spindles, shooting galleries, knife racks, red lemonade, fortune tellers, faith healers, witch doctors, and a thousand other interesting, instructive and amusing features" appeared "to please the old and the young." A carnival midway and a couple of dozen "shows, museums, exhibitions, vaudevilles, and spectacular sensations" entertained the crowds.[11]

Beginning in the late 1870s, the New Hampshire Veterans' Association developed a "campground" on the shores of Lake Winnipesaukee that consisted of a number of permanent buildings as well as campsites. Annual reunions of all the state's veterans and meetings of regimental and auxiliary organizations were held at the camp. The decade-long building program, partly subsidized by the legislature and by private donors, represented a boon to local contractors. The four-day reunions also proved profitable: in addition to the typical speeches, parades, sham battles, fireworks displays, balloon ascensions, and games for veterans and their families, a motley collection of "peddlers and hustlers . . . strung themselves out in booths and stands . . . in 'fakirs row.'" As many as two hundred entrepreneurs sold souvenirs related to the reunion (badges, canes, ornaments); offered carnival games (baseball throwing and ring tossing); coaxed veterans and their families into dime museums with "mermaids," miniature cattle, and whales; and offered Punch-and-Judy shows and demonstrations of the magic of electricity.[12]

Such veterans' events thus resembled state and county fairs more than military or patriotic celebrations. Encampments could also sometimes be used to boom a city or region, thereby annoying the men whom the reunions were supposed to honor. In addition to a lack of organization and an apparently understaffed local arrangements committee, complained the *Confederate Veteran*, Atlanta organizers focused more on prominent officers and dignitaries, sponsors, and the bevy of "maids of honor" that appeared at most Confederate reunions than on the common soldiers. The information bureau was completely swamped with requests, accommodations were difficult to find, and costs were decidedly higher than they had been a year earlier in Nashville. In a not-too-thinly veiled swipe at Atlanta's reputation as the New South's rising commercial center, the *Veteran* criticized the "deplorable spirit of Atlanta to gush and to permit extortion."[13]

The slick brochure distributed for the 1890 "Reunion of the Blue and the Gray" at Vicksburg revealed the commercial opportunities that often lay behind such events. In addition to listing typical reunion activities, the official program promoted the healthy business climate of the little city of twenty-two thousand. Manufacturing was on the increase, the city government mimicked that in any other American city, the waterworks were efficient, the streetcars were modern, cultural institutions abounded, and the educational facilities were unequaled in the South.[14]

At the 1902 National Encampment in Washington, the Kansas GAR took over the Oxford Hotel, promising a "Western Welcome" at a permanent open house that featured a band, the Modocs singing group, and displays of sunflowers, corn, and other Kansas agricultural products. An elaborate, profusely illustrated souvenir booklet highlighted GAR members' role in the state's politics over the preceding four decades and detailed opportunities for businesses and individuals in the "soldiers' state," a "land of Moral Citizenship, Sobriety, Churches, Schools and Kindly Climate." Like other Gilded Age publications, often issued by railroads or land companies, that touted the western states, the Kansas GAR's booklet offered statistics and illustrations describing economic growth, educational and cultural institutions, and laws friendly to old soldiers (including measures providing headstones for burials and exempting GAR property from taxes and veterans from peddlers' license fees). In this case, the GAR acted as a kind of chamber of commerce for the state most commonly associated with veterans.[15]

Commercial instincts joined veterans' nostalgia in the sham battles that attracted many paying customers. Reunions large and small featured well-choreographed and noisy re-creations of long-ago battles. Evansville, Indiana, celebrated the reconciliation of the North and the South marked by the successful war against Spain by hosting the huge "National Reunion of the Blue and the Gray" in October 1899. The entertainment included boat races on the Ohio River, cycloramas of Civil War battles, fireworks, and a "monster steamboat parade." In addition, veterans and private militia companies held a "large sham battle" and competitive drills, which numbered among the most striking examples of the commodification of war and of veterans.[16]

One of the biggest imitation battles was staged at the 1889 Milwaukee reunion, where a temporary amphitheater was constructed along Lake Michigan so spectators could watch the event's climactic amphibious "assault." An estimated three hundred thousand people paid a dollar each (though Pabst paid the admission fee for old soldiers) to watch the attacking fleet trade volleys with land-based batteries. The two thousand men taking part in the reenactment sang old army songs before the action started, but once the attack began, they eagerly fired fifty thousand blank cartridges. Of course, the Union carried the day: two Confederate vessels burned to the waterline, and the Yankee "victory" was celebrated with even more fireworks. The affair cost ten thousand dollars.[17]

That the spectacles were intended more for civilians than for veterans was reflected in complaints in the *Milwaukee Sunday Telegraph*. "The sham battle is the shammest of shams," declared the paper in 1884 after the premature firing of a cannon tore both arms off a veteran taking part in a July 4 reenactment in Union Center, Wisconsin. Two old soldiers lost an arm and a thumb, respectively, in a separate incident; two years earlier, another veteran had lost an arm. "An accident of some kind occurs at nearly all of them," stormed the *Telegraph*, and such reenactments "ought to be prohibited." The editors also excoriated sham battles staged to increase attendance and thus gate receipts at July 4 and other public celebrations. Although civilians might "imagine that the methodically and mechanically placed lines of battle, the play forts, prancing steeds and the bellowing bands afford a truthful picture of a battle," they are instead nothing "but a cheap show . . . to get money." Such performances did not educate observers about the nature of war or inspire courage but rather demoralized participants and audience alike. Fake and real battles were so unlike "as to disgust the old veterans who engage in them to a degree which leads them to overstep the bounds of a battle for fun," taking risks and behaving in ways that almost inevitably led to injuries or even death. "All of the gate money ever taken in connection with sham battles is not worth the life of one poor veteran."[18]

Veterans hosted calmer entertainments, too, usually to raise money for the fund maintained to help comrades in times of need. One of the more ambitious chapters in this regard was the largest post in Worcester, Massachusetts, which repeatedly presented a patriotic tearjerker of a play, *The Drummer Boy*, that was very loosely based on the story of John Clem and had all the plotlines of a typical Civil War melodrama. Through five acts, thirteen scenes, and four tableaux, a large cast of stereotypical characters marches through the sectional conflict, including families whose ancient friendship has been destroyed, an enthusiastic youngster determined to become a drummer boy, a kind old "darky," a brave Yankee spy, a sinister South Carolinian, a mother who sacrificed three sons to the Union cause, and a suffering prisoner and a cruel guard at Andersonville prison. With only one professional actor in the company—he played the villainous South Carolinian—veterans, members of their families, and other community members would often play the same roles for years at a time. The play ran nearly every year, typically for a week, and raised a total of thirty thousand dollars for the post.[19]

Scenes of Continuous Pilgrimage

Worcester veterans were in complete charge of their not-quite-annual production, and the GAR, UCV, and other organizations created much of reunion content. Yet veterans did not necessarily control the ways in which the free market memorialized their service. Another point of conflict was the establishment of national military parks as tourist destinations late in the century. Usually led by veterans, the movement to protect and develop the great battlefields of the war found willing partners in communities hoping to attract tourists. Veterans welcomed the recognition of their valor on the killing grounds of their youth, but tensions arose when economic motivations seemed to overwhelm patriotism and propriety. The potential for friction between veterans and entrepreneurs had flared up even during the war, when soldiers began erecting monuments on battlefields. Individual regiments and brigades commissioned stone tributes to fallen leaders and markers on spots of noted actions. Confederate soldiers had put up small wooden markers around the battlefield at Chickamauga by the time President Jefferson Davis visited a few weeks after the battle. But battlefields had also attracted sightseers and entrepreneurs as soon as the armies moved on to other battles. Civilians combed the fields for collectibles or other objects to sell, and coffin makers and undertakers raced to cash in on the carnage. Members of the emerging profession of embalming drew criticism for making money from tragedy and for promising more than they could deliver. Families complained to the army about extortionate prices and poor workmanship that did not deliver natural-looking bodies to mourning parents and wives.[20]

The battlefield at Gettysburg became a tourist attraction almost as soon as the guns fell silent. As the site of only major fighting in a northern state, it became America's most commercialized battlefield. Souvenirs and tour guides quickly appeared, and one reporter commented on the "rapacious urchins" who fought over visitors' baggage at the train depot on behalf of the town's leading hotels. Commerce and patriotism operated in tandem, at least according to this observer, who approvingly reported that "by the wise forethought and patriotic zeal of the citizens of the town, all the salient points of the battle-ground have been purchased and secured in perpetuity for the public benefit." Some of the entrenchments and lines of battle would also be preserved; more important, "scholarly and practical men" had undertaken the chore of verifying important facts and places related to the battle. Like most observers, the author believed that the "now sacred" Soldiers' National Cemetery would remain the centerpiece of the visitors' experience. Indeed, the cemetery raised the purpose of a trip to Gettysburg from a mere vacation to a meaningful journey. Better rail connections would "make Gettysburgh the scene of an almost continuous pilgrimage."[21]

Gettysburg's status as a patriotic destination was enhanced by the mythology surrounding Lincoln's address there and by the national cemetery the speech had consecrated. Thousands of visitors came to view with dignity, reverence, and sadness the site of what most Americans believed to be the turning point of the war and of the largest single concentration of Union soldiers' graves in the North. But investors and town boosters actively sought to capitalize on Gettysburg's historic significance. In modern terms, they sought to exploit the Gettysburg brand.

One of the first postwar efforts to make money on the Gettysburg name was the "discovery" of healing springs west of the town. In an age when medical science still allowed for the belief in the natural curative power of certain kinds of water, such a discovery could be a windfall for hotel owners, physicians, guides, and numerous other townspeople. The mythology created overnight for the Katalysine Springs, as they came to be known, included the supposed healing of wounded Confederates during the battle. In addition, the marketing of the resort built around the springs and of the water bottled for retail distribution took advantage of the name recognition inherent in the presence of the battlefield. One of the directors of the first hotel constructed near the springs was David Wills, the most important promoter of the creation of the National Cemetery. By 1869, the site hosted a four-story, three-hundred-room hotel. The establishment of a soldiers' home near the springs was also planned, although it was never built.[22]

The veterans' interest in developing battlefield parks stemmed at least partly from their dismay about the possibility that commercialism would pollute the solemnity of the sites. As James A. Kaser has shown, old soldiers wanted the historical meaning of the battles to trump any other use or consideration. They hoped their stories—or at least those of their regiments— would be told correctly. They insisted on what they believed to be precision in the text on the markers honoring their units and in the locations of the markers establishing positions and movements. Behind the pomp and celebration of the reunions that accompanied the opening and development at the battlefield park at Chickamauga lay countless arcane debates about the ebb and flow of the battle and individual units' roles in the Confederate victory. What one historian has called the "golden age" of battlefield preservation occurred in the 1890s for several reasons: veterans seized on their encroaching mortality to urge the nation to commemorate their sacrifices and heroism in accurate and respectful ways; they recognized that Gilded Age economic and urban expansion would soon threaten the integrity of the old fields of battle; and many of the state legislators and members of Congress who would have to mobilize government resources to create the battlefield parks were themselves veterans.[23]

At Gettysburg and on battlefields throughout the South, monuments to specific regiments, batteries, and other units became the most direct way of honoring the courage and sacrifices of Union and later Confederate soldiers. Individuals and veterans' organizations donated money to pay for the monuments, although after 1884 state governments also began paying for shrines to their regiments. Veterans enthusiastically raised money and attended dedications.[24]

But even the campaigns to establish historical accuracy and recognition through careful placement of markers became part of the battlefields' business plans. Most decisions about site administration and development were made with commerce in mind. By the late 1880s, civilian and veteran groups alike were promoting the idea of allowing Confederate units to be memorialized in stone. Union veterans had come to believe that only by showing where Confederate units fought would the stories of and monuments to northern valor make sense. Businessmen believed that the presence of Confederate monuments would not only soften remnants of sectional bitterness but also encourage tourism from the thus far underrepresented southern states. In addition, the solemnity of marble slabs carved with names of the noble dead was being supplemented by the 1890s with monuments featuring soldiers firing weapons, leading charges, and striking otherwise dramatic poses.[25]

As the historian of the battlefield has written, "Everyone seemed to profit from the frenzy" to honor the men who fought the great battle at Gettysburg, from the monument companies that advertised their work there to the local businesses that profited from the crowds drawn to each new dedication. Con artists targeted veterans, offering to get their names carved on monuments—in exchange for a small fee, of course. Hotels offered tours, guidebooks, and souvenirs, and when veterans' groups or other organizations came to town, they were greeted by brass bands in striking uniforms and by red, white, and blue arches and banners. Four versions of the Gettysburg Cyclorama were created, enabling huge crowds in multiple locations to view Philippoteaux's masterpiece during the 1880s. In addition to veteran lecturers who provided commentary regarding the ambitious painting, "guides" and "maps" of the cyclorama were available, adding further verisimilitude to the experience. These and less fully realized artistic representations of the battle were presented around the world, from Paris to Sydney and from world's fairs to department store walls. When one of the originals found a permanent home at Gettysburg, investors believed it would provide additional profits for battlefield interests.[26]

Gettysburg became less a place to honor the living than to remember the dead—and increasingly to have a good time. In addition to veterans' organizations, which were naturally attracted to the site, fraternal, religious, and other organizations as well as large groups of day-trippers from Philadelphia and Baltimore made their way to the site. Dance pavilions, beer halls, amusement parks, movie houses, and other attractions eventually drew as many tourists as did the battlefield and cemetery. Popular sites included Round Top Park, where rules against drinking beer on Sunday were easily ignored.[27]

A quarter of a century after the battle, the editor of the *Ohio Soldier* expressed concern about reports of "exorbitant charges" at Gettysburg, a town living "almost entirely off of tourists." His investigation did not substantiate the charges, but he was disturbed by the "constant" reference of guides, guide books, and residents to "the Confederacy," a "thing that never had an existence except in the diseased imagination of rebels." Although the term was no doubt attractive to southern travelers, "it doesn't look nor sound patriotic in the citizens of the locality of the only battle fought on loyal soil to honor rebellion by referring to it by the name which indicates that it was a nation." At the very least, guides should preface the term with "so-called." If "old rebel sympathizers" visit, they can "call it what they have a mind to, but the loyal people of Gettysburg should call it by a name which designates its character—rebellion or conspiracy."[28]

Confederates had easier and cheaper access to other battlefields, and former Rebels were among the first and most consistent entrepreneurs offering guided tours of important spots and monuments. But battlefields became big business when the Chattanooga and Chickamauga battlefields were converted into a national military park in the mid-1890s. City and county governments not only granted permission for markers, monuments, and informational tablets to be placed at points around the city but also connected Chattanooga's main streets to the roads leading into the park itself. "The practical result of this liberal action," wrote a contemporary, "has been virtually to add to the National Park the entire city of Chattanooga and its surroundings." Most visitors to the new national battlefield parks in the 1890s were veterans and their families.[29]

Although the establishment of national military parks in the 1890s has often been framed in the rhetoric of reconciliation, the creation of parks could also lead to tension and conflict, especially when battle narratives were created in the form of permanent stone monuments. Hundreds of markers were dedicated to specific regiments, batteries, and commanders and were often placed at points on the field where these individuals or groups made important contributions. Gallons of ink were spilled in veterans' publications, in private correspondence, and in the records of the commissions charged with approving monuments in debates over just how far a regiment advanced, exactly where it turned the enemy's flank, the spot on which a general was wounded. One such controversy, clothed in fairly polite rhetoric but of deep importance to both principals, arose when William C. Oates, who had commanded the 15th Alabama during its attack up Little Round Top on the second day at Gettysburg, tried to get a monument to his regiment mounted inside the lines commonly understood to be held during the stand by Joshua Chamberlain's 20th Maine.

But larger issues than a stone and brass marker were involved. Over the nearly thirty years since that fateful day, both men had made the bloody affair into a centerpiece of their memories of the war. Chamberlain's career as college president, governor of Maine, federal appointee, and popular speaker was founded on his courage and decisiveness during his first battle as commander of the regiment, which had earned him the Medal of Honor. Although the 15th Alabama had failed to carry the position, its valiant and repeated assaults over difficult terrain also dominated Oates's view of his leadership and service. He had fought through the war and lost an arm, but his career as a lawyer, congressman, and governor was also based largely on his role in the battle. That his brother, John, had been mortally wounded that day lent a poignant sense of survivor's guilt to his memories and added a potent edge to his desire to establish in the public mind how well his regiment had fought despite the odds.

In the end, the 15th Alabama did not get its monument. Although on the surface the issue seemed to hinge on rather inconsequential details—after all, the 20th Maine had held, the 15th Alabama had retreated—the matter bore extraordinary importance for these two proud men whose reputations and sense of self-esteem depended on maintaining their memories of the fight. How far did Chamberlain's flank bend? Did the 15th withdraw in order or retreat in disorder? Even after lifetimes of recognition and accomplishment, such matters loomed important to these two old warriors.[30]

Relics of Priceless Value

As the sale of souvenir relics on the great battlefields indicated, the magnitude and meaning of the conflict imparted almost mystical importance to the detritus of war. War artifacts held special significance for soldiers, who naturally hung onto uniforms, haversacks, mess kits, even weapons. Some put them to use in civilian life, but for most veterans, these reminders of their military pasts, in the words of a veterans' newspaper, "remain dear to the individual for some peculiar act connected with it." One man cherished a tin plate he had carried in his haversack for three years; it saved his life when, during the Atlanta campaign, a bullet creased the tin and ricocheted harmlessly away. The *Milwaukee Sunday Telegraph* occasionally ran a feature, "The Old Knapsack," that reported on objects found in attics or closets by soldiers or their families. In 1883, a Chicagoan wrote of opening a knapsack carried by his brother throughout the war and untouched for nearly twenty years. It contained parts of a uniform, a rubber blanket, a "dog" tent, a pair of veteran's reenlistment stripes, a gun plug, three musket caps, a piece of flannel wrapped around three sewing needles, a tintype photograph, a jack of spades, and a June 24, 1865, pass to leave camp.[31]

But tools of war also attained an almost grail-like status in the minds of both northern and southern civilians and became a kind of currency of memory and patriotism. Predicted the *Sunday Telegraph*, as "our late comrades become gray and one by one pass away to the last roll call, our future generations will . . . treasure up the relics of the late war." Although collectors and curators might put a price on these objects, they were literally priceless to those who imbued the items with patriotic and tragic meanings. As a result, even if they were not part of moneymaking schemes, they attained a currency recognized by every American. Veterans and nonveterans agreed that these objects were valuable, but the more they became collectibles, assigned a price on the open market, the less they were relics of sacrifice and of causes lost and won.[32]

A largely northern market for Confederate artifacts developed in the latter decades of the century. With an enthusiasm not unlike the insatiable appetite for stories of plantation life and local color that appeared in northern magazines in the 1880s and 1890s, Yankees sought to buy up anything related to the Confederacy. The *Confederate Veteran* reported that northern collectors were paying between $12 and $250 for Confederate postage stamps. Another article suggested that veterans in need of money might find a market for their "war relics" in the North, where newspapers frequently ran notices from Yankee collectors. Some southerners were outraged that old soldiers and their families were selling their Confederate heritage. A member of the United Daughters of the Confederacy (UDC) wrote that she had seen advertisements for Confederate war relics in almost every newspaper she had seen. "What are our people thinking of?" she cried. "Are they selling these relics that should be held as sacred treasures in every Southern household to enterprising relic hunters, who in turn place them in museums North, and charge the seller a big price to visit and see what they considered worthless?" She urged people who no longer wanted such items to turn them over to local chapters of the UDC for care and preservation.[33]

Individual collectors were important players in the relic market, but the war also inspired museums to collect war artifacts such as guns, battle flags, splinters from Confederate and Union ships, and various pieces of soldiers' equipment. Civil War exhibits tended to be of the cumulative variety—amassing items was more important than explaining them—but were nevertheless a small stream in the emerging science of museum display, which became a central part of the broadening Gilded Age notion of cultural education. Eclectic, crowded displays of such items had been popular objects of public curiosity through the war and were often featured at the U.S. Sanitary Commission fairs held in most northern cities.[34]

Events held for the benefit of veterans after the war also featured mini-museums. In the late 1870s, the Massachusetts GAR held a number of Grand Army Fairs, at least some of which featured an exhibition of war items intermixed with objects connected to sensational incidents from the Police Museum. A wide variety of weapons, sections of rope from nooses used to hang infamous murderers, and tools used by notorious counterfeiters, gamblers, and burglars could be viewed alongside war-related "curiosities, relics, and mementoes" such as Confederate officers' swords, spurs, and pistols, manacles taken from slave pens in the occupied South, a button from John Brown's coat, and a collection of photographs of Massachusetts soldiers and sailors who died during the war. The 1881 Boston Soldiers' Home Bazaar featured dozens of "relics from Gettysburg," most of them Union and Confederate artillery shells and shell fragments.[35]

The war created artifacts enough for countless large and small museums. An Iowa veteran created an exhibition that he showed around the Midwest and Plains states in the 1890s. The "museum" filled three wagons and included Indian artifacts and a few stuffed and mounted animals along with items from the Civil War. The memorabilia seem to have been fairly typical, ranging from a Confederate belt buckle and canteen to scores of photographs of men from his old unit, the 3rd Iowa Cavalry.[36]

Many of the better-heeled GAR posts filled their headquarters—often substantial buildings with offices for the Woman's Relief Corps (the GAR ladies' auxiliary) and other organizations—with paintings, engravings, objects, and miscellaneous ephemera and reminders of the war. A tin cup carried by a New York veteran as he was shipped to and from nearly half a dozen Confederate prisons was displayed at his GAR post, while a Kansas post displayed a shirt bearing blood shed by one of its members when he was wounded at Chancellorsville. In addition to paintings and photographs of battle scenes and post members, the Lewis P. Buckley Post in Akron, Ohio, owned a wreath from President James Garfield's funeral car; gavels made from wood collected at Little Round Top, Andersonville, and Chickamauga; and a silk flag presented to the post by local merchants that was to be used, according to a label, "as a winding sheet for the last survivor of Buckley post." Members of Philadelphia's GAR Post No. 2 organized a museum of objects donated by veterans. Items in the museum, which was later taken over by descendants of Union veterans and was known for many years as the GAR Museum and Library, included a tree from the Chickamauga Battlefield pierced by a cannonball; a section of the wooden stockade at Andersonville; items belonging to General George Gordon Meade, a Pennsylvanian; miscellaneous bullets and bones; and a surgeon's kit. In addition, the museum possessed the handcuffs that John Wilkes Booth planned to use when he kidnapped Abraham Lincoln and a strip of cloth purporting to be a scrap from the pillowcase on which Lincoln lay when he died. Although the George H. Ward Post No. 10 in Worcester, one of the more active GAR posts in the Northeast, had intended to inventory its large collection of artifacts, a true reckoning of its holdings was not recorded until 1937, when a locked room in its now underused hall was opened to reveal two hundred lithographs, photographs, documents, and paintings, including a facsimile of the South Carolina ordinance of secession; the last official document signed by the post's namesake, who was killed at Gettysburg; and a photograph of the 25th Massachusetts, the regiment whose veterans formed the nucleus of the post.[37]

The Illinois State Legislature led the way in creating a major Civil War museum by chartering the state's Grand Army Hall and Memorial Association in 1887. A few years later, when a new public library was built near Dearborn Park on land originally intended for a soldiers' home, the legislature ordered that the library house a Grand Army Memorial Hall. Fitted with marble walls, Tiffany windows, and Italian mosaics, "this temple of patriotism" also became a museum, displaying nearly five hundred photos, pieces of equipment, memorabilia, and documents in four wall cases and six floor cases. In addition to the more typical items, the collection devoted an entire case to Lincoln objects and papers and included a few items related to the American Revolution, the war in Cuba, and Custer's Last Stand. The museum also housed a piano purchased at Chicago's 1865 Great Sanitary Fair; a cane made by a prisoner at Andersonville; the drum used by "Bill Nevins, the Drummer Boy of the Rappahannock," the "champion drummer" of the Ellsworth Zouaves militia unit; a model of the USS *Monitor*; the last telegram sent by Abraham Lincoln; documents related to slavery; and a pair of manacles.[38]

Southerners pursued similar strategies to keep soldiers' past contributions and current plight before the public and to attract visitors to important events. Sue Monroe kept a small museum in a store in her hometown of Wellington, Virginia, near the Second Manassas battlefield. Herself a "veteran" of the battles—she recalled the gunfire and the passing of the troops following First Manassas—she had gone over the battlefield countless times, "and every time brought home something, either a shell, balls, bayonets, or ramrods, and everything else I could find." She had found buttons from the uniforms of men from most Confederate states as well as "a little tin cup picked up where Jackson's troops charged."[39]

Although the managers of the 1895 Atlanta Exposition did not organize an exhibit of Confederate relics, the UDC, UCV, and Sons of Confederate Veterans procured sites within the exposition for displays. These groups appealed for contributions of money and artifacts through the *Confederate Veteran*. Two years later, a similar exhibit appeared at the Tennessee Centennial Exposition in Nashville, where the Confederate display occupied a prominent place in the History Building. The exhibit contained several dozen uniforms, parts of uniforms, and hats (dutifully labeled when their owners had been killed, wounded, or married while wearing them); flags; personal possessions; weapons; a wreath made from the hair of Jefferson Davis, Andrew Jackson, Robert E. Lee, Nathan Bedford Forrest, Kirby Smith, James Longstreet, and other Confederate celebrities; and a hoof from one of the horses shot out from under the famously lucky General Forrest.[40]

But these ad hoc efforts were joined by a campaign led by the *Confederate Veteran* and a number of women's memorial organizations to create a museum representing the entire Confederacy. After much discussion, the Richmond mansion that had been used as the Confederate White House became that museum. The Confederate Memorial Literary Society in Richmond began a campaign to obtain funding and donated relics in the early 1890s, with the goal of restoring the mansion to its wartime appearance. Rooms were named after Confederate states, and veterans and supporters from those states were asked for funding and artifacts.[41]

The Confederate Museum opened on Washington's Birthday 1896. The chilly, damp late winter weather gave way to balmy sunshine—as if, according to an article in the *Southern Historical Society Papers*, "it was . . . the approving smile of the Lord of hosts upon the truly reverential efforts of our most excellent women in the perpetuation of the truth." Most of the artifacts had not yet been installed; a huge crowd was expected for the opening, and most of the rooms contained only a few pieces of furniture, wall decorations, and refreshments. Most of the items displayed were portraits or busts of Davis, Lee, and other prominent Confederates; battle flags; and ceremonial swords. The museum also exhibited a few framed documents (among them firsthand accounts of First Manassas, Lee's Farewell Address, and fairly mundane muster and pay rolls); the uniform and equipage of an Alabama general; and a pair of slippers made from the carpet that covered one of the rooms in the Executive Mansion during the war.[42]

Two years after the museum opened, organizers were still soliciting items for display. A Tennessee woman wrote to the *Confederate Veteran* urging old soldiers and their families to contribute the "souvenirs, relics, records, letters, orders, and other data of priceless value" before the "ceaseless march of time, the destroyer" takes away the "battle scarred veteran defenders of the Southland" and the chance to preserve "the truth of history." She asked interested donors to forward the items, along with "a short descriptive sketch of same or of [the] battle, march, siege, person, or event which they commemorate."[43]

The soldiers' homes established in most of the former Confederate states late in the century also provided logical sites for the safe storage and display of artifacts. The home maintained by Richmond's R. E. Lee Camp actively

In 1898, the Relic Room at the Maryland Line Confederate Soldiers' Home held hundreds of artifacts from the war. Courtesy of The Maryland Historical Society.

solicited contributions of memorabilia in a circular published in the late 1880s. The home's managers had set aside a locked brick building for this purpose; the home would accept donations or even buy relics from people "who have no means of preserving . . . War Relics and Antiquities."[44]

By the early twentieth century, the Confederate Home in Pewee Valley, Kentucky, had become a repository for original paintings, artifacts, and records related to the war. In a sense, the homes seemed to be trying to surround the old soldiers with artifacts and pictures that would help them recall their youthful exploits. The home newsletter frequently reported on contributions of artwork and relics and raised money among veterans and others to pay for a portrait of Kentucky's favorite Confederate, John Hunt Morgan. On another occasion, the home's managers solicited a flag that had flown in the service of the Confederate States of America, which they "would value . . . beyond all possessions." The home eventually received several flags, including the standard of the Fourth Kentucky, part of one of the most famous units in the Confederate Army, the Orphan Brigade. Eight color bearers had been killed or wounded carrying that flag. A gift of six lithographs of realistic paintings by popular artist Gilbert Gaul "tell the story . . . of the life of the Confederate soldier in camp and on the battle-field so faithfully that one cannot fail to appreciate the hardships as well as the amusing side of war."[45]

The Maryland Line Confederate Soldiers' Home in Pikesville, just west of Baltimore, accumulated hundreds of items, large and small, in its "Relic Hall," which was used only for special occasions. Alongside the usual battle-field paintings and photographs, uniforms and field equipment, guns and swords (many belonging to notables such as Lee, Jeb Stuart, and Wade Hampton), and letters and other ephemera, the home displayed a lock of Lee's hair, a piece of the doorsill from the room in which Stonewall Jackson was born, and the handkerchief used by Louis T. Wigfall when he approached Fort Sumter to demand its surrender in April 1861.[46]

The most famous nineteenth-century Civil War museum appeared in one of the least likely places when a northern entrepreneur moved the building that had housed Libby Prison from Richmond to Chicago in 1889. Chicago consumers and entrepreneurs alike had long been interested in Civil War displays, and "Colonel Wood" displayed some Civil War items in his dime museum immediately after the war ended. The Great Fire destroyed Wood's museum and otherwise distracted Chicagoans for a decade, but huge audiences thronged exhibits of the Gettysburg and Shiloh Cycloramas in 1883 and 1885, respectively. Seeking to exploit northerners' curiosity about the war, insurance executive W. H. Gray raised two hundred thousand dollars from a group of investors to purchase, dismantle, move, and rebuild the somewhat decrepit stone warehouse that had comprised the main section of the old prison. A total of 132 freight cars were needed to carry the four-story building from Virginia to Chicago; some of the stones were carried off as souvenirs after a railway accident in Kentucky. The structure was then rebuilt inside a gothic-style stone wall on Wabash Avenue between Fourteenth and Sixteenth Streets and filled with an eccentric collection of artifacts, documents, and pictures divided into the Confederate and the Union departments. The museum's most notable objects included the desk at which Grant and Lee drew up the surrender terms at Appomattox; tableware, chains, and bracelets carved by prisoners from wood and bone; and bricks and floorboards from the prison etched with names and game boards. Rooms were named for their function (the Reception Room, for example), for the commanders of the units whose officers were imprisoned in them, or for the battles at which the prisoners were captured (the Chickamauga Room). Museum advertisements touted the bricked-up entrance to the tunnel used by more than a hundred prisoners during an 1864 escape attempt.[47]

Unlike most other war-related tourist destinations, the Libby Prison War Museum purported to show at least a part of Union soldiers' actual experiences. Although cemeteries near battlefields drew many visitors and inspired much rhetoric, tourists visiting battlefields could separate the drama of the military side of the war from the horror and boredom experienced by the men. Doing so was impossible at Libby Prison museum, however. No group of veterans drew more sympathy and interest from the civilian population than the men who had survived horrid conditions in Confederate prisons. (Conditions were just as deadly in Union prisons, but that fact was rarely mentioned in northern circles.) Libby and Andersonville were the most infamous prisons; because Libby existed for most of the war, because it had housed mostly officers, and because it was in the Confederate capital, it was perhaps the best-known site in the Confederacy. The investors in the Libby Prison War Museum Association counted on the general public's continuing interest in the plight of Yankee prisoners; in this case, the commercial exploitation of the war was directly related to the experiences of Union soldiers. Despite its rundown condition and the structure's postwar reversion to its original function as a warehouse, the prison had still attracted tourists during the time between the end of the war and its relocation. One veterans' newspaper suggested that the hack drivers, hotel keepers, and souvenir hawkers who already profited from Yankee curiosity about the famous building would be ruined by the building's removal. That curiosity might have been piqued by Richmond African Americans' purported belief that the old prison was haunted.[48]

Criticism of the plan to open the museum in Chicago emerged almost immediately. Southerners clearly did not care for having the alleged horrors of Confederate prisons thrown in their faces in such a one-sided way; one southern newspaper suggested that if the enterprise proved profitable, southern investors should "organize a prison association in the South for the purchase of the prison pens at Elmira and Point Lookout and Fort Delaware and Johnson's Island, where thousands of Confederate prisoners were put to death by slow torture." Critics in both sections worried that the museum would fan sectional antagonism by reminding both northerners and southerners of one of the most bitter memories of the war. Worse, some commentators complained that making a museum out of the prison would disrespect the men who had suffered and died there and would make morbid curiosity profitable. Perhaps most shocking was the idea that Gray and his investors clearly had no patriotic motives but simply sought to make money. "There is no idea of waving the 'bloody shirt' in this," said one of the partners; "It is simply a business speculation for what there is in it." One veterans' paper argued that despite many people's "ardent desire" to see old prisons, they should be left where they belong. "They are the relics of the most inhuman barbarism that has ever been inflicted upon humanity, and they should not be permitted to pollute any loyal state."[49]

The rhetoric cooled after the old warehouse, fitted with electric lights and blue and red flags, its whitewashed walls decorated with thousands of relics and artifacts, opened in September 1889. The only truly "National War Museum in America" according to its own advertising, the institution claimed that "one of the most interesting and important points about the exhibit . . . is the fact that it contains the most complete and valuable collection of Confederate relics in existence." Contradicting its founders' earlier admission, the museum's catalog billed the establishment as not only educational but also a "Shrine of Patriotic Memories." But there was also room, as always, for commerce. Visitors could buy Libby Brand cigars, replicas of bullets, spoons, medals, Confederate money, flags, lapel pins, jewelry, photographs of Chicago, and pieces of the original floorboards. Interest in the museum reached its height during the 1893 Columbian Exhibition, whose managers had deliberately omitted Civil War–related artifacts from the historical exhibits to prevent sectional discord and thus left that market to the museum, located a couple of miles north of the exhibition grounds. The museum ran a prominent ad in the July 1893 *Confederate Veteran*, inviting veterans to visit the museum while in Chicago for the world's fair.[50]

Veterans generally supported the Libby Prison museum, which logged hundreds of visits by former inmates each year. The Chicago Association of Ex-Union Prisoners of War hosted formal reunions of midwestern prisoners at the museum roughly every six months, while other groups met there more informally. Further catering to the interests of veterans was the *Libby Prison Chronicle*, named after a wartime inmate newspaper and published by John Ransom, a former prisoner at Libby and a famous diarist. Although any visitor could purchase the publication, it contained news and information of particular interest to former prisoners and to veterans in general. Finally, former inmates could pay to have plaques installed on the floor space where they or one of their comrades had slept during their incarceration. More than four hundred men purchased plaques.[51]

Yet another example of the commodification of veterans and veteranhood was the score or more of veterans' newspapers that combined advocacy for veterans' issues and outlets for the veterans' voices with an entrepreneurial patriotism. Although quaint compared to the mass-market periodicals that offered sensationalistic crime stories, women's fashions, and tales of international adventure—all paid for with dynamic and colorful advertisements—the soldiers' newspapers nevertheless were part of the explosion of popular media that helped propel Gilded Age consumerism.[52]

The first of this genre, William Oland Bourne's *The Soldier's Friend and Grand Army of the Republic*, appeared in 1868 but ran for only a few years. In some respects, the flagship soldiers' paper was the weekly *National Tribune*, which was published in Washington, D.C., beginning in 1879 and served for many years as the national GAR's unofficial organ. Perhaps no other paper pushed as hard as the *Tribune* for soldiers' pensions and benefits; in fact, its masthead included the passage from President Lincoln's Second Inaugural Address that inspired efforts to aid disabled and needy veterans: "To care for him who has borne the battle, and for his widow and orphans."[53]

The halcyon days of veterans' publications came in the 1880s and 1890s, when a number of newspapers were published in the North and West. Many were allied formally or informally with state departments of the GAR, although St. Paul's *Relief Guard* was affiliated with the Union Veterans' Union and *Neighbor's Home Mail*, published in the 1870s and early 1880s by Lieutenant J. W. Neighbor in Phelps, New York, was nearly as much a temperance organ as a veterans' paper. The *Milwaukee Sunday Telegraph* was one of the more political soldiers' papers and almost singlehandedly brought about the 1880 reunion of soldiers in Milwaukee that helped resuscitate the slumping GAR; however, the *Telegraph* resembled a general interest newspaper more than most soldiers' publications did. The Des Moines–based *Grand Army Advocate* served as the organ of the Iowa GAR for several years after 1889. The *Soldiers' Tribune* of Lyons, Kansas, was more of a local paper with strong soldiers' interests than a soldiers' paper; it seemed to have a closer relationship to the Sons of Union Veterans than did other newspapers. A very different sort of soldiers' paper appeared for several years in the 1880s as a kind of newsletter for the Southern Branch of the National Home for Disabled Volunteer Soldiers (NHDVS) in Norfolk, Virginia. In addition to offering news items from the home and the larger community, including occasional articles about African American residents, the *Home Bulletin* also followed events at other branches of the NHDVS and offered brief reminiscences by soldiers and biographies of generals.

Perhaps the most strident of the GAR-allied papers was the weekly *Ohio Soldier*. In its first issue, published in August 1887, the paper described itself as "an organ of the Grand Army of the Republic in the sense that its editor is a member of that body, in full sympathy with its objects." GAR news would be reported, and the group's interests would be protected, but the GAR was not responsible for any stories or opinions that appeared in the *Ohio Soldier*; the organization "does its own talking, through its regularly authorized officers." Within a couple of years of its first issue, the *Ohio Soldier* bought out a competitor, the *National Picket Guard*, and added its name as a subtitle.[54]

In an age when newspapers and magazines filled their pages with ceaseless self-promotion, commerce and public service were inextricably related, at least rhetorically. Editors of soldiers' papers did not differ from their civilian counterparts in constantly pushing subscribers to prove their loyalty by renewing subscriptions and recruiting new readers. The *Milwaukee Sunday Telegraph*, for example, claimed in 1882 that it was the only newspaper "in the west" to devote as much as five columns in each issue to soldiers' concerns. The paper touted its promotion of the 1880 reunion in Milwaukee, its role in "hunting up hundreds of witnesses whose testimony was essential in procuring pensions of worthy comrades," and its willingness to perform "all kinds of work which tends to the benefit and pleasure of comrades." It also met the needs of businessmen, who, a late-1882 editorial suggested, were clamoring to advertise in its pages, which were read by the "most intelligent and the well-to-do classes of the people . . . who are the best customers of the best establishments." But the *Telegraph* also implored veterans grateful for its news and advocacy to "devote the small space of half an hour to personal work among their acquaintances" to increase circulation.[55]

Like all nineteenth-century periodicals, soldiers' papers offered premiums for readers who helped enlist subscribers. The *Ohio Soldier* sought to bolster profits in early 1891 by offering a 9' by 4.5' "imitation bunting" American flag to every GAR chapter in Ohio that recruited a "club" of ten subscribers, while chapters organizing twenty subscribers would get a "genuine bunting flag." No post should be without a good-quality flag, for "nothing contributes more to the life and vigor of a post than the proper paraphernalia . . . and nothing will set off a post room and make it more attractive than a number of flags appropriately draped about its walls." Any individual who "got up" a club of one hundred subscribers would receive a watch with a solid gold case. The *National Tribune* offered a column-long list of books, pictures, watches, clocks, and knives for anyone who sent in paid subscriptions.[56]

The *Neighbor's Home Mail* billed itself as the "most intensely interesting Soldier paper published in this or any other country." Leaving his work as a printer and editor to serve with the 148th New York, Neighbor had returned "the merest skeleton all broken down in health and bodily strength." He now made a living at his trade but relied on his fellow veterans for sustenance. Neighbor reminded his readers of the wartime cry, "Rally on the Colors, men," and asked them to recall the last words of gallant comrades, the shattered silence as survivors drank coffee and chewed hardtack after a bloody battle, the poignancy of the ever-thinning ranks. "Remember all this? Yes, thrice times yes, and in the most sacred cherishings of fond memory will ever live these realities. Comrades, rally around the Home Mail. It is doing a noble work—every surviving Soldier has an interest in its mission." The more men who fulfilled their duty by subscribing, "the grander and more complete will be" the paper's "preservation of the little incidents and precious memories which fill the bosom of every honored veteran." The drumbeat was incessant. An 1880 call for subscribers claimed that for seven years, "this paper has stood sentry guarding the best interest of those and the rightful heirs of those who fought down the Rebellion." As a result, "no true soldier can be indifferent to the sustaining of such a paper and be true to the faith that is in him." "Every Ex-Soldier should Subscribe for it!," declared a huge ad in the same issue; "Every Grand Army man should read it! Every friend of the Soldiers should take it! Every Soldier should write jokes for it! Every lover of Liberty should help it!" And if the call to duty failed to inspire, the readers who solicited the greatest number of new subscribers could win prizes, including a "Splendid 14-Stop Beatty Organ," a spring wagon, a sewing machine, or one of several different styles of watches. In 1881, an editorial asked, "Was You a Soldier?," the ubiquitous greeting extended to old soldiers by other old soldiers, and went on, "If you was, allow us, comrade, to grasp you by the hand and appeal to you—looking you straight in the eye as we used to peer into the darkness cross the lines on vidette duty—to do a true-soldier's duty toward the *Home Mail*."[57]

But even the *Home Mail* was outdone in the arenas of self-promotion and articulating the connection between patriotism and profit by the *Confederate Veteran*, official paper of the UCV, UDC, and Sons of Confederate Veterans. Editor S. A. Cunningham enthusiastically pushed, prodded, and cajoled readers to believe it their duty to subscribe. Cunningham, a veteran of some

J. W. Neighbor, editor and publisher of *Neighbor's Home Mail*, frequently urged "true soldiers" to subscribe and to recruit other subscribers. *Neighbor's Home Mail*, December 1880.

of the war's hardest fighting, expected his fellow Confederates and their families to make sure that he could fulfill "the great mission of the *Veteran*": "to leave to posterity our side of the Civil War." Toward the end of his first year of publication, Cunningham argued that the *Veteran* was actually "more for those who were not in the War, since its contents will make them more patriotic and prouder of their ancestry." He assured readers sensitive to sectionalism that "the war was not against the system of government to which all give allegiance now."[58]

Cunningham frequently suggested that subscribing to the *Veteran* was the peacetime equivalent of doing one's duty as a soldier. As "one of the ordinary soldiers in the service," he described himself as just "as powerless to accomplish its patriotic and holy purposes as would have been our army commanders to win victories without the co-operation of the soldiers." Calling the *Veteran* "the most important medium that has ever been printed to represent the principles for which you suffered," he asked "all who believe in the good faith of Confederates" to "rally now to their advocate, and the world will yet honor them more and more in what they did." In mid-1894, when hard times meant that a thousand subscribers had failed to renew, Cunningham wrote simply, "Comrades, this won't do." His magazine was "commended officially, yea, sacredly, by more organizations of noble men than has ever been any periodical, no doubt, in history," a reference to the often-reprinted three-page list of local chapters of the UCV and other organizations that had sanctioned the *Veteran*. "Think of the thousands all over the South who, after bending the stiffened knee in prayer during their business proceedings, while providing for afflicted comrades and other sacred duties, say, upon their love of country and sacred honor, that the *Confederate Veteran* deserves the support of all good men." And those good men not only should maintain their subscriptions but should go out and recruit five other men to subscribe. In that way, comrades could answer the roll call of patriotic former Confederates with a resounding "Here!" Cunningham reached the pinnacle of hyperbolic self-importance in June 1895, when he wrote, "There is nothing printed of equal benefit" to his magazine "save only 'the book of books,' and its holy mission will be maintained." He may have matched that prideful statement when he said three years later that "the Veteran is approved and endorsed by a larger and more elevated patronage, doubtless, than any other publication in existence."[59]

Some evidence indicates that Cunningham earned his readers' loyalty. In 1899, a veteran wrote that the magazine "is just what I have been looking for many years. Often I have wondered why we old soldiers of the Confederate States of America, who are beginning to live so much in the past, had nothing with which to refresh our memories and our children of the trials and struggles endured by their fathers and mothers during the great war." Although plenty of books had been written about Confederate leaders, the *Veteran* provided "avenues for privates" to tell their stories. "I wait for the

Veteran like the little boys wait for Christmas." Cunningham's confidence in readers' goodwill led him to straightforward demands: "Comrades. are you faithful in your duty? The *Veteran*, it is true, is a personal property, and, in the ways of the world, it is a plea for your patronage to sustain that personal interest. But do you put that estimate upon it? Those who have been students of its course have long since been assured of the absolute consecration of its owner and manager, and that he would spend all and be spent that he would surrender life itself that its principles be maintained." "Are We All Doing Our Full Duty?"[60]

All veterans should "rally to the *Veteran*," making it the topic of conversation at every reunion event. In 1894, readers were urged to give subscriptions to the *Veteran* as Christmas gifts. Cunningham frequently suggested that comfortably situated readers subscribe on behalf of the thousands of veterans unable to afford the publication. Circulation steadily climbed past 160,000 by 1896, but Cunningham did not rest. When one man could no longer afford his subscription, the editor entreated "all who are so situated [to] consider how important it is for each one to stand firm? Won't such as feel they can't afford to renew, procure four subscribers, and thus continue [to receive the magazine for free]? Do let us all stand together, making a true record as long as our lights hold out to burn." After "five years in harness the necessity of diligence is ever apparent. The responsibility increases continually, and the appeal is just as earnest and necessary as it was for comrades to rally and re-rally in battle when the war was in progress." Cunningham urged readers to make "whatever the necessary sacrifice to maintain this truthful record of what you are proud of and what you wish incorporated in history hereafter." The "reward will be greater than in anything else in which you can invest the small sum of $1 a year."[61]

We, Too, Have Fought for a Principle

In addition to becoming a kind of brand name by late in the century, veterans were also a recognizable market segment. The Ex-Soldiers Mutual Life Assurance Society of the Northwest in Goshen, Indiana, sold life insurance—at the lowest prices anywhere, it assured potential customers—only to ex-soldiers and their "families, heirs, and relatives," while the Union Publishing Company would print personal service records on a chart containing "thrilling battle scenes," framed and ready for hanging, for $1.25.[62]

GAR, UCV, and other veterans' associations provided additional opportunities for the marketing of keepsakes and official memorabilia. Clothiers offered uniforms meeting the often exacting regulations established by organizations. Numerous retailers also offered ceremonial and personal flags, patriotic bunting and banners, and ceremonial swords, rifles, and drums. Former Rebels could buy battle flag lapel pins and Confederate States of America Veteran grave markers, while Yankees could buy business cards with the GAR seal and their regiment and company engraved in gold in "a neat and tasty style." Cincinnati's Pettibone Brothers Manufacturing Company published a twelve-page catalog of uniforms, insignia, ceremonial weapons, caps and hats, lapel buttons, cufflinks, belts and belt buckles, and ladies' hat pins for UCV and Sons of Confederate Veterans. A full dress uniform with hat, the appropriate collar and sleeve insignia, and a few accoutrements such as buttons and cufflinks for a regular member of the UCV could cost as much as thirty-five dollars; the cheapest sword would add five dollars, while fancy gauntlets would add two dollars. A tiny ad for the Chicago's Rubber Supply Company that appeared in the *American Tribune* testified to the development of a number of modern marketing innovations, including sexually tinged advertising: "Ladies and gentlemen can *have fun* with our rubber goods *without danger*."[63]

Reunions provided a special market for goods and opportunities for advertising. One Indianapolis business specialized in renting tents to "encampments and fishing parties." Ads in local newspapers or special publications produced during major reunions targeted veterans' needs for uniforms, insignia, flags, and other "official" items. Manufacturers produced GAR watch fobs; others made of gold were shaped like small military-issue canteens. Other GAR souvenirs included a small cast-iron GAR hat, a glass tray engraved with the GAR seal and name, a napkin ring, a cigar box imprinted with "Campfire G.A.R.," and a folding comb. As part of its sponsorship of the 1889 National Encampment in Milwaukee, Pabst Brewing distributed thousands of beer glasses engraved with the GAR medal, an eagle, crossed cannons, and the U.S. flag. The printed program for the encampment, a "Souvenir of the Pabst Brewing Co. for Members of the Grand Army of the Republic," featured a full-color cover depicting battle scenes.[64]

Soldiers' homes and other Civil War sites became part of this commercialization of veteranhood and of the war. Dozens of examples of soldiers' home and battlefield kitsch were mass-produced and sold during the late nineteenth and early twentieth centuries. Crippled residents of the Milwaukee soldiers' home were allowed to sell bound versions of a short history and description of the institution "for their own benefit." In addition to this and other guide and picture books, tourists and visitors could buy plates, dishes, vases, pitchers, and glasses as well as toothpick holders, salt and pepper shakers, paperweights, silver spoons, and candlesticks. The huge NHDVS Central Branch in Dayton offered nearly a dozen different items, while the tiny state home in Hot Springs, South Dakota, offered a mustache cup, book-ends, a book-shaped ceramic figurine, and a bar of soap boasting a color picture of the home and the words "Souvenir Soldiers' Home." The state home in Quincy, Illinois, sold a tiny white glass pipe, while the Erie, Pennsylvania, Soldiers' and Sailors' Home featured a pink ceramic boot with a high heel, turned-up toe, and four-color picture of the home. At least fourteen homes in every part of the North participated in these marketing efforts. The Ohio Soldiers' and Sailors' Home allowed a local stationer to sell souvenir postcards—"useful as well as beautiful, a token of that visit to the Home or a memento as a gift to another"—as well as a cheery memoir by one of the inmates. Far fewer southern homes, which were also much smaller and less likely to be tourist attractions than their northern counterparts, sold collectibles, although the Confederate Home in Kentucky offered a series of ten-cent postcards with full-color pictures of the home.[65]

Soldiers' homes and other Civil War sites and commemorations were also etched onto decorative spoons and plates, both of which became popular souvenirs in the 1890s. Tourists could purchase spoons featuring hundreds of buildings, events, and monuments, including the U.S. Soldiers' Home near Washington, D.C.; Civil War battlefields; prominent generals; and Old Abe the War Eagle, mascot of the 8th Wisconsin. Late-century spoons fitting perfectly into the Lost Cause imagery featured Stonewall Jackson's birthplace, the great seal of the Confederacy, various statues of Confederate soldiers, and the Lee Monument in Richmond. Other spoons marketed to the GAR featured the elements of the organization's seal, dates of annual encampments, and replicas of reunion medals. Plates featured views of soldiers' homes, Pickett's Charge, and Libby Prison.[66]

Many businessmen sought to increase their trade by associating their products with veterans. For some, it was simply a matter of making sure potential customers knew that the advertisers were also veterans. A Washington, D.C., business notified readers of the *American Tribune* that "Your Comrade, CHAS EVERSON, is with Kelleher, the Leading Hatter," and featured a picture of an official GAR hat in the advertisement. Other advertising simply tried to connect products to the war or more often to the veterans. The newsletter of the Kentucky Confederate Home regularly ran an advertisement from a Louisville coffee company that called itself the "Old Veteran's Friend" and noted that it was run by the "earnest son of a Confederate." The

A collectible plate from the soldiers' home in Hot Springs,
South Dakota. Author's collection.

annual report of the Florida Confederate Home contained more advertising
than information, including an ad from a milk company stretching the link
between Confederate patriotism and commerce by declaring, "We, too, have
fought for a principle—the idea of quality in milk." Ayer's Sarsaparilla compared the company's winning a gold medal at the 1893 World's Fair to the
"grizzled veteran" who had earned a medal for valor in the Civil War. A furniture business linked Union heroes' defense of hearth and home with the
company's commitment to quality. In effect, Union soldiers had "fought for
a bedroom set and a fireside chair: so choose your furniture well." Although
it is not clear whether or not any former soldiers were involved in the firm,
Brewster, Gordon Company, a wholesale grocery business in Rochester, New
York, sold a variety of goods under the "Veteran Brand." The label featured a
silver-haired, blue-coated general and the phrase, "A Winner Since 1866."[67]

National advertising campaigns also featured veterans, who grew pro-
gressively older in the illustrations for various products. In 1918, Colt Fire-
arms portrayed an old Confederate and an old Yankee absorbing a lecture
from an earnest young officer in the American Expeditionary Force on the
merits of its newest military pistol, with the tagline, "Through All Wars

the National Standard." Two years later, an ad for the Grinnell Automatic Sprinkler System drew on veterans' heroism and their declining health by featuring one old Yankee pulling another out of a burning soldiers' home. The text began "Once a hero" and argued that veterans should not be expected to perform such feats forever. As late as 1934, the General Tire and Rubber Company ran magazine ads featuring an old Civil War veteran arm in arm with a pretty young girl.[68]

The Toledo-based Woolson Spice Company, one of the world's largest coffee roasters, featured veterans in a number of advertisements for its Lion Coffee that appeared in the *Ohio Soldier*. Drawing on the frequent scenes in veterans' memoirs that recalled the hurried building of fires to boil coffee during long marches, one ad for "The cup that cheers but does not inebriate" declared that "IN WAR TIMES, during the long and dreary marches, how the soldier relished his cup of Coffee! TODAY, a peaceful citizen, he enjoys it just the same, and finds Lion Coffee the best of all." Others drew readers' notice with giant letters that borrowed military terminology—"ATTENTION COMPANY" and "COMPANY, HALT! STACK ARMS!"—to promote "the best beverage on earth." A large drawing of the 1891 Sons of Union Veterans Encampment included a Lion Coffee pennant flying over the quartermaster's tent, which was decorated with the phrase "Good Coffee is Life to the Soldier and we Drink Lion Coffee." Happy drinkers could cut eight lion heads from Lion Coffee labels and exchange them for a free collection of war songs "dedicated to the G.A.R., W[oman's]. R[elief]. C[orps]., and S. of V."[69]

They Would Not Be Able to Do Business without Them

The dark underbelly of the commercial connection between soldiers' homes and their communities revolved around alcohol: soldiers' desire to drink it and entrepreneurs' desire to sell it to the soldiers. Every town or city with a home had a neighborhood or street known for cheap bars and brothels frequented by the veterans. By 1896, more than thirty saloons clustered near the northern and southern entrances of the Northwestern Branch of the NHDVS in Milwaukee. Veterans may have been attracted to dives boasting familiar names such as Lincoln, Sheridan, and Sherman or to bars employing fellow veterans, among them August Miller, a GAR member, and George Eagan, an inmate who moonlighted as a bartender (and for which he was disciplined by home authorities). John Christerford admitted that he and perhaps eleven other men held the same jobs, although he had conveniently forgotten their names. The far western stretch of the city's National Avenue, with at least seventeen establishments, came to be called the Line; one veteran wrote disapprovingly to his son that it was "filled with old Soldiers from morning to night." Outside the soldiers' home near Leavenworth, Kansas, was Klondike, a village of thirty one-story frame houses, at least two-thirds of which were "whisky saloons, gambling houses, or dens or the grossest immorality," according to one disapproving reformer. The equivalent row of dives and bars near the Togus, Maine, branch straggled down Hayseed Avenue. In Dayton, the seedy area was simply known as the West Side.[70]

The presence of these rough and disreputable areas reflected that class of opportunists who had emerged to take advantage of the old soldiers. As one Kansan complained, "vile women and men" had come from other towns to "prey on these men, to drug them, thug them, and rob them." Such entrepreneurs were less savory than their counterparts in the GAR uniform trade, the publishing business, or the battlefield promotion game, but all were part of the larger process of commodification of veterans.[71]

John Bettelon, the mayor of Dayton and a lifelong resident of the city, testified in 1884 that the last dozen or so years had seen bars and saloons spring up on the West Side, where they were "as thick . . . as the hair on a man's head." The new establishments took advantage of the residents of the home, but because most of the bars were beyond the city limits, authorities could do nothing. Bettelon agreed with a questioner's statement that the saloon keepers "lay for the men and undertake to inveigle them into their places." The owners of these "'dives' and saloons" could not make a living without the old soldiers: "If the soldier has any money they are certain to go for their share of it, and they go for it in any way they can get it." Prostitutes, too, plied their trade on the West Side, which was also notorious for robberies and other crimes.[72]

An official at the Togus branch of the NHDVS told a congressional investigating committee that rather than buying their liquor a drink at a time in shops, residents of the home bought it by the bottle from "men in buggies" who "hang round in the vicinity of the Home, because this is the place for them." Other vendors slipped into houses along the roads or in the nearby woods; some of the residents also were illegal providers of alcohol. The practice was hard to "break up," according to one sergeant, because local law enforcement was indifferent to the problem. The sellers were also aided by discharged men who acted as lookouts for the undercover detectives sent out by the home authorities.[73]

"These men do not go back until they have spent their money," stated a longtime Dayton policeman, and the proprietors of the more than two dozen saloons clustered near the home's entrance did their best to separate the men from their pensions. The saloon keepers stood in doorways, offering warm rooms and cheap drinks, but only until the men spent all their money, when they were put out. Another attraction was the women: "There is not one but which has a harlot in it," reported Officer Shoemaker. "They would not be able to do any business without them."[74]

Many late-nineteenth-century firms could not have remained in business without the old soldiers' market. Most efforts to commercialize the veteran experience were, on the surface at least, harmless enough—they were simply part of the vigorous expansion of advertising, marketing, and other elements of the Gilded Age economy. But as the growth of the alcohol and vice industries near soldiers' homes indicates, the commodification of veterans had complications that would have major ramifications for the relationship between old soldiers and the civilian communities in which they lived.

chapter four **Regiments So Piteous**

SOLDIERS' HOMES, COMMUNITIES, AND MANHOOD

When a reporter for a Cleveland newspaper visited the construction site of the Central Branch of the National Home for Disabled Volunteer Soldiers (NHDVS), he referred to the buildings going up on the low hill two miles from Dayton as the "Home of the Soldier." Sixteen years later, an article about the NHDVS in *Harper's New Monthly Magazine* suggested that "there is little left to sharply remind one of the fratricidal conflict, save the invalid and disabled soldiers gathered together, under the auspices of the government, into a stupendous institution, designed by special enactment to be considered as a home, in contradistinction to the asylums founded by charitable or legislative policy."[1]

As the *Harper's* correspondent implied, midcentury Americans distinguished between asylums and homes. Simply put, the former housed the desperately poor, the insane, and other adults unable to care for themselves. The latter housed orphans, redeemable delinquents, and other more sympathetic persons who deserved government assistance. The soldiers' homes established by the federal and state governments in the decades following the war were called "homes" for a reason: they were meant to be safe, comfortable, respectable environments for the men who had fought but were now unable to survive without help.

But the effort to care for the men who had borne the battle turned out to be more complicated than proponents imagined. Local communities, counties, and states had slowly accepted responsibility for creating such institutions starting very early in the nineteenth century, but most of the occupants were the poorest of the poor, the neediest among the needy, or members of the specific ethnic or religious communities who sponsored the homes. The creation of the NHDVS and of dozens of state soldiers' homes created a new class of Americans eligible for public charity. These persons' claim to government care—their military service—was unique in American history; as a result, the public understood the homes as a positive and necessary innovation. Yet old assumptions die hard, and the reputations of the old soldiers living in the homes, perhaps inevitably, began to crumble almost immediately. The question, "Who could be more deserving than the men who had risked all for their country?" did not ultimately have a straightforward answer.

As Chad Alan Goldberg's recent book reminds us, value judgments have always been applied to expansions of government-funded social welfare programs. Policy makers and politicians have normally assumed that anyone in need of help from the government was almost by definition incapable of fulfilling his duties as a citizen. This attitude at times was stated baldly and at other times was implicit in the rhetoric and procedures designed to implement new forms of welfare. The expansion of "state involvement in social provision," writes Goldberg, "often generated intense struggles over whether to model the new policy on or sharply distinguish it from traditional poor relief." A lot was at stake, including "the citizenship status and rights" of beneficiaries, "who struggled not only to acquire new social rights but also to avoid losing their civil and political rights in the process." In other words, Americans who submitted to confinement in homes and asylums had, simply by allowing themselves to become dependent, made themselves less than complete citizens. According to Goldberg, Americans still assumed "that poverty was a consequence (or, alternatively, a cause) of poor morals and poor habits."[2]

That Americans had decidedly mixed feelings about the veterans living in homes—and by extension about veterans in general—can be gleaned from a number of sources reflecting the ambiguity in the attitudes and perceptions of the residents and managers of the homes as well as of the civilians who lived nearby. The Committee on Military Affairs of the U.S. House of Representatives conducted an investigation of the NHDVS in the late summer of 1884 and issued a one-thousand-page report on its findings. The Grand Army of the Republic (GAR) conducted an investigation of the New York state home. Local press reports appeared. And a few home residents left records of their feelings in diaries, letters, and other documents. As in all other relationships between veterans and the public, the association of soldiers' homes with the communities in which they were located was made complex by old ideas about poverty and disability, by practical issues related to the boundaries—both geographical and jurisdictional—between the homes and other government agencies, and by the behavior of the men as it clashed with the expectations of communities with fairly specific notions of how old soldiers should act. Finally, the veterans' responses indicate that the institutions in which they slept and ate and waited to die were less like homes than their creators had hoped.

Our Citizens Delight

The relationship between the Northwestern Branch of the NHDVS and Milwaukee residents illustrates many of the ways in which soldiers' homes became a part of the fabric of nearby towns and cities. To the extent that Milwaukeeans' contact with the home consisted of enjoying the parklike grounds and of viewing the kindly old soldiers from afar, the relationship was quite positive. Conversely, when residents of the city encountered residents of the home face to face, that relationship became much more fraught.

The Northwestern Branch's history began with a short but sharp public debate over the link between ongoing efforts by Milwaukee women to build a permanent home for Wisconsin veterans and male community leaders' efforts to attract a branch of the newly formed National Asylum. The conflict reflected the way that locals often took ownership of the homes established in their communities. Milwaukee's West Side Soldiers' Aid Society had managed a haven for sick, disabled, or merely weary soldiers at a downtown location throughout the war. A great fair held in the summer of 1865 raised one hundred thousand dollars toward the purchase of land and the construction of a permanent institution. When Congress began looking for NHDVS sites, George H. Walker, one of Milwaukee's founders; Alexander Mitchell, a banker, railroad executive, and future congressman; and other city fathers urged the women to give up their plans in favor of the National Home. In the summer of 1866, although construction of a building apparently had already begun and despite concerns that Wisconsin veterans would not receive preference at the National Home, the women reluctantly turned over their money, enabling Milwaukee to become one of the first three locations in the NHDVS system.

As the skirmish between Milwaukee's town fathers and leading women indicated, the city community was clearly invested in the presence of a soldiers' home. Almost from 1869, when the first residents of the Northwestern Branch moved into temporary housing a half hour's buggy ride west of Milwaukee, city residents were encouraged to visit. In fact, home officials nurtured the impression of the grounds as a park, and the head landscaper gave a speech in late 1868 in which he urged locals to utilize the grounds.

Milwaukee had reached the point in urban development, he declared, that "demands parks for those who ramble, and for those who ride and drive." Other cities would have to spend millions of dollars to rescue their residents from urban ills; Milwaukee needed only to look westward to the welcoming hills on which the home perched. By the end of its first decade, sixty thousand people were visiting the grounds each year.[3]

The facilities were improved over the years specifically to make the home more attractive to visitors. In 1875 alone, a dance hall, a bandstand, three summer houses, two "outside water closets, for use of pic-nics," and a new street gate were built. In addition, new and existing roads were graveled and graded, and six hundred shade trees were planted. When a new amusement hall was built in 1878, it was located near the railway that wound through the grounds to ease visitors' attendance at performances. By the 1890s, a restaurant sold light lunches and desserts, and docents led guided tours of the institution. The home governor acknowledged that "the judicious betterment and tasteful adornment of the grounds" not only benefited the old soldiers by beautifying their surroundings but also made their lives less monotonous by attracting "large numbers of visitors."[4]

The event that brought out the biggest crowds each year was July 4, the most popular public holiday of the Victorian era. A fairly small gathering in 1869 was ushered in with thundering cannon followed by a somber reading of the Declaration of Independence. A sumptuous dinner was followed by "a grand display of fire works." The celebration grew over the years to include concerts by the home band, military parades by the inmates, afternoon and evening dances, and hundreds of Chinese lanterns encircling the largest of the four ponds with "picturesque and grand" illuminations. Games eventually were added; residents and visitors chased greased pigs and raced on foot, in tubs on one of the lakes, in sacks, in wheelbarrows, and on crutches. By 1879, the party was in full force. The *Milwaukee Sentinel* described special trains unloading their "human freight bedecked in gay dresses and black broadcloth" and hundreds of wagons and omnibuses winding toward the home entrance. "Flags fluttered from every tree," the miniature lake sported small boats decorated for the occasion, and men and women decked out in red, white, and blue swarmed the grounds, which "fairly foamed with sightseers like a choppy sea." A thirty-eight-gun salute marked high noon, after which the home band "struck up dancing music" for hundreds of couples swirling around the pavilion. As afternoon gave way to evening, revelers sang patriotic and camp songs, "and from the shadows" cast by the illuminated lakes "came the most human kind of laughter." By dusk, between fifteen and twenty thousand spectators had gathered to watch the fireworks, a fitting end to a memorable day. The next year, with the addition of illuminations along the curved avenues and transparencies tucked under arching trees, the *Sentinel* pronounced that the "Centre of Attraction" of a "Fiery Fourth" was "at the National Soldiers' Home."[5]

The gala Independence Day celebrations were only the biggest of the numerous attractions that drew people to the area's newest public institution. A few months after the home opened, the *Sentinel* ran a public invitation for the flag raising over the nearly completed Main Building. The "Veteran Variety Troupe," which included a dozen amputees, presented the first public performance at the home in early 1868. By 1871, nearly a hundred city residents attended the home's Christmas concert. If attendance at home events serves as an indicator, local residents' interest grew by leaps and bounds. The home band began presenting summer concerts in the early 1870s. A program for the "Eleventh Promenade Concert" of the National Home Silver Comet Band also announced weekly "social parties" with entertainment by the home orchestra. Tickets cost fifty cents, transportation would be provided from the streetcar terminus to the home, and refreshments would be available. By the 1880s, the Sunday performances were a Milwaukee tradition, with nearly two dozen held each year. Theatrical presentations also became quite popular. In 1871, the temperance melodrama *Ten Nights in a Barroom* enjoyed a large attendance. Residents often presented complete theatrical seasons, with free performances given each week, "simply for the amusement of Inmates and citizens generally, who favor the veterans with their presence." The 1872 season, for example, featured *The Poacher's Doom*; a comedy, *The Toodles*; an "Irish farce," *Barney the Baron*; *The Cross of Gold*; and *Poor Pillicoddy.* Winter debates staged by the home's "literary and philosophical association" included city residents, and local citizens were invited when acts such as magician Shoo Shon appeared at the home.[6]

Milwaukeeans clearly considered the home a community resource, with many local organizations holding meetings, picnics, and parties among the groves and meadows. "Our citizens delight in the" home's "sylvan shades," reported the *Sentinel*. Other organizations that came out for their social events included the Knights of Templar Lodge, the local dancing school, the Old Settlers' Club, the employees of the St. Paul Railroad, and four hundred residents of Columbus, Wisconsin. For the first fifty years of the home's existence, the Milwaukee Gun Club and Milwaukee Balloon Club met there. The grounds were featured in tourist booklets, often illustrated more with images of civilians than of soldiers. A souvenir pamphlet published in the

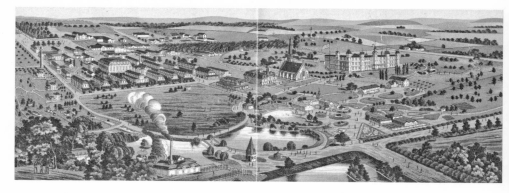

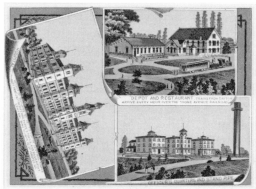

Scenes from the NHDVS Central Branch, Dayton, Ohio, as presented in one of the heavily illustrated guides to soldiers' homes published for tourists. *The Soldiers' Home Book* (Columbus, Ohio: Ward, 1887).

early 1880s showed not only the most prominent buildings but also tourists and visitors strolling the grounds, ladies gracefully floating on swings hanging from trees near the hospital, and couples admiring a picturesque fountain.[7]

Other homes also became tourist attractions. In 1884, a visitor to the Central Branch in Dayton, Ohio, declared it "the 'beauty spot' of the West." Eight years later, an admiring article claimed that 315,000 people had visited the grounds, including forty-eight large groups staging special excursions. Many of the visitors were locals, who could take one of three different streetcar lines to the home. Its five thousand acres contained a small city with scores of buildings large and small, about six thousand veteran inmates, and hundreds of staff. "To see in one day everything to be seen would more than tire out a vigorous walker."[8]

Visitors could take tours led by inmates or other volunteers and could purchase guides that provided detailed descriptions of the grounds and buildings. One section, "As a Public Attraction," described the extensive plantings and greenhouses open to the public—plants native to the region, landscaping "beautified to a high degree of perfection," and a large herd of deer that was of special interest "to the young, who love to visit the Home." Like the home in Milwaukee, the grounds of the Dayton facility "present a rare combination of the urban and suburban, that public opinion has pronounced the best and most attractive in this country." At the end of their tour, visitors "usually avail themselves of the privilege to secure souvenirs of the Home, which are found here in variety."[9]

Although much smaller in scale, Confederate soldiers' homes, according to their historian, were also "places where people could congregate and reaffirm their devotion to the dear principles of the Lost Cause." People visited on Confederate Memorial Day, on Robert E. Lee's and Jefferson Davis's birthdays, and on the Fourth of July. Individuals as well as groups of schoolchildren and ladies' associations regularly visited; administrators encouraged and often organized outings by the most able-bodied veterans to concerts, parades, funerals, and other ceremonies related or unrelated to the memory of the war. The five-hundred-volume library at the Confederate Home of Kentucky was available to civilians, while the septuagenarian Confederate Choir sometimes entertained guests. Both on Decoration Day 1910 and at the party in honor of Lee's birthday the following year, members sang "Tenting on the Old Camp Ground."[10]

Let the Government Worry about the Veterans

At the most superficial level, civilians found the soldiers' homes pleasurable distractions. But meetings between grateful veterans and gracious civilians were tempered by other, less positive encounters. The Texas Confederate Home's relationship with its surrounding community was somewhat more complicated than most; it was located in the middle of Clarksville, an African American community that sprang up on the outskirts of Austin just after the war. Neighbors remembered the two hundred or so veterans living at the home late in the nineteenth century as a rather frightening presence. A few recalled encounters with veterans who would appear on porches or shout racial epithets at passing children; most area residents simply remembered parents and preachers issuing warnings against venturing too close to the forbidding complex that represented the racist society in which they lived.[11]

As late as 1916, the superintendent of the Arkansas Confederate Home felt the need to defend his institution from the common belief that it was "a humiliating refuge for pauperized men and women, where the conveniences are meager and rude and crude, where the sunlight of happiness never creeps in, and where a visitor may go, only to pity and minister." Nothing could be further from the truth: residents enjoyed "a healthy normal wholesome atmosphere" and were "average—morally, mentally and socially—only they are old. They do not want to be pitied," although "they do not object to common human sympathy." Some years earlier, a former inmate of the Milwaukee home wrote to the local newspaper, "Some ladies who visit the Home look upon the soldiers as a blot upon the fair landscape." On one occasion an "exquisite being" visited the grounds and declared that it was "too, too lovely. If they would only take those disgusting soldiers away, it would be too heavenly." According to a witness during the 1884 congressional investigation of the NHDVS, the public's attitude seemed to be "'There is your Soldier's Home' and let the government worry about the veterans." By the 1870s and 1880s, this negative perception of veterans was more prevalent than anyone could have predicted in 1865.[12]

The government indeed attempted to take care of the neediest veterans. But it frequently encountered resistance to its policies and procedures as local communities and branches of the NHDVS tried to locate a mutually acceptable set of boundaries for institutional obligations and prerogatives; determine local, state, and federal jurisdiction; and adjust the inmates' behavior and the home managers' priorities to the context of local standards and assumptions. The conflicts that arose from these clashing attitudes could range from the outrage in Ohio when the Central Branch starting serving oleomargarine instead of butter in the 1890s to much more serious controversies over criminal justice and social welfare. The peculiar relationships between these large and growing federal institutions and local authorities in Milwaukee again serve as an example.[13]

Old soldiers suspected of serious crimes could spark major conflicts between home officials and local law enforcement agencies. The home resembled other military installations in that it existed as a federal reservation over which U.S. authorities had sole jurisdiction. Complicating the situation, however, was the practice of allowing residents to vote in local and state elections, even if they had come to the NHDVS from other states. Many observers believed that this practice made the men subject to local laws and jurisdictions. A law passed by the Wisconsin legislature ceding jurisdiction to the United States over "certain lands" exempted that property from taxation. Yet it specifically stated that "civil or criminal process issued from courts in the State of Wisconsin, may be served within the territory hereby ceded."[14]

This contradiction was tested in the spring of 1874, when Samuel Hynes, an inmate at the Northwestern Home, accused fellow residents Peter Manning and John O'Conner of assaulting him. When home governor Edward Hincks refused to turn the two men over to sheriff's deputies, he ignited a rhetorical and political firestorm. Hincks's supporters included the city's major newspaper, the Republican-leaning *Milwaukee Sentinel*. On the other side were a Democratic municipal judge, sheriff, and district attorney as well as the *Milwaukee Daily News*, the Democratic organ published by Alexander Mitchell, a congressmen and president of the Chicago, Milwaukee, and St. Paul Railroad. (The home had been built on land purchased from Mitchell's son, John, a Union veteran who would later serve in the U.S. Congress and on the NHDVS Board of Managers.)

Hincks argued that the incident simply constituted a minor infraction of home rules and was thus subject to internal procedures. Moreover, the law allowed authorities to serve "criminal process issued from courts in the State of Wisconsin" only when a suspect tried to take refuge at the home after committing a serious crime outside its environs. Despite the original warrant, the incident had occurred on home grounds, where most people on both sides of the issue believed the governor had sole jurisdiction. Hynes had been discharged from the home rather than given a furlough, as he claimed, and he was subsequently arrested and jailed as a material witness in the case.[15]

About two weeks into the crisis, the sheriff led a posse straight onto the home grounds, barged into a workshop, and took O'Conner into custody. According to the *Daily News*, when the posse returned for Manning, the home provost guard and a crowd of 150 soldiers turned him away. For its part, the *Sentinel* referred to the arrest as a "kidnapping." The debate then shifted to the habeas corpus case brought on O'Conner's behalf, which went all the way to the state supreme court.[16]

The resolution of the affair represented a clear victory for supporters of the National Home's status as a federal reservation. On June 10, the Wisconsin Supreme Court granted O'Conner a writ of habeas corpus, perhaps because his attorneys reminded the court of O'Conner's "shattered body and mind," suffered in defense of his country, and turned the case over to the local courts. He appeared in municipal court the next day, about six weeks after the first article about the assault appeared in the *Daily News*. When O'Conner complained that he had no counsel, the judge responded, "You have had too much counsel already," before dismissing the case because the alleged assault had occurred on home grounds.[17]

Despite the peaceful ending, the rhetoric had nearly gotten out of hand in numerous news stories, outraged editorials, and extensive interviews with Hincks and the other characters in the melodrama. Early on, the *Daily News* claimed that Hincks, who had charge of several hundred men at the time, had told the unarmed deputies who first visited the home that they could not take the men "unless you are stronger than we are." A second visit by the sheriff and a deputy had the same result; when the sheriff warned that he would appeal to the state's governor, Democrat William Taylor, Hincks again said he would "not yield, except to armed force." A letter from an inmate supporting the *News*'s portrayal of the governor as violating the law reported that in response to Hincks's tough system of discipline, in which he acted as judge, jury, prosecutor, jailer, and collector of fines, inmates had dubbed him the Tycoon. Toward the end of the controversy, a long summary article followed the only slightly tongue-in-cheek headline, "From the Front."[18]

If the relationship between the NHDVS and the community was not already politicized enough, the voting practices of inmates at the National Homes sparked further controversy. A *Home Bulletin* article justifying the voting rights of residents of the Southern Branch in Norfolk was headlined "Veterans' Rights" and quoted extensively from the U.S. Constitution in support of the notion that inmates at National Homes had a right to vote in the cities where they lived. The *Richmond Dispatch* countered with the argument that since the land on which the home stood had been ceded to the federal government, it actually was not a part of the Commonwealth of Virginia and no one residing on it should have the franchise in state elections. "It is a preposterous absurdity," responded the *Bulletin*, that the soldiers "should have fought the civil war to an end, and with the result of *enfranchising* the Negro and *disfranchising* themselves."[19]

The veteran voting bloc could equal hundreds or even thousands of votes and had the potential to swing an election in unexpected ways. Veterans living at the Northwestern Branch voted in Wauwatosa, the village abutting the home grounds. Although area residents were divided more or less evenly between Democrats and Republicans, the large contingent of veterans made the town a Republican stronghold in the 1880s and 1890s. A similar situation developed in the Democratic-leaning St. Paul, where veterans from the Minnesota Soldiers' Home tended to vote Republican in local elections. Some opponents, complained the *Relief Guard*, had tried to eliminate the soldiers' vote, partly by "stigmatiz[ing] them as paupers, idiots, drunkards and everything else that is mean and contemptible." Such attempts led the veterans to close ranks to create "a unity of sentiment and feeling."[20]

Another source of tension grew out of the home's role as one of the first federal agencies to intervene in the lives of the poor, the sick, and the mentally ill. When the governor of Mississippi recommended the construction of a state home in 1902, he referred to "a well defined certainty of conviction . . . in the public consciousness . . . that a duty rests upon" the state to shelter "indigent old Confederate[s]" in a place where they could pass their "few remaining days on earth free from the disturbing annoyances of want and helplessness." Those men who had been forced "to take refuge in these hovels of misery" called poorhouses and "to exist on what by a strange perversion of language is denominated public charity" would be rescued, and "justice" would be achieved. The governor thus captured a sense of how Americans finally came to view soldiers' homes at both the state and federal levels. Although unaccustomed to federal intervention in individuals' social welfare, the skeptical American public also believed that if the government was going to accept responsibility for veterans, it should do so without exceptions. The real debate occurred when the military discipline in the homes or the disdain of some veterans for life as inmates clashed with local institutions' distaste for spending precious resources on men believed to belong in the home.[21]

A case in point occurred in 1883, when Patrick O'Connell, superintendent of the Milwaukee County workhouse, asked the home governor to readmit Joseph Williams, a one-legged "lunatic" who had recently been discharged from the Northwestern Branch. In the following weeks, Williams was ordered to the county workhouse three times. A local judge refused to send him to the county insane asylum, suggesting that he was the responsibility of the soldiers' home. O'Connell testified to a congressional committee that Williams "became insane" after he was thrown out of the home for "connecting himself with some disreputable . . . women," including an African American whom he had apparently married.[22]

The case highlighted the difficulties raised by the presence of a large federal institution. Veterans were allowed to come and go almost as they pleased; the home had no authority to force men who had been discharged to return to their families or native states. Like Williams, men who required medical or psychological treatment or who were simply unable to support themselves often fell through the cracks. Although local agencies—workhouses, jails, asylums—might grudgingly take in such men, institutions could also refuse to do so on the grounds that the men were not legal residents of the community. Moreover, none of the NHDVS regional branches had facilities to care for seriously deranged men, who were supposed to be sent to the asylum for insane veterans in Washington, D.C.; however, it was usually over-crowded. According to a letter from the home's governor, Marsena Patrick, submitted as evidence to the investigators, the home steadfastly refused to admit Williams because of overcrowding and the lack of appropriate facili-ties—insane residents were sometimes kept in the guardhouse or "other im-proper places"—and suggested that he would be admitted to the asylum in Washington as soon as space was available. Patrick suggested that the court appoint a guardian for Williams and give the appropriate county institution access to his twenty-four-dollar monthly pension.[23]

Jacob Clements, director of the county infirmary, reported that since he had taken office eight months earlier, "eight or ten men" claiming to have been discharged from the home had sought admission to the infirmary, and some had been admitted. "They all claimed that they were decent and re-spectable and that they were discharged wrongfully," but Clements believed them to be "bad men, and the officers at the infirmary 'kick' because this Soldiers' Home has all the facility of police, &c., and they can keep these men better than they can be kept at the infirmary." When one of the in-vestigators suggested that the veterans were "pretty hard cases generally," Clements replied, "Yes, sir." William D. McKemy, the county probate judge who had declared Williams insane, confirmed that the mayor and the courts had turned over several former inmates of the home to the workhouse. Some were merely destitute or vagrants, but others had been charged with larceny and drunkenness.[24]

The problem still roiled the relationship between the home and the county five years later. A *Milwaukee Sentinel* reporter found fourteen former inmates of the Northwestern Branch living at the county farm in the win-ter of 1889. All had been discharged from the home after being punished for drinking and going absent without leave. Some were more belligerent than others, but to a man, at least according to the reporter, they preferred to live outside the home rather than submit to its strict discipline. The superin-tendent of the county farm believed he had no responsibility toward these men, none of whom were residents of Milwaukee County. He refused to put them out in the winter cold but suggested that only this approach would force home authorities to readmit the men. "Those fourteen men take the places of others," he complained. "They have their faults," he admitted, but rather than be "turned loose as a tramping disgrace to the old Union army, they ought to be kept at the home."[25]

A cordial but clearly tense correspondence between McKemy and Patrick about veteran James Murray shows how a situation with multiple shades of gray could spiral into controversy. Murray had wandered into town with an injured wrist and foot just a few weeks before the congressional hearing began. The police let him stay at the station house for a night, but his unstable mental condition became apparent, and he was sent to the county jail, where a "lunacy inquest" pronounced him insane. Judge McKemy asked Governor Patrick to admit Murray to the home because he was a veteran of a New York artillery battery and thus ineligible to be cared for in a county facility. Patrick replied that the New Yorker had applied for admission but had been turned away by the home doctor, who believed that his injuries did not amount to a disability "contracted in the service of the United States." Moreover, "even if he were eligible we could not receive him or any other insane person until some fifty cases of insanity now present" could be transferred to the Washington asylum.[26]

The city infirmary in Dayton had a similar problem. Its director claimed that at least two applicants per week alleged that they had been unjustly discharged from the home. Whether they were guilty or innocent, he testified, "they are all a burden on us. . . . They have no money, and we have to pick them up and keep them from starving during the winter time. They cost a great deal of money."[27]

No one liked the state of affairs, but no satisfactory solution could be found. A member of a Milwaukee GAR post's relief committee spoke to the dire straits in which many men found themselves: "They had been buffeted about from place to place . . . broken down in health and spirit, and . . . about ready to die." But the homes had no room. As a result, the old soldiers sought help from Grand Army posts, which nationally spent a total of five hundred thousand dollars for temporary relief of veterans in 1884. When that help ran out, veterans went "to the county or city authorities and [tried] to get into the hospitals, poorhouses, homes for the aged, or other public institutions." Many were turned away there, too, and some committed suicide. The angry GAR man argued that Congress needed to build additional barracks at the NHDVS. In the meantime, however, he suggested that men should be admitted to the homes even if they had to sleep on floors. Such accommodations would be better "than to lie down in a jail with no other crime charged against them than that they were old soldiers and homeless wanderers over the country they had fought to save."[28]

Some former Confederates, too, became homeless wanderers. Several letters to administrators of the Confederate Soldiers' Home in Richmond suggest that some old soldiers were forced to rely on county institutions. In 1892, Fitzhugh Lee, president of the home's Board of Visitors, received a letter describing Lucien Godwin as "utterly unable to provide for himself on account of age and infirmities." He was currently living in the county jail, "preferring to stay there with the jailer who is a comrade than go to the poorhouse." The superintendent of the Western Lunatic Asylum at Staunton asked if John Thompson, "an old wounded veteran who has no home and no Future beyond this Asylum for Life," could be admitted to the Richmond home. Thompson had been found in unspeakable poverty in an old cabin on the outskirts of town. A thrice-wounded veteran, Thompson's bad hip and leg had led to a "form of insanity" that caused him to be "very morbid taciturn and despondent." He believed himself to have "no friends," and the superintendent hoped that living "with old army associates" would improve his condition.[29]

In the North, questions about the relationship between inmates and local institutions were played out in the local press, a process that no doubt compromised relationships between communities and homes and indirectly between all veterans and civilians. Local newspapers provided disgruntled veterans with a venue in which to express their dissatisfaction with the homes' living conditions and organization. Indeed, less than a decade after the *Milwaukee Sentinel*'s spirited defense of Governor Hincks over the issue of federal versus local jurisdiction at the soldiers' home, the Milwaukee daily waged a major campaign against the home. The first real complaints that appeared in the summer of 1882, like most grumbling by inmates, related to bad food and erratic medical treatment and died down fairly quickly. Despite home officials' insistence that resident complaints were exaggerated, isolated examples cited by discontented men who constantly violated house rules, rumors and accusations swirled in Milwaukee for most of the next two years, and according to the *Sentinel*, "There seems no abatement in the interest manifested by the public in the condition of affairs at the National Home."[30]

The *Sentinel*'s interest in the soldiers' home certainly did not abate. Less than a year later, headlines blasted the Board of Managers' inspection procedures. Although "it is the duty of this Board to thoroughly inspect all the various National Homes . . . and to listen to all complaints which may be made against the management," the "numberless complaints" the board received seemed to "find a speedy tomb in the depths of the waste-basket." Rather than conducting a thorough inspection, the managers were seen "Dodging In and Out of Bed-Rooms and Testing the Wine and Viands." They ignored complaints about arbitrary punishment, poor food, and an inefficient surgeon and missed the fact that four men had taken advantage of the current

Governor, General Jacob Sharpe, to form a "Ring of Four" to "Run the Place to Suit Themselves." These four men—the provost sergeant, quartermaster sergeant, commissary sergeant, and engineer—had set things up so their jobs were secure and their authority unchecked. A member of the Board of Managers protested in an article published ten days later, saying that despite the constraints of time and resources, he and his colleagues followed accepted practices for inspecting such institutions. Because the home was a "mere human institution," "understrappers" naturally would take advantage of their small authority to abuse others, but the board member believed that most inmates were content and that the "complaints are made for the most part by a few chronic grumblers and croakers."[31]

Such dismissals aside, criticism of the home seemed endemic. Complaints against home officials in Milwaukee and elsewhere tended to focus on quality-of-life issues, especially the decision to put residents under the military code of discipline. At the end of a long attack on the home's management, the *Milwaukee Sentinel* quoted an inmate at the Northwestern Branch who complained of its "niggardly and parsimonious" refusal to buy "any of the many little delicacies which are so necessary to the palate of an invalid." "There was nothing too expensive for us in '62," he sighed, "but times have changed since then." Another letter asserted that the beef served the men was of poor quality and was usually boiled; it was often placed on the table long before the men arrived to eat, "so as to give the flies a chance to take the nutriment out of it." Many of the potatoes served in the spring were rotten and had been boiled with skins on; the bread was "sour and moldy," and the "butter is strong enough to speak for itself." But old soldiers could apparently adjust: "Some of the boys are getting so that they can eat about anything they get if it is dead."[32]

Perhaps no other situation in which a veteran might find himself threatened his manhood more than living in a soldiers' home, where he inhabited the uneasy ground between civilian freedom and military discipline, between dependence and independence. Two witnesses before the congressional investigators offered conflicting approaches to balancing manhood and the need for order. One of the most hard-nosed governors of a branch of the NHDVS was General Marsena Patrick, who had commanded troops in the field during the war but was best known as provost marshal of the Army of the Potomac. When he first arrived at the Central Branch, he told the congressional committee, "a man would sit down and put his foot up on the table, and squirt his tobacco juice all around, and keep his hat on and talk to me. I required him to stand up when he addressed me, and take off his hat;

put himself in the position which an inferior does to a superior in service." He expected residents of the home to salute him when they passed, but not everyone did so. The "old soldiers have a pride in it," he reported, but "there are a lot of soreheads always, who call themselves citizens of Ohio, and they would like to get out of the way of doing it. It is a great hardship to them."[33]

Patrick's approach was "fundamentally wrong," said James M. Weaver, a physician who had been an administrator at the home prior to Patrick's arrival and who still lived in Dayton. According to Dr. Weaver, Patrick "considers the Home a garrison, which should be governed by rules and articles of war. I think he came here with the disposition to govern the men as very bad men." Weaver's work among the old soldiers had convinced him "that they are just as good as any other class of men to be found anywhere else. There are good and bad men there, intelligent men and ignorant men, but as a community they are as good as you will find any where else." Although the Articles of War could be applied, they should not be used at all times against all men. Indeed, Weaver had been among those who persuaded Congress to change the name of the institution from the National Asylum for Disabled Volunteer Soldiers to the National Home for Disabled Volunteer Soldiers: "Everything gathered around that word; and everything that made it more of a home we did; that is, instead of giving shelter and food and raiment, we tried to look after their spiritual wants, and gave them employment and amusements."[34]

W. G. Haskell, an old soldier at the Eastern Branch of the NHDVS, published a pamphlet in which he argued that although home officials studiously refused to refer to the men as "inmates," a term associated with criminals in prisons, the men in homes were indeed "helpless." Their lives were shaped by others, their reputations were besmirched by political opportunists, and their behavior was analyzed and criticized by all manner of authorities and supervisors. Haskell's pamphlet urged Congress to expand pension benefits to residents of soldiers' homes, who, despite having their food and most other necessities provided, still had to buy underwear, toiletries, and other small items. But the booklet's dozen pages went far beyond economic matters to include the ways in which men living at homes were not really men at all but rather guests requiring permission to come and go or to visit family members or attend funerals; propertyless men who, when discharged on furlough or permanently, had to turn over the uniforms issued to them; former laborers and farmers and craftsmen who could no longer earn their livings.[35]

"Badger Veteran," who lived at the Northwestern Branch, wrote several incendiary letters along the same lines to the *Milwaukee Sentinel*. He alleged that men were fined for the slightest offenses, deprived of their right to lodge complaints, forced to eat substandard food, and made to maintain the extensive park and buildings without pay. "The National Home for disabled volunteer soldiers has never been anything but an ostentatious fraud and sham," he declared. "Thousands of disabled soldiers can trace their ruin directly to its influence." He made a similar comment in a later letter: "The men now living at the National Homes are not . . . in the military service of the Government, they are not criminals, neither are they paupers. . . . They are also free American citizens, and no unnecessary restriction should be placed upon their liberty."[36]

Such complaints prompted an investigation by a local post of the GAR, which resulted in a fairly positive report. The U.S. House of Representatives Committee on Military Affairs also conducted an investigation of the home in the late summer of 1884. Although the committee had received a "numerously signed" petition and two individual letters against the management of the institution, former general and committee chair William Rosecrans denied that the committee was responding to formal charges. Indeed, he suggested, he and his colleagues expected to be in Milwaukee for only a brief time and did not plan to make any major recommendations.[37]

That prediction held true. In its extensive reporting of the investigation, the *Sentinel* focused on clashes between Sharpe and a former surgeon at the Home, Dr. A. F. Hare, who, Sharpe testified, was a drunk and a liar and had resigned before he could be discharged. According to the governor, Hare, assisted by a local lawyer, was using the complaints of several former patients to get back at Sharpe. The committee seemed to side with former general Henry Slocum, now a member of Congress, when he declared, "I don't believe in lawyers to argue the case of veterans." The accusations of inmates' drunkenness and meddling by outsiders tended to overshadow the other evidence presented at the hearing. By the end of the testimony, the committee had determined, in the words of one member, that "on the whole . . . the home [is] well conducted, and [we] are well pleased."[38]

Providing an important undercurrent throughout the often very public discourse on inmates' behavior were the assumptions articulated when the federal homes were organized: they would be less like institutions than like homes. The cozy images of hearths and homemade bread, fondness and collegiality, tolerance and generosity, and peace and quiet were rarely sustained in any soldiers' homes, federal or state. The former military men who administered the homes were almost entirely drawn from the regular army, at least in the first decade or two, while nearly all the residents were volunteers. Daily schedules, terminology, and even uniforms were borrowed from the regular army, and the men had to submit to a modified form of the army's disciplinary code. Adding to the institutions' decidedly undomestic organization were living conditions that featured barracks with large numbers of men sharing quarters, scheduled bath times, eating in shifts, and work assigned to able-bodied men. Although most of the veterans living in the homes accepted the situation in which they found themselves and followed the rules, a significant minority could not or would not do so.[39]

Living Ornaments of the States

Although northern state homes were often created expressly in opposition to the hard-nosed reputation of the federal homes, they too encountered problems. At a meeting of managers of state veterans' homes in Milwaukee in 1894, a trustee of the Michigan home admitted that "the State Homes are dumping" men he called "habitual drunkards" on the NHDVS. Yet despite such practices and their operation on a smaller scale than the federal homes, state homes were not immune from problems of discipline and manhood.[40]

The state homes had been conceived as a kind of "anti-NHDVS." Louisa May Alcott showed the popular image of a state home in a serialized story that appeared in *The Sword and the Pen*, a journal published during the 1881 Soldiers' Home Bazaar in Boston. "My Red Cap" follows the narrator's friendship with a soldier named Joe, whom she meets while handing out fruit to a regiment passing through Boston. She is taken by his dignity, his kindness, and his simple patriotism. They encounter one another again six months later in much less pleasant circumstances; she is working in a Washington hospital, he is a patient whose arm has been shot off. The narrator nurses him back to health and writes on his behalf to his fiancée back home. When the woman ends their relationship, Joe is heartbroken but characteristically determined to get on with his life. Years later, the narrator encounters him again, working as a "Red Cap" messenger, and discovers that he has lost his family and his farm and is alone in the world. He has not adapted well to living without a right arm and is bothered by rheumatism acquired while in the army. He perseveres, telling his friend that he would be able to "scratch for a livin'" and then go to the almshouse and hospital when he could not make it on his own. He is cheered when she suggests that Massachusetts might build a soldiers' home for men like him, and during the next few months she organizes her neighbors to help by hiring him to do errands and deliver messages. Inevitably, Joe's condition worsens. He is forced to quit his job, and after some difficulty—at one point, someone tells her that he has died—the narrator finds him boarding with a poor widow, doing housework and minding the woman's children. Joe has been ill and has lost a shocking amount of weight: "There ain't much left of me but bones and pain, ma'am." She takes him to the newly opened Soldiers' Home, and Joe, alone in the world, with no prospects except a pauper's grave, joyfully moves in. "A happier man or a more grateful one it would be hard to find, and if a visitor wants an enthusiastic guide about the place, Joe is the one to take, for all is comfort, sunshine, and goodwill to him; and he unconsciously shows how great the need of this refuge is, as he hobbles about on his lame feet, pointing out its beauties, conveniences, and delights with his one arm, while his face shines, and his voice quavers a little as he says gratefully,— 'The State don't forget us, you see, and this is a Home wuth havin'.'"[41]

This idyllic version of a state home did not jibe with reality for all veterans. A former inmate, A. C. Smith, waged a major battle against the Wisconsin state home in 1906 and 1907, sending letter after letter and a few telegrams to the governor of Wisconsin complaining about corruption (deceased and absent veterans and widows were carried on the roll so that administrators could still collect government subsidies) and autocratic discipline. Smith called for an investigation of the home by a committee consisting of a Democrat, a Republican, and a Socialist; when that idea failed to move the governor, the agitated veteran attempted to launch a newspaper, the *Veterans' Voice*, in which he promised to reveal "Red Hot Stuff" about the home's management. A circular written by another resident, Jesse Cornish, and sent to major newspapers around the state purported to tell the truth about the home's "beautiful location" and "splendid management" and to debunk Smith's claims. According to Cornish, a veteran of the 38th Wisconsin, Smith had never been a captain, although he signed his name with that title, and had served for only four months. When he entered the home, he had gotten the home governor to waive certain eligibility rules to allow his wife to join him but had then constantly criticized the home with "malicious letters and circulars in which he is doing his best to malign and abuse the Home and its officials." Smith had been dismissed, although his wife remained at the home. "Perhaps," Cornish suggested, "it would be more appropriate" to name Smith's proposed newspaper "The Kickers' Voice."[42]

At the Youngville Veterans' Home in California, an attempt to require men to turn their pension money over to the commandant "for safe keeping" sparked a riot that resulted in the expulsion of two inmates and the arrest of the commandant for assault. Officers were forced to arm themselves before civil authorities were called in. More than 160 old soldiers pledged to resist; one observer believed they were being encouraged by local saloon keepers. Home administrators typically blamed drinking for most disciplinary problems.[43]

The behavior of the men in the much smaller Confederate homes also challenged administrators and communities. R. B. Rosenburg's catalog of conduct deemed unacceptable at southern homes matches the behavior that plagued northern homes: "indecent exposure, begging, using profane language, aggravated assaults against fellow inmates or employees, habitual drunkenness, chronic kicking, 'cohabitating with negro wretches,' disturbing religious services, and propositioning female servants." Inmates found their bunkmates to be intolerable and beat one another bloody; bickered about politics; bridled at requirements to perform modest labor and bathe regularly; and frequently broke pledges to abstain from alcohol. And like their northern counterparts, administrators of southern homes had the authority to dismiss men for these and other chronic misbehavior but rarely used that power. The *Atlanta Constitution* reported in 1901 that twelve or fifteen of the residents of the Georgia home inclined to drunkenness; several of them "had been giving much trouble by begging on the streets"; when they got enough money, they spent it in bars and later in the evening staggered back to the home. One inmate of the Florida home reported that there was "no dignity or decorum practiced by some of the inmates, acting more like a lot of hogs and wild animals and making use of language that is anything but pleasant to the ear." Female visitors to the new Confederate home near Louisville were dismayed at the poor food, substandard heating, bad manners, and terrible hygiene of the men living there.[44]

The report of the 1883 investigation of the New York State Soldiers' and Sailors' Home in Bath revealed the extent to which the rights and self-respect of the residents were contested throughout the system of state homes, especially the larger institutions. Complaints had arisen throughout the summer, as a number of residents swore accusatory affidavits before local lawyers and justices of the peace. The press fanned the flames. "Another morally run and prayerful establishment [has] come to exposure and disgrace," sneered the *National Police Gazette* in an article on inmates' assertions of "canting managers practicing shocking cruelties on their victims, the crippled inmates, until the Home was transformed into a hell." Although the Grand Army no longer controlled the home, the group remained a prominent force in the administration, and the Board of Managers appointed a committee to look into the allegations. In July, investigators interviewed more than thirty witnesses and, through the GAR's New York Department, issued a report basically exonerating the administration of cruelty and abuse, although two of the accusations that a sergeant had used unnecessary force were supported.[45]

But the board's questioning of the inmates and administrators revealed the huge gap between what soldiers believed they needed and what administrators and trustees believed residents deserved. Despite the GAR's acute interest, the board, which included three former generals and at least two other Civil War officers, seemed to treat the complainants as poor men throwing themselves on the charity of the state rather than as honorably discharged soldiers. Investigators clearly sought to disprove the inmates' claims and undercut their character and reliability rather than to assess the validity of their complaints.

The first witness, a man named Cowan, made many different accusations: he had witnessed abuse of other inmates; residents received inadequate clothing, bad coffee, and poor cuts of meat; and he had been unfairly dismissed as a chaplain. Apparently anticipating trouble, Cowan produced a petition with more than two hundred names of inmates and others attesting to his sterling character. As soon as he finished testifying, the committee immediately presented evidence gathered prior to the hearing that challenged Cowan's reliability. Committee members had written earlier in the month to his former senior officers, who reported that Cowan's military record "was very bad, he would get drunk and also steal." One officer repeated rumors that Cowan had defrauded donors in a postwar scheme to collect money for the freedmen. Another letter called Cowan, a former army chaplain, "a disgrace to religion and a dangerous and wicked man whose word is not to be relied upon." Yet another writer accused him of fraudulently trying to obtain a disability pension, and still another suggested that he was no longer an ordained minister, having been dismissed from the Congregational ministry while serving a sentence for forgery in New York's Albany Penitentiary. Court records provided further nails in Cowan's coffin. Cowan's subsequent testimony, which takes up nearly a fifth of the committee's proceedings, included confusing and often contradictory statements about his military service, his family, and his various residences. Whatever Cowan's personal shortcomings—he was clearly a poor soldier and, perhaps, a bad man—other witnesses and administrators failed to address his specific charges regarding the home, and the aggressive manner in which board members grilled him and their enthusiasm for questioning his motives and character indicated a defensive and even presumptuous attitude about the inmates at the home.[46]

The board showed more restraint with other witnesses. The next inmate to testify, James Turner, had published three affidavits in the local press with the help of one of the members of the board of trustees, Grattan H. Wheeler, a native of Bath. One accused a sergeant of manhandling a "sick and dying" veteran, the next accused the superintendent of fining Turner for his work on behalf of the Democratic candidate in the previous election, and the third claimed that another sickly inmate had died after being forced to go out to the field to pick stones. Although no parade of witnesses castigated Turner's character, the board members picked away at his testimony, asking him to repeat certain facts and making sure that Turner's stay at Blackwell Island (as a hospital patient rather than a convict) and at the almshouse from which he came to the home were read into the record. Investigators brought up information about minor infractions committed by Turner, such as missing roll call and overstaying a pass on Election Day. The home surgeon and several other witnesses were called to talk about the case of Tuit, the man who had died. Charles K. Emery, the sergeant in charge of the dead man's barracks, asserted that picking stones was not compulsory and that Tuit had not complained about the assignment. He also pointed out that Tuit had not been too ill to walk into the village the night before and return to the home drunk.

When one board member asked Emery if a number of men in his company were "partially insane" or "cracked," he replied, "Yes, sir." When asked if he had "much trouble with the men," he answered, "Not until lately." He had generally let them complain as much as they wanted, but in recent weeks men such as Turner "began to make these affidavits." Emery apparently satisfied board members that the treatment of inmates was reasonable and without compulsion.

The corporal who supervised Tuit on the fateful day contradicted Emery's testimony, however. The corporal had no knowledge of Tuit having been drunk, the man had clearly been ill the day before he died, and everyone had to go out to work "except a few favorites of that drunken Sergeant Emery." The corporal also asserted that "every man was satisfied with me, nine-tenths of the men hated that Sergeant Emery, I hated him." The corporal's sour attitude did not help his case, nor did the fact that, when Turner was recalled, it became apparent that he was mistaken about the dates on which the events regarding Tuit occurred. Board members again undercut the charges against home officials by focusing on fuzzy memories, the inmates' conflicting motivations, and the possibility that a key witness had been drunk.[47]

The emphasis on getting physically able men outdoors and to work indicates a certain attitude about how the men should spend their time that resembled a workhouse or almshouse more than a soldiers' home. A disdainful general order discharged Turner from the home for "refusing to do anything that has the slightest appearance of labor, even to preparing his own vegetables, or joining his comrades on the ground engaged in picking up stones. . . . [T]his man claims immunity from all work on account of his age, yet he can go to the village as often as and as quick as most any man in the home." Another witness, who had signed an affidavit complaining that his varicose veins prevented him from picking stones, became uncooperative and somewhat belligerent when the board tried to get him to admit that he was able to walk several miles to a nearby town. Several witnesses declared that the work was good for the men. The former home surgeon "suppose[d] men are sent here to make it a home, and each should contribute what he is able to make it such." But the testimony from the men suggested that the policy was more about working for the sake of work than about finding useful work for the men to do. One inmate claimed to have been rushed back to work after breaking his arm and said he really was not able to pick stones. But "no man was allowed to lay down in quarters, and being 66 years old it was pretty hard work to carry my arm all day. I saw old men on the hill picking up stones that should not even been asked to walk up there." Whether the work was, strictly speaking, compulsory, the inmates certainly felt as though they had little choice in the matter.[48]

The most spectacular witness of the hearing was Rudolph Knopp, who accused the Republican managers of mistreating the old soldiers, most of whom, he claimed, were Democrats. "These poor men have been waiting for over three years for a change of state government and administration," he testified; such a change would "relieve the inmates from all their tormentors and from those selfish men who made a rich sinecure for themselves out of a charitable institution and have, in [an] illegal way, deprived the invalid veterans of their pensions." He accused the administration of poisoning home residents with "fraudulent vaccines," committing "willful and systematic manslaughter" in five cases, intercepting pension checks and correspondence, and allowing the murderer of an inmate to "disappear unmolested." Finally, he accused the administration of turning this "living ornament to the State, established for charitable purposes," into "a poor house or a penitentiary for professional tramps, habitual drunkards, and worn-out veterans out of all kinds of prisons." After confirming that he had sent messages to the governor several times and had circulated the letters, the investigators refused to listen to his charges regarding "murders" at the home. According to the record, Knopp's examination was "suspended . . . it being plainly apparent to the trustees that the witness is insane."[49]

Some of the factors that helped form the policies at Bath emerged from the testimony of General Thomas G. Pitcher, a West Point graduate who had been wounded at Cedar Mountain and had served as commandant at West Point for several years following the war. When he took over the home in 1880, he "found here something like five hundred men that were badly clothed, I think badly fed, apparently without any discipline, I think some of the hardest customers I have ever had to deal with." He made "some summary dismissals" to clear out the worst men—a practice that he understood alarmed area residents of Bath—and instituted a strict pass system. Another of his "greatest troubles," he said, was to "find occupation for the men." So he instituted the stone-picking details. "There was no force used at all," he said, and as a result, some of the more defiant men simply "lounge[d] . . . around under the trees." Indeed, Turner was one of the worst malingerers. Another apparently able man named McComber was sitting on a bench while his company was out picking stones; Pitcher drove by in his buggy and asked McComber why he was not with the other men. McComber looked the governor in the eye and said, "I am not going out, and I want you to distinctly understand that." Pitcher, who had been shot in the knee during the war, claimed, "If I had had two good legs I would have got out of that buggy, but I did not." Instead, he ordered the man to the barracks and dismissed him from the home. "If I allowed men to defy me in that way, where would the home be?"

Pitcher complained that the men were lazy and difficult to manage, were in the habit of calling their sergeants "all the vile epithets he could imagine," declined to do required work, and refused to understand the necessity of turning over all but a small portion of their pensions to their families. If they had unlimited access to their pensions, Pitcher contended, the men "would get their pension in one day and squander it in drunkenness very soon." In fact, Pitcher believed that many veterans sent their money not to family members but to friends who surreptitiously returned it to the veterans.[50]

The board responded much more sympathetically to Pitcher's frustration than to his contempt for the men. The final report declared that "the discipline of the home has been much improved in the past three years, and your committee desire emphatically to assert that if there has been any error on the part of the superintendent in the government of the home, it has been on the side of kindness rather than severity." Health care, clothing, and food were excellent; the men were well taken care of. Such tended to be the company line whenever home policies and conditions were challenged. But despite the fact that their frequent complaints tended to focus on food and work, the men were really, sometimes consciously, sometimes unconsciously, mourning the loss of their sense of manhood.[51]

During their investigation of the national homes, congressmen often probed the notion of manhood as it applied to the inmates. But investigators sought not to gauge how home policies failed to recognize the veterans' manhood but to determine the extent to which they failed to deserve to be treated as men. At one point, members of the panel asked the head of the Central Branch, "What effect does long continuance in a Home have upon the individual life, on the manhood of the men?" Governor Patrick responded by suggesting that even men who entered the home temporarily, who thought, "If I am kept here for a while, that before six months or a year I will get straightened out so that I can take care of myself," ultimately stayed permanently. "Men who, if there were no Home, would take care of themselves, in my view, hang on. They do not want to go away." At a recent annual examination, seventy-eight men had been recommended for discharge; many protested, and only about a dozen left, although many more were deemed able to take care of themselves. The questioner responded, "Then the effect seems to be they lose their independence—they become sort of children?" "That is it," Patrick replied; "You have hit it."[52]

Another witness was asked whether "they would be more manly and independent by being amongst their kinsfolk, provided they would not waste their money in that way and live in the same way there as they live here?" Although noncommittal, the officer suggested that many men went to live with their families but virtually always returned. During the testimony of the city's mayor, the committee chair asked "whether there is anything that you have seen that indicates the men deteriorate in the self-directing power, become more like children." A later witness indicated the extent to which the adoption of the military's Articles of War as the basis for home discipline could be a problem. The chaplain called it "the saddest calamity that ever befell" these men, who "fail to understand . . . why it should be necessary, that men called into the service of their country, who have volunteered in the service of the country, who have served the country until the rebellion was crushed, after they have been wounded, disabled by disease, enfeebled in body and mind" should be placed under the same rules as recruits in the regular army. That policy has caused "great unrest," and "its insertion" in the act establishing the home had been "a disaster."

> The men are, in every case, disabled either in mind or body, and very many of them are mentally and physically afflicted. They are not like well men outside. Sick persons are in the habit of complaining; you know they usually do, and they are discontented anyhow. Whatever military discipline they learned during the war is already knocked out of them. They cannot be soldiers; it is out of the question for them to be soldiers. They want to forget the past. Their series of afflictions, the breaking up of their families, and their mental and physical disabilities, put them in a position which causes them to absolutely hate everything military.

Even the good men "cannot abide it."[53]

Such conflicts threatened to spoil the reputations of all veterans. Later in his testimony, the chaplain worried that the nature of the witnesses called before the committee and the information they provided would "leave the impression that the men at the Home are the hardest cases under heaven, and hardly allowing that there are any good men in the Home." The "drunkenness and debauchery" displayed by inmates in the city threatened to cause civilians to think "that they are all a body of the very worst men in the Army and the very worst men living." He asserted that among the 4,000 men at the Home, "there are certainly 3,000 who are as well behaved men as you will find anywhere in this country—weak in mind and body, many of them, but they don't harm any person." The respectable majority "are very much humiliated by reason of the bad character given to the Home outside, and something to sustain the reputation of the disabled volunteers of the Republic ought to be done." He concluded this part of his testimony by saying that "one great benefit to this Home would be to defend the character of these men rather than seek to debase it."[54]

Some men who testified in the various investigations seemed to understand that simply accepting a spot in the home had compromised their manhood. The burden of proving their character led veterans to try desperately to fulfill their duties as men. Fifty-year-old Charles Morgan of the 13th New York had been shot through the lungs at the Seven Days' Battles, which left him "consumptive sometimes" and spitting blood. He lived at the Dayton home for a few months in 1871, then moved to the Hampton, Virginia, home for a year and a half in the belief that the warmer climate would help his lung condition. When he asked for a transfer to Togus, Maine, where he hoped to get work in the shoe shop, he was denied. Incensed, he jumped the fence and was dishonorably discharged. He complained to the Board of Managers as well as to the congressional Military Affairs Committee. He remained outside, living on a small pension and odd jobs, until he "got poor again"—when he was admitted to Togus. He stayed there for a couple of years, but in March 1879 he left to live with his wife, whom he had married two years earlier. "I can pretty near make my own living," he said, and "I would rather half live outside than to be with the class of men I had to be with here." While in the home, he had a run-in with another inmate about the Hayes/Tilden election. After he moved out, he brought his wife to an entertainment at the home but was forced to leave by a guard who still bore a grudge. Another altercation had arisen when he was caught taking bones from the scrap heap for his dog. When asked if he would apply for readmission, he declared, "No, sir. I will come pretty near starving to death before I do."[55]

An exposé of alleged abuses at the Togus branch of the NHDVS complained of a nonsensical pass system, the governor's absolute control of pension allotments, the automatic arrest of men who seemed slightly drunk, beatings of men who complained, discharges of old men who refused to work, and terrible food (moldy meat, little or no butter, soup and hash made of rancid beef). Although the abuses were bad enough, the anonymous author of the document seemed to be more concerned that the residents were not considered men: "Oh shame, shame! That such things should be allowed." Togus should be "a Soldiers' Home instead of a military prison. These men are not all saints, neither should they be treated as if they were all criminals."[56]

As an aside in his testimony to the congressional committee, Isaac L. Rawlings referred to his attempt to leave the home and get a job elsewhere: "I made an effort to try to make a man of myself and went down there to get employment, but was baffled." "I am nothing more than a man," one inmate testified, "and I want to do the duties in this Soldiers' Home as I should do them, but I am treated wrongly." An applicant for admission to the Dayton branch of the NHDVS visited the home several times, but "finding that a soldier could not be treated like a man, I could not stay there."[57]

Home officials apparently remained unconvinced. A trustee of the Michigan soldiers' home thundered in 1894 that soldiers' homes contained a class of residents who, despite the care provided to them, had never been good citizens. "I have come to believe that there is such a thing as the old soldier who has forfeited every right he had to the protection of the state. . . . When

he goes so far as to lose all manhood, punish him just as you would a criminal." Although the trustee was not suggesting that all veterans fit this category, the fact that he could articulate such a policy indicates the complexities of northern attitudes about veterans.[58]

The veterans who entered federal and state soldiers' homes during the
Gilded Age could not have escaped the prevailing notion that men were expected to support themselves and their dependents and that men who had
failed to save money for their old age deserved whatever happened to them.
The veterans seemed to know that the all old soldiers' reputations could be
threatened by the downfall of one. The charitable enterprises of the GAR and
other veterans' organizations were motivated chiefly by sympathy for poor
soldiers and their families, but these efforts to keep comrades out of poorhouses when alive and out of paupers' cemeteries after death also indicate
sensitivity to public perceptions: the fewer soldiers who demanded community resources, the less likely that veterans could be stereotyped as failures
and drags on society.[59]

A different dynamic prevailed in the South, where, argues Elna C. Green,
the Confederate homes and pension systems were intended to prop up veterans by providing small incomes or dignified living conditions. These practices would allow former Rebels to live up to their roles as exemplars of masculinity and to be held up to impressionable children as clean-living heroes.
The failure to abide by the rules of soldiers' homes, to drop out of the ranks
of the deserving poor, meant not only a fall from Confederate grace but also
a dismissal from the social welfare systems meant to protect and support the
very poorest—and most patriotic—old Confederates. Confederate homes at
times experienced the same scrutiny and criticism as northern homes. In
Kentucky, for example, the clash between the idealistic version of the home
as a place for worthy veterans to live peacefully and quietly and the reality
that the residents were no more or less likely than any other set of old men
to drink alcohol, resent authority, and refuse to bathe caused a fairly public
debate over the extent to which the institution could be a haven rather than
a military post. Yet generally speaking, Confederate homes avoided the controversies that plagued at least some northern homes.[60]

By the turn of the century, poorhouses increasingly became old-age
homes for men and came alarmingly to resemble soldiers' homes. Most inmates of both types of institutions had never married, and three-fourths
had only one or no children. In other words, they were more or less alone
in the world, without the resources to escape the stigma attached to charitable institutions. Residents were perceived as lazy, shiftless, and often alco-

holic—just a step or two above common vagrants. That stereotype colored the attitudes of both the men entering the homes and their families. Not incidentally, the Gilded Age also witnessed a speeding up of a trend begun in the antebellum period of celebrating youth over age, of reducing the natural respect extended to elders, of integrating the elderly less thoroughly into communities and the economy by encouraging retirements, and of turning old age into a "social problem" rather than an acceptable if bittersweet phase of life. As a result, from a certain vantage point, institutionalized old soldiers came to represent a rather extreme version of all men trapped in the inevitable spiral of age.[61]

Inside the Bug House

The discourse regarding the manhood of residents of soldiers' homes raged within as well as without homes. One member of the state home in Ohio remarked on the tensions caused by being "thrown together" into a sort of "brotherhood," which could be violated by a member "who talks Civil War too much, dishonesty especially thievery of a dead-beat as no one cares to have the finger of suspicion on them when they must face their comrades day in and day out or to have it said that while away on furlough they were spreading slang or fabrications of the Home."[62]

The most spectacular criticism of the residents of a soldiers' home, revealing a great deal about their manly attributes, came from Henry Clinton Parkhurst, who lived in state homes in California and Iowa early in the twentieth century. Parkhurst was a particularly irascible and intolerant man, and the veterans about whom he wrote had already survived the Gilded Age. But his scathing account of life in soldiers' homes nevertheless offers insights into the tensions that shaped veterans' place in society. "Some men enter soldier-homes from necessity or for temporary convenience," wrote Parkhurst in 1910, while "others find in a soldier-home a luxurious hotel—a glorious place where they can eat, sleep, play cards, blather by the hour, and wear out clothes, without having to work."[63]

Parkhurst opened an unpublished manuscript, "The Soldier Home Troops," with a dismal paraphrase of Dante that summed up his point of view: "Who enters here leaves pride and self-respect behind." Parkhurst had been in and out of homes all over the country throughout his middle and early old age, and he hated them thoroughly, although he claimed that he had voluntarily checked into the homes so that he could write. He completed at least one book manuscript, and it and his other writings are filled with conflict with other veterans and with himself, not to mention an un-mistakable sense of self-loathing.[64]

Parkhurst had seen hard service during the war as a member of the 16th Iowa Infantry. He entered the army as an eighteen-year-old in 1862 and re-enlisted in 1864. He fought at Iuka and Corinth and was captured at Atlanta, spending six months at the Andersonville and Florence prison camps. Dur-ing his peripatetic career as a journalist in Iowa, New York, and California, he sometimes found it financially and personally convenient to enter state and national homes.

Although he had benefited from living in the homes, he held the institu-tions and their inmates in absolute contempt: "It is not worth while com-plaining about soldiers' homes or scribbling much about them. They are all alike — rotten with graft — and a man of intelligence who is forced to live in one of them is to be pitied." He complained about officials' negligence and poor management, inmates' bad habits and foreign birth, and the "fact" that most men living in the homes by the 1890s and early 1900s were not veter-ans but short-timers, militiamen, or out-and-out frauds. He referred to the residents as "cattle" and "human hogs"; out of any one hundred inmates, "not more than four or five would be worth talking to [for] five minutes. They are the utter scum of civil and military life — the ignorant refuse of jails, alms-houses, insane asylums and penitentiaries." Such men were hardly the stereotypes of old soldiers presented in sentimental stories and articles. Al-though Parkhurst clearly exaggerated his fellow inmates' vices, he seemed to capture a version of old soldiers' character widely accepted by the American public.[65]

Parkhurst's contempt stemmed from his difficult service and from his conservative belief, apparent in his writings, that real men should be able to stand on their own two feet. "No man should be maintained for life at pub-lic expense, and be allowed a pension besides, unless he could prove he had served six months at the front, in actual warfare." Even disabled men who could not prove such service should be sent to the poorhouse, along with the "riff-raff" of the regular army and navy. "To establish expensive places and call them 'soldier homes,' and then make them dumping grounds for the filth and scum of society — for professional paupers, army deserters, insane persons, tramps, jail-birds, men fresh from penitentiaries, men who have no shred or sign of military papers, or who have found or bought the papers of dead soldiers — to do this is a sham and hypocrisy and an imposition on tax-payers."[66]

Parkhurst's catalog of criminals and miscreants was impressive. He claimed that at least five thousand men were living in soldiers' homes under the assumed names of dead soldiers. His evidence was anecdotal but powerful: a hardworking mechanic who had retired to the National Home in Hampton after happening across discharge papers in the drawer of a bureau purchased at an auction; an acquaintance who surveyed the roll of members of the National Home near Los Angeles and found his own name. Parkhurst had been assigned to barracks under the authority of sergeants with highly suspect records: one, a career criminal and member of a home guard company in Nevada, had lived for thirty years in the home; another had been a gambler and pimp, a brawler and saloon keeper, a forger and an inmate of San Quentin (after shooting a man in a fight); a third had been put in charge of a captured vessel filled with cotton during the war and had immediately deserted to the Rebels.[67]

In "The Bug House," written about two weeks after the "The Soldier Home Troops," Parkhurst continued his screed with the story of a knife attack by a "vicious inmate" on an inoffensive barber—the second knife fight in the home in two weeks. Parkhurst broke up the fight by battering the attacker with a board. Punishments were rare: "No criminal is ever turned over to the civil authorities, lest public criticism should be excited." Murders at the National Homes were "not infrequent," but perpetrators were regularly pronounced insane and shipped off to the asylum in Washington, D.C. After they were "cured"—usually in about a year—they were sent to another home, "to probably kill another man there." Parkhurst admitted that "there are many good fellows, and many good soldiers in every soldier-home." However, he estimated that "two-thirds of the inmates are low, dirty, lazy, ignorant, drunken, obscene European paupers and 'dead beats' whom it is a burlesque to call 'old soldiers.' . . . They are simply human scum, and when the last one of them is dead, it will be a blessing to the country."[68]

Not quite three years later, Parkhurst was living at the Iowa Soldiers' Home in Marshalltown. He was about sixty-nine years old, but age and the change of scenery had not moderated his disdain. Reflecting quaint notions about germ theory, he reported that he resisted using common drinking cups, kept his towel separate from those of other veterans, and always scrubbed out the tub before bathing for fear of contracting cancer or syphilis, the latter of which apparently raged at epidemic levels. His litany of accusations continued: one of the "captains" of a veterans' company "is a favorite at Headquarters, not withstanding the fact that he was convicted of the degraded crime of sodomy." The sentencing judge had allowed the man to choose to go to the penitentiary or to the soldiers' home, "an insult to every soldier of the Union army." Another "filthy vagabond" suffered from venereal disease but was nevertheless a pet of the home governor, carrying on conversations "so obscene and disgusting that it would not be allowed in an ordinary house of ill fame."[69]

Parkhurst could not believe that these men had ever been soldiers—at least not good soldiers. They were "so ignorant of military drill that they can't 'keep step,' and any brief march throws them into confusion." They mishandled their guns and could barely get off the volleys required at official funerals. Many spent their time tracking private pension bills in the *Congressional Record*; others plotted ways to scam the government with crutches, fake illnesses, and forged documents. A number of men who claimed complete disability carried on businesses outside the home grounds. Rather than talking about generals and battles, as "real" old soldiers would do, the old men engaged in "incessant filthy talk about women; and angry blathering about pension bills." Such qualities were hardly celebrated on Memorial Day, but they were certainly part of the package of wildly contradictory characteristics that civilians selectively applied to old soldiers.[70]

Parkhurst hardly spoke for all old soldiers, and the bitter tone of his writings betrays blinding scorn leading to exaggeration. Yet the specifics and fervor of his reports suggest that they contain nuggets of truth. Parkhurst's comrades, at least as he described them, lived down to the worst versions of Civil War soldiers.

My Pride Has Full Succumbed

The reputation of home residents doubtless played a role in many families' reluctance to accept the fact that their fathers and husbands needed help. One of those men, T. H. Flow, lived with his son's family, and although they tried to make him comfortable and he contributed to the household income with his pension, they had three little children, the son worked hard, and his wife was in "indifferent health." Flow's own declining health and inability to work outside the home made him feel like he was not only in the way but also a drain on their resources. When he mentioned his intention of applying to the Ohio soldiers' home, they had protested "that it would be a call for charity and to this as long as my son had health and willing hands they would never agree." Yet Flow persisted and, despite having to give up playing with his three grandchildren, whom he often led in military drills, he took advantage of the family's absence one day and in effect ran away from home. He made his way to Sandusky, where he was admitted with little fuss or bother. His forebodings immediately dissolved as he enjoyed the airy rooms, the well-cooked meals, and the respectful treatment by the staff. He wrote to his family, enclosing a souvenir booklet that explained the home's charitable and patriotic purposes. His daughter-in-law's response reflected her family's relief and acknowledgment that they had been wrong about the nature of the home. Flow penned a memoir describing his minor duties, his stay in the hospital, visits to and from his family, the enjoyable and mildly military rituals that shaped his life, and the homey atmosphere that embraced the old men.[71]

Others badly wanted their kinsmen to go into homes, not necessarily because people were unaware of the social ramifications but because the veterans in question deserved no better. William R. Williams, an inmate of the R. E. Lee Camp Confederate Home who was discharged for chronic disobedience and habitual drunkenness, had clearly worn out his welcome with his family. A letter to home officials from Williams's sister-in-law complained that he was "going around here like a Vaga[b]ond picked up on the street sick in the night and carried to jail he does not come to my House I don't want him." She asked that the home tell Williams that his belongings had been left in a box at the depot, where he could retrieve them. "I am truly sorry I got in that family. . . . I have not got but a short time to live and I want to live in peace."[72]

These two veterans and their families occupied opposite ends of the spectrum of families' responses to the prospect of kinfolk living at soldiers' homes. The two cases also reflect broader public attitudes about the homes and the men who lived in them. Although most veterans living in soldiers' homes had no immediate families, those with families had chosen to leave them. Wives and children could visit, of course—most state homes provided housing for at least a few wives and widows—but the decision to enter a home required men to make hard choices about their own and their families' reputations. As a result, unlike the pension system, which one historian has suggested was meant to "reconstruct" families in the Union, the system of National Homes established to care for and to honor the veterans who had sacrificed the most removed them from their families and eliminated the possibility of establishing "normal" lives. Already considered less than whole because of their disabilities, they were further emasculated, within the conventions of Victorian manhood, by their dependence, their isolation, and their uselessness.[73]

The idea of living in a soldiers' home had acquired unfavorable connotations as early as 1867. The first report of the short-lived Soldiers' Home of Louisiana acknowledged that at least at first, even the neediest soldiers hesitated to apply for admission because of their "deep-rooted prejudice" that such a place was "no better than prisons or penitentiaries." That dread continued to exert a powerful influence on veterans throughout the century. Some veterans deplored the necessity of relying on friends and even family members. "My folks are willing to do all they can for me," one man wrote to the administrator of the R. E. Lee Camp Home, "but I can't impose on them any longer if I can do any better." He had tried to survive on his own, but "circumstances that I have no control over" compelled him to ask to be readmitted to the home he had left voluntarily several years earlier. Part of his hesitation stemmed from the effect of such a move on the family's place in the community. E. L. Cobb lost his job during the 1890s depression but waited nearly a decade before applying to the NHDVS because his family "looked upon such a step as a great mistake which reflected upon them and their social standing. There was a disposition on my part not to boast about it." Most families also wanted to do everything they could to help their veteran relatives. When the family of one old Confederate learned that he had applied for admission to the home in Richmond, they asked for his immediate release: "I don't want him to stay at a Soldiers home while I am able to take care of him," wrote his sister.[74]

Despite loved ones' resistance, veterans usually got their way. But a number of men sought to convince their families that they were being treated in a dignified and kindly manner. Benjamin Rogers wrote a four-page letter to a friend a week or two after arriving at the Confederate home in Richmond early in 1904. Rogers carefully reported on the clothes residents were issued (four pairs of shoes a year), the food (not "fancy" but plentiful and "well-cooked"), the orderly manner in which meals were served, the minimal duties expected of the men (scouring their own chamber pots, maintaining their silverware, serving "guard" duty a few hours a week at meals), the fairly generous rules regarding passes and travel within Virginia, the free tobacco and toiletries, the comfortable beds. In short, he worked to convince his correspondent that the home met soldiers' needs. Using a phrase often employed by supporters of homes North and South, he assured his friend that "we have a home in the true sense of the word for the old boys." But he really meant that he would be cared for in a certain basic way—without luxury, but more than he could expect crowded into a family member's extra bedroom or in a county poorhouse. He betrayed a hint of uncertainty about what daily life would be like. Although the grounds were beautiful, "the sameness of seeing a lot of old men in all conditions of decrepitude day after day will I fear grow monotonous to me."[75]

Like many men, George Crosby had come to the Northwestern Branch of the NHDVS partly because he feared becoming a "dead-wait" to his family. His son, George Jr., had apparently supported or at least helped to support both his father and mother, and the elder man wrote, "I know that I have held you back for years all though you have never had us feel that it was so." He later speculated that he might have been the cause of some of his son's indebtedness, "but I suppose it is useless to ask." Young George apparently did not want his father to enter the home, but the veteran asked that his son "not think anny the worse of me because I see things in a different light from what you do, so let us think no more about it. I am here, and will stay." He had also arranged to have twenty-four dollars of his thirty-six-dollar pension sent to his wife, instructing the younger George to help his mother decide how to spend it and to teach her how to "make her mark" on the blank checks in a way that the bank could identify them. The home apparently provided the older man with needed medical care, resulting in a noticeable improvement in a malady affecting his hands. In later letters, George Sr. attempted to make his family more comfortable with his decision to spend his winters far away, describing occasional visits from friends, his work as a watch repairman—"So you see I ain't dead broke"—and the fine treatment he received, which included a napkin at every meal.[76]

Another inmate with a positive attitude was Temple Dunn, who entered the NHDVS in 1904. Dunn had mustered out of the 49th Indiana as an eighteen-year-old corporal; following the war, he became a respected educator and a failed businessman. After a decade of hard luck after the Panic of 1893, the sixty-year-old finally checked himself into the Central Branch in Dayton.

Dunn knew that his admission to the home carried connotations unbecoming to a Gilded Age male, and he fought to maintain his honor and confidence. He seemed to make a conscious effort to be happy, but his daughter, Bettie, was deeply disturbed by the idea of her father accepting the nation's gratitude in this way. She and many other Americans saw shame in wearing the NHDVS's plain blue uniforms. Newspapers and GAR magazines published frequent articles and editorials assuring Americans that veterans living in soldiers' homes were not paupers but warriors receiving their just rewards. But the rather defensive tone of the articles indicated that just the opposite assumption was common currency among Gilded Age Americans.

During his three years at the home, Dunn wrote chatty missives to his daughter, with whom he was clearly close. But Bettie did not want her father living in a soldiers' home, and Dunn desperately wanted to convince her that accepting support from a grateful nation was not shameful. That he felt the need to do so suggests his awareness that public attitudes toward old soldiers were more ambiguous than most public rhetoric would suggest.

A deeply religious man, Dunn began his first letter with a biblical reference, "Let not your heart be troubled." He apparently hoped that his evocation of John 14:1 would make the news easier for Bettie to take. His decision had "been coming a long time," he wrote, but "I have not been able to command courage enough to speak to you about it." He assured her that he had thought and prayed and wept about the move, satisfying himself that it was the best thing to do. "All my regrets are for you, and all the tears it has cost me have been for you. . . . I beg of you not to make it harder for me to bear by bemoaning more than you must my situation." Dunn hated the thought of being a burden to anyone, especially Bettie, and he desperately wanted to avoid cashing in a life insurance policy that would be his only material legacy to his only living child. He assured her that he would be well fed, well clothed, and well housed and that there would be "a great many arrangements to contribute to my religious, social, and intellectual life." Moreover, he believed the country owed him the security and limited comfort that the home could provide: "I deserve, and richly deserve, everything that can be done for me here. The debt can never be overpaid." He took pains to suggest that his job search would continue and that he might stay at the home only over the winter. He was "sure I may trust you to put only the most generous construction upon my actions."[77]

But his sunny outlook could not erase an uncomfortable sense that going to the home had given him a status that would raise neighbors' eyebrows and inspire family members' guilt. Dunn inadvertently revealed much about common middle-class attitudes about the home that ran counter to public admiration for veterans and patriotic rhetoric about the homes' function in rewarding worthy saviors of the Union: he sent his first letter to his daughter "in a Home envelope, making no effort at concealment. Let us be right out with it. My pride has fully succumbed, and I trust yours will yield without too much pain to you." He later asked Bettie to "not try for a moment to conceal my whereabouts. Just say I cannot bear to be a burden to others who have their own burdens to bear."[78]

Dunn's assurances and proud descriptions of the home grounds failed to move his daughter, at least at first:

Your sorrow-burdened letter—and the preceding one—are here this morning. You make a powerful appeal, but you are wrong. My course is the soul of honor. I am not making a disgraceful surrender. I am not physically able to prosecute a determined fight, and am doing the only thing that is open to me as I see it. I am as anxious not to become a burden upon you as upon others—though I know—O, how well I know it—you would bear it as no one else in the wide world would. . . . Step by step I have fought it out with myself, for a long time; and I do not think of changing my purpose. . . . [A]s I see my situation, I have done the right thing.

Dunn continued, "Out of respect to your mistaken notion," he would write virtually all subsequent letters on plain paper rather than NHDVS stationery. "I am sorry I may not just use the Home envelope. It will very soon be known, and it would be better not to attempt any concealment." He closed, "*Sorry* to give any answer which is the opposite of what you ask for."[79]

Dunn's acceptance of his position grew over time, as small comments and bits of news he conveyed to Bettie indicate. He supervised a crew of three men in a "pleasant" job; kept his promise to send her money from his quarterly pension, much of which she used to refurbish her house; decorated a letter written on Flag Day 1905 with a hand-drawn American flag; described from time to time the tasty food served; reported his progress in reading the Bible from beginning to end; suggested ways for her to view a partial eclipse of the sun; and began brushing up on Latin.[80]

Dunn exemplifies the veteran who accepted his nation's charity but did not surrender his self-respect. He remained a clear-thinking, engaged father, unbowed by what he apparently perceived as a temporary situation. He coaxed Bettie through an apparently disorienting religious crisis and provided kindly romantic advice. By the summer of 1906, Bettie was engaged and Dunn was preparing the wedding invitations. Perhaps because she appreciated the fact that the home had not, as she must have feared, deprived her of her father, Bettie eventually came to accept her father's point of view, visiting him on at least one occasion. After her departure, many of the veterans came to Dunn "with warm handshakes and warmer congratulations over my having you. I was very proud of the way they sized you up." He was also proud of the kindness and maturity she showed in speaking to "my friends." Your "manner was *superb! God bless you!!*"[81]

Dunn's last surviving letter to Bettie described his new job at the home— difficult but rewarding—and expressed his determination that when he came to live with Bettie and her husband, he would not be a burden but a help around the house. For the first time in nearly three years, he wrote a letter on NHDVS stationery. Dunn apparently left the home shortly thereafter, although no record of his later life exists.[82]

On the surface, Dunn's cheerful resignation and his determination to make the best of an imperfect situation make him the stereotypical inmate of a soldiers' home. His response reflects the attitudes Americans assumed that their veterans possessed. But Dunn was also aware that a significant portion of the population believed that something was lacking in the character of the men living on government largesse. Of course, entering a soldiers' home also suggested that one's family was unable to assume one's care, which put the family in a bad light. Optimistic and comforting letters written by Dunn and others may well have reflected their true attitudes about life in soldiers' homes but were also intended to deflect stereotypes and overcome familial embarrassment.

At Rest and Happy

Some residents of soldiers' homes displayed less pragmatic equanimity than Temple Dunn. Indeed, most evidence points to exactly the opposite conclusion. For most men, living in a soldiers' home brought decidedly mixed experiences. Yet the public expected veterans to be thankful for the government's generosity. A line had been drawn, and veterans must not cross it if they wanted to remain in their countrymen's good graces. Complaining about the benefits extended was clearly over that line. The undeserving poor could be ignored, but the ungrateful poor could not be tolerated: "What are we to think of the man or woman of the Home who receives all the comforts and courtesies and ministrations of the institution and then goes out among other people and slanders and knocks and criticizes?" asked the *Arkansas Veteran* in 1915.[83]

"Kickers," as soldiers called chronic complainers, probably outnumbered unreservedly satisfied customers. Yet a few men publicly and without qualification accepted their lots with gratitude and contentment. A poem written by an inmate at Togus in the 1870s painted an idyllic if bittersweet picture of life at a soldiers' home:

Here at rest and happy we abide,
Our army record, our only pride;
Down life's unruffled stream we glide,

Unnoticed—not unknown.
Thus living in our quiet way,
Contentment gilds each passing day,
And pleasure's ever genial ray
    Illumes our Togus Home.[84]

An even more satisfied member of the Idaho Soldiers' Home contrasted the meager fare and harsh living conditions that soldiers had experienced in the army to the treatment at the home and suggested that his dignity was maintained simply by the fact that he was provided with a clean bed, three square meals served by waiters, and a chair and locker for his possessions. When he heard "unkind remarks about our food-supply, and cooks, by some unthinking comrade, my heart has been made to cry out, O man! Whence comest this ingratitude towards your most noble benefactors." A resident of the Pennsylvania Soldiers' and Sailors' Home in Erie who had lived quite a hardscrabble life before entering the home now had regular meals, a comfortable bed, clothing, and tobacco. "And all of this free of charge," he wrote simply. "I have little or nothing to do but make myself comfortable."[85]

Most residents of soldiers' homes recorded neither their frustrations nor their gratification. Like Joseph Buck, who lived at the Northwestern Branch of the NHDVS at the turn of the century, they kept their heads down and went about their business. Buck started a new family while in his seventies, and his children lived with their young mother in Milwaukee and received visits from their father once a week. He used the pages of a twenty-year-old almanac to keep a kind of journal covering a year or two of his time at the home, recording his children's birthdays, pension days, and efforts to find work both inside and outside the home. He listed items he needed to buy and complained mildly about his health. He reported the day he exchanged his worn-out clothes for a new set, a pickpocketing incident in a neighborhood saloon, the loss of a razor, an inspection by the home managers, and numerous other small events. On one occasion, he noted that he had spent a Sunday afternoon going "arround the home," perhaps visiting friends or strolling on the grounds. Although Buck wished he could live with his family, his journal entries paint a picture of man who was a little bored but not unhappy.[86]

But those few men who left behind accounts of their time in state or federal soldiers' homes generally seem to have occupied opposite ends of the spectrum of satisfaction. As a result, the Henry Parkhursts and Temple Dunns, the Marsena Patricks and newspaper reporters, the townspeople and public servants, and all the others who wrote or testified about life in and around soldiers' homes have to shape our impressions about the place of veterans in Gilded Age America. Touted as the material representations of a nation's gratitude, the homes also constituted part of an unprecedented effort to bring the government to bear on social problems. At the same time modern in organization and traditional in conceptualization, soldiers' homes placed veterans in a kind of limbo between freedom and dependence. Although the number of residents never topped a few tens of thousands at any given time, the fact that they lived in places often visited by tourists and townspeople, were frequently seen on the streets and in the shops and courtrooms of nearby towns and cities, and appeared in the local and national media in both positive and negative ways made them one of the most identifiable groups of veterans. As such, especially in the North, their presence encouraged the public to view them and perhaps other veterans as unmanly and useless. The homes thus helped create two extreme stereotypes of veterans: feeble and incapable, or drunken and irresponsible. Americans seemed to think of the residents of soldiers' homes as less than truly men, and at least some of the men trapped in these stately prisons of gratitude agreed.

PENSIONS AND PREFERENCE

When the magnificent redbrick U.S. Pension Building opened on Washington's F Street in 1887, the Parthenon-style frieze that stretched around the building just above the first range of windows reminded passersby of the structure's real purpose (they still do; the restored structure now houses the National Building Museum). It shows a column of men marching, riding, and limping to their next battle. Some are grizzled veterans, some smooth-faced drummer boys. Some are joking and chatting, others look grimly determined, and still others betray fear. Most focus on the road ahead or on the trials that await them; a few glance out at the viewer. In the middle of the procession is a band of walking wounded, arms in slings, leaning on canes or crutches. This is how Union veterans—Confederates, too, no doubt—saw themselves and wanted the civilian public to see them: determined, enduring, and patriotic. They were good men, worthy recipients of the country's gratitude. Such might have been the most popular representation of Civil War veterans.

But competing images existed. When a congressional investigator asked the governor of the Central Branch of the National Home for Disabled Volunteer Soldiers (NHDVS) to explain the "source and cause of [the] irresponsibility" of the men under his command, he suggested that "it is due, first, to the generosity of the nation, which has provided for all its disabled soldiers. They believe it is the duty and indeed the privilege of the nation to provide for them. A large number of these men believe that they should be taken care of, wholly regardless of their conduct." This assumption led to a certain kind of arrogance on the part of residents, who had become "exceedingly wasteful, extravagant, and greatly given to breaking" government property. Although he was describing residents of the NHDVS, the governor's attitude reflected how many Americans had come to think about veterans receiving

Detail, Pension Bureau Frieze by Caspar Buberl (1834–99). Photo by F. Harlan Hambright, courtesy National Building Museum.

any form of government aid. Even worse were the overheard comments of a weary letter carrier in Newark, Ohio, while distributing yet another round of pension vouchers to the veterans on his route: "I wish every soldier was dead; they are nothing but a damned nuisance anyway!"[1]

As the foregoing demonstrates, the pension issue complicated northerners' attitudes about Union veterans. Old soldiers, especially those represented by the Grand Army of the Republic (GAR), came to believe that the nation's gratitude must take concrete form through the pension system. Many Americans found the veterans' continuing insistence on expanding pensions beyond the disabled to violate certain assumptions about independence, the role of government, and manhood. Simply put, they believed that veterans were not expressing enough gratitude for the unprecedented programs already created by the federal government. Veterans never seemed to say thank you for the homes and pensions at least some men received; the public never quite understood the ways in which veterans, even those who seemed to have emerged from the war sound in body and spirit, could demand so much of their fellow countrymen.

Unlike disabled veterans—including both those who were home-bound and those living in soldiers' homes—pensioners comprised an ever-growing number of old soldiers. Their number reached almost three-quarters of a million by the early 1890s. As a result, the complicated attitudes toward Union veterans caused by the pension issue did not affect merely a few marginalized, broken-down men. Rather, the political and rhetorical fights over pensions and the related issue of job preferences for veterans became the greatest source of conflict between the American public and hundreds of thousands of Union veterans. Doubts about the transparency, fairness, and integrity of the pension system left veterans at the center of a kind of Gilded

Age culture war about American values that included competing notions regarding loyalty, the role of government, and manhood but also descended into a bitter conflict over whether gratitude should flow from the nation toward the saviors of the Union or from those disabled and helpless veterans toward a beneficent government. And running close to the surface through all of the debates were Gilded Age anxieties about change, truth, and identity.

An Army of Pension Beggars

One of the complicating factors in attitudes toward former Union soldiers was partisan politics; the Republican Party favored generous pensions, while the Democratic Party opposed pensions for all but truly disabled veterans. Such divisions had arisen earlier in American history. Colonial governments had sometimes provided support for men disabled while serving in militia deployments, while the Continental Congress created a small pension for soldiers disabled by wounds or disease during the revolution. Yet by the 1810s, veterans' benefit programs had become intertwined with the debate over the national debt, states' rights, and fraud in the delivery of pensions to Revolutionary War veterans as well as Congress's decision to award lifetime pensions to officers in the Continental Army. These conflicts foreshadowed the pension and preference fights of the Gilded Age.[2]

But the politicization of pensions loomed much, much larger in Gilded Age than in Jacksonian America. The pension debate that raged in Congress during the former took often predictable turns: Republicans supported expanding and increasing pensions, while Democrats opposed further drains on the treasury. The authors of the *Republican Campaign Text-Book*, an 1884 handbook of talking points for candidates, called the section on their opponents' stance on pensions "Democratic Hatred of Union Soldiers." The debate took on an inevitable sectional element, as southern representatives tended to vote against pension bills and southern newspapers and Confederate veterans' publications railed against the escalating pension drain on southern taxpayers. But debate also concerned whether the pension program was being administered effectively, the apparent presence of widespread fraud, and the worthiness of some of the veterans receiving pensions.[3]

The rhetoric soared in 1887, when President Grover Cleveland vetoed the most generous pension bill to date and at roughly the same time angered veterans by advocating the return of captured Confederate battle flags. Cleve-

She Sends her Young Husband in response to Father Abraham's 300,000 call. | They Go in answer to Grover's Veto call.

A *Soldiers' Tribune* cartoon laying out the stark choices facing poor veterans in the face of President Grover Cleveland's veto of a service pension bill. *Soldiers' Tribune*, February 16, 1888.

land's reelection campaign the next year claimed that Americans were suffering from the high tariffs partly devoted to paying for the pension system and argued that fairness required a "reduction in the revenues" collected by the federal government. Although Cleveland was defeated by Benjamin Harrison, who lost the popular vote but won the electoral college, the *Grand Army Advocate* wondered how long the Democrats would continue to hammer away at the "fictitious issue": "Common justice and National honor require that the country discharge its obligations to the men to whom it owes everything before it strips itself of its power to pay." The image of veterans spending their last years in almshouses, on county poor farms, or at other charitable institutions that elicited long-held notions of fear and contempt was a powerful emotional and political tool that had helped spur the building of state soldiers' homes in the 1870s and 1880s.[4]

The mass media usually described Union veterans in admiring terms. But the pension issue could lead to extraordinary antisoldier rhetoric: after Cleveland's veto of the 1888 pension bill, the *Chicago Tribune* editorialized, "Thank God! The claim-agents, the demagogues, the dead-beats and . . . deserters and coffee-coolers and bounty-jumpers, composing our great standing army of volunteer me[n]dicants have been defeated." The *Tribune* refuted the claim that the veterans had "saved" the country: "No country, no nation, political constitution, system, or establishment, has ever been saved by . . . citizens that are not in the habit of depending on themselves." Indeed, the "army of pension-beggars" were "more dangerous enemies of the nation than undisguised rebels." Ex-Rebels, deprived of the opportunity of living off government pensions, had become thrifty, hardworking, independent men. Conversely, the majority of Union veterans, encouraged by Republican Party demagogues, had been "indoctrinated . . . with the pestilent notion that it is becoming to a savior of his country to fulfill the character of a dependent upon its bounty[,] . . . of a pauper without character or self-respect." The editorial ended with a kind of premature epitaph: "It will be a happy day for the republic when the last beggar of the Grand Army humbug is securely planted."[5]

Pensions were almost entirely a northern issue; no one would ever say that about Confederate pensions or pensioners. The lack of debate over Confederate pensions reflected not only their small scale but also their administration by individual states rather than the federal government and their availability to only the neediest applicants. Moreover, southerners maintained an almost mystic regard for Confederate veterans. A sample of the worshipful rhetoric that appeared from time to time in the South appeared in an editorial welcoming the United Confederate Veterans to an 1893 encampment in Fort Smith, Arkansas: "How nobly you did [your] duty the world knows. In marble and bronze posterity shall read it, and tongues tipped with fire from the altar of all that is pure and holy, shall tell it to the ages to come. And when the everlasting stream of time shall reach the great ocean of eternity's wealth, the character of the Southern soldier will tower grandly above all that finds lodgement there." The men had grown old, and "bent and tired you pick your doubtful way." Yet in obvious contrast to Union veterans, "no grateful government helps to bear your burden. No monthly pension aids your tottering steps. . . . No exemption from the general load is yours. But you have the proud consciousness of duty nobly done, and the blessings of that line of patriots of which Washington was one, Jeff Davis another, and Lee and Jackson a sainted two."[6]

The subject of Confederate pensions hardly appeared in the press, and when it did, commentators rarely challenged the system or the men who benefited from it. When the South Carolina legislature doubled the appropriation for old soldiers' pensions in 1901, the vote was led by its younger members, many of them the sons of Confederate veterans. The amount to be spent on pensions was only $200,000, which made the program much easier to defend from a fiscal standpoint, but the fact that little debate took place and that the original proposal had been to increase the amount only from \$100,000 to \$150,000 suggests a very different attitude about pensions in the old Confederacy.[7]

Although they were never as deeply embroiled in partisan politics as Union pensions, Confederate pensions formed part of southern Democrats' efforts to retain the loyalty of former Confederates, especially in the 1880s, when the pension systems of most southern states were inaugurated, and 1890s, when the former Confederates who controlled most state governments, county commissions, and pension agencies sought to keep pensioners from deserting the Democracy for the Populists.[8]

Not a Veteran in the Poorhouse

The conflict in the North found expression in two remarkable Memorial Day speeches delivered only a few years apart. Although Memorial Day speakers usually followed a script highlighting the worthiness of the Union cause and the valor of Union soldiers, these Union veterans offered competing interpretations of the pension program. The first laid out the typical arguments for expanding the roll of pensioners; the second presented the case against the blithe awarding of pensions to virtually all old soldiers. That both speeches were delivered by veterans suggests that the public debate raging over the pension system was also taking place within the veterans' ranks.

Charles W. Johnson, chief clerk of the U.S. Senate, highlighted the distinction between the true heroes of the war and the false heroes of the Gilded Age in his 1887 address in Minneapolis. "Old age, decrepitude and disease are reaping an abundant crop" among Union veterans, he declared. Like a ghost of Memorial Day past, he offered images of martial glory during the fight for the Union nearly a quarter century earlier; like the ghost of Memorial Day present, he asked his audience, "Look at these soldiers! Look at their gray hairs, their furrowed cheeks, their bent forms, their tottering limbs and trembling hands. They cannot carry rifle, knapsack, ammunition and rations, and march over rough roads, ford streams, stand on picket in pelting rains, endure exposure and fatigue. Their eyesight is dim. They cannot aim. They are not fit for service. They are not soldiers. They cannot undertake new enterprises in civil life. They cannot learn new ways." Johnson suggested that such decrepitude encouraged Americans to ignore these men and even to hold them in contempt.

Yet as they returned from their victory in 1865, Johnson suggested in words reminiscent of Whitman's "Return of the Heroes," these young soldiers had taken "up the burdens of civil life cheerfully, ardently,—they went west, north and south; they entered public lands, they felled forests, broke the virgin soil of wood and prairie . . . ; they built cities and railroads; they opened mines, manned the looms." In short, the veterans had saved the Union on the battlefield, then helped that Union grow more powerful in their peaceful pursuits. But now, with encroaching wounds, sickness, and old age, they needed to collect on the moral debt owed to them by their fellow citizens. The debt would be paid by men "who did not enlist; who perhaps sustained the war in an honorable way while it was going on; or [by] that other citizen who was too prudent, too prosperous or too young to enlist, or the foreign born citizen who has come to America since the war."

Acknowledging the raging controversy over pensions, Johnson connected public reluctance to accept responsibility to the growth of materialism, which he defined as the love of wealth and a misplaced admiration of men whose only accomplishment was making money. The glittering celebrity of the capitalists and the dynamic consumerism encouraged by the growing economy had distracted the public from its former veneration of old soldiers. Rather than honoring veterans, "in our day the men who grow suddenly rich in speculation, in chicanery and vulgar cunning, whose flashing equipages go rolling by, are shown the highest seats and sway the world." But living up to the promises made or at least implied to the veterans when they went off to war, honoring those men for their sacrifices in the modest ways made available by the government, would serve as counterpoints to the "corroding influence" of the undue worship of material wealth. In a sense, the Union heroes were conducting one last campaign for America's soul. "The presence of the Veteran of the Union is a constant reproach against the tendency of our times," thundered Johnson, awakening "an impulse toward a better and higher citizenship."

These men could be materially honored and the nation could pay its moral debt to them by retaining the preference given to veterans for federal jobs, now threatened by civil service examinations and patronage handed out by the resurgent Democratic Party, and by granting pensions to all elderly or disabled veterans, even if their disabilities were not caused by military service. "These Veterans have done and are doing every duty" asked of them, concluded Johnson, and now "it is the duty of the citizen to see that there is not a Veteran in want; not a Veteran in the poorhouse."[9]

Although few Americans believed that aging veterans should be allowed to die in degradation, many people still believed that not all veterans needed government help. The premise that the nation had a duty to its old soldiers had been turned upside down by another veteran a few years earlier. On the same day in 1884 that Oliver Wendell Holmes Jr. described veterans' hearts as "touched with fire," Theodore C. Bacon held forth in Canandaigua, New York, on "The Veteran Soldier's Duty to His Country." Bacon, who had served in the 17th Connecticut Cavalry and as a staff officer for General John Buford, began his talk to the Albert M. Murray Post of the GAR by saying that he had little to add to the traditional "wisdom" and "eloquence" that had become commonplace in Memorial Day speeches. He could hardly "add a new resplendence to the halo of eulogy with which, from year to year, we have been wont to crown the memories of those who have died for us."

But after this bland opening, Bacon fired a volley in the culture war by turning the tables on the veterans in his audience; rather than telling the nation what it should do for its old soldiers, he suggested that the veterans maintained a further debt to their country. Rather than suggesting that the American people would be judged based on how they treated veterans, he argued that veterans had to live up to higher standards simply because they were veterans.

After delivering an admiring and idealized account of the way in which Oliver Cromwell and the veterans of his New Model Army blended peacefully and prosperously back into society after the English Civil War, Bacon declared that "the first duty of the veteran soldier to his country, in this nineteenth century as in the seventeenth, in America as in England," is "that he shall be in time of peace its best and most active citizen." He should of course obey the law, but he should also help restore the nation's prosperity, repair the damage wrought by war, and "be . . . most diligent of all in restoring that frightful waste." Bacon urged veterans to make themselves available to state militias, which had deteriorated disgracefully since the war. In a comment that revealed as much about his attitudes toward the poor as about the pension issue, Bacon complained that state and local militias had declined so much that they would be unable to put down the riots that were sure to come in cities teeming with immigrants and dissatisfied poor folks who were only a demagogue away from becoming "armed and raging multitudes." Finally, because their military training and their sacrifice had made the veterans "in some sense a superior caste," they must "not forget the duties that belong to superiority." They should proudly display their uniforms, flags, weapons, and medals, but only at times and in places that honored those symbols of their service. "If you have fallen into vicious or criminal ways, shelter yourself from the cold with anything rather than that old blue coat," he ordered. Former officers could display their framed commissions in their shops or offices but not "in your tippling house or your gambling hell."[10]

In short, old soldiers must live up to their responsibilities as heroes and continually justify the public's high esteem. And they must remember the patriotism that led them to war. Bacon distinguished between soldiers who had volunteered and those who came into the army late in the war, when bounties inspired unworthy men to don the blue and substitutes entered the army only for monetary gain. "There were still noble men—patriotic men, unselfish men—breasting the storm of bullets, with higher motives than the bounty, the so-many-dollars-a-month-and-found, or the future claim upon the public treasury, impelling them." But they had become more and more rare as the war dragged on. The connection of material gain to military service at the expense of pure patriotism had "demoralized our armies, lost our battles, depraved the public sentiment, and burdened nations, states, counties and towns with prodigious accumulations of indebtedness."

The "evil influence" of mercenary self-interest "is even now persistent and efficient" in politicians', claims agents', and greedy old soldiers' calls for the so-called service pension, "the most stupendous schemes of retroactive payments that the world had ever dreamed of." "True soldiers" would never associate themselves with this large-scale public larceny. Yet the aggressive promotion of such programs by a few GAR newspapers, opportunistic politicians, and profit-seeking agents had earned all veterans reputations "as mercenaries, haggling for their pay; or as mendicants, begging for alms." Old soldiers owed it to the nation to "give the lie" to such stereotypes, to reject the burden placed on poor taxpayers by the "pretended demand of veteran soldiers."[11]

Johnson and Bacon were talking about two different kinds of men. Some Union veterans—the men Bacon suggested were too proud to beseech the government for aid—had fit back into civilian society. Others really were the broken-down old soldiers described by Johnson. Indeed, the debate over service pensions also raged within the GAR as some members decried the seemingly mercenary demand for pensions for all veterans rather than just the neediest as choosing "money" over "manhood." Yet most members saw expanding the pension system as an extension of their commitment to providing relief to poor veterans. This approach, as historian Stuart McConnell has suggested, required a new guiding principle: "The saving of the Union had been such a great service that anything given in return was of necessity incomplete." Need was not the issue; rather, the men sought respect and gratitude. Union veterans' "claim on the nation's treasury" channeled through the pension system would not be seen "as a compensation for illness, not as a gratuity, but as an absolute *right*."[12]

The values-laden rhetoric about soldiers' worth and a nation's duty to its soldiers would continue to provide a hard-edged counterpoint to the sentimentalized celebration of veterans' heroism and sacrifice. Years earlier, the idea of providing pensions to Revolutionary War veterans had sparked a debate over the most appropriate form of gratitude for the sons of liberty. As Sarah J. Purcell has pointed out, "The democratization of military gratitude" to include common soldiers—indeed, anyone who had participated in the sharp end of the revolution—"was far from a smooth process. Gratitude was traditionally a conservative cultural force and therefore difficult to put to new purposes." As early as 1788, Philip Freneau, a poet and former British prisoner of war, complained that the "maimed and unrewarded soldier" was being forgotten by businessmen and moneylenders who had grown "fat upon the miseries of the soldiery" during the war but now refused to recognize and reward those sacrifices in a meaningful way. The ambiguities in the relationship between the first American soldiers and their countrymen and -women foreshadowed the storm over Union veterans' pensions.[13]

Get a Pension

According to a brief report in the *Home Bulletin*, a newspaper published at the NHDVS in Hampton, Virginia, a "Hampton belle" said, "O! I would be the happiest woman alive if I could only marry a man with $24 a month pension." Like this possibly apocryphal woman, many Americans believed that the pension system was rife with opportunities for ethically challenged pension agents, soldiers, and even dependents and potential dependents. The *Bulletin* ran this anecdote as a joke that left out the main villains in this alternative view of old soldiers: the claims agents who, critics complained, encouraged veterans and their families to act on their baser instincts.[14]

A supposedly typical agent appeared in a direct attack on the pension system in *Puck* magazine in 1882. "I am a pension agent . . . and I am proud of it," declared the fictional entrepreneur. "A disreputable business? What! To succor the distressed, to get justice for the faithful servants of the government—that a disreputable business? But I'm not obtaining justice for the faithful servants of the government, I'm getting fat pensions for people who never earned them? Well, now, don't you judge my business too lightly. When you take into consideration the trouble of mind, the wear and tear of intellect that is required to run up cases of neglected vets and impoverished widows—when you consider the labor I have in teaching them what to say [to government investigators]—why then you'll admit that I'm earning my money." A later editorial argued that most "deserving veterans" had gotten "their pensions long ago." After that source of income dried up, "the pension agents had to make business. They made it by seducing old soldiers; by persuading them to swear that their present weaknesses and ailments were the result of injuries incurred during the war. These agents have got their commissions, and have tarnished the honor of thousands of men who were brave and honest before they were tempted beyond their strength." Although critics of the pension system frequently accused soldiers of fraudulent and conspiratorial behavior, such attacks on veterans were often camouflaged by castigations of pension agents, who received blame for the "organized debasement of patriotism" that was the bloated and scandalous pension system.[15]

Although hundreds of agents helped soldiers redeem enlistment bounties and make various kinds of claims against the government immediately after the war—the *Daily Missouri Democrat* devoted a separate category of advertisement to "war claim" agents during the second half of 1865—that market had pretty much dried up by early 1866, when the number of agents declined. The agent population quickly began to rise again when the pension system started to expand after the Arrears Act of 1879 and especially after the liberalization of the pension in 1890. Pension laws did not require veterans to apply through agents, but most veterans apparently used such services, and hundreds if not thousands of pension agents opened offices large and small to help veterans process their claims. Because their income was partly based on the number of claims they processed, with requests for increased pensions counting as "new" cases, agents were interested in pushing ever more veterans to claim greater disabilities and pursue larger pensions.[16]

Pension agents mounted modern and aggressive marketing campaigns. In the late 1870s, according to the commissioner of pensions, "the country was flooded with addresses, circulars, and other printed matter, addressed to pension claimants and soldiers in general," along with personal letters and other correspondence. Enterprising agents with offices in Washington, D.C., took advantage of the common newspaper practice, especially in small towns and cities in the West, of publishing the names of men who had recently been awarded pensions. The Washington pension attorneys would then write to pensioners suggesting that they had been rated too low and should receive higher pensions. The enclosed brochure offered the attorney's services—for a fee of ten dollars—to prosecute the claim. Congress created an extremely useful resource for agents when it ordered the publication of the entire *List of Pensioners on the Roll: January 1, 1883*, which provided the name, address, cause of disability, and rate of pension for every veteran, widow, and dependent. On four thousand pages in five volumes, the names of about three hundred thousand pensioners were made available in alphabetical lists organized by county and state.[17]

Some agents employed emerging hard-sell advertising techniques. Former Union soldier Milo B. Stevens, who had offices in Washington, Cleveland, Detroit, and Chicago, created a marketing plan that included the publication of a journal, *The Soldiers' Bulletin*, and advertising town meetings with agents whose arrival would be announced by circulars sent out weeks in advance.[18]

Charles J. Alden, who had served with the 21st Wisconsin, distributed a brochure with the startlingly direct title of *Get a Pension*, that listed all of the conditions that might be covered by pensions, summarized ways of getting desertion charges cleared from one's record, explained how lost discharge certificates could be replaced, and informed potential clients of ways to get on the pension rolls even when they had entered the military under assumed names.[19]

The most commonly employed advertising tactic was simply providing information to potential clients. Pension agents seem to have divided veterans into two categories: those who were already receiving pensions and those who were eligible but were ignorant of their rights and opportunities. Chicago's E. S. Weeden specialized in obtaining pension increases for men victimized by examining surgeons who had "cut a pension [rating] down, or off, with or without cause, from ignorance, prejudice, or pure meanness." In addition to his twelve years' experience, his "corps of clerks," and his capacity for hard work and efficiency, Weeden presented as a credential his experience as a frontline soldier who had been "confined in rebel prison pens until my health was permanently injured," a status that allowed him to "present claims a 'mere outsider' does not."[20]

"Never despair," declared the pamphlet from Washington's W. H. Wills agency. In some cases, according to Wills, soldiers were ignorant of bounty laws that had been passed after discharges were issued, the fact that sailors could obtain prize money long after the war, and recent laws had eased the process for dropping charges of desertion and for declaring long-gone soldiers dead, enabling their heirs to collect pensions. The pamphlet trumpeted Congress's recent 1883 authorization of $101 million for pensions and the hiring of more than a hundred additional clerks for the pension office. The agency promised a full range of pension-related services: in addition to the regular pensions granted to men who had lost limbs or ruined their health while in the service, Wills would help men file claims for horses and equipment lost in the service, resubmit claims for higher allowances, procure "veteran muster" papers required to obtain certain bounties, and process claims for twenty-five cents for every day a soldier was a prisoner of war or was home on sick furlough (to pay for the rations they had not consumed). Correspondents were asked to enclose stamps with their queries, to pay the postage for the firm's reply. But the pamphlet's most important message was that most veterans were deserving but were often ignorant of what they had coming.[21]

Indianapolis's Philander H. Fitzgerald, who for decades ran one of the country's largest pension agencies, made his aggressive interpretation of the pension law very clear in an ad appearing in his own *American Tribune*: "Every Soldier Disabled while in line or discharge of duty, and who is now laboring under disability, either by accident or otherwise, is entitled to a pension. The loss of a finger gives a pension. The loss of a toe gives a pension. Rupture, though but slight, gives a pension. Inguinal hernia or varicocele gives a pension. Varicose veins of legs will give a pension. Deafness a pension. A gunshot wound entitles to a pension. Where piles or hemorrhoids were contracted while in service of the United States a pension is granted if the disability still exists." Fitzgerald's ad assured potential clients that many claims "have been filed by incompetent and unskilled persons" and thus were rejected because the paperwork had been prepared incorrectly, the wrong disability had been claimed, or disabilities had been described inaccurately. As Congress debated the 1890 disability pension bill, the *Tribune* published a long questionnaire that soldiers could fill out and send to Fitzgerald's office, where agents would calculate and then apply for the correct pension for which the sender was eligible. Within twenty-four hours of the bill's passage, a completed pension application would be sent to every applicant for his signature. The rush of applications would, Fitzgerald warned, swamp the Pension Bureau, and "a week's delay in filing a claim is likely to cause many months delay in a final adjustment."[22]

Fitzgerald; James Tanner, a disabled former commissioner of pensions and prominent GAR leader; and George E. Lemon were perhaps the most influential pension agents in the country. Lennon's Washington office employed a hundred clerks and agents at any given time; his newspaper, the

National Tribune, reached one hundred thousand subscribers. The *Tribune* published a "valuable book for all ex-soldiers" consisting of the official roster of regimental surgeons and assistant surgeons, including their last known addresses. Originally compiled for the use of the Pension Office, the volume was now being offered in a "handsomely bound" edition to soldiers for $1.50; it would be sent free to anyone who recruited ten subscribers. Unlike other published rosters of soldiers and officers, this compilation had a particular purpose: helping old soldiers locate the men whose testimony was vital to proving claims of wartime disability. Lemon was one of the most conspicuous lobbyists for expanded pensions, appearing frequently as a witness before congressional committees. After almost singlehandedly waging a six-year-fight, he persuaded Congress to repeal a law regulating fees; on another occasion, he orchestrated the defeat of an effort to tighten the medical examinations given to applicants. His most infamous accomplishment, however, was pushing through an 1884 provision raising the fee agents could charge to twenty-five dollars and making the fee retroactive.[23]

Although the North had hundreds of pension agents, a group that included local lawyers, retired Union generals, and even inmates at soldiers' homes (perhaps a dozen residents of the Central Branch of the NHDVS acted as agents), a few giant agencies—Fitzgerald and Lemon, especially—dominated the market. In 1880, commissioner of pensions J. A. Bentley estimated that perhaps ten firms controlled half of all pending claims.[24]

Critics of the federal pension system believed that such agents' aggressive, optimistic marketing lay at the root of the pension problem, encouraging veterans to seek ever-larger payouts based on unrealistic expectations and only modest disabilities. W. H. Wills's 1883 pamphlet quoted the pension commissioner's comment that a million deserving men were not receiving pensions and reported that clerks in the pension office had been directed to "work as fast as possible" to process pensions for worthy veterans. "A faithful attorney who never allows one link of evidence to be lacking in the prosecution of a claim," Wills promised, "never fails to bring a just claim to a successful issue." Passages declaring that "nearly every pensioner is NOW entitled to an increase" and that "any disability, no matter how slight, entitles the soldier to a pension" simply encouraged men to submit claims. Despite the confidence with which the pamphlet presented its case, it used careful language and offered no guarantees. It simply encouraged all veterans, even those already receiving pensions, to submit new claims. And it treated applications for new or increased pensions as a kind of duty, framing the words

"Rally, Soldiers! To the Aid of your Good Cause" with American flags flapping in the wind.[25]

Soldiers' newspapers were part of the system. Indeed, they explicitly sought to help individual veterans obtain pensions and typically became clearinghouses for requests for information on surgeons, officers, or fellow soldiers who could swear affidavits supporting old comrades' claims. Although few advertisers were as obvious as John Clouser, who hoped to hear from "any of the boys who remember . . . his getting wounded at Bulls Run, Va., July 21, 1861, in the left side"; William Robinson, who sought "some of the late officers and comrades of his command, who recollect of his becoming disabled in the army and can assist him in his claim for pension"; or Manasses Waters, who hoped that some of his old friends remembered "his sickness in the army and can assist him in his claim for a pension," such agendas clearly lay just under the surface in the dozens of requests for information and contacts that appeared every month. The *Milwaukee Sunday Telegraph* bragged in its second year of publication that its gathering of veterans' names and addresses had "been the means of putting tens of thousands of dollars into the pockets of worthy soldiers who ought long ago to have received their pensions."[26]

A Raid upon the Treasury

After his 1887 veto of an enlarged pension, President Cleveland sent a message to Congress that directly criticized the measure's supporters. Cleveland complained that the new pension would have been extended to "enlisted men who have not suffered the least injury, disability, loss, or damage of any kind incurred in or in any degree referable to their military service including those who never reached the front at all" because they had enlisted too late. He also hated the provision that would extend pensions to men "suffering from mental or physical disability not the result of their own vicious habits or gross carelessness which incapacitates them for the performance of labor." The bar was set too low for government aid, he believed; too little burden was placed on the soldiers, who would receive pensions only because they could not earn a living, with no need to show that they were without property or dependent on others. He pointed out the relatively high pay, especially in bounties, received by men who had served in the war and suggested that the "really needy and homeless" soldiers—the men who he believed actually deserved government aid—were already cared for in soldiers' homes. He refused to allow additional costs to be passed on to the American people, who were already paying for what amounted to a "large standing army" of pensioners. He also doubted whether most honorable veterans wanted the bill to pass: "I cannot believe that the vast peaceful army of Union soldiers" would want "to be confounded with those who through such a bill as this are willing to be objects of simple charity and to gain a place upon the pension roll through alleged dependence."[27]

But that "standing army" refused to give up. While Congress debated the Dependent Pension Bill and after the measure passed in 1890, opponents vigorously and harshly attacked veterans. Whether the old soldiers were being misled by agents, blinded by greed, or allowing wishful thinking to get the better of them, they were clearly jeopardizing their reputations as loyal Union soldiers. The attacks on their character sometimes distinguished between true veterans—the men who had enlisted early in the war and who had served steadily throughout—and those who had been conscripted, had joined as the war was winding down, or had served as teamsters, sutlers, or in other rear-echelon posts. But the rhetoric usually ignored differences among veterans, instead painting all with the same broad strokes.

The cost of the pensions sparked considerable opposition. In an 1889 essay, Leonard Woolsey Bacon, a minister and theologian, used as his title the common description of pensions as "a raid upon the treasury." He compared the pension system to gambling, particularly lotteries, in the sense that many Americans did not realize that pensions came with heavy costs. Two years later, another critic declared that as a consequence of the pension system, the United States was "no longer on the verge of socialism" but "in it, far advanced in both the principle and practice of what was but a very few years ago an abhorrent doctrine to all Americans." As late as 1911, the rhetoric could still be shrill, as evidenced by the title of former Union general Charles Francis Adams's diatribe against the pension system: *The Civil-War Pension Lack-of-System: A Four-Thousand-Million Record of Legislative Incompetence Tending to General Political Corruption.*[28]

With so much at stake, the middle-aged and elderly veterans collecting pensions became a threat to the same Union that they had saved in their youth. The *New York Times* launched its harshest attacks on the pension system as well as on veterans and the GAR during the weeks just before and after the bill became law. Rather than "saving the veterans from the humiliation of [actual] pauperism," the dependent pension bill would "offer a large premium for professed pauperism, and the number of the unworthy who will receive its benefits will be so large that they will throw discredit upon all who share with them." Indeed, as soon as the bill went into effect, reported the *Times*, the "grand army of pension hunters" besieged the pension office with thousands of new applications. The *Times* targeted lazy farmers—Populists calling for economic reforms that would benefit them—and GAR pension-ers who were not the truly disabled but who had collected large bounties when they enlisted late in the war. "When the war ended, these men had enlarged views, good health, and as time passed an avaricious enthusiasm that caused them to elbow back to the rear the sick and infirm, the disabled, and the widow and the orphan." These "pension sharks" were clamoring for government aid both as farmers and as unworthy recipients of pensions. By the end of the summer, the *Times* had turned a moving wartime song, "We Are Coming, Father Abraham, Three Hundred Thousand More," into an anthem promoting expanded pensions. The editors even complained that the 1890 census of Union veterans, which would include the names of veterans and their physical condition, was simply "a means to help the grasping pension agents" find new clients.[29]

The *Chicago News* went even further when it suggested that the muster rolls of Civil War regiments "were cumbered with men that at all times shirked a soldier's duty—ever in the rear as stragglers, never on the front line on a battle field. These non-combatants, the scum and riffraff, wore the blue for the revenue only and were a disgrace alike to the army, the uniform and the flag." Such men had become the chief promoters of pensions, turn-ing the GAR into "mercenaries" comparable to the Hessians who had fought for the British during the American Revolution.[30]

In the rather grotesque cartoon style of the time, *Puck* magazine periodi-cally and mercilessly attacked the pension system in the 1880s and 1890s. Several cover illustrations offered full-color portrayals of the unnecessary generosity and outright fraud within the system. The first, which appeared in December 1882, featured "The Insatiable Glutton," a many-armed man wearing a Civil War–era forage cap labeled "U.S. Pensioner," crouching on the floor, and scooping coins out of an overflowing bowl labeled "U.S. Trea-sury." The sleeves on the man's two dozen or so arms bear such labels as "Fraudulent Attorney," "Bogus Widow," "Bogus Grandpa," "Bogus Grandma," "Bogus Orphan," and "Agent." A few years later, a sinister-looking James Tan-ner was depicted outside the U.S. Treasury building holding a horn of plenty with a long tail, labeled "Pension Bureau," snaking back into the building. Coins, bills, and bags of money are spilling into dozens of grasping hands. In 1893, pensioners were cast as a weary old "U.S. White Elephant" happily munching on the treasury notes being scooped into his mouth by a sweaty, perturbed Uncle Sam. In a clever commentary on both pensions and the "elixir of life," a new headline-grabbing cure for impotence invented by French physician Charles-Édouard Brown-Séquard, *Puck* showed Tanner injecting gold coins into the pockets of decrepit veterans, who then dance away, visibly younger and throwing away their canes and crutches. The caption read, "Tanner's Infallible Elixir of Life for Pension-Grabbers Only."[31]

Some veterans also criticized the government's generosity. William Conant Church, a journalist, former Union army officer, member of the Military Order of the Loyal Legion, and cofounder of the *Army and Navy Journal*, argued in 1893 that Congress had "ignored the distinction between the duty soldier and the 'coffee-cooler,'—the man who lingers in the rear to take his comfort or to escape hardship and risk." Most soldiers appreciated the life lessons that military service had provided; they would not accept the commonly held theory that military service "is necessarily demoralizing, or destructive to health, or that . . . it diminishes a man's ability to compete with his fellows in the struggle for existence." Church recalled the words of Andrew Jackson, who had declared in the context of the debate over pensions for Revolutionary War veterans that "the honest veteran has nothing to fear from such a scrutiny, while the fraudulent claimant will be detected and the public treasury relieved."[32]

In a sermon delivered the day after Memorial Day in 1890, Unitarian minister and former army chaplain Edward H. Hall called the recently expanded pension system "an indignity to our citizen soldiers." The debt the nation owed to its saviors could not be "measured in dollars and cents," and attaching any "monetary value" to those debts "cheapens the sentiment of patriotism." For Union soldiers, "as with all brave men who had gone before them, the victory of the cause . . . was their sufficient recompense," and whatever additional provisions were made after the war "were accepted with dignity and gratitude." But pension agents and veterans' organizations had wanted more. "The country was flooded with circulars and appeals, military societies were led on step by step to countenance these friendly efforts in their behalf, public sentiment was quietly and successfully played upon to sympathize with the soldier's sufferings and to forget that anything had yet been done to relieve him, politicians were reminded of the rich party capital to be secured by coming forward as the soldiers' friends." The 1879 Arrears Act was the inevitable and tawdry result. But even after this major expansion, the "recipients of that magnificent plunder" continued to proselytize the pension issue, leading to the recent passage of the 1890 bill, which turned "pension roll from a roll of honor into a monstrous charity list" that

Corporal James R. Tanner as an overly generous commissioner of the Pension Bureau. *Puck*, May 29, 1889.

removed "all distinction between heroic and non-heroic." This "lavish appropriation for the country's defenders . . . removes the distinction between brave men and cowards and offers a splendid premium on pauperism." Now, "instead of expressing gratitude to the country for its unparalleled munificence," rather than "waiting for others to extol their merits," the old soldiers had begun "to speak themselves of the debt the country owed them."[33]

Partly because of agents' aggressive marketing campaigns, almost every nonveteran and even some veterans assumed that the system was rife with fraud. The percentage of fraudulent pensioners is impossible to determine; contemporary estimates ranged from 5 to 33 percent, although the percentage of exaggerated (as opposed to wholly fraudulent) claims added significantly to the amount of waste. Even the commissioner of pensions admitted in 1879 that although the commonly cited estimate that 30 percent of pension claims were fraudulent was greatly exaggerated, perhaps 10 percent were indeed falsely sworn. A decade later, another veteran, General H. V. Boynton, a Washington reporter, argued that at least a quarter of all pensions were counterfeit. He blamed the pension agents, "who, with their advertising dodgers and their circulars, have kept the veteran element in constant ferment on the subject of pensions." Although some agents acted honestly and in the best interests of the old soldiers, most "have held out false expectations, and led thousands upon thousands to apply for pensions who, except for these confidence men, would never have entertained the idea."[34]

Claims agents generally were perceived as acting more in their own interests than in those of the veterans. Agents' hard-driving strategies bore as much responsibility as any other factor for the unsavory reputation that the pension system gained during the 1880s and 1890s. Another contributing factor, however, was the congressional practice of passing private pension bills. Although perfectly legal, the thousands of private bills adding pensioners to the rolls or more often increasing the amounts paid inspired a sense that some men were garnering undeserved benefits through backroom deals. Such bills covered less than 2 percent of the number of pensioners and of the total cost of pensions but accounted for more than half of all bills passed by the Senate in the late 1880s. Friday nights were unofficial "pension nights" in the Congress; despite the absence of quorums on most of those evenings, private bills were customarily passed without debate or individual votes. Because some bills declared previously disqualified veterans eligible—men listed as "deserters" in the official records could have their records cleared by congressional fiat, for example—and because most applicants for private bills had first been rejected by the Pension Bureau, the uneasy sense of systemic corruption grew.[35]

The debate over pensions—or, rather, the debate over the worthiness of men receiving pensions—paralleled the controversy that has accompanied any extension of economic benefits to the disabled, the poor, and other dependent classes from the early nineteenth century through the era of welfare reform in the late twentieth century. A survey of coverage in the Gilded Age press found not only a widespread belief that the pension system was riddled with fraud but also a firm commitment to separate "true" soldiers from the "skulkers who had suffered neither hardships, danger nor disease," as one editorial put it. The latter were taking advantage of the reputation won by the former on the battlefield. Another editorial referred to legitimate pensioners as the "righteous core of a generation of men."[36]

The outrage against pension fraud that erupted intermittently, especially in election years, was paralleled by Americans' common belief that many recipients of poor relief were fraudulently obtaining benefits. As Michael B. Katz has shown, even reformers betrayed a certain amount of contempt toward aid recipients, and it is not difficult to see how easily similar attitudes could be transferred to the pension system, which affected far more people and cost the government far more dollars than did local welfare efforts.[37]

The skepticism extended beyond the men who purposefully committed fraud against the government. By the early 1890s, critics had decided that all veterans and veterans' organizations were tainted by association. Any man or GAR post that failed to stand up to fraud or to admit that pensions were a drain on the treasury and a blight on the Union was no better than a man who lied on his pension application. The GAR, *Puck* declared in 1893, continued to push for bigger and broader pensions despite the fact that the government annually paid out a fourth of its revenue—$160 million—in pensions. "It is hard to realize how the Grand Army of the Republic could have been placed in its present shameless attitude. Is it any wonder that the people should doubt the patriotism of men who seek to join it? Can not the rank and file of the G.A.R. be brought to see that the element which controls it is gradually placing the Order on a par with the women who sell their bodies?" The historian and reformer William M. Sloane agreed: When "the hero covered with honorable wounds, the faithful and courageous soldier who served long and bore the brunt of battle" associated with pension frauds and their agents, he was "no better than the deserter, the straggler, the bounty-jumper, and the coward."[38]

The rhetoric on both sides of the issue challenged a number of basic values: proponents of personal accountability clashed with advocates for a newer sense of government and communal responsibility. The idea that a citizen-soldier who volunteered gave up the possibility of future reward or material gratitude conflicted with the theory that paying soldiers a monthly salary and rewarding them with bounties and other benefits established precedents for negotiations for additional concrete recognition. The rather vague promise in the American compact that the government had a responsibility to provide "life, liberty, and the pursuit of happiness" ran up against the suggestion that the government had quite specific duties in regard to its citizen-soldiers. True "men" would not accept pensions unless absolutely necessary; true "men" should stand up for certain principles.

Long Losts

The discourse regarding pensions drew ammunition from the general unease with the magnitude of the program—the cost, the number of men receiving pensions, the size of the bureaucracy required to administer it. Moreover, a creeping sense of distrust—of strangers, of authority, of organizations—that emerged during the Gilded Age added to the conversation about pensions and pensioners. Part of this phenomenon can be traced to the unreliability of "truth" and the seemingly fungible nature of identity that came out of the war. These cases went far beyond the common stereotype of political opportunists who used the war as a kind of credential for public office, such as the Kentucky colonel whom Ambrose Bierce accused of lying when he claimed to have led a regiment up Missionary Ridge. "It is my opinion that he was never a soldier at all or he would have known better than to make statements so easily refuted." The Kentuckian was hardly the only man to exaggerate or fabricate a military record; California had a number of "military impostor[s] . . . whose bubble of glory" Bierce could "prick when so disposed. I have hitherto abstained because the bubbles are so gorgeous that I admire them myself." In another column, Bierce mused, "One would think war horrible enough without the monstrous exaggerations that seem inseparable from the story of it."[39]

The antebellum suspicion of demagogues and gamblers, the uneasy transition to the anonymity and uncomfortable interdependence of urban life, the decline of deference and of the influence of religion, and the fear that disorder and community declension would threaten republican ideals and virtue prepared Americans to expect the worst after the Civil War. The extraordinary disorder caused by the mobilization and then demobilization of millions of men, the upheaval in politics, and the major changes that the war had wrought on society, at least in the short term, raised the specter of disorientation, disrespect for authority, and criminality.[40]

Countless reports of swindles aimed at veterans or at civilians appeared in the decades following the war. The *Confederate Veteran*, which, like many magazines at the time, encouraged readers to recruit subscribers by offering free subscriptions or other premiums, occasionally warned of confidence men taking subscription money without delivering it to the *Veteran*. John C. Brain, a "smooth tongued, bold faced man" claiming to be a disabled veteran of the Confederate Navy, traveled through the South in the mid-1890s, appealing to members of United Confederate Veterans camps to contribute money to various monument funds. The *Veteran* exposed him as a fraud. He had never been a regular member of the navy, his scars and lameness—which were effective selling points to the old soldiers—were not the result of battle wounds, and he never turned in the contributions he gathered. Five years into its long run, the *Veteran* complained, "There has been a good deal of this."[41]

The very visible disabilities suffered by thousands of Union and Confederate veterans attracted vast sympathy among veterans and civilians alike but also provided openings for opportunists. Just a few months after the war, the *Soldier's Friend*, perhaps the most steadfast proponent of aid to deserving veterans, warned that many of the apparently disabled veterans begging on the nation's streets were really "shameless imposters, who play upon the popular sympathy for the soldier to secure a larger income than ordinary beggary would produce." A man who had truly been disabled in service would not, the *Friend* suggested, be reduced to wearing a placard reading, "This man has lost his sight in the service of his country, and is trying to make a living." A federal pension would take care of true heroes. The *Friend* worried that "such shameless mendicancy" would not only turn the public against deserving veterans but also embarrass the United States. Beggars claiming to be soldiers should be chased off the streets by the police. "Let not the blue coat, made glorious by the heroism of a hundred battle-fields, be now degraded into the badge of pauperism."[42]

A one-legged man who claimed to have lost the limb at Gettysburg subsequently admitted that the injury was not incurred during war service — but not before he had used the disability to beg meals from patriotic farm families. Another disabled man who might or might not have been a veteran showed up at the National Home in Norfolk claiming to be a Confederate veteran and "imposing" on the home's Union veterans. The *Milwaukee Sunday Telegraph* reported the appearance in Wisconsin of a man claiming to be commander of a GAR post in Pennsylvania and asking for help from local GAR members because he had been robbed. A little checking provided the information that he was "unquestionably a fraud, a type of a considerable class which roams about the country preying upon soldiers and soldier societies." GAR members "owe it to themselves and the worthy men who deserve help to discover these swindling tramps and expose them."[43]

One of the largest cases of fraud occurred in Elmira, New York, in the 1880s, when "Blind Patterson," a cantankerous, alcoholic, and sightless street beggar, received a pension of seventy-two dollars a month plus thirteen thousand dollars in back funds. A charge of desertion had held up his pension for years, but an attorney managed to get the charges dropped and the pension awarded. It soon became apparent, however, that the case was a fraud; a local pension agent had bribed former soldiers in the 154th New York, including a captain, to swear false affidavits. Most of the money was retrieved but went to lawyers handling the government case against Patterson and his agent.[44]

The problem of trying to distinguish between deserving veterans and imposters persisted throughout the Gilded Age. A short history of the Dayton branch of the NHDVS admitted that even a decade after the war, many men still haunted railway cars and city streets, begging for money or playing hand organs. These "apparently disabled men, who claim to be soldiers," were often "never soldiers at all, or [were] deserters, or were dismissed for crimes." The author urged citizens to refrain from giving such beggars anything: "This prostitution of the honorable wounds and the uniform of the soldier [could] only be saved" if "every man, and especially . . . every woman, whose kind and patriotic hearts are touched by such exhibitions of apparent want," were to ignore the imposters.[45]

The general suspicion of soldier-beggars emerged in the context of the "tramp problem" of the 1870s and 1890s. Particularly during the earlier period, tramps were seen as a "distinct and dangerous class" that had evolved from a "nuisance" to a "menacing nuisance." Commentators suggested a direct link between demobilized soldiers and the homeless men, hobos, and drifters who clogged the nation's roads and railroads. Historian Todd Depastino has argued that during the 1870s, most Americans blamed habits gained in the army for the problem. Many commentators and more than a few soldiers worried that men would not smoothly adapt to peacetime, and the presence of so many tramps less than a decade after the end of the war seemed to prove the point. Civilians might respect soldiers' valor on the battlefield, but they did not admire the "lazy habits of camp-life" developed during the long periods between battles. Nonveterans were especially alarmed by the soldiers' careless disregard for property and social norms, a phenomenon perfected by Sherman's "bummers" during the March to the Sea in 1864. Many observers saw Sherman's troops as a kind of foreshadowing of the tramp army threatening the United States. The presence of so many shiftless, unattached, and potentially dangerous men, some of them clearly veterans, contributed to the taxpayer distrust and veteran resentment that characterized the pension debate.[46]

Not all tramps were veterans, but both groups of men were caught up in the Gilded Age insecurities caused by mass production, labor unrest, mobility, and depression. If Civil War veterans often felt as though they had been left behind by the men who had remained at home, if disability or the lack of education or denial of opportunity excluded veterans from the apparent if illusory affluence of the Gilded Age, then these men shared many of the same traits as itinerant laborers constantly searching for work. Although most tramps took to the road for only a few months or at most a year or two, popular opinion saw them as a permanent underclass in which immigrants were overrepresented and traditional American values such as hard work and reliability were underrepresented. Indeed, ignoring economic realities, editors and politicians blamed the tramps for failing to thrive. If only they would root themselves, shake off their laziness, and commit themselves to becoming productive citizens, they could be woven back into the fabric of American life.[47]

The Reverend John James McCook, a Trinity College professor and pioneering researcher of homelessness as well as a veteran, published a series of articles in the 1890s on the adventures of William Aspinwall, a veteran who had been on the road since the 1860s. Aspinwall differentiated himself from other tramps, who he believed fit the lazy, shiftless stereotype: he was simply an independent soul living out his republican principles. Aspinwall critiqued the industrial system and the wealthy men who controlled it, romanticized himself as a "Gentleman of the Road," and separated his voluntary, nomadic existence from those of the unlucky or lazy men who had no choice but to become desperate "common tramps."[48]

Veterans earned something of a reputation for living off the small-time charity of their friends and neighbors, accepting reduced rates on railroads, free tickets to concerts and circuses, and free drinks in neighborhood saloons. The stereotype was so prevalent that even as fierce a defender of veterans' rights as the *American Tribune* had to admit that "there are too many old soldiers who join the Grand Army for the amount of sponging they can do." Such men "take it for granted that favors belong to them," rarely pitching in to help organize GAR events but eagerly accepting the free meals served at meetings and enjoying the easy credit granted by doctors and merchants. Most poor veterans were honest men, "but there are just enough dead beats to lower to an appreciable degree the standing of comrades in general. They should be repressed with vigor." A week later, the *Tribune* complained about "show comrades," men who only kept up their dues so they could participate in Memorial Day and Fourth of July parades and other big events and thus accept the cheers and admiration of their civilian neighbors. Yet they did not do their part in the hard work of the chapters—serving as officers, visiting sick comrades, or offering relief to poor veterans.[49]

But the anxiety about veteran identity went beyond whether old soldiers or men claiming to be old soldiers were cheating the Pension Bureau, scamming GAR posts, and selling fake subscriptions to magazines. In an age when, despite the many hundreds of thousands of photographs taken of new recruits during the course of the war, most people had no more than one or two pictures of themselves or anyone else, the war had caused a small surge of cases of mistaken or lost identity. These curious stories appeared as tiny articles in newspapers, as short stories and poems, and on a few occasions in court records. They were usually presented as heartwarming tales of adventure, perseverance, and homecoming; sometimes they were cast as sinister attempts by men to join or to defraud families or communities to receive undeserved benefits or recognition.

It is tempting to cover these incidents and concerns with an existentialist template—an upheaval on the scale of the Civil War would inevitably cause victims and victors alike to question their national and personal identities. Americans asked themselves how they fit into the new economy, the new political system, and the new set of assumptions about race and government. At least subconsciously, such concerns shaped the responses of families, towns, and government officials. This apprehension was also an extension of the wartime fear that soldiers who died on the battlefield would not be properly identified. The scale of the war made it impossible to track down every dead soldier, but even more appalling was the mutilation that complicated efforts at identification. Families, the U.S. Sanitary Commission, and eventually the U.S. Army strove to put names to bodies buried in trench graves or found in fields or forests of battle.[50]

The vastness of the war, the frequent absence of men for two or three years, the difficulties of communication, and the enormous number of men killed, wounded, captured, and missing created conditions that could at times lead communities and even family members to question returnees' identities. Indeed, observers feared that war had the power to change men, to wipe out their identity, and to threaten the communities to which they returned.

Several versions of lost identity appeared in postwar popular literature. In a long poem, "The Veteran's Bride," a soldier is reported dead, leaving behind a wife and small daughter. The widow marries a kindly farmer, and the daughter grows to adulthood. The soldier, however, was not killed, but only captured. He subsequently escapes from the Rebels, losing his memory, though, as a consequence of wounds and illness; after his recovery, he remains in the South working on a plantation. Years later, he falls from a horse, bumps his head, and recovers his memory. He goes home, where he finds that the farmer has died. He reestablishes contact with his daughter, and he and his wife eventually remarry.[51]

Even without lost loves, the stories of homecomings by middle-aged men who had last been seen as young men or even boys caught the imagination of Americans for years after the war. That most of the stories contained the improbable coincidences and sudden changes in fortune familiar to readers of Victorian fiction suggests that a certain wariness should be applied to the tales.

Two heavyweight authors offered their particular takes on the genre. Kate Chopin's "A Wizard from Gettysburg" (1894) starts with the teenage son of a once prominent planter family discovering a feeble old man along the side of a road. The boy had been away at boarding school, but the economic depression had forced the family to withdraw him. The mysterious stranger asks if they are in Louisiana and says enigmatically, "I've been in all of them since Gettysburg. Sometimes it was too hot, and sometimes it was too cold; and with that bullet in my head." The boy's grandmother and parents are distracted by their economic crisis and barely notice the old man, who sits quietly in a corner of the veranda. Later, unable to sleep, the youngster reflects on the man's plight: "On that field of battle this man had received a new and tragic birth. For all his existence that went before was a blank to him. There, in the black desolation of war, he was born again, without friends or kindred." A few hints of the inevitable appear: the man calls the boy by his father's name and insists that despite the family's economic troubles, he "must go to school." Increasingly agitated, the tramp drags the teenager out to the orchard and orders him to dig. They eventually find a tin box filled with gold coins. When the boy presents the "wizard" and the treasure to his family, his grandmother nearly faints—it is her long-lost husband who had been believed killed at Gettysburg.[52]

Even Bierce contributed to the genre in his distinctive way. In "A Resumed Identity," he presents a Union officer who suddenly wakes in the middle of an empty road. He watches a silent, ghostly army pass and over the next few hours tries to figure out why the battlefield on which he had been fighting has disappeared. He assumes he has received a glancing blow from a bullet, rendering him unconscious; perhaps he has just awakened from a coma. A doctor in a nearby town is inexplicably surprised to hear that the officer is in his early twenties. He finally finds a battlefield monument indicating that his brigade had fought there many years earlier, and when he peers into pool of clear water and sees the reflection of an old, graying man, he collapses face-first into the water and drowns.[53]

But a number of real-life stories also challenged the public's notions of fiction and reality: The wife of a Georgia soldier is persuaded to leave the South with their three children during the federal occupation; the husband returns to an empty house and has no idea where to find his family. After several years, he obtains a divorce from his missing wife, remarries, and has another child. Somehow learning of the divorce, the first wife also remarries and bears three more children. After both of the second spouses die, the grown children of the first marriage make contact with their father, and following separation of a decade and a half, the man and woman remarry. A man leaves a wife and baby at home to join the 133rd New York, is captured, and is driven insane by hunger and ill treatment at Andersonville. He spends years at various asylums, unaware of his past or his surroundings. He makes a surprising recovery, finds his wife and daughter, and journeys back to Connecticut. A less happy ending awaits a man named Kean who joined the 1st Wisconsin Battery in 1862, leaving behind a wife and child in Milwaukee. Although he survives stints in Libby and Andersonville prisons, he starts drinking and wanders the country. Twenty years later, he finally returns to Milwaukee, where he finds no wife, no child, no house. "I am a poor old wanderer," he tells a policeman, "only a tramp."[54]

Another man remembered his identity only after reading an obituary in a northern newspaper. The man had been discovered in a little coastal town in South Florida, where he compulsively tried to board fishing boats, steamers, or any other vessel heading out to sea. With no memory of his past, he could not explain his mania, and he became a nuisance to the community. After he reached Key West, his insanity subsided, though his memory remained clouded, and he became known as Schooner John. He found he could read and write; he worked hard, made some money, and bought a plantation, having by then acquired the name John Schooner. He also grew to believe he had played some role in the war but could not figure out exactly what it might have been. Years later, he read the obituary of a man killed in an accident in Brooklyn, New York, who had left behind a destitute widow and several children. The widow had had a brother who disappeared during the war, and "she, of all the family, had cherished a faith that he would return." The article "proved to be the touchstone that restored" the man's memory of his life as John B. Hotchkiss, who had been a prisoner of war at Andersonville. He had escaped and worked his way south, looking for a port from which to head north, before apparently falling ill and losing his memory.[55]

No one could blame a seriously wounded man for failing to return home. In some instances, however, long-lost soldiers were not ill or injured but had chosen to take different identities or to stay away from home and family, a phenomenon that enabled communities to doubt the motivations of prodigal soldiers. From time to time, soldiers' papers published requests for information about missing parents, siblings, or children. Although such notices do not necessarily suggest that the soldiers had lost their memories, they certainly indicate such a profound change in the relationship between a man and his family that he cut off contact for many years. A Sheboygan, Wisconsin, soldier who was thought to have been killed turned up seven years after the war in the Sandwich Islands. Another fifteen years went by before he was heard from again; he was then a first mate on a merchant vessel docked in Bombay. One South Carolina man did not hear of his brother for thirty-eight years after he was left in a hospital during the Antietam campaign. A Minnesotan's children sought his whereabouts in 1890, a dozen years after he was discharged from the National Home in Milwaukee.[56]

Yet another story concerned a man from Akron, Ohio, who suddenly reappeared in his hometown late in 1880. According to the *Akron Tribune*, residents thought the man had been interred in a local cemetery for sixteen years, but no one had opened the casket. The soldier admitted that he had read the report of his own funeral and "concluded to let it go at that," although he gave no reason for his actions. He subsequently worked at a variety of occupations, including as a sailor, a clerk, and a trader, in Asia and Europe and "the whole big world." He boasted tattoos all over his body and told an exciting story of nearly being eaten by cannibals. When asked why he had not written to his folks, he responded that they had not written to him. He soon disappeared again.[57]

Although generally reported as credible, these stories of forgotten identities generated disbelief among at least some readers. The *Milwaukee Sunday Telegraph* referred to "those newspaper fellows who devote themselves entirely to writing up 'long losts,' live dead men, poverty stricken counts . . . and all that sort of thing. When a clever newspaper liar wants to make the gullible public swallow his biggest yarn without a grimace he sticks up at the top of it this threadbare saw about . . . 'truth being stranger than fiction.'"[58]

Perhaps the most intense effort to separate truth from fiction unfolded over several years in the 1890s, when a man claiming to be William Newby returned to the little town of McLeansboro in southern Illinois. Newby had been shot in the head at Shiloh, and several comrades in the 40th Illinois recalled burying him on that chaotic battlefield. But other former friends and neighbors positively identified the stranger as Newby. His wife had begun collecting a widow's pension and now lived with a son in Texas. Newby's arrival created a stir, and a number of men and family members who had known him in earlier years visited him in the local poorhouse, where he showed them scars from childhood fights and accidents and answered questions about the family and the community that no stranger could have known. Although he did not look much like people remembered William Newby, such changes could be explained by the passage of twenty-nine years; harsh conditions at Andersonville, where he claimed to have spent some time; and the rough life of a tramp, with frequent stays in poorhouses and jails. His apparent feeblemindedness—he spoke in a disjointed way, often interrupting himself—worked in his favor, seeming to support his claims of hardship and to explain some of the inconsistencies in his account of the past.

The Newby story became the Newby case when, encouraged by friends, Newby applied for a pension. Because he had never been mustered out of the army, he was owed not only disability but also back pay, a sum totaling ten thousand dollars. The Pension Bureau, already under pressure from the Democratic Party, which was gearing up to use pensions as an issue in the 1892 election, decided to investigate. William Newby's wife, Fereby, returned to Illinois and immediately identified the man as her husband. Flocks of friends and neighbors visited the farm, a birthday party was held, and the GAR post invited Newby to tell his story. Some doubts remained, but most residents and the first agent sent by the Pension Bureau to check Newby's claim believed Fereby Newby. However, the story unraveled after two witnesses abruptly changed their testimony. Another pension agent interviewed dozens more people and developed a theory that "Newby" and some of the witnesses had concocted a plan to obtain a fraudulent pension. The agent believed that the impostor had met one of the Newby brothers in a Mt. Vernon poorhouse, where he learned enough about the family to hatch the plan. The conspiracy eventually grew to include McLeansboro residents and Fereby Newby. The claim was then denied.

With Cleveland's reelection to the presidency in 1892, the appointment of a new pension commissioner less inclined to spend the national surplus on pensions, and a Democrat-controlled local board of pension examiners, the Newby case became a centerpiece of the administration's tough new policy on pension fraud. Yet another investigator came to believe that "Newby" was actually "Rickety Dan" Benton, a southern Illinois native who had grown up in Tennessee. Benton had lived a listless and careless existence during the years since the Civil War, and in June 1893, he was indicted for pension fraud.

The case went to trial, transcending the tribulations of one tired, rather confused old man. According to historian Stuart McConnell, both sides sought to "fill this essentially blank slate"—everyone agreed that "Newby" did not have a strong grip on reality—"with a culturally compelling narrative." Republicans and Democrats turned the trial into fights over wartime loyalty (the presiding judge was an infamous Copperhead), the government's duty to provide pensions versus fears of the spreading tendrils of big government, and the clash between fraudulent tramps and deserving returned soldiers. That "Newby" claimed to have been incarcerated at

Andersonville provided yet another context, since no set of veterans was believed to be more deserving of federal aid than the men who had survived Confederate prisons. The trial was held in Springfield, the state capital, and the government and the defense called a total of more than two hundred witnesses over three weeks. The GAR helped the defendant with cash and by arranging a speaking tour by "Newby" and the publication of a supportive book by C. J. George, *William Newby: The Soldier's Return: A True and Wonderful Story of Mistaken Identity* (the mistake being the identification of the man as Dan Benton).

The jury took only nineteen minutes to return a guilty verdict, and Newby/Benton served two years in prison. But neither he nor his wife ever recanted their stories even though they never lived together again and even though Fereby Newby was denied a renewal of her widow's pension partly because she refused to testify that her husband was dead. Newby/Benton lived for more than a decade longer, apparently dying in a poorhouse in Georgia.[59]

The Newby case was a spectacular example of a question that nagged Americans: Could the men who claimed to be heroes or even veterans be trusted? "An old broken down Confederate Soldier" wrote to the administrator of the Robert E. Lee Camp Confederate Soldiers' Home offering assurances that he would bring "proof to show you that I am no imposter."[60]

Incidents such as the Newby case as well as the generalized anxiety over the scope and purposes of the pension system helped to construct an alternative version of the returned soldier that all but obscured his heroism by focusing on his opportunistic demands for greater, unprecedented benefits from the country he had served. Although most Americans did not share this view of veterans, the fact that attacks on "pension sharks" and "coffee-coolers" explicitly criticized all veterans—including honest pensioners and loyal GAR men—simply for associating with their less savory comrades caused veterans and their organizations to counterattack.

A Distinction with a Difference

Veterans' organizations also worried about men claiming falsely to have served—the Kansas legislature made it illegal for nonmembers to wear a GAR or Loyal Legion badge—but tended to support any man claiming to be an old soldier. And these groups struck back at their critics with a vengeance, challenging the moral authority of men too timid or too young to have served and concluding that pensions were, as one veteran stated, "an *obligation*," not a "*gratuity*." In so doing, veterans' organizations not only made the pension issue one of the most divisive topics of the era but promoted a theory of government responsibility and individual entitlement unprecedented in American history.[61]

Veterans and their allies used as their main avenue of counterattack the pages of the dozen or more "soldiers' papers" published around the country in the decades after the war. Supporters emphasized the old soldiers' sacrifices, reminding the nation of its appropriate expressions of gratitude immediately after the war and attacking Democratic pension opponents as "Copperheads." Responding to a typically virulent attack by *Puck*, one veterans' paper declared, "Any school boy can correctly caricature Puck. All he has to do is draw a long circular line, put a flat head on it with a forked tongue sticking out of the mouth, and daub the head a coppery color. That's *Puck*, and a favorite lurking place of the slimy creature is around the pension office, ready to strike any maimed and dependent soldier who comes there seeking relief."[62]

Perhaps veterans' strongest argument in the debate over who could best define loyalty, manhood, and gratitude was that they had seen combat. This approach was rather circular—because we have served, we are best able to judge how to reward those who have served—but nevertheless remained a constant theme in veterans' writings. As one supporter admitted, any large body of men would contain "a certain percentage of badness." Even civilian organizations devoted to fraternity and peace had bad apples, as when "the society for the prevention of cruelty finds its secretary whipping his wife." But despite the inevitable presence among a million men of examples of cruelty and bad character, "no such other aggregate of men was ever seen on the earth as composed the Union army." A quarter century later, however, enemies "assail . . . their characters, attempt . . . to mar the glory of their work and record, [and] cast . . . an innuendo against the purity and nobility of their motives."[63]

According to the *National Tribune*, suggestions that "the substitutes and bounty-jumpers form the bulk of the veterans, and the men who left their homes from pure patriotism, and sacrificed everything to save the country are so few as to be hardly worth considering" were "mean and cowardly slander, and the men who utter it are the ones who, if old enough to bear arms during the war, were poltroons who did not dare go where they would hear a cap burst. They are the sneaks who at the first mention of a draft perjured themselves as to their bodily condition, or begged foreign protection, or sneaked off to Canada." The stereotype that Canada offered a haven for draft dodgers appeared in a ditty published just after the war. Sarcastically using the same title as the popular sentimental song, "Mother, Is the Battle Over?" the parody shifted the point of view from a young boy waiting to learn if his father had survived a recent battle to a young man who had escaped conscription by hiding in Canada.

I've been so long, in Canada,
I long to get away!
They say the war is ended,
Indeed I hope 'tis so,
You know I love my country well,
But the "Drafting" made me go.[64]

"There is not power enough in this nation nor on the earth to effectually rebuke the veterans," thundered the *Soldiers' Tribune* in late 1887. And that power flowed directly from the moral high ground veterans occupied: they had fought and bled for their country. This version of the "bloody shirt" was simple, direct, and devastating: How dare noncombatants, even those who had been too young or were not yet born while the war raged, challenge the rights of disabled and elderly veterans to the pittance of a pension offered by the government? "All the soldier haters," wrote a veteran of the 4th Michigan to the *American Tribune*, should "be placed in line armed as for war, with the same number of Johnny Rebs in their immediate front . . . as at Gettysburg," with old soldiers armed with bayonets stationed behind as file closers. "Now the battle begins. . . . [O]bserve the weakening knees, listen to the abject howl of these valorous home heroes. . . . They would need no stronger cathartic for a sluggish digestion. . . . What a spectacle! These home braves cringing before these abused and hated old veterans." A similar refrain appeared in a letter from a Kansas veteran who declared, "If the men who denounce us as the offscourings of the earth could have had the courage to face death on the battle field, they would sing a different tune." He continued, "When there is no danger they have brave hearts, but in the hour of the country's need, they had cowardly legs." Such cowards now praised bondholders whose only contribution was to loan money to the government at a profit: "Their bonds would not have been worth any more than Confederate script [*sic*], if they had not the seal of patriotic blood upon them."[65]

Grover Cleveland, the only Democrat and the only non–Civil War veteran to serve as president between 1869 and 1901 and an inveterate critic of expanding the pension system, served as a lightning rod for veterans' contempt. One old soldier, Henry Gibson, lashed out at Cleveland in particular and Democrats in general in a speech delivered in the U.S. House of Representatives in the spring of 1900. Gibson had spent two years as a commissary officer in the Union Army before attending law school and becoming a carpetbagger in East Tennessee. Unlike many other northerners who moved South, however, Gibson stayed, working as a lawyer and filling a number of appointed positions, including a post as an agent for the U.S. Pension Bureau. A Republican, he served five terms in Congress beginning in 1895, and during the campaign of 1900, a rematch between William McKinley and William Jennings Bryan, Gibson vented about the last Democratic administration. Cleveland had come "into power breathing threatenings and slaughter against the pensioners" and claiming that "thousands of neighborhoods had their well-known fraudulent pensioners." Yet three years later, such claims had proven "false, slanderous, and scandalous." Postmasters appointed by Democrats had acted as "spies, scouts, and guides," and the government had encouraged friends and neighbors to turn in suspected frauds. "Every device that partisan prejudice or personal malice could invent was resorted to," Gibson declared, and in a reference to a brand-new medical technology only barely understood early in the 1890s, he claimed that "the records of 970,000 pensioners were searched as with X-rays." Gibson compared the attempts to cull the pension rolls to the "massacre of the innocents by the bloody Herod" and claimed that only thirty-nine cases of fraud had been discovered.[66]

Veterans took special delight in criticizing Cleveland's decision to hire a substitute rather than submit to conscription. *Judge* magazine, founded by refugees from *Puck* and not coincidentally allied with the Republican Party, helped with a pair of cartoons during the 1892 election. A full-color, two-page illustration, "Their War-Records Contrasted," showed a rotund Cleveland enjoying a beer in a Buffalo Beer Garden and his running mate, Adlai Stevenson, delivering an anti-Lincoln speech in 1864, while their substitutes—one too fat to be an effective soldier, the other too old—march off to war. The other panel of the cartoon shows their Republican rivals, President Benjamin Harrison and his vice presidential candidate, Whitelaw Reid, in valiant poses as an officer and as a frontline war correspondent. Later in the campaign, a *Judge* cartoon featured the Democratic candidates in ragged attire, much like the tramps that some veterans supposedly had become, being turned away when they try to enlist. The recruiting agent, dressed as Uncle Sam, gestures toward the highly decorated Harrison and the uniformed Reid and says, "I do not need your services. These two gentlemen will go to Washington as your SUBSTITUTES!" In 1887, about midway through Cleveland's first term, the *Ohio Soldier* reported that the man who allegedly had served as Cleveland's substitute had died in the soldiers' home in Bath, New York, of consumption he had contracted in the army. The Polish immigrant had been paid $150 at the time of his mustering-in (when, claimed the *Ohio Soldier*, the typical amount was $500), with the promise of more to come if he survived the war. He never saw another dime, never received a pension, and had spent time in a poorhouse prior to entering the soldiers' home.[67]

Veterans' counterattack against "soldier-haters" involved other elements as well. Veterans customarily—and in some federal and state government positions legally—received employment preferences, reflecting the argument that veterans had lost valuable time during which they could have earned money or learned trades. This position first appeared immediately after the war, when soldiers arriving home faced unsure prospects, an uneasy sense that they were no longer fit for civilian life, and the feeling that life had passed them by. An 1895 history of the GAR suggested that soldiers had saved the Union and preserved the "business life" of the nation but had returned to find "another hand busy at their loom, and another web prosperously progressing where they had hoped to resume their own." Boys too young to fight had grown into strong men eager to work; "able-bodied 'stay-at-homes' had comfortably grown fat on the unprecedented business opportunities growing out of the necessity for maintaining an army." Although soldiers "had imagined a future filled with the peaceable fruits of loyal devotion," they realized they had to look out for themselves, too.[68]

Recent research has suggested some merit to the assertion that veterans had indeed lost economic ground to their peers. Residents of Dubuque, Iowa, who served and then returned to the city tended to remain in the generally low-paying occupations in which they had worked before the war, whereas those who did not join the military proved more likely to rise along the occupational ladder. Russell L. Johnson has argued that spending several years as tiny cogs in the giant military machine made veterans more content with limited economic opportunity than were their civilian counterparts. Economist Chulhee Lee has shown that Union veterans who were wounded or suffered from chronic illnesses and even those who had simply experienced combat had less economic and geographic mobility than nonveterans or uninjured veterans.[69]

Many entrepreneurs had made fortunes during the war, and veterans saved their most bitter denunciations for men who had not served in the war but had profited from it. Just as the image of the Union veteran as a tramp became a stereotype for some observers, the civilian who became wealthy while less fortunate and more patriotic men did their duty became a stereotype in veterans' circles. The image cropped up almost immediately after the war. A poem by a veteran of the 14th U.S. Infantry in the *Soldier's Friend* lauded the loyal soldier who had gone off to war, leaving behind classmates and friends who thought him foolish for risking his life and well-being for principle. Now, disabled but with his mission accomplished, the soldier returns home and asks about his friends, who have become doctors, lawyers, and successful businessmen. "All are far above him now, for the soldier boy has fell / Below the circle in which he moved." In the same year, a song inscribed "To the People of the South" and titled "Why Can We Not Be Brothers; or, We Know That We Were Rebels" offered reconciliation to defeated Confederates but attacked

> the coward band,
> Who in the conflict dire,
> Went not to battle for their cause,
> 'Mid the ranks of steel and fire,
> Yet now since all the fighting's done
> Are hourly heard to cry
> Down with the traitors, hang them all!
> Each rebel dog shall die.[70]

"Almost every day," declared a magazine a year after the war, "we see men in the honored livery of their country, with that eloquent token of their patriotism, an empty, looped-up sleeve, forced to grind hand-organs and beat tambourines on the street corners for a few paltry pennies." Conversely, throughout the country, post offices, customs buildings, and other federal agencies housed "fat, sleek and hearty men and boys, who never heard a hostile gun, or the whistle of a bullet, but who took care to keep their precious bodies at home, occupying places as clerks, messengers, porters, and the like, to the exclusion of the men who have saved the country." The article praised the southern states' "determination" to give veterans "the preference above all others." A few years later, a two-panel cartoon revolving around a typical nineteenth-century pun called "A Distinction with a Difference" appeared in *Punchinello*, a short-lived humor magazine published in New York. The drawing contrasted "Heroes of the War"—a one-legged soldier and one-armed soldier, dressed neatly but begging on the street—with a portly, unpleasant-looking, ostentatiously dressed man with walking stick and pinky ring standing before a sign advertising "shoddy" clothing. The caption read, "He Rose by the War."[71]

The refrain persisted throughout the Gilded Age. "As time passes we grow more impatient with the grudging objections which many are so ready to make whenever some material benefit is bestowed on an ex-soldier for the reason that he was a soldier," complained an 1885 article in the *Milwaukee Sunday Telegraph*. All soldiers carried some physical "memory" of the war, whether a chronic disease, a scar from a wound, or a searing recollection of horror. But an equally long-lasting effect of the war was the devastation it wrought on men's economic prospects. Few soldiers could save money while in the army, which "consumed . . . four years of [their] business life," while the soldiers' friends "had had great business opportunities; fortune had knelt at their feet." But when veterans limped home, they "found the choice places occupied; the strategic points strongly entrenched." A soldier "could not well ask any one to step down and out that he might step up and in." Many soldiers nevertheless succeeded, but some lost "their grip in the weary campaigning and falling down and down, even to the depths of tramp-hood." And whatever had been done for the soldier, "the debt has not been so fully paid that we can hear the sharp and thoughtless criticism often made when some ex-soldier had received a pension from the government, or a civil office . . . without being angered by its free and ready injustice."[72]

The image of veterans suffering economically as a consequence of their patriotism was powerful enough to be noticed by fiction writers. A pro-GAR novel that appeared in 1871, just as the society's first iteration was beginning to wind down, offered all the stock characters of a wartime and immediate postwar melodrama. Daniel Garvin is the evil half-brother of Allen Paige, a dead veteran whose family is now living in poverty because of Garvin's treachery. Garvin represents the archetypal civilian who lets others do the fighting while he grows rich—an atheist, a profiteer, and a cotton specula-tor. On a wider level, the society in which the drama unfolds deeply mis-trusts returned veterans and all but ignores them. Nevertheless, a band of noble Christians led by a character known only as the Veteran comes to the rescue of Paige's widow. Along the way the motto of the GAR and one of the novel's many subtitles—"Fraternity, Charity, and Loyalty"—is represented as the best possible combination of virtues and the inevitable product of the old soldiers banding together as comrades. The Paige family's fortune is re-stored, the veterans' reputations are redeemed, and Garvin commits suicide when his fraud and deceit are revealed.[73]

William Dean Howells's *The Rise of Silas Lapham*, published in 1884 during the period of the most intense debates over pensions and prefer-ence, turns on its head the notion that soldiers missed out on opportunities to improve themselves. Lapham, a veteran who carries a bullet in his leg from Gettysburg and who attends army reunions, has done very well with his paint business after the war. He also believes that the war has hardened young men who previously were interested only in frivolity and girls. Howells sometimes downplays the value of the veteran experience when other characters, themselves combat veterans, suggest that the sallow young men sitting at the club could become heroes or even that nonmortal crises could inspire a similar spark of heroism. But even though most of the people who come to know Lapham admire him as a shrewd businessman, Howells clearly presents Lapham as more than simply a rags-to-riches success story; his rise after the war reflected the same values and "moral seriousness" as did his wartime dutifulness.[74]

But a more balanced presentation of the ways in which a veteran in either section might feel held back by his war experiences appears in "Decoration Day," by Sarah Orne Jewett. Known for her elegant stories of country manners and local color, Jewett begins this tale with three old soldiers talking about crops and the weather. Their conversation soon shifts to the community's apparent lack of interest in commemorating Decoration Day. A nearby town had held a procession, but their little village had barely noticed the occasion for several years. The men move on to discuss brothers and friends who died in or after the war: one had never quite managed to fit back into society and had taken to drinking, while several others were buried in the paupers' graveyard. All had had a tough time recovering after their return. "I don't know why 'twas we were so beat out," one shrugs. The ground-down young men just back from the war had struggled, and the community noticed but took the wrong lesson. "The fellows that staid at home got all the fat places, an' when we come back we felt dreadful behind the times," one man grumbles. "They begun to call us hero an' stick-in-the-mud just about the same time," says another.[75]

An Absolute Necessity

Although it was never as controversial as pensions, the policy of veterans' preference was directly related to the theory that veterans had missed their chance to benefit from the booming wartime economy. Like pensions, preference was a new concept for Americans. Prior to the Civil War, no formal veterans' preference statutes existed. Former army officers, but rarely rank-and-file members of the military, were often appointed as collectors of customs, surveyors, internal revenue officers, and other patronage positions in the federal government. Congress established the first law formally establishing a preference system for all soldiers just as the war was winding down. The measure said that "persons honorably discharged from the military or naval service by reason of disability resulting from wounds or sickness incurred in the line of duty" would have preference for civil offices, provided they had the "business capacity" necessary for discharging the duties of those offices. As civil service reform seeped into the federal appointment process, veterans' preference was upheld by interpretations of the law by successive attorney generals. At first, disabled veterans had preference if their qualifications were equal to those of other candidates for positions; later, when civil service examinations led to a ratings system, disabled veterans were moved to the tops of lists of possible appointees if they received a rating of sixty-five, although a passing mark for nonveterans was seventy. Finally, an 1876 law gave veterans, war widows, and orphans preference when an executive branch agency reduced its workforce, provided that these persons possessed qualifications equal to those of other employees.[76]

Veterans' preference preceded the pension issue in the minds of returning Union soldiers. According to one of the first histories of the GAR, veteran "clubs" were formed in the closing weeks of and immediately after the war largely because men were disappointed to discover that they had been mistaken in their assumption that soldiers with good records or who were wounded or disabled "should be entitled to consideration in the distribution of offices under the local, State, or national governments." Although the idea sounded "prettily" in editorials and speeches encouraging men to enlist, it ran into "practical politics" and "entrenched politicians" unwilling to give up their places for "merely sentimental whims." Thus veterans found it "an absolute necessity" to organize into groups to promote "the advancement of soldiers and sailors in and to positions of trust and emolument."[77]

Pensions and preference came together in the early 1890s when President Cleveland's new commissioner of pensions not only established a Board of Revisions that led to the reduction or elimination of pensions for fifty thousand disabled soldiers but also fired, "without cause or reason," about sixty old soldiers, many apparently "maimed," according to the *American Tribune*. Such actions led at least some veterans to mobilize on behalf of their unemployed comrades. The Union Veterans' Union, greatly overshadowed by the GAR on most issues, stated among its goals and purposes a provision for obtaining preferential treatment for veterans. A 1903 flyer issued by the commander of the Union's Illinois Division declared that the group was "fighting for our political rights, for our recognition at the hands of those who control the politics of the country, and who have relegated you to the rear and regard you as a 'back number' when it comes to appointments to positions." Old soldiers were just "as capable" of filling government jobs "as the young men who were not born when you were suffering and sacrificing so much to preserve this Government from disruption." Without those sacrifices, "those who are now preventing you from enjoying some of the fruits of your four years of agony, would yet be living under a foreign flag and be ignorant of the blessings of liberty." "Stand by your rights and fight for them," the commander thundered; "You want bread more than bouquets and this is the way to get it."[78]

Even the patriotic quarterly magazine *Acme Haversack*, which usually printed good-natured and sentimental songs, poems, and anecdotes, published a surprisingly bitter poem by the wife of legless pension commissioner "Corporal" James Tanner that challenged the prevailing shift toward civil service in government. "Heroic Service, or Civil Service: Shall Faithful Soldiers or Delving Book Worms Be Promoted?" said a great deal about veterans' attitudes toward those who had not fought.[79]

On a more practical level, the minutes of the St. Paul "regiment" of the Union Veterans' Union are filled with discussions and resolutions related to veterans' preference. Job issues appear in the minutes nearly two dozen times between 1897 and 1904, the most frequent entry in the records of the biweekly meetings. Some of the entries were simply a matter of one comrade recommending another for a job, but the organization also appointed a standing employment committee; sent a resolution to the secretary of war regarding the hiring of civilian and regular army veterans at the army headquarters at Fort Snelling; communicated with the local postmaster, the mayor, the city's school board, and the president of the public works system regarding the candidacy of specific veterans; and sent a resolution to the Civil Service Commission seeking a revision of new regulations regarding veterans and the civil service exam. On several occasions, committees were appointed to call on the mayor and other public officials about the applications of specific men for specific jobs, down to the level of custodian at the post office. The St. Paul UVU's resolution to the secretary of war accused the Civil Service Commission of "depriving and debasing the old soldiers and creating places for life for those who sought the disruption and overthrow of this nation." They implored the secretary to take up this issue "with such attention as in your wisdom you deem proper, and to the best interest of a large number of most worthy men who have been ignored and deprived the rights a Republic should grant to brave & loyal freemen." The *Relief Guard*, published by the St. Paul UVU, also acted as an employment agency by keeping a list of unemployed veterans and veterans' widows and publishing their occupations. (Successful placements were also noted.) The desired jobs included steamboat pilot and janitor, watchman and clerk, lumber sorter and "business man," teamster and "wash and scrub" woman. "These are men and women that are in want of daily bread, that cannot get work and are really in need of help," the *Relief Guard* told its readers. "They are willing to work but cannot labor hard but can do light work, and we think that the people should apply here and give these worthy citizens their patronage."[80]

The search for jobs became a kind of military campaign pitting deserving soldiers against ignorant and uncaring civilians. The *Relief Guard* upped the rhetorical decibel level when it moved from the common belief that veterans had been denied jobs *despite* their service to the suggestion that they were being denied jobs *because* they had been soldiers. "Right smart get, double quick into line and join the rest of your comrades in the Veterans Union," trumpeted the *Guard*, "and let us have a Grand Organization of every old soldier in this city, and we will not go hungry and wonder [*sic*] around the streets looking for work and be refused it because we are old soldiers. Let us stand together, and if we must starve let us starve together, and the disgrace that will accrue to an ungrateful people will be a just retribution."[81]

Although the GAR was somewhat less single-minded in its drive to obtain jobs for veterans, an 1884 pamphlet outlined some of the efforts by the twenty-two posts of the Brooklyn GAR on behalf of veterans. In addition to offering free aid for veterans who believed they might be eligible for pensions, the GAR posts had established a bureau of employment that tried to connect veterans with jobs and lobbied local businesses and government officials to hire veterans. The pamphlet contained testimonials from employers of old soldiers (including the newly opened Brooklyn Bridge), remarks by local veterans (including the one-armed postmaster), and an acknowledgment that many civilians believed that "all soldiers were of a doubtful character" because of the many instances of street begging and other poor representations of veterans. The Bureau of Employment would help deserving men get off the streets. Moreover, the brochure argued that "where the qualifications are equal, and the choice is to be made between a veteran of the war, and one who has not served, we ask that the place shall be given to the soldier or sailor."[82]

Nearly thirty years after the war, the *Ohio Soldier* commented on the perception that the young men seeking positions in government were impatiently waiting for the old soldiers to "get out of the way of the rising gen-eration" and hoping that the preference law would be repealed. Young men seemed to be asking, "Will they never die?" The *Ohio Soldier* roared back: "Half a million died when you were in your cradle. . . . Many thousands of them died in prison or in rebel hospitals," while "many other thousands of them to-day hobble on crutches or flap empty sleeves." Ambitious young men needed to be patient—the veterans "are dying fast enough"—and they should never forget that "but for them there would be no government for you to serve, nor to protect you." The old soldiers "are marching off the field, and they will soon, all too soon for me, be out of your ungrateful way, God bless them." "Their deeds are blazoned upon the history of more fields than your weak brain can remember. They will soon be out of the way; but while they are here the republic will give them the preference."[83]

Their Pensions Shall Be Paid in Full

Drew Gilpin Faust has argued that the United States accepted certain re-sponsibilities when it "mandated the obligation of the citizen to fight" in its defense: "Citizenship represented a contract in which the state and the individual both assumed certain rights and duties, for which either could be called to account." The reinterment and identification of scores of thou-sands of dead Union soldiers was one way in which the government fulfilled its part of the bargain.[84]

But Union veterans came to understand that contract in much larger terms than getting a decent burial. Despite opposition, they, like their Con-federate counterparts, persuaded state and federal governments to take their issues seriously. Federal homes and pensions cared for most Union soldiers, and by the early twentieth century, virtually all northern states and most southern states had at least one home for disabled or elderly sol-diers; many of these establishments included housing for veterans' wives and widows. A few northern states also offered pensions; most also paid for veterans' burials (and in a few instances made it illegal to bury a veteran in a potter's field), offered exemptions from property taxes up to one thousand dollars (or more in one or two states) and from poll taxes, provided for the care of veterans through county property taxes, and prevented veterans and their families from being cared for in county institutions (poor veterans were to be provided with relief in their own homes, not in almshouses). A number of states set aside rooms in state capitol buildings for GAR headquar-ters, while many mandated that local governments would provide funding for respectable Memorial Day celebrations. Rhode Island took on the responsibility of prosecuting all claims for pensions and bounties (to relieve claims against the state), while Vermont offered free hospital care for all veterans, Colorado excused veterans applying for state jobs from taking the civil service examination, and New Jersey exempted ex-soldiers and sailors and their widows from most state taxes.[85]

Pensions apparently had a positive effect on the lives of recipients. In 1900 and 1910, according to Dora Costa, the only significant statistical difference between Civil War veterans and nonveteran white males was the fact that the veterans were more likely to be retired and to be heads of households. The pension system clearly had eased their way to independent retirement. In some ways, the Civil War pension system foreshadowed the social security system created in the 1930s. Despite widespread criticism of the pension, including the alleged corruption within and politicization of the system, reformers during the first two decades of the twentieth century frequently held Civil War pensions up as models for old-age pensions.[86]

Veterans had come a long way since the end of the war, when the *Soldier's Friend* warned them not to "arrogate to themselves some *special* distinction for what they have done" or to "suppose themselves worthy of *special* reward." The *Friend* recognized that some soldiers had received higher enlistment bounties than other volunteers, and the war had wreaked greater havoc on some survivors than others. But veterans must resist "putting themselves in the position of those who would drive a hard bargain with the country for the part which they were proud to take in her defence, in defence of all that made her dear, precious and sacred." The article, tellingly called "Plain Talk with Our Returned Volunteers," also urged veterans to recognize that not all patriots served in the army and not all sacrifices were made by soldiers: "What self-respecting man who has served as a soldier would not be ashamed to make out a bill against his country for additional compensation beyond what he had bargained for at the onset?"[87]

A quite different attitude about duty and gratitude emerged in a poem published nearly a quarter of a century later and set to the tune of "Marching through Georgia." The author laid out the veterans' basic position on the pension issue:

When peril came through deadly foes who tried to crush our land.
The nation saw there must be raised a mighty soldier band,
And so they said, "We'll care for you, if in the breach you'll stand,
Oh! save the Flag of Liberty!"

Chorus: Hurrah! Hurrah! To promises be true!
Hurrah! Hurrah! give veterans their due!
It's small enough the nation votes to martyrs saving you,
Now be their pensions paid full![88]

A couple of years later, a much more elaborate description of the contract that had been arranged between veterans and their government came from the pen of Green B. Raum, a former congressman and brigadier general who was halfway through his four-year term as U.S. commissioner of pensions. "All civilized nations have for centuries granted pensions in some form to the soldiers who fought in their great wars," he declared in "Pensions and Patriotism," published in the *North American Review*. Raum argued that a generous pension system reflected "the fact that the noblest duty a man can perform is to risk his life for his country" and that all citizens shared an obligation "to make suitable provision for the men who have fought under the national flag, and for their widows, orphans, and dependent parents." Pensions were a necessary part of national defense, helping to inspire patriotic men to take the risks needed to defend their country because they knew that they would be cared for if they were disabled and that if they died, their families would be cared for. Raum outlined three "well-defined grounds upon which pension laws and other beneficial legislation for soldiers rest: first, to stimulate the spirit of patriotism . . . by honouring the love of country exhibited by the soldiers; second, a recognition that the monthly pay of the soldier was not a suitable equivalent for the services rendered; third, a broad sentiment of gratitude upon the part of the people to men who have died in defence of their country and to those who have risked health and life under the flag." To Raum and to the Republicans who promoted liberal pensions, such federal generosity was not "prompted simply by a spirit of almsgiving." Rather, building federal soldiers' homes and extending federal pensions "were prompted by patriotism, justice, and gratitude—to bestow benefactions on the living, benedictions on the dead."

Raum spent several pages explaining the problem faced by hundreds of thousands of men: although they had seen hard service, suffered from various maladies and injuries, and gone home weaker than they had left, they were not technically disabled. Twenty years of pension examinations revealed that many men whose energy and health had steadily dissipated since leaving the army could not directly tie their disabilities to their military service. Yet they suffered from poverty and from high mortality rates— Raum estimated that two out of seven survivors of the war had already died and that perhaps six hundred thousand had "lost at least twelve years of the usual expectation of life." Many others were physically incapable of doing the manual labor expected of most American men and consequently were mired in desperate poverty.

"The men who fought to save the Union," Raum assured his readers, "were not mercenaries. They did not preserve this country for the purpose of looting its treasury." Moreover, their pride would not allow them to receive unwarranted charity: "They feel that an old soldier can receive a pension as a recognition of honorable service with a feeling of pride, while he would turn his back with shame upon an offer of charity." No new taxes would be required to pay these pensions; the U.S. government's fiscal situation was solid. The public debt had dropped from more than sixty dollars per American in 1865 to less than ten dollars. The country's population was soaring, its economic power was multiplying, and its institutions had become the envy of the world. And Americans needed to understand that these developments resulted in large measure from the men who now received pensions of a few dollars a month: "The generation of people who have come upon the stage of action since the war closed should understand that the blessings of peace and prosperity now enjoyed by the people of the United States are due to the patriotism and valor of the soldiers of the Union."[89]

DESPITE PENSIONS, EFFORTS TO PROVIDE employment, and the building of literally dozens of soldiers' homes, Union veterans shared the sentiments expressed by the commander of an Ohio GAR post in 1888: "The world is too busy to care for the old soldier. He has had his day of glory. Those who are coming in our places know nothing of war, and neither should they want to know, nor should we want them to know." Civilians may "think they honor and respect the soldier, and no doubt do so as far as the rush and whirl of a selfish world will allow." But ultimately, "like the old musket and the sword father and brother brought home, battered and rusted from the war," veterans "are becoming curious relics of the past, worthy to be remembered for our history." Veterans had become a major cultural, political, and economic force during the Gilded Age. But the partisan attacks on the programs created for their benefit did not distinguish between deserving and undeserving veterans and represented an important step in the process of the separation of veterans and civilians in Gilded Age America.[90]

chapter six **Sad, Unnatural Shows of War**

VETERANS' IDENTITY AND DISTINCTIVENESS

Less than two years after the Civil War ended, the *New York Times* noted that the "heroic generation" that had won the war already "seems to be gathered away from life. It is the universal experience of history that almost before a nation has made ready to do justice to its heroes, the most of them are gone." But more than 1.8 million veterans were still living—more than 5 percent of the country's population. As Susan-Mary Grant remarks, "The paper's anticipation of the eventual disappearance of the 'race of heroes' at a time when most of the heroes in question were still young men highlighted the ambiguity attendant on the return of the citizen-soldiers of the Union from war." A decade later, the editor of a soldiers' newspaper expressed frustration common among northern veterans: the public's disinterest in the veteran. "He is dead. Or lost. Strayed or stolen, possibly. We do not know where he is, but he is not here. He has gone away to some place. Perhaps he has ceased to be necessary." Although he "occasionally . . . appears on the pension list, with one leg, a wife and seven children and $8 a month," not much was known about him. He never ran for office; perhaps he had moved out west, "where the Indians could get at [him] more easily." There used to be many soldiers, the editor wrote with mournful sarcasm, and they were important in a number of ways. One had to have one hundred men to be commissioned a line officer and a thousand to become a field officer. "They dug trenches, they constructed long lines of breastworks, and then, when an enemy came in sight, they climbed over them and went outside of them to fight." Indeed, "some historians have even gone so far as to maintain that without them the war could hardly have been carried to a successful termination. They were really quite useful." But "now they are all gone. It seems sad, looking back at the war, that none but the Generals, and Colonels, and Majors . . . should have survived its dreadful ravages." Some are now in business or teaching or farming, "but all the same they are all gone, and its [sic] seems dreadful lonesome without them. There used to be so many of them."[1]

Another decade later, after the rebirth of the Grand Army of the Republic (GAR) and the huge growth in publications aimed at telling the stories of Civil War soldiers, the *Soldiers' Tribune* perceived a prevailing attitude that veterans should recognize that the "war is over" and get on with their lives. To such people, the *Tribune* posed several questions: "Have the four hundred thousand Union soldiers who 'died that our nation might live,' been restored to life and health, and home and happiness? Has the weeping mother who sent her darling and only son to defend the flag had him safely returned to her? Have the dependent and orphaned children whose brave father was miserably starved to death in Andersonville prison pen, again been given his fostering love and care? Have any of our one-legged comrades who have been hobbling about these twenty years or more, felt . . . a new growth of the limb that they left on the battlefield at Gettysburg?" Veterans had every right to remember the war, the *Tribune* declared, to remind the nation of their sacrifices, and "to urge their just and legal claims upon the attention of even the great and powerful democratic party."[2]

The relationship between veterans and their communities was very different in the South, but Confederate veterans also struggled to define themselves and to find productive ways to make their experiences relevant. "A 'Confederate Veteran' was not a fact before the war," the historian of the Fulton County, Georgia, Confederate Veterans' Association pointed out in 1890. "We frequently hear of things which existed 'before the war.' Some people were rich before the war. Some people were slaves before the war. . . . There were governors, senators, judges and 'militia majors,' but never a 'Confederate Veteran' before the war. A Confederate Veteran is to-day a unique figure in life, and will ever be unique in history." The narrative went on to describe in effusive detail the nobility and originality of the Confederate Veteran, but the author made his main point early on: "Nothing else, and nobody else on earth to-day [is] like a Confederate Veteran."[3]

These rather defensive comments indicate the degree to which veterans felt the need to turn to other old soldiers for respect and support. These men continued to rely on the cohesion that developed among soldiers, on the relationships and communities they forged in camp and on the battlefield. In combat, those soldiers' networks, which clearly separated military men from civilians, could overcome a man's urge to flee or fuel survival in a ghastly prison camp. And such networks remained a way that soldiers identified and separated themselves from civilians after the war. In the late 1860s, several northern states attempted to distinguish between men who had served honorably and those who had not by disfranchising men convicted of or in some cases simply charged with desertion, but not all of the laws were enforced, and a few were struck down by the courts. Moreover, as Dora L. Costa and Matthew E. Kahn have discovered, although deserters were more likely than nondeserters to move away from their homes after the war, the former did not play a significant role in postwar memory. It is not surprising that deserters failed to write memoirs explaining their actions, but it is somewhat more surprising how quickly they receded from virtually everyone's memory during the Gilded Age. In the end, simply having been a soldier was more important than having been a good soldier. Indeed, the veterans' ethos depended on it.[4]

George M. Fredrickson has argued that the separation between soldiers and civilians grew as the former gathered more experiences that the latter would never acquire. For example, the Lowells, the Cabots, and the Shaws, men who came out of the northern elite with abolitionist principles firing their patriotism, came to realize that the war was more complicated than their boyish sensibilities, which civilian adults still maintained, could fathom. The experiences of combat, of occupying the South, and of meeting contraband slaves had hardened these men and made them realize that principles alone could not sustain their commitment to finish the job they had started. War was very different than they had imagined, and they believed that they were the only Americans to comprehend that fact.[5]

Several versions of Civil War veterans emerged in Gilded Age culture. One stereotype portrayed them as dangerous tramps, helpless drunks, and institutionalized amputees. A parallel, perhaps equally powerful, and certainly better-known stream of commentary on Civil War veterans also existed. They were brave, and they had lived through exciting times that most Americans could hardly imagine, much less articulate. But beyond the immediate admiration for the old soldiers' perseverance and courage, Americans held up the men who had saved the Union and those who had fought on behalf of the Confederacy as archetypes of the modern volunteer soldier, the "highest type of fighting man the world has yet produced," according to a speaker on Memorial Day 1902. They had rallied 'round the flag, of course, and for that the nation was grateful, but the outpouring of soldiers' memoirs in books and magazines eagerly consumed by the Gilded Age public also highlighted the skill with which these men had fought, the efficiency with which they had killed. Yet even this admiring version of the Civil War veteran set him apart as much as it embraced him as part of the larger community. As militarism and the strenuous life promoted by Theodore Roosevelt and others seized the imaginations of many Americans in the late 1890s, the old men who had demonstrated those values on bloody battlefields seemed to become quaint antiques, their roles in manufacturing or at least inspiring these new attitudes somehow forgotten. Everyone knew that such men did exist or had existed, but the memory of their youthful exploits was more likely to capture the attention of the general public than the awareness of their current prospects and plights.[6]

Neither stereotype was particularly useful for real-life veterans. As civilians struggled to grasp the complexities of veteranhood, veterans sought to maintain their dignity as individuals and their moral authority as a group. It was easiest, perhaps, to accept the heroic version of veterans, but doing so required time to stand still—for the men touched with fire to become as static and immovable as the statues that took up their eternal posts in cemeteries, town squares, and courthouses. Civilians also found it fairly easy to accept the most negative versions of veterans as grasping pensioners or hapless drunks. In very general terms, the former version was most popular in the old Confederacy; the latter at times seems to have dominated in the North.[7]

In an influential 1944 book, *The Veteran Comes Back*, Willard Walker pessimistically predicted that men returning from World War II would create a disaffected class unwilling to blend into peacetime society. In effect, they would form a subculture characterized by a particular sense of humor, moral standards, and even language. Their martial skills would be useless. Their capacity for suffering and resigned willingness to take another person's life and their particular psychological profiles—Waller suggested that "every veteran is at least mildly shell-shocked"—alienated them from society. Waller's book reflected and no doubt encouraged a certain amount of anxiety about the return of veterans.[8]

Civil War veterans were similarly set apart in Gilded Age America—as static monuments to the Lost Cause in the South, as grasping pensioners and residents of huge federal and state institutions in the North, as men out of step with the rest of society to at least some extent. Yet these definitions of veterans came from outside the communities of old soldiers. Civil War veterans also saw themselves as men set apart, but not in quite the same ways as civilians did. As a result, the old soldiers spent much of the Gilded Age justifying their existence. In their search for a common denominator that could maintain their place in a society seemingly in a hurry to forget their contributions or to change the ways they were remembered, old soldiers in the North and South turned to their most powerful quality: they had once been soldiers. That key to their pasts, while superficially matching civilians' impressions, actually went deeper. By stressing their wartime service as opposed to their need, their disabilities, and their age—qualities that highlighted their loss of manliness—veterans could remain relevant to "modern" society, stop the erosion of the public's memory of the war and of the men who fought it, and exert an influence on civic society that they were particularly equipped to wield.

A New Generation

"The natural sympathy which was at first felt for these men has worn off," a Union veteran complained in the 1890s. "A new generation has come upon the stage of action, and the present day sees a great change in many respects as regards the Union volunteer." Indeed, even as veterans attempted to stay relevant, publications such as the wildly popular *National Police Gazette* held up as masculine ideals those men who had gained flashy, individualistic, even shallow fame based on sensationalistic sporting events, public stunts, and even crime. That the stories describing the exploits of athletes and daredevils shared pages with stories about "new" sexual mores and pictures of pretty girls further cheapened, at least in veterans' eyes, the kind of manliness and recognition that contributed to the decline of veterans as representative men. Although they too could lay claim to feats of daring, those accomplishments had been recorded within a structure of military discipline and for the sake of the nation—not for economic gain or celebrity.[9]

One current of postwar thought argued that the war had been won not just on the battlefield but also on the home front; rather than emphasizing only the bravery of soldiers, many observers highlighted the superior character of all Americans and gave equal credit to the efforts of home front volunteers and organizations such as the U.S. Sanitary Commission and the U.S. Christian Commission. Although Frances Clarke has argued that the movement by middle-class writers to describe an enthusiastic and united northern home front was directed toward European criticism of the United States as fragmented and selfish and of the northern armies as foreign-born mercenaries, such writings could easily antagonize soldiers who had done the actual fighting.[10]

Confederate veterans also worried that their sacrifices would be forgotten, that the link between the values and interests for which they had fought would be lost in the rising commitment to commerce and reconciliation that were hallmarks of the New South. Edward Ayers has suggested that respect for Confederate veterans dwindled a bit even among southerners and that the heroes of the Lost Cause themselves "seemed lost in the New South." He even relates the ironically tragic incident of an old soldier being run down by a streetcar on his way to a Confederate reunion. With the rise of new southern principles and attitudes, Confederate veterans could easily be seen as relics. At the very least, the representation of Confederate veterans remained focused on the past, when they had endured extraordinary sacrifices for clear principles. As a result, southern civilians, perhaps inadvertently, ensured that old soldiers would remain heroes uncomplicated by modern concerns such as pensions, preference, and politics.[11]

Some of those same old soldiers — the men Peter Carmichael has called "the last generation" of Virginians reared before the war — had initially approved of the New South's spirit of commercialism and progress; as college students just before the war, they had criticized their fathers' generation as "old fogeys" who were allowing Virginia to slip into irrelevance. Their military service, mainly in the Army of Northern Virginia, had confirmed in their minds the importance of economic development and modernization. Despite the personal trauma of defeat, they believed that the Old Dominion could learn a few lessons from its industrialized enemy as well as from the surprising way that military necessity forced the South to devote vast resources to industrialization. In addition, Virginia could take advantage of wartime Confederates' toughness and dedication to rebuild and reimagine a South that could regain its stature and economic influence. These young men, working as lawyers, educators, community activists, and politicians, used their status as honored veterans to fight for progressive policies, an effort that generated mixed results. These men also steadfastly supported reconciliation between the North and South, believing that Confederate valor could survive an acceptance of defeat and reunion. Yet even these proponents of the New South eventually fell back on stereotypes as they neared the ends of their lives, embracing the Lost Cause mentality that celebrated not only veterans but also the Old South.[12]

Post-Reconstruction racial politics also helped to ensure that Confederates would remain relevant and honored symbols. Threats from reformers such as the Virginia Readjusters in the 1880s and Populists in the 1890s prompted the Democratic establishment to contrast the new parties' biracial constituencies with the Confederate sacrifices of white conservatives. Displaying empty sleeves as prominently as northern Republicans had waved bloody shirts, crippled veterans became symbols of patriotism, racial superiority, and southern honor ignored by these upstart politicians. Directly linking reform parties' success to the rejection of the Confederate past, Democrats enshrined veterans even more securely, making them unassailable and uncomplicated.[13]

Although its effects were felt far more deeply in the North, the rapid demobilization of the army in 1865 and 1866 and the continued marginalization of regular army and militia service during the 1870s reflected a decline in the relevance of military service as a proof of manhood. The tiny army manning frontier outposts was made up of professional officers and what most Americans believed to be the immigrant refuse of eastern cities. As a result, the public men of the generation who came of age after Reconstruction had to find other ways to demonstrate their manly qualities. Many men chose politics as their battlefield. The younger generation of politicians and civic leaders toasted and memorialized their forbears—the men who had represented an older idea of American manhood by risking their lives for their country—but fulfilled their own destinies in metaphorical rather than actual warfare, thus tending to isolate Civil War veterans from an important part of the public ethos of manhood. Whatever currency veterans received as a consequence of having endured combat and sacrifice was, like paper money and the value of veterans' pensions, deflated during the Gilded Age. This process did not happen overnight; veterans remained very prominent at all levels of politics and society throughout the 1870s and 1880s. But their wave crested soon thereafter, and despite the continuation of much of the admiring rhetoric, veterans remained isolated from the rest of society. Kristin Hoganson has argued that the dwindling influence of veterans as leaders and as models led to a reinvigorated sense that only through a personal experience with war could men truly demonstrate and earn honor, a belief that helped inspire the jingoistic foreign policies of the late 1890s and early twentieth century.[14]

But that brief turn to martial enthusiasm followed a period in which a vague antimilitary feeling crept into the public mood. Soldiers were wastrels and immigrants and drunks who lay around western forts and massacred Indians. Once the "bloody shirt" had done its duty during the political wars of the Reconstruction era, military service was seen as less of a qualification for public service and fame. Andrew Carnegie, whose purchase of a substitute during the war did not affect the public's admiration for his success, spoke for many when he said in 1881 that "the real glory of America lay in the fact that she had no army worth the name." Even when Americans woke to the presence of the heroes in their midst in the 1880s, admiration was layered on top of a decade and a half of ignoring the old soldiers and was characterized by an appreciation of the glory of war rather than its bloody reality. Both emotions contributed to the wall erected between veterans and civilians.[15]

I Was There

Yet the most important and the simplest distinction between Civil War veterans and other Americans was the fact that the former had offered up their lives to their country, enduring disease, hardships, and mortal combat. Even those who had not fought in the great battles—the men who had garrisoned towns, guarded prisoners, or spent months in hospitals recovering from illness—believed that their willingness to risk their lives gave them a moral authority that civilians could never have. Not long after the war, one Confederate felt his memory of the war "slipping away, down, down, sparkling as it sinks, but ever growing dimmer, dimmer." But if veterans could rarely create a coherent account of any battle in which they fought, they could re-create at least some of the feelings of fear and comradeship and the sense that they had endured something terrible and wonderful. Carol Reardon's thoughtful interpretation of soldiers' combat memoirs suggests that fighting men often felt that they could not adequately describe their experiences and that they should keep the horror of battle away from sensitive civilians. Furthermore, veterans believed that however limited their true understanding of what had happened to them, they had endured a special kind of trial by fire that no civilian could really understand.[16]

Veterans, like all Americans, had a hard time grasping the scale of the war, which threatened to wipe out soldiers' sense of themselves as individuals. Millions of men served in the armies; scores of thousands fought in even the most forgettable "skirmishes"; casualty lists filled columns and pages of newspapers; hundreds of thousands ended up on pension rolls and membership lists of veterans' organizations. In the face of this perception that they were generic cogs in the war machine, nameless numbers in a pension clerk's ledger, or just another ragged column of aging men in vaguely military uniforms in a Memorial Day parade, veterans exerted their individuality by putting pen to paper or voicing their thoughts. Most recalled their service proudly and rarely expressed regrets at having followed the flag of either side into battle.

Old soldiers' efforts to make others understand that they were not faceless cannon fodder had to overcome the sheer scale of the war, which was documented in a number of efforts to enumerate casualties in the late nine-teenth century. The compiler of one of those efforts, William Fox, wrote, "It is hard to realize the meaning of the figures. . . . It is easy to imagine one man killed or ten men killed; or, perhaps, a score of men killed." But when the totals topped a few thousand, even a veteran "is unable to comprehend the dire meaning." Soldiers were inspired to tell their stories at least in part by that awful scale of death as well as the army's unprecedented size, the un-countable resources spent to fight the war, and the vast distances covered by campaigns. By making sure even the smallest war stories were heard or read, by insisting that any experience was worth repeating, soldiers could redeem their individuality from the numbing magnitude of modern war. Equally important was the fact that, unlike practices in previous wars, when the dead were often and intentionally grouped together by unit, great pains were taken to identify and bury the Civil War dead as individuals.[17]

A first step in establishing veterans' roles in the great war was to ensure that their names were spelled correctly and that some basic record of their service was available. Northern states strove to produce complete and accu-rate rosters of the regiments that had been mustered into the Union Army. The *Roster of Wisconsin Volunteers, War of the Rebellion, 1861–1865* was pre-pared after Governor Jeremiah M. Rusk, a veteran and former member of the Congressional Committee on Invalid Pensions, convinced the legisla-ture to replicate the state's records, which were in danger of being worn out by men seeking information for pension applications and Grand Army activities. The preface to the Michigan roster claimed that the state legisla-ture was responding to the wishes of the "enlisted men" who "considered it due themselves and their children that their names should appear . . . in the archives of their country and their services noted, that future generations might know the honorable part their ancestors bore in the memorable con-flict." GAR posts were surveyed to complement the already crumbling official records. Once the roster was published, all honorably discharged Michigan veterans and their survivors could request and receive copies of the appro-priate volume. The Ohio roster was distributed even more widely, with GAR, Union Veterans' Union, Union Veteran Legion, and Sons of Veterans posts, public libraries, public institutions, county officials, and adjutant generals of all states and territories receiving copies and each legislator receiving forty-seven copies.[18]

Filling out the various questionnaires distributed by organizations or gov-ernment agencies offered a much more personal way of preserving one's individual place in history. The most famous of these efforts came in the late 1910s, when the state archivist of Tennessee collected more than six-teen hundred questionnaires including basic information about the military service and personal backgrounds of men from the state. An even more ambitious enterprise was initiated in 1893 by the Confederate Memorial Literary Society, which collected into a "Roll of Honour" thousands of completed forms containing answers to twenty-three questions about the respondents' military service. Led by Bessie L. C. Dunlop, the society corresponded with United Confederate Veterans (UCV) camps and advertised in dozens of newspapers across the South. Over the next thirty years, more than sixty thousand former Confederates returned forms with basic information—name, unit, and so forth—and about fifteen thousand provided "further comments" about the battles in which they had fought and other memories. The forms were bound into 346 volumes and stored in the Museum of the Confederacy in Richmond.[19]

Veterans of both armies also insisted on keeping their stories alive—accounts not just of leaders and strategies but of privates, whose anecdotes were granted virtually the same attention as tales spun by their commanders. According to Alice Fahs, "The sense that war had created an inexhaustible supply of stories, that there were innumerable 'incidents and anecdotes' of the war to be collected and told," lent to the Civil War an unprecedented, unrepeated, and "profound sense of narrativity . . . centered around the abiding faith that every individual experience of the war was not only worthy of but demanded representation." By the 1880s, Fahs suggests, "veteran-oriented war literature" had taken over the market, and "the military stories of the war became pre-eminent." Over the twenty or thirty years during which soldiers' newspapers were published, thousands of separate anecdotes, short stories, and major essays appeared, describing battles large and small, memorable marches, amusing incidents, and poignant remembrances. The veterans' stories became a kind of oral tradition whose chroniclers' only credential was that they had been in the war.[20]

Less permanent but equally popular was the favorite part of any veterans' encampment, the "campfire," where veterans and their friends and families would gather round a real fire or, in inclement weather, in a meeting hall to hear formal as well as informal recitations of war incidents. National encampments featured huge campfires held in convention halls with formal speeches, eulogies and benedictions, poetry readings, sing-alongs, and other entertainment. Local affairs could be much less elaborate, however: at Menasha, Wisconsin, in March 1883, about forty members of the local GAR post and forty nonmembers answered an open invitation to a campfire. "There was no formal programme," a correspondent to the *Milwaukee Sunday Telegraph* reported, but "a good deal of story telling and lots of fun." The traditional meal of baked beans, hardtack, and coffee was served, and although the writer claimed that no one had brought liquor, after supper "we had a regular circus." Every man received a clay pipe to smoke, and the crowd sang old army songs such as "John Brown's Army," tossed a few comrades in a blanket, and after obtaining a "lot of sticks," "limped around, 'drilling for a discharge'"—apparently an old soldiers' joke in which injuries were exaggerated in hopes of convincing the army that the men were too injured to fight. Confederates followed similar traditions at their reunions and meetings.[21]

According to Stuart McConnell, the speeches and talks at GAR campfires served as word monuments. Casting the result of the Civil War as not a foregone conclusion—the Union had almost been destroyed and would have been if not for the heroic efforts of Union soldiers—and focusing on details such as tactics and anecdotes of personal experiences rather than the messy bloodiness of war, campfires provided evidence for why the federal government should fulfill the open-ended commitment to rewarding veterans and examples of the ways in which veterans distinguished and separated themselves from civilians.[22]

The outpouring of battle reminiscences that appeared in books, magazines, and soldiers' newspapers during the Gilded Age also constituted an important part of veterans' efforts to retain their individuality in the face of the war's unimaginable scale. Most battle narratives were long on tactics and action and short on feelings, attributes that frustrated some younger contemporaries. As Stephen Crane exclaimed, "I wonder that some of those fellows don't tell how they *felt* in those scraps. They spout enough of what they *did*, but they're as emotionless as rocks." Yet those emotions sometimes broke through: "Would to God I could tear the page from these memoirs and from my own memory," Sam Watkins wrote of the Confederate bloodbath at Franklin. "I was there. I saw it. My flesh trembles, and creeps, and crawls when I think of it today. My heart almost ceases to beat at the horrid recollection. Would to God that I had never witnessed such a scene!"[23]

Earl Hess has traced the evolution of soldiers' experiences of combat from innocence through shock to resigned acceptance. Although few veterans put their traumas behind them, most old soldiers resisted sharing their experiences widely for a number of reasons: propriety, a decision to describe camp life or comrades rather than misery and death, a softening of battle memories, and the need to emphasize the noble purposes over the tawdry realities of war. Despite the horrors it contained, the experience of combat—the act of putting oneself in a place to face combat—was an important distinction between veterans and nonveterans that mattered very much to the former. In an eloquent and angry essay on the difference between surviving and describing battle, Paul Fussell has suggested that his experience as a young lieutenant commanding a rifle platoon in World War II resembled Civil War soldiers' experiences at their most substantive levels. Unlike the rationality that nonveterans try to apply to warfare, Fussell writes, it is a "culture dominated by fear, blood, and sadism, by irrational actions and preposterous (and often ironic) results."[24]

Some soldiers did not shy away from detailing battlefield horrors in letters to wives and children. Many started battle passages in their correspondence with the disclaimer that they could not adequately describe what they had seen. A few scenes were almost ubiquitous in their accounts: amputated limbs piling up near field hospitals, fields that could be crossed only by stepping on dead bodies, the irrational impulse to lean into enemy fire during an advance as though the bullets and shells were really just gusts of wind or sheets of rain. Other accounts were shockingly detailed. After First Bull Run, a Yankee described for his family the effect of a bullet hitting a man's head: "It makes a crash among the bones that can be heard for some feet . . . and a torrent of blood from his mouth gush[es] all over your face." Another man described the effect of a single artillery shell on four men: "The first man's head was taken off, the next one's face was blown off against my head, the next lost his underjaw, and fourth had his throat tourn entirely out. . . . I saw a man's brains spattered all [over] the next man's head and other sights as bad."[25]

Whether or not they chose to impart to their reminiscences and memoirs the jagged edge of trauma, Civil War veterans hesitated for a few years before publicly claiming their authority to describe the war to nonveterans, at least in print. To be sure, regimental histories began to appear soon after the end of the war. Yet Gerald F. Linderman has referred to the late 1860s and the 1870s as the period of "hibernation," when neither soldiers nor civilians talked or wrote much about their personal war experiences. Not until the 1880s and 1890s, during what Linderman has called the "revival" of the war, did soldiers begin to publish and speak out about their individual roles in the conflict. The surge of book-length memoirs and of articles in *Century Magazine*, the *Southern Historical Society Papers*, and countless other periodicals confirmed veterans' status as the only true authorities on what happened on the battlefield; it was the most public way in which veterans distinguished themselves from other Americans.[26]

That status seemed to grow in importance as time passed. As one Virginian wrote in 1895, "There is not enough money in the coffers of all the banks to buy the proud claim that I was a loyal soldier." A Yankee labeled veterans "the aristocracy of the land," who had recorded "deeds . . . immensely superior to the devotees of fashion, or the worshippers of gold." At least in their own minds, old soldiers became not only the heroes of the war but its most important historians and, although they would not have used the word, sociologists. A particularly thoughtful description of the extent to which combat changed men and made veterans the only reliable witnesses to the truth of war appeared in B. F. Scribner's description of the Battle of Chickamauga, where Scribner's army was routed:

> There is nothing that produces upon a man so profound an impression as a great battle; nothing which so stirs and tests the soul within him; which so expands and strains the functions of sensation and so awakens all the possibilities of nature! There is nothing which so lifts him out of himself; so exalts him to the regions of the heroism and self-sacrifice; nothing which so surcharges him and permeates his receptive faculties, and so employs all the powers of his mind and body as a great battle!

What stockbroker, store clerk, mechanic, or farmer could match such an experience? As historian John Pettegrew suggests, Civil War veterans, however mundane or desperate their postwar lives, had acquired a set of memories that created "a heroic identity that transcended ordinary ways of being a man."[27]

That transcendence could be difficult to articulate, but a few veterans put into words the special nature of their experiences. In the most famous passage from the most famous Memorial Day address, delivered in 1884 to the GAR post in Keene, New Hampshire, Oliver Wendell Holmes Jr. coined a phrase that has become deeply evocative to Civil War historians and enthusiasts alike: "Our hearts were touched with fire." The line comes from a longer passage: "Through our great good fortune, in our youth our hearts were touched with fire. It was given to us to learn at the outset that life is a profound and passionate thing. While we are permitted to scorn nothing but indifference, and do not pretend to undervalue the worldly rewards of ambition, we have seen with our own eyes . . . the snowy heights of honor, and it is for us to bear the report to those who come after us."

Holmes firmly reminded his listeners that veterans were not only noble symbols but also a separate breed of men "set apart by [their] experience."

He spent much of the talk listing impressions and images that a man who had not fought in the war could never know but that a participant would never forget. "You see a battery of guns go by at a trot, and for a moment you are back at White Oak Swamp, or Antietam, or on the Jerusalem Road. You hear a few shots fired in the distance, and for an instant your heart stops as you say to yourself, The skirmishers are at it, and listen for the long roll of fire from the main line." Twenty years after firing their last shots in anger, he admitted, old comrades met and reminisced—not about their families or careers, as most men would do, but about such terrible and manly moments as "when you were nearly surrounded by the enemy, and again there comes up to you that swift and cunning thinking on which once hung life or freedom—Shall I stand the best chance if I try the pistol or the sabre on that man who means to stop me?" In another passage, Holmes cataloged the members of his generation of Boston aristocrats who did not survive the war—Cabot, Putnam, Lowell, Revere, Abbott. Holmes recalled a scene from the Seven Days' Battles, the last time he saw James J. Lowell alive: "When I looked down the line at . . . the officers . . . at the head of their companies. The advance was beginning. We caught each other's eye and saluted. When next I looked, he was gone." This "old soldier"—he was all of forty-three— was talking to other old soldiers. But the civilians in the audience would have realized that Holmes was setting out differences between those who had fought in the war and those who had not. He was not necessarily glorying in the pageantry of war. He had been wounded several times and as a young man had been bitterly disillusioned by the rhetoric of martial glory. By 1884, however, he seemed to have recovered some of his pride in having served bravely, and his speech highlighted the ways in which the war had improved the character of the men who had fought and the seriousness of purpose that army discipline and the bonds of comradeship had nurtured among survivors.[28]

Certain sacrifices could not be shared; certain nightmares could not be explained. And those experiences had cemented relationships among soldiers stronger than any other connection. As the commander of the 154th New York said to the remnant of his battered regiment during their farewell ceremony, "I would not exchange my three years' connection with this little band for all the rest of my life together; for I feel that, in after years, I can look upon these as of more value than them all." This was a remarkable statement, as Mark Dunkelman, the historian of the 154th, points out: despite twenty years of civic service and prosperity before the war and the confidence that his service and the respect of his townsmen would continue after the war, despite the fact that he was in a successful marriage with two healthy sons, this lieutenant colonel "was ready to dismiss all the years he had spent, and all the unknown years to come, as lesser than the three years he served with the 154th New York." Dunkelman's great-grandfather, who served for the last nine months of the war with Sherman in Georgia and the Carolinas, made that short time the central experience of his eventful, eighty-five-year life. His war service was featured in biographies published in local history books, appeared in the headline of his front-page obituary, and became an important part of the personal folklore he passed down. His descendants kept a kind of museum of the *carte-de-visite* he had taken in Washington, D.C., on his way to the front, his bayonet and uniform insignia, and souvenirs he had collected during the March to the Sea as well as his GAR uniform buttons and ribbons, postcards, and memorabilia from reunions and trips to battlefields. Those nine months, the younger Dunkelman has written, "echoed resoundingly" through the rest of the old soldier's life.[29]

The GAR relied on that sense of separateness. An admiring 1895 chronicle of the organization referred to veterans' "hearts joined by mutual sorrow and danger." In a flowery passage that echoed Holmes's sentiments if not his manly prose, the author described the "somber hours" just before a battle, when "men whose reticent silence had never before been broken looked into each other's eyes, and each committed his solemn heart-secrets to the other's keeping as they promised that if either one fell in battle that day," the other would deliver a letter, lock of hair, or photograph to a loved one back home. "And they sealed this compact with one last strong clasp of hands; for the set lips dared not speak lest they should quiver, and the eyes gazed away to the blue hills, because a soldier must not shed tears." Although most soldiers may not have pictured themselves in such an idealized and oddly romantic exchange, many no doubt agreed that nonveterans were jealous during the celebrations, parades, and fetes held during the 1876 Philadelphia encampment. Any civilian wishes himself "a 'veteran,' when watching the good times that they are having" during "the brilliant parade, and the reunions, and the interchange of courtesies that bind society with an unwritten statute."[30]

Many years after Holmes's speech, Bruce Catton, who, perhaps more than any other popular historian of the Civil War, managed to impart in his books the kind of bittersweet manliness that Holmes evoked, described the old veterans Benzonia, Michigan, as "men set apart." Their gray beards, "natural dignity," and roles as "keepers" of the town's "patriotic traditions" gave "an especial flavor to the life of the village. Years ago they had marched thousands of miles to legendary battlefields, and although they had lived half a century since then in our quiet backwater all anyone ever thought of was that they had once gone to the end of the earth and seen beyond the farthest horizon." As a grown-up newspaperman and historian, Catton could see "something faintly pathetic about these lonely old men who lived so completely in the past that they had come to see the war of their youth as a kind of lost golden age." However, "as small boys we never saw the pathos. We looked at these men in blue, existing in pensioned security, honored and respected by all, moving past the mounded graves" on Memorial Day "with their little flags and their heaps of lilacs, and we were in awe of them." It was as though veterans had stepped out of the schoolbooks and into real life.[31]

The experience of combat—or the lack thereof—at times threatened to divide veterans, too. The Union Veterans' Union, a poor cousin to the GAR (although many union members also belonged to the GAR), initially limited its membership to "battle men"—those who had served in battle or at the front for six months or had been discharged because of injuries or disease acquired in such service. Members had to have enlisted prior to July 1, 1863, "before the large bounties were offered," and to have served at least two years. No draftees or substitutes were admitted. This requirement differentiated the Veterans' Union from the GAR, as did the explicit goal of entering politics to "exact from the Government proper appreciation of the services of the Union soldier," including electing veterans to public office, obtaining support for veterans and their widows and orphans, and securing recognition of the "right of the Union soldier to preference" in government employment. By the turn of the century, after a great deal of controversy, the national organization had decided to admit all veterans regardless of the nature of their service as well as the sons, sons-in-law, and grandsons of veterans. The decision caused a near riot at the Union Veterans' Union's 1902 convention and an unsuccessful attempt to unseat the group's commander in chief.[32]

Camp Ways Are Prevailing among the Old Boys

Reunions of national, state, and local veterans' associations always included civilians and activities unrelated to the war. The 1900 reunion of the W. L. Moody Camp of the UCV, for example, included a baseball game and concerts by the ladies' Mandolin Club and the local brass band. But several facets of the program were intended to highlight the distinctions between veterans and nonveterans. The UCV's James Breathed Camp held a two-day gathering every August at which the 130 members would camp overnight, "do our own cooking, make real coffee and . . . have a good time generally." The climax would always be a sham battle, "which all seem to enjoy," at least partly because the Sons of Veterans of Pulaski participated by manning the old Confederate ten-pound cannon.[33]

Organizations utilized military jargon and ritual to at least some extent. The program for the huge 1880 reunion of Union soldiers in Milwaukee included "General Notes" that could have been labeled "General Orders." Commanding officers of the various state divisions were asked to appoint staffs and to organize their field officers; all were requested "to appear mounted and wearing side arms." No uniforms were required of the men, but they were asked to wear "dark clothes and slouched hats or fatigue caps." Men were required to bring their own blankets, tin cups, and eating ware, and although they would not be required to perform guard duty, they would have to "care for and protect public and personal property in their respective Camps" and set up and take down their tents. Throughout the instructions, military terminology reminded the men that they were indeed veterans of military units. Finally, each regiment would post at the general headquarters in Milwaukee the flag that it had carried through the war: "Let the storm tattered flag, riven by shot and shell on a hundred fields of battle, once more be unfolded to the breeze before they are forever laid away to moulder into dust." As many as twenty thousand old soldiers slept in a tent village along Lake Michigan during the encampment. As a local newspaper commented, "Camp ways are prevailing among the old boys. . . . Thousands of them appear to want to renew their army experiences as veritably as they can for a few days," sleeping in tents, cooking "grub" in canteen halves, and using wool blankets ragged enough "to be the same articles that were brought home in 1865." Veterans had been places civilians could never go, and they intended to revisit those places—without the explosions and dysentery—to the greatest possible extent.[34]

The soldierly behavior at times got out of hand. The first Ex-Union Soldiers' Inter-State Reunion was held in Cherokee County, Kansas, in 1883. The event became an annual affair and within several years drew up to fifty thousand people, but the first reunion featured unbridled "enthusiasm and . . . effervescent loyalty" that led, recalled a county history, to "quite a number of casualties" during the traditional sham battle. Furthermore, during the night the old soldiers carried out a "terrific . . . sortie" in which they "seemed to forget that the war was over, or that Kansas might be a loyal State." They raided henhouses and pigpens, milked cows, and "bombarded" gardens. "The entire night was made hideous with jay-bird bands, tom-toms, hew-gags, and other musical instruments of warfare, accompanied by war songs, war whoops and rebel yells." It was "sure enough war times."[35]

The ritual aspect of the national orders provided further demonstrations of separateness. Mark Carnes has argued that the aggressively ritualistic ceremonies of fraternal organizations helped create a masculine space and community outside the purview of women and lesser men, enabling older men to pass along knowledge and responsibility to younger men. Although the GAR's second incarnation rejected the military caste system that had doomed the first attempt to organize, its rituals remained rooted in formality, hierarchy, and conformity. In some ways, members of the GAR were replacing the actual manhood they had demonstrated in their military service with the artificial manhood of the organization's formulaic and purely symbolic rituals. The GAR had an especially elaborate set of rituals for every occasion—initiations, funerals, Memorial Day parades, installations of officers.[36]

In any context, ritual lends dignity to occasions, distinguishes participants from observers, and provides formal markers of certain kinds of passage. But former Confederates went even further in ritualizing their commemorations of the war. As Charles Reagan Wilson has shown, the merging of southerners' Protestantism and the Confederate response to defeat created a "civil religion" that revolved around the Lost Cause: "Southern ministers and other rhetoricians portrayed Robert E. Lee, Stonewall Jackson, Jefferson Davis, and many other wartime heroes as religious saints and martyrs." At monument dedications, funerals, veterans' reunions, and other public ceremonies, politics, religion, and memory came together as a tightly focused demonstration of southern unity and Confederate loyalty. Bibles used by Confederate leaders and uniforms worn by Confederate martyrs became precious relics, while certain religious songs became "Confederate hymns," with "How Firm a Foundation" sung most often at Confederate funerals.[37]

The rituals of the Lost Cause embraced veterans but became in effect bigger than the old soldiers' efforts to commemorate their service. When a former Confederate died, the official burial ritual assured listeners that "he fought a good fight and has left a record of which we, his surviving comrades, are proud, and which is a heritage of glory to his family and their descendants, for all time to come." Reunions of the UCV tended to be more religiously oriented than GAR gatherings; each day started with a prayer and a hymn, and every reunion featured a memorial service at a local church. Indeed, the 1897 reunion in Nashville was held at the Union Gospel Tabernacle (later the Ryman Auditorium, home of the Grand Ole Opry). Churches raised money for Confederate monuments, Confederate periodicals featured religious subjects, and the *Confederate Veteran* was published at the press of the Southern Methodist Church in Nashville. The link between living veterans and the martyrs of the war could only be completed when the former died, but while on earth the latter were revered in ways that might have made at least some veterans a little uncomfortable.[38]

Inside jokes and self-deprecation are universal ways for groups and organizations to separate themselves from others, and old soldiers were no different. As their rituals suggest, veterans took themselves and their organizations very seriously, but they also reserved the right to make fun of themselves. The "Old Guard" of the R. E. Lee Camp No. 1 parodied the hardships they had endured as Confederate soldiers in an invitation to their winter 1893 "Big Eat," warning that "no Comrade shall come to the table in his bare-feet, or without a shirt on," nor should he "put his feet on the table, nor pick his teeth with a bayonet." The menu was divided into three "reliefs"— the wartime term for a shift on guard duty—plus "cold dishes" and "luxuries." Included was such traditional army fare as beans, stew, and bacon as well as other items familiar to hard-pressed Confederates, including rye coffee and sorghum pies. Cold dishes were limited to various manifestations of ice, while the "luxuries" included "cold water and Irish Whiskey, and more Whiskey." A number of inside jokes also appeared: the "meal" included "corn cobs (Appomattox style)," "Dead Beats," "Greyback Stew," "Stewed Boot," and "Fish Balls, Minie Balls, and Base Balls."[39]

"Burlesque" initiation rituals constituted an even more elaborate mode of self-deprecation. The same firm that provided uniforms, badges, regalia, and other "lodge supplies" to fraternal orders of all kinds published J. P. Van Nest's *Ceremonial of the "Munchers of Hard Tack," or "Jordan Is a Hard Road to Travel."* An ad in the *Ohio Soldier* indicated that Van Nest was a former Union Army lieutenant; his burlesques were apparently very popular among a number of organizations, although the fifth edition was "especially adapted to G.A.R. Posts, Sons of Veterans' Camps and Military Organizations, and written for the purpose of creating an interest in meetings and driving dull care away." The ritual mocked virtually all aspects of a Gilded Age fraternity. There was a surfeit of officers: "Grand Muncher," "Grand Assistant Muncher," "Grand Past Muncher," and "Grand Keeper of Spondulix" (slang for cash); elaborate costumes and props (including a giant head of a jackass available from the publisher for $1.50); pages of dialogue and stage directions with references to "treating," conscripting new members, and "significant ceremonies" in which initiates "will be exposed to dangers both seen and unseen, as great and more terrible than those you encountered on the field of battle." The over-the-top dialogue referred to new members as "victims" and included mildly abusive language ("You son of a gun," says the Grand Muncher at one point, "it now becomes my duty . . ."), while the initiate was forced to "be tried with hard tack" (a piece of leather or hard soap) and answer questions humorous ("Will you agree to set up the rot-gut whiskey to all the Munchers present?"), racist ("While in the service of your country were you ever guilty of playing peek-a-boo with a niggerwench with your knapsack and accoutrements on?"), and surprisingly risqué ("Have you ever had any . . . disease common to the urinary organs?"). The ritual was rather demanding physically, with much kneeling and marching and other machinations conducted while blindfolded or wearing the donkey head. The ritual for the "third degree" involved a certain amount of beer drinking.[40]

Aside from the consumption of alcohol, crusty old soldiers may well have been somewhat less than willing to exert so much effort on a frivolity. But GAR chapters staged mock courts-martial for members—an advertisement for Van Nest's "Moot Court Martial, or Let'er Go, Gallagher" appeared in the back of the *Ceremonial of the "Munchers of Hard Tack"*—and some reunions featured parodies. From the late 1870s to the mid-1890s, Philadelphia veterans staged burlesque parades, courts-martial, executions, and even monument dedications. With elaborate uniforms, send-ups of patriotic rhetoric, and makeshift band instruments, the shows suggested that veterans had the privilege of honoring their service by lampooning it. Another exaggerated account of a GAR initiation came from H. P. Marsh, a Rochester, New York, writer and local historian. The narrator of *The Greatest Burlesque of the Day! The G.A.R. Exposed! By Drumhead* claimed to be exposing the GAR's inner secrets. The volume was one of a few books published in the late nineteenth century that parodied both the societies they "exposed" and the muckraking journalists who presaged the Progressive Era. "Drumhead" took as his inspiration an 1884 book by "Bricktop," *The Knights of Pythias Shown Up. The G.A.R. Exposed* purported to describe the initiation into the organization of a veteran who had "served my country and fought her battles for three months in the barracks at Elmira." Along the way, the man scrambled to discover small injuries that might earn him a pension; made offhand remarks like "I did not think that a war where they killed one another was very civil"; described a violent and abrupt initiation; and welcomed the chance to march in the Decoration Day parade and appear the hero—his goal all along. The secret password for his post was "More Pension"; the sham battle on Decoration Day featured "veterans" who had never fired a gun. Marsh dedicated his "little book of absurdities" to "all those who can look sometimes on the funny side of life, and can appreciate a little harmless sarcasm." A full-page ad for a Rochester manufacturer of artificial limbs appeared at the end of the book, along with an ad for "Patriotic, Humorous and Miscellaneous" recitations to be used at GAR posts, campfires, schools, and other public entertainments.[41]

Peaceful Invasions

Visiting battlefields, especially those with large soldiers' cemeteries, was a way to honor the dead and to celebrate the contributions of the living. For veterans, the commercial and patriotic contexts of battlefield tourism simply provided a veneer for a deeper appreciation for the sacred spaces over which they had fought years before. Old soldiers believed that their personal knowledge of the battles connected them almost mystically to those places. Thus, soldiers' journeys to the fields of battle became pilgrimages that demonstrated their unique relationship to the sites that all Americans knew but only a small percentage had seen when they were consecrated by soldiers' blood. As John Neff has argued, mourning and honoring the dead was a highly ritualized experience that brought Confederate and Union veterans most closely together. "The dead were the measure of the living," Neff asserts, "and reshaping their memory to a focus on the virtues of duty, dedication, and sacrifice" reflected well on the qualities of the men who had survived.[42]

Union survivors had begun visiting the battlefields of the South soon after the war ended, but the impulse grew dramatically in the 1880s. These veteran tourists sought landmarks on the battlefields, and although, like civilians, they often picked up small souvenirs—bullets, canteens, fragments of equipment—they really used their trips to relive the past, to connect with other veterans, to renew their sense that they differed from other Americans. In groups large and small, individually or with families, as major outings or quiet hikes, veterans reacquainted themselves with the spots where they had been touched with fire.

Those veteran travelers who put their feelings into words marveled, like Holmes, at the passage of time and the peculiar ways in which the intervening years could disappear in a moment. Standing at the summit of Missionary Ridge outside Chattanooga, C. O. Brown wrote, "Present company and momentary incidents are forgotten. The past rises before me like a dream." Despite new-growth trees, the breastworks, forts, roads, and trenches remained quite visible. "It seems just yesterday that I stood here. Then these works had been but freshly made and were bare. Now, behold they are covered with a forest! What mighty Aladdin has rubbed his lamp that these things can be?"[43]

An 1890 visitor to Shiloh expressed a similar uneasiness with the changes a quarter century had brought to the bloody field. Referring to landmarks well known to the men who survived the battle and to Americans who had memorized them in the years since, he remarked that the old church had been carried away by relic hunters and replaced by a new one. "The spring where thousands who are now gone, beyond the All quiet river, once quenched their thirst, is as dry as a powder keg; the Duncan field is abandoned; the peach orchard is a thing of the past; the old sunken road is entirely disused and the red brush that grew so thickly at the hornet's nest and was mowed down by the deadly shower of missiles on each side, has again overgrown the ground." The woods in which Confederate general Albert Sidney Johnson died had been cut for timber; his death spot was now marked by a single cedar tree growing in the middle of a cotton field. Yet some features remained startlingly recognizable: "The limits of the battlefield can be made out by scars of shot and shell, which still show on the trees. The bullets have been mostly cut out, thousands of them having been gathered and sold, and thousands collected by relic hunters."[44]

Participants in GAR chapters' more elaborate excursions sometimes published formal accounts of their planning, the correspondence between the visitors and their hosts, and excerpts from newspaper stories about the trip as well as detailed descriptions of banquets, parades, and tours. Authors used military terminology as much as possible. The account of a Newark GAR post's visit to Richmond referred to the touring party as the "Brigade" and to the trip itself as the "invasion"; the committee set up to explore the logistics of the journey "boldly attacked" the problem; while waiting for a train connection, the men "foraged" for snacks; the veterans wore uniforms of new broadcloth overcoats and silk hats, carefully designed badges, and matching bamboo canes. The trip began with a formal march from the Academy of Music and to the train station, with cheering crowds and blaring bands in the mode of long-ago farewells. Similar scenes awaited the veterans in Richmond, where the reconciliationist rhetoric soared and metaphors strained to keep up with the fraternal feelings espoused by one speaker after another. The Yankees, accompanied by their new Rebel friends, visited Libby Prison and the battlefields outside the city where many post members had fought during the Peninsular Campaign. At Seven Pines, the northerners bought up the collection of relics from the field gathered by the proprietor of a ram-shackle country store. At Petersburg, the orderly column became "a band of vandals . . . poring over the ground in search of bullets, bits of shell, or what-ever else came to hand," including a thighbone and a skull.[45]

A somewhat more typical expedition set out from Peoria, Illinois, for the battlefield at Shiloh in the spring of 1884. Men from Illinois, Iowa, and Min-nesota gathered at the train station, renewed friendships, shared a sumptu-ous breakfast, and boarded a train for the South. Bands serenaded the trav-elers, crowds waved farewell handkerchiefs, and the Evansville, Indiana, GAR post transported the old soldiers from the train station to the riverfront, where local veterans saw them off. Steamships took the travelers down the Ohio River and up the Tennessee. The party consisted of about 250 people, perhaps thirty of them wives and daughters, who came from all walks of life: "Here was to be seen a banker, and there a hale, hearty farmer from the fields of Iowa. Here stood a member of the Iowa legislature, and there a mechanic from Indiana—all on a common level now, although twenty-two years ago the one was a general and the other a high private in the rear rank." General J. M. Tuttle, an Iowan who had headed a brigade at Shiloh, was declared "commanding officer of the expedition." The overnight voyage was a mini-reunion, with "joyful meetings of old comrades . . . songs, stories, screams of laughter, and practical jokes." In the tone taken by northerners during and after the war in describing a South that was very different from the North, the Yankees left behind "the thrifty and modern Northwest," and entered "the South of fifty years ago," with ramshackle cabins, slack-jawed farmers, snuff-dipping farmwives, and ubiquitous yellow dogs watching stolidly as the travelers passed. Here and there a Confederate veteran would greet them. "But the [Union] veterans came not to visit the living, but to re-view the past and pay tribute to the dead." For two days, the party explored the battlefield, stopping first at the cemetery. After a formal procession, the bands played appropriate songs, a prayer was said, and a speech was given by General T. Lyle Dickey, a member of the Illinois Supreme Court and a veteran of the battle. The ceremony ended with the hymn "Nearer My God to Thee." Then the men and their guests fanned out across the battlefield, looking for campsites, landmarks, and spots where comrades had fallen or memorable incidents occurred. Although local guides and maps made espe-cially for tourists proved virtually useless, most men found what they sought. When darkness fell, the tourists returned to their boats, where they were served an "old soldiers'" meal of beans, pork, coffee, and hardtack on tin plates. Afterward, "old army songs, music by the bands, and a perfect Babel of conversation served to pass the hours until 'taps.'" The next day was spent searching for battlefield relics, including pieces of shell, fragments from the ruins of the old Shiloh church, cannonballs, bullets, buttons, ramrods, gun barrels, and camp kettles. Those who failed to find relics could purchase them from any of the locals who made a living selling souvenirs. Monday evening, to the strains of "Home Again" and accompanied for a time by a small group of Confederate veterans who reminisced with their old enemies, the northerners steamed back to Indiana. The trip ended on Thursday, when the old soldiers "scattered in the direction of their homes, perhaps never again to meet." The trip had gone so well, however, that plans were already being made for a similar journey to Vicksburg and New Orleans.[46]

A small percentage of Union soldiers mounted pilgrimages to the most infamous sites in the Confederacy: the former prisons in which they had been held and in which many of their comrades had died. An 1880 visit to Richmond by a former prisoner brought back a flood of memories: "I remember how I felt as I staggered along the principal streets of the gay confederate capital; how proud the grey-dressed captors marched beside us down Main street; how the fashionably dressed ladies, from their liveried turnouts, watched us; how the young girls laughed at us; and the smart young bloods made remarks about the 'Yanks,' [and] how the crowd of sunny 'niggers' and 'white trash' saluted me with, 'say, mista, what-yer take for them boots?'" Much of the city through which he and his fellow prisoners had been marched remained unchanged. He entered an abandoned building whose crumbling walls and deserted stairways brought images of haggard prisoners and a long-forgotten memory of the death of an elderly Virginia Unionist jailed with the Yankee prisoners. The visitor found that the Ligon and Company tobacco factory in which he had been housed for some time had been torn down and replaced; he climbed the stairs of the new building to gaze out a window that offered roughly the same view of the city he had had while imprisoned. His last stop in the city was at the old Henrico County Jail, where the names and pictures scrawled onto the walls had been obscured by many coats of whitewash. On an upper floor, however, he found that the prisoners' names and regiments scratched into the wooden window sills and floor were still visible. He noted that family members had cut out and taken away several sections of cedar plank bearing the names of prisoners who had died there.[47]

As the specific memories of these men suggest, the more than four hundred thousand men who had been prisoners of war, especially Union soldiers incarcerated by the Confederacy, carefully separated themselves from other veterans, becoming an even more victimized and honored subset of old soldiers. Former prisoners created separate veterans' organizations (among them the Association of Union Ex-Prisoners of War, the National Society of Andersonville Survivors, and the Chicago Association of Ex-Union Prisoners of War) and acquired the status of martyrs. Indeed, a quartermaster titled one report, *The Martyrs Who for Our Country Gave Up Their Lives in the Prison Pens in Andersonville, Ga.* One of the first accounts of the suffering of Union prisoners called itself a "complete history of the inhuman and barbarous treatment of our brave soldiers by rebel authorities" and lent an even more somber tone to the exposé with a passage from John 3:11: "We speak that we do know, and testify that we have seen." If old soldiers who had survived combat were distinguished from civilians by the sights they had seen and the hardships they had endured, former prisoners were distinguished from their fellow veterans by the even more appalling treatment inflicted by their captors. Moreover, the conditions that killed more than a quarter of all prisoners were caused at least partly because the prisoner exchange system had broken down over the Confederate treatment of black captives, thereby connecting the suffering and death even more closely to the root cause of the war. Former prisoners carried the most bitter memories of the war, and their particular sacrifices appeared from time to time as extreme versions of soldiers' peculiar status in Gilded Age America.[48]

Journeys to old prisons consequently took on a rather different tone than did excursions to battlefields. Just as old soldiers who had been prisoners of war attracted an inordinate amount of attention from civilians, so did Andersonville, where many northerners had been imprisoned. By the early 1880s, only a fragment of the stockade remained, the stream that had run through the camp had dried up, and most of the site was covered by brush. Little had been done to make it more attractive: "It is a plain spot. There is not much attempt made to ornament this city of our martyred dead." According to one soldiers' newspaper, "Southerners shun the spot." But the cemetery, which held the graves of more than 13,700 Union soldiers, was a popular stop for northern tourists. Some wrote personal messages in the register kept in the superintendent's office; one asked the "forgiveness of God for the murder of her brother," one of the prison's victims. A few of the tourists were former prisoners. The superintendent reported that such men, "whatever their natural temper . . . can almost be distinguished by the effects of fear, dread and vivid recollection, which come back like a shock into their faces as they again stand on the now quiet and sunlit scene of their war experiences."[49]

Although battlefield tourism seems to have been less important to former Confederate soldiers than to Union veterans, members of both groups participated in blue-gray reunions at Gettysburg and other sites, and individual chapters of the UCV traveled to southern battlefields. A former Confederate captain and current UCV leader, for example, led an 1896 veterans' tour of Vicksburg and Jackson, Mississippi.[50]

A few thousand Union veterans undertook a permanent "change of base," to use a military term often used by veteran pilgrims, when they formed "soldiers' colonies" in the South and West. Although the founders sought primarily to make money, moving to new communities was another way that veterans could separate themselves from nonveterans. In Jackson County, Kansas, veterans from Illinois founded Soldier Colony (later renamed Colony), while Kansas's McPherson County (named for Civil War general James B. McPherson) became home to the Ashtabula colony, founded by a group of Ohio veterans soon after the war. An apparently short-lived colony was established at Geraldine, Texas, around the turn of the century, while North Dakota's Red River Colony was advertised in the spring of 1872 in the *Prairie Farmer*. Grantville, a San Diego land development, offered lots near the GAR Soldiers' Home there and subsequently became a community within the city.[51]

Blue and Gray magazine featured advertisements from real estate companies and railroads offering land, lumber, and other business opportunities in the Blue Ridge Mountains, Florida, and other points south. E. C. Robertson of Cincinnati promoted investment in southern timber and mineral lands, booming the South as the "Coming Country," "Nature's Most Favored Land," and the "Poor Man's Paradise." A regular "Bureau of Colonization" section featured letters touting the benefits of certain regions of the South, reporting on the progress of northern emigration, and offering large tracts of land as investments. An illustrated four-page article in the advertising section of the May 1894 *Blue and Gray* described in glowing terms the "Land of the Sky"—western North Carolina—and recommended it for "home-building and fortune-seeking."[52]

A more substantial colony developed in Dakota Territory in 1883 when a group of Union veterans founded the town of Gettysburg and some surrounding farms. The community of about two hundred old soldiers from nearly a dozen eastern states came to be called the GAR Colony. The National Tribune Company established the Seminole Land and Investment Company to organize St. Cloud Colony in Florida's Kissimmee Valley, but its colorful brochure highlighted the climate and the economic opportunities rather than the settlement's status as a veterans' colony. Although early newspaper accounts frequently referred to St. Cloud as the "Old Soldiers' Colony," relatively few veterans seem to have settled there permanently. Some former soldiers journeyed to La Gloria, Cuba, shortly after the end of the Spanish-American War, although the outpost was not marketed specifically as a "soldiers' colony." Lynn Haven, a for-profit "Union Colony" in Florida, lured scores of Yankees and hundreds of other settlers to North Florida between 1910 and 1920.[53]

But the most famous and arguably most successful of the veterans' colonies was Fitzgerald, Georgia, where Union and Confederate veterans came together to celebrate the soldiers' ethos they shared near the spot in southern Georgia where Union cavalry had captured Confederate president Jefferson Davis in 1865. Thirty years later, Georgia's generous response to a severe drought in the Midwest encouraged Philander Fitzgerald, a noted Indianapolis pension agent and publisher of the *American Tribune*, to set in motion a movement to create the colony that would bear his name. He promoted the scheme heavily in the *Tribune* and a broadly distributed pamphlet, and hundreds of veterans and investors from Georgia and other southern states ultimately bought stock in the American Tribune Soldier Colony Company, which purchased land and prepared to receive the pioneers expected to flow south from northern states. Other settlers simply moved in to take advantage of the developing town's commercial possibilities. Within two years, Fitzgerald had more than six thousand residents, perhaps a thousand of them southerners.

As a model of purposeful reconciliation, Fitzgerald was organized to ignore sectionalism. Streets on the east side of town were named for northern generals, while streets on the west side honored Confederate commanders. GAR and UCV posts coexisted peacefully along with a Blue and Gray organization, and for years, the aging veterans from both armies gathered in a vacant lot on an apparently daily basis to play horseshoes and rehash their war stories. By the early 1900s, however, the sham battles fought at the town's intersectional reunions consisted of fights between the army and Indians rather than Yankees and Rebels. After the town's first decade or so, advertisements tended to focus on commercial development, public health, cultural institutions, and schools rather than the settlement's symbolic role in the easing of sectional tensions, but Fitzgerald remained famous as the "Old Soldiers' Colony."[54]

In the same way that the founding of Fitzgerald was often held up as a perfect model of sectional reconciliation, so, too, were the journeys of northern veterans to the southern scenes of their martial youth associated with the happy reunion of North and South. Indeed, tourists self-consciously chose to emphasize the similarities rather than differences between Union and Confederate veterans. When a group from the Trenton, New Jersey, GAR post arrived in Richmond in 1882, the travelers' chronicler wrote, "It was soldier greeting soldier." The post commander told his hosts, "We have all suffered like yourselves, in many ways not now to be recounted, the afflictions consequent upon the unhappy civil discord from which our country so lately emerged." Years earlier, both sides had "gallantly displayed upon the battlefield the qualities we claim for our race and nation"; he especially appreciated the Confederates' "having had the courage of your convictions—a virtue not so nearly universal as it should be in this favored land of unfettered speech and action."[55]

Several tour histories featured effusive rhetoric about patriotism and reconciliation that reflected a sense that the war was the veterans' war. The preface to the grand account of the Newark veterans' "Fraternal Visit" to their Richmond counterparts left the philosophy and politics of the war to others: "Every page of this work"—and by extension every event on the carefully orchestrated tour—"was constructed with the most cordial sentiment of regard for the men of the late Confederate army as well as for our beloved Comrades-in-arms." The author stressed that neither he nor his fellow Union veterans cared to comment on the South's social customs or politics. Such statements would only prove "personally obnoxious" to him and the ninety other men who had experienced the extraordinary fraternity displayed on that fall weekend. In 1889, members of the 3rd Georgia invited members of the 9th New York to attend a reunion for the stated purpose of reconciliation. The regiments had fought each other on several battlefields; individual survivors had communicated intermittently after the war, and the invitation to a "Georgia barbecue" was eagerly received. A later visit to New York by members of the 3rd completed the circle.[56]

We Knew We Were Right

A minor success on the vaudeville circuit and a major success at soldiers' homes and reunions were Colonel J. A. Patee and his Old Soldier Fiddlers, all Union and Confederate veterans who promoted the cause of reconciliation by performing old folk tunes and army songs, telling stories, and, after nearly getting into a staged fistfight when the jokes veered into attacks on Rebels or Yankees, assuring their audiences that the war was over and they were all Americans. Nevertheless, despite the best efforts of entertainers such as Patee and his fiddlers and veteran colonizers, old Rebels and Yankees retained lingering resentments and antagonisms that simmered beneath the calm surface of reconciliation. Even in Fitzgerald, Union settlers and Confederates disagreed about the appropriate ways to commemorate the war and the ways in which the Union and the Confederacy were presented in classrooms and schoolbooks. Moreover, Union veterans made a yearly pilgrimage to decorate graves at the National Cemetery near Andersonville, annually renewing a potentially explosive issue. The disagreements between northern and southern veterans often reflected not only remnants of wartime enmity but also resentments against fellow northerners and southerners who sought to ignore the old soldiers' contributions and attitudes.[57]

The most complete realization of the reconciliationist vision appeared in the form of *Blue and Gray: The Patriotic American Magazine*, published for several years beginning in 1892. The magazine featured military memoirs by Yankees and Rebels as well as editorials, advertisements, and correspondence from readers constantly urging reconciliation and betraying impatience with any lingering sectional attitudes. Yet a letter from a hotheaded Kansas pension agent indicates that reconciliation was never as complete as the rhetoric would suggest. The letter, which the editors published verbatim, had been sent with the promotional card for the *Blue and Gray* that the writer was returning. Undoubtedly speaking for many others, this veteran retained substantial feelings against Confederates: "Observe their ungrateful and damnable treachery treason and virulent abuse of power by flaunting their . . . treason and love for their cowardly rebellion by nullifying the pension laws and depriving the destitute and needy defenders of our Union & Nation and their dependents of their legal vested pensionable rights." Former Rebels' use of terms such as "paupers mendicants hirelings and sand baggers of the treasury" to describe Union pensioners raised the question of "if or whether the time has come for it to be patriotic to mingle the Blue and Gray in honorable connection and thereby allow the cause we sacrificed health means opportunity and life for to become obliterated & swalled into the subteranean abysses of eternity by a hord of cowardly ingrate traitors to our government."[58]

A pugnacious 1893 communication to the *Confederate Veteran* from the superintendent of the Maryland Line Confederate Soldiers' Home provided "a little insight into the way we do [things] in Maryland" and another example of the limited attraction of fraternization: "We have no ex Confederate societies, but several large, strong, and active Confederate societies.

We have never mixed in any manner with the other side[. We] have no joint reunions, no joint banquets, no decoration or memorial days in common. In fact, we do not mix, we go our way and they go theirs, and we find we gain more respect by so doing. We do not belong to that class of Confederates that believed they were right. We knew we were right in 1861, we knew we were right when the war closed, and we know today that we were right."[59]

Yankee veterans felt the same way. The speaker at an 1880 Memorial Day celebration in Cincinnati stated with equal conviction that the Union soldier had been "battling for the liberty of a nation . . . and that the other was seeking to tear down and destroy that nation . . . ; that the one gave his life that a great nation might live and its liberty be transmitted to generations unborn[;] that the other died seeking to rivet the chains of human bondage." Less pointed but more condescending were the words from an address delivered on the same day in Baltimore: "Our late troubles were an illustration of patriotism and loyalty to country on the one side, and on the other, of the children of rebellion fighting only for a fancied wrong."[60]

The issue of wrong versus right dwindled in importance as reconciliation came closer to reality, but old principles sometimes popped to the surface. In 1881, a man who had risen from private to colonel during the war, lost a leg, and gone on to become a professor at Wisconsin's Lawrence University gave a Memorial Day address in which he remarked that "there is a marked tendency in these days to excuse high-handed crimes, to admit rogues to good society, and to retain in good standing in churches, members, who violate the common morality and the everyday principles of honesty." It seemed to have become "an era of good nature and lax moral principles," in which rebels were celebrated for being rebels, a practice tantamount to the "paying of honors to the tories on Independence Day, and to Judas on the Christian Sabbath." In the case of the newly admired old Confederates, "charity slops over and becomes maudlin sentimentality when it attempts to decorate rebels as rebels." Such a course would "obliterate very important distinctions," making "patriotism cheap and treason respectful." "If the time should ever come when you can no longer pay unsullied honors to our dead heroes," he demanded, "I beg of you [to] forget that they ever lived or died, and drop Decoration Day from the calendar." Just a few years later, a Bangor, Maine, newspaper published an article complaining that "when Memorial Day ceases to be an occasion when the voice of the old soldier or the old sailor's friend can be heard—when the grey is lauded equally with the blue—when they who sought to tear down are made equally the subjects of laudation with those who sought to preserve—and an insult to the old soldier, no matter how high the source from whence it comes, can go unrebuked—then will the ceremonies of strewing the graves become meaningless and vapid."[61]

One of the sharpest protests against reconciliation appeared in the *Ohio Soldier*'s coverage of a dustup between General Samuel Hurst, a volunteer who had been brevetted a brigadier after commanding the 75th Ohio, and General Henry Boynton, former commander of the 35th Ohio and also a brevet brigadier. Boynton, the Washington, D.C., correspondent for the *Cincinnati Commercial Gazette*, was one of the leaders in the movement to establish the Chickamauga and Chattanooga National Military Park, an effort often hailed as an important step in the reconciliation of the sections and a frequent stop for veteran tourists. In early 1891, Hurst, who had served for most of the war with the Army of the Potomac, complained that "the only battlefield the army of the Cumberland ever abandoned is selected to mark its history, and that the cause of the nation is to be degraded, by lowering it to a par with the rebellion." Accepting the equality of Yankee and Rebel motivations and patriotism might prevail in Washington, where Boynton's views had been shaped by "frequent thrusting of knees under the rebel mahogany," but back in Ohio, veterans "still call a hoe a hoe, and a rebel a rebel." Former rebels should be treated well personally, and no one would deny their rights to citizenship, but Ohio veterans "still think a dead patriot is better than a dead rebel, and will resent the efforts of those who attempt to degrade their dead to a level with criminals."[62]

Former Confederates' continued veneration of the Confederate battle flag particularly raised the ire of their northern counterparts. Although veterans rarely clashed over substantive issues such as politics or race, they readily threw out skirmishers and fixed bayonets over symbolic disagreements, and no late-nineteenth-century subject was more guaranteed to spark sectional differences among veterans than the Confederate flag, with the matter at times stretching thin the sincere desire to reconcile. A New Jersey GAR post's 1884 visit to Richmond was cut short by a day because some of the men felt insulted by the absence of American flags and spectators during their ceremonial march from the train station to the hotel, which they had made with their Confederate hosts. Most of the visitors did not share this view, but "some of the boys got it into their heads that the lack of display . . . was an indication that they were not welcome guests." Even the GAR's generally positive response to the idea of building veterans' homes in the South could be derailed by the tiny Confederate flag that appeared on funding appeals for a Missouri home sent by the St. Louis Daughters of the Confederacy. Not a single Yankee responded.[63]

The issue flared up briefly during preliminary and ultimately unsuccessful discussions about holding a Confederate Day or Blue and Gray Reunion during the 1893 Columbian Exposition in Chicago when the *American Tribune* blasted the notion of Confederate flags flying on the shores of Lake Michigan. "There will be but one flag," thundered the *Tribune*. Southerners seemed not "to understand that the Rebel flag and the cause it represents was knocked out twenty-seven years ago." The *Ohio Soldier* declared that the GAR had so far "taken no part in these mongrel exhibitions" and should continue to resist. Such reunions "only add to the vilest conspiracy that ever existed, and cost millions in life and money, a dignity and character which it can never have on its own merit." Moreover, "if the southern people want to appear at Chicago it should be as the representatives of live and loyal American states, and not as the remains of a dead and rotten rebellion."[64]

Although late-century Confederate ceremonies generally featured the Stars and Stripes at least as prominently as the Stars and Bars, the ubiquitous waving of the old battle flag could sometimes set Union veterans' teeth on edge. Crowds cheered the Confederate flag and waved handheld versions of it at the dedications of memorials to Stonewall Jackson, Robert E. Lee, and Nathan Bedford Forrest and at reunions of Confederate veterans throughout the period. Partly in response, the GAR resolved in 1896 that "those who wore one uniform and fought under one flag, fought for their country and were right, while those who wore the other uniform and fought under the other banner, fought against their country and were wrong, and no sentimental nor commercial efforts to efface those radical differences should be encouraged by any true patriot." Three years earlier, the GAR had formally criticized what it believed to be excessive respect for the Confederate flag at public ceremonies in the South, connecting such displays to a desire to encourage younger southerners to rebel against the United States. Furthermore, although individual units had been returning flags to one another for years, when President Grover Cleveland authorized the War Department to begin returning 550 captured Rebel banners still in storage, Union veterans defeated the effort. When the Confederate flag again garnered cheers at the 1896 UCV reunion, the GAR lodged still another protest. Although Congress finally settled the issue in 1905 when it authorized the return of the many flags still in the possession of the federal government, the subject had for at least two decades been the issue most likely to threaten reconciliation.

As late as 1914, the rumor that Union veterans in Little Rock would refuse to march in the UCV reunion to which they had been invited because the Confederate flag would be flown inspired a condescending blast from the *Arkansas Veteran*. Any man who "feels that he is less of a patriot because of the occasional sight of the Confederate flag [is] to be pitied, rather than censured."[65]

Another point of apparent disagreement actually indicated a deeper if unrecognized shared value. Although veterans on the two sides disagreed pointedly about causation and blame, they were more alike than different in their earnest desire to influence the way that their histories were presented to students and the general public. The national commander of the GAR told New Jersey veterans that although they might be materially poor, they were "rich in the possession of a [veteran's] badge[. M]en would give millions if they could purchase it and the glory it represents." And that unique possession made them particularly suited to chaperoning the nation's schoolchildren through their history education. For its part, the Joint History Committee of the Confederate Veterans Organizations of Alabama could have been speaking for virtually any veterans' group when it declared its goals to be "the better preservation of all the facts, events and incidents" of the war, "the correction of errors in relation thereto in published works, especially school books, and the stimulation, through a study of the war, of a broader and more intelligent patriotism." In short, Union and Confederate veterans wanted the truth to be told about the war. But in this case, the "truth" meant respecting one side's motivations and valor more deeply than the other's.[66]

Union veterans seemed unsurprised that some Confederates belittled the Yankees' cause and fighting abilities but they were especially incensed by northerners' lack of appreciation for Union soldiers' contributions. In particular, they worried that schoolbooks marketed to northern schools by the 1880s and 1890s did not appreciate the competing motivations behind northern and southern responses to the sectional conflict and did not present a right side and a wrong side to the war. "The efforts to be impartial and non-sectional," complained an 1887 Wisconsin GAR committee report, "have in many instances gone beyond the bounds of reason." One of the most successful school histories of the Gilded Age was *Barnes's Brief History of the United States*, by Joel Dorman Steele, which appeared first in 1871 and in three revised editions by 1885. Using the passive verbs and the noncommittal tone that still characterize history textbooks, the author's evenhandedness incensed GAR members. They protested that the book's straightforward chronology seemed to make the Confederates victors in battles that were really draws, including Cold Harbor, the Wilderness, and Spotsylvania. The sectional conflict was presented as a chronicle of political debates rather than a struggle between right and wrong; Reconstruction was presented fairly objectively, although carpetbaggers made a brief and slimy appearance. Even worse, the author deigned to use southern as well as northern sources, including Edward Pollard's books on the history of the Confederacy. The overreliance on Pollard and the very temperate discussion of issues that no Yankee in his right mind would view temperately inspired an exaggerated response. The *Milwaukee Sunday Telegraph* castigated the "entire work" as "a matter of love on the author's part to applaud and extol the enemy upon all occasions; there is a warmth shown which is not to be mistaken when they are mentioned, while coldness or indifference follow Union troops." To the extent that the text briefly mentions the hardships faced by the outnumbered Confederates, the accusation was not false. Yet the *Telegraph* concluded that "the whole tone of it is calculated to smother the fires of patriotism instead of causing them to blaze up afresh."[67]

Ironically, a similar outcry came from former Confederates. In words matched by resolutions passed at countless local, state, and national UCV encampments, the *Confederate Veteran* complained in 1894 that most books about the war, even those written by southern men from a southern point of view, constituted defensive apologies rather than aggressive justifications for southern principles. "How few of our children know that Jamestown, Virginia, was settled before the Pilgrim Fathers came to this country, or that the vast domain which forms four fifths of the United States was won by Southern men, or that slavery was forced upon this country by England, seconded by New England, or that in 1860 one tenth of the slaves were communicants in churches." The true history of the United States involved *northerners'* "overthrow of the Constitution as it was originally adopted." "Upon our Confederate veterans lies the duty of securing this vindication of their cause from the facts of all our past history."[68]

Nevertheless, even when they clashed bitterly, veterans could find common cause. A southern veteran argued that the glorification of Union soldiers in a sense validated the foes who had fought the northerners nearly to a standstill: "They can't glorify themselves without witnessing to the patriotism, valor and constancy of the Southern people . . . in every book they print, in every song they sing, in every eulogy they speak, in every monument they set up, in every pension they draw."[69]

As the textbook issue reveals, veterans who expressed reservations about certain aspects of reconciliation often sought to protect their legacies within their communities, states, and sections. They lashed out at anyone who seemed to belittle the causes for which they had fought or the status of veterans themselves. This anger often took the form of rhetoric that indicated the brittleness of the reconciliationist veneer. In a Memorial Day address in Savannah in 1895, Pope Barrow, a Confederate veteran and former congressman and senator from Georgia, contradicted the growing belief within the South that its differences with the North had been healed. Those differences had existed since the establishment of the United States, declared Barrow, and the defeat of the armies fighting for those southern principles did not destroy those principles. Yet thirty years after the year, "new men, men with new names, mentioned for the first time in history, names that are not to be found on any muster roll of any army, go about prating of a 'New South,' and sneering at the Old South." They were attempting to replace a society based on sacred beliefs with one in "which they are the apostles, and mammon is the titular divinity." Like most veteran speakers, Barrow believed that dedicated service to his country recommended a man more than did the amount of money he had.[70]

Confederates at times seemed more concerned about protecting their legacy from other southerners than from Yankees. In fact, New South advocates often ignored the Confederate veterans in their midst. By the 1880s, Confederate veterans were commonly recognized at public events such as state fairs and exhibitions; however, the 1881 Atlanta International Cotton Exposition, widely considered the official launch of the New South ideology, ignored Confederate veterans but held a "Freedmen's Day."[71]

Speaking for the Union side, an 1889 screed in the *American Tribune* authored by "Bitter Sweet" described the process that had put Union soldiers on the defensive and had made them wonder what had happened to public sentiment since the years just after the war, when "the air was heavy with 'God bless the soldier.'" According to "Bitter Sweet," "the idea was asserting itself that the man who dropped a dollar in the sanitary or christian commission hat was as much entitled to credit and honor as the man who dropped his leg or his life in the valley of the Rappahannock or along the course of the Mississippi." Politicians' and civilians' subsequent desire to treat old Rebels and Copperheads "with compassion and love" meant that an old soldier could not tell his war stories "without giving offense to his stay-at-home neighbor" or being accused of "flaunting the bloody shirt." As the sole remnants of the true war spirit—as the conscience of the Union—these veterans naturally came together in the GAR. Even then, when presenting themselves to the public, they had to take care not to wear, literally, their principles on their sleeves: If a veteran "wears his [GAR] badge continually on a suit of good clothes he is playing for popularity, and if he fastens it every day to a shabby coat he is scheming for a pension."[72]

In many ways, the northern and southern veterans' hesitation about complete reconciliation was less a function of their distrust of one another than a demonstration of their shared insistence on not brooking challenges to the kind of "war spirit" or patriotism that had sustained their war service and acceptance of the horror, disabilities, and hardships they would endure and remember for the rest of the lives.

Bands of Brothers

Oliver Wendell Holmes Jr. claimed late in his 1884 Memorial Day speech that he had not set out to suggest that the men he described or the old soldiers in his audience were better than other men. But he may have been disingenuous. If Henry V's speech before the 1415 Battle of Agincourt (at least as imagined by William Shakespeare two centuries later) sought to inspire his followers to fight because surviving would separate them from and even raise them above their fellow Englishmen, then Holmes's stirring words to the aging veterans of New Hampshire provide a parallel suggestion that gentlemen too young or too timid to have fought for the Union would "hold their manhoods cheap" when those deeds were remembered on Memorial Day.

That attitude found perfect expression in Stephen Crane's "The Veteran." Published in 1896, a year after *The Red Badge of Courage*, the story projects Henry Fleming into a calm, contented early old age. Younger neighbors listen to Henry's war stories, including the tale made famous in the novel, and are surprised that any old soldier would admit to having been frightened. The townsmen laugh a bit, but Henry's little grandson, Jim (named, no doubt, after Jim Conklin, Henry's brave comrade mortally wounded in that long-ago first battle), is troubled that his hero could ever have run from danger. Later that night, a drunk hired hand accidentally starts a fire in the barn. The other men, not having been tempered by the far harsher trials of battle, rush haplessly around, fumbling with buckets and trying to get a stubborn pump to work, but the old veteran keeps his head and runs grimly to the barn. Henry makes half a dozen trips into the inferno to retrieve the horses; he smashes his hip, and his hair and whiskers are burned off. When someone remembers the two colts trapped in a back corner, Henry "stared absent-mindedly at the open doors. 'The poor little things,' he said.

He rushed into the barn." The roof collapses a few seconds later. In celebrating Henry Fleming's eventual redemption, *The Red Badge of Courage* fit well into the notion that war could bring out a man's positive and even ennobling qualities. "The Veteran" showed that once a man came to grips with mortal peril in battle, the strength he drew from that special brand of terror and accomplishment would last the rest of his life.[73]

But the transformation that made veterans different from their nonveteran countrymen was not always positive. Ambrose Bierce would probably have scoffed at the notion that war could ennoble a man. Although both he and Holmes had served as junior officers, sustained serious wounds, and spent much of their lives thinking about the ways in which war changed—or failed to change—men, Holmes and Bierce came to espouse almost opposite sides of the deeply held notion that men who had endured war differed fundamentally from men who had not. For Holmes, surviving combat could make a man appreciate life, aspire to important things, and value effort and determination—in short, it could make a man take advantage of the great second chance he had been given and work to find both large and small ways to contribute to the public good. Although Bierce was dismayed at the failure of Reconstruction and had little patience with the grasping pension agents and politicians who pandered to veterans' interests, he took a basically apolitical approach. His "target," according to historian David Blight, "was Civil War sentiment and romance"; surviving war simply underscored the cruelty and randomness of life and death. Veterans, Bierce seemed to believe, should come away from war knowing better than anyone that they were helpless in the face of death.[74]

Although he was not necessarily known during his lifetime for his Civil War stories, Bierce wrote just over two dozen of them, and several were published in his 1891 collection, *Tales of Soldiers and Civilians*. A precursor to Crane's realistic approach to Civil War combat, Bierce wrote of war not as a grand adventure, although some of his characters believe it to be one before they experience it, and not as an occasion for pride or national honor, although a recurring theme is the folly of such attitudes. Instead, his characters are buffeted by bad lack and worse generals and die squalid deaths for dubious reasons. Bierce was drawn to satire and became quite good at it, at least partly because he had reached "a deep understanding that in the Civil War men had died for causes they did not understand, died to have their manhood recognized according to history's definition at the time: courage, honor, duty." Yet Bierce believed the realities of heartless and faceless warfare had led them to kill and to die "as honest, if highly deluded, foemen."

His cynicism ran counter to the celebratory memoirs that began to appear during the last twenty years of the nineteenth century.[75]

The protagonists and antagonists caught up in this vicious fighting were privates and lieutenants, spies and martinets, pompous politicians and fatalistic common soldiers. Among the sometimes humorous, often pathetic, and virtually always tragic characters Bierce invented for his Civil War stories were Parker Addison, a doomed but philosophical Yankee spy who chats with his captor about the nature of death and life; a smooth-faced orderly who reluctantly agrees to don women's clothing to trick a fatuous and evidently lonely staff officer; a frantic captain whose company suffers a single casualty on the fringe of a battle, though the captain himself, undone by stress, subsequently plunges his sword through his breast; a scout who waves his company away from the spot of a Rebel ambush an hour after being killed; and the generally silly Brigadier General Jupiter Doke, a bumbling braggart of a commander whose farcical military career is told through a series of confusing dispatches and exaggerated newspaper stories.

Bierce used his short stories to vent his frustrations with the follies of humankind, to exorcise the demons that often plague veterans of harsh combat, to distinguish himself—his intellect, his detachment, his objectivity—from the pedestrian feelings and emotions of his fellow Americans. He certainly believed that soldiers were the only true experts on the war, writing to a potential publisher that "no man who has not been a soldier is ... competent" to judge "war stuff." But he could somewhat grudgingly accept at least a sliver of the Holmesian view of war—the notion that the common soldiers of both sides were forever linked by their experience. Bierce did so in 1903 when writing about the burial grounds at a tiny battlefield in West Virginia. Bierce remembered the skirmish well. The casualties had been light on both sides, but a small national cemetery had been created and maintained for the few Union dead. But little had been done for several Confederate graves lying a short walk from their enemies' well-manicured resting places. The Confederate graves were merely indentations in the dirt, with a handful of scattered, incomplete stone markers. Bierce ended his famous essay "The Bivouac of the Dead" with a plea to do something for these worthy opponents: "They were honest and courageous foemen, having little in common with the political madmen who persuaded them to their doom and the literary bearers of false witness in the aftertime. . . . Among them is no member of the Southern Historical Society. Their valor was not the fury of the non-combatant; they have no voice in the thunder of the civilians and the shouting. Not by them are impaired the dignity and infinite pathos of the Lost Cause."[76]

In his nonfiction work, Bierce could veer rather close to Holmes, only to take a characteristically sharp turn away from the Boston Brahmin's point of view. Bierce's account of the Battle of Shiloh effectively re-created the confusion and horror of that fight, ending with the words,

And this was, O so long ago! How they come back to me—dimly and brokenly, but with what a magic spell—those years of youth when I was soldiering! Again I hear the far warble of blown bugles. Again I see the tall, blue smoke of camp-fires ascending from the dim valleys of Wonderland. There steals upon my sense the ghost of an odor from pines that canopy the ambuscade. I feel upon my cheek the morning mist that shrouds the hostile camp . . . and my blood stirs at the ringing rifle-shot of the solitary sentinel. Unfamiliar landscapes, glittering with sunshine or sullen with rain, come to me demanding recognition, pass, vanish and give place to others. Here in the night stretches a wide and blasted field studded with half-extinct fires burning redly with I know not what presage of evil. Again I shudder.

Although he betrays echoes of Holmes's bittersweet recollection of fellow officers marching to their deaths at the Seven Days' Battles, Bierce dwells not on individuals or bravery but on the impersonal if memorable sensory perceptions that all soldiers—and only soldiers—faced. Although he wrote about particular soldiers—especially officers he despised or admired—in other contexts, Bierce saw as the interesting thing about war not its relationship to men and manhood but its absolute indifference to both. War becomes the main character in the tragicomedy that Bierce created out of his experiences, with the brave and bumbling officers and common and uncommon foot soldiers mere props.[77]

If combat made Holmes's veterans more aware of the preciousness of life, it made Bierce's characters more aware of its meaninglessness. If Holmes believed that experiencing the sharp end of war transformed a man into a better version of himself, Bierce believed that war might make a man different—but not better. If Holmes believed that war should make men more committed to their values and ideals, it made Bierce believe that life's fragility lessened its value and made it best observed—and lived—from a safe distance. Most veterans could not articulate the ways in which they differed from their countrymen as well as Holmes and Bierce did, and many old soldiers may not have recognized themselves in the words of either. But even if neither version of the war fit perfectly into a veteran's perceptions, even if neither Bierce's nor Holmes's demons were the ghosts that haunted a particular old soldier, all veterans understood the gulf that stood between them and their civilian neighbors.[78]

A third voice provides a quite different sense of how the experience of combat might affect veterans. Walt Whitman, a noncombatant, drew from his travels over battlefields, his work in hospitals, and, perhaps, in conversations with his veteran brother an idea that few civilians understood: many men enjoyed combat. More accurately, Whitman recognized that soldiers appreciated and found meaning in the excitement, the adrenaline, the drama, the vivid sensations that civilians could only dimly understand by reading histories and memories and viewing paintings and panoramas. In "The Veteran's Vision," Whitman's narrator lies beside his sleeping wife, his infant breathing quietly in the next room. The man suddenly awakens, and "the engagement opens there and then, in my busy brain unreal." He is not dreaming but reliving in precise detail an unnamed but very specific battle; he can re-create the varied sounds of the different projectiles, the detail of an artilleryman checking his fuse, the grand sweep of a regiment charging ahead, the constant roar of cannon, the file closers preventing gaps in the regiments peppered with canister. But, he remembers parenthetically, "the falling, dying, I heed not—the wounded dripping and red, I heed not." This is the memory not of a traumatized veteran but of a man who, while not quite missing the action, appreciates it as something that he will always hold close to his heart and will revisit late at night, when he is alone in his wakefulness.[79]

That speculative description of the difference between a veteran and a nonveteran may not accurately gauge the attitudes of most Civil War veterans. They rarely suggested that they loved war or killing, enjoyed camp life, or welcomed forced marches. But they almost universally expressed their appreciation, their love for having been soldiers. Their service defined them, made them different, provided unique rewards and self-esteem beyond anything most Gilded Age Americans could muster. Perhaps they took this point of view because the true meaning of the experience could never really be explained coherently.

Whitman offered perhaps the second-most-quoted phrase on the Civil War when he wrote, "The real war will never get in the books." He seems conflicted in that realization. On the one hand, in perhaps the least prescient passage to appear in his writing, he claims that "future years will never know the seething hell and the black infernal scenes" of the war: equal horrors would challenge Civil War soldiers' grandsons in the Argonne and their great-grandsons on Okinawa and on countless other battlefields. And he admits that perhaps "it is best they should not." Yet he worries that the "the fervid atmosphere" and events of this particular war will be forgotten, lost in the bustle and growth and change in the United States that he so often celebrated.[80]

That tension between the need to forget and the need to remember symbolized the conflict between veterans and civilians. It complicated soldiers' homecomings, created additional burdens for the disabled, soured attitudes about government programs meant to sustain old soldiers, and encouraged confrontations between veterans and nonveterans. Even in the South, where dramatically less conflict arose over gratitude and rewards, old soldiers were committed to distinguishing themselves from those who had not fought for Confederate independence. Even though sectional divergence and personal disabilities caused dramatic differences in veterans' postwar lives, old soldiers were more like one another than they were different. As a history of Atlanta's veterans suggested in 1890, "Nothing else, and nobody else" in Gilded Age America was like a veteran of the Civil War.[81]

Notes

Introduction

1. See, e.g., *Atlanta Constitution*, April 27, 1901; *Richmond Dispatch*, February 21, 1893; "Confederate Veteran Alumni Reunion"; *Milwaukee Sunday Telegraph*, September 18, 1881; *Confederate Veteran*, December, October 1895; Bancroft, *Book*, 88, 607.

2. Thomas Nelson Page, "How the Captain Made Christmas," in *Novels*, 371–97.

3. Sandburg, *Always*, 45–48.

4. Rowell, *Yankee Cavalrymen*, 257.

5. Brooks, *Lost Sounds*, 215–33.

6. *Yankton Press*, December 11, 1872.

7. *New York Times*, June 21, 1878, January 8, 1880, October 1, 1881, December 13, 1884, February 17, 1886, August 31, 1891, May 9, 1893, March 14, 1898.

8. Cather, "Sculptor's Funeral," 173–74.

9. Fleche, "'Shoulder to Shoulder'"; Gannon, "Won Cause." Hagaman's close analysis of pension records suggests that black veterans in Maryland experienced many of the same physical, economic, and personal problems that plagued white veterans ("Personal Battles"). See also Shaffer, *After the Glory*.

10. Costa, *Evolution*, 198; Escott, *Military Necessity*, 165–66.

11. Eleventh Census; *Wright's City Directory*.

12. Lembcke, *Spitting Image*, 101–26; Fred Turner, *Echoes*, 45.

13. Grant, "Reimagined Communities," 507; Beecham, *As If It Were Glory*, 228.

14. Chamberlain, *Passing*, 271–72.

15. Garland, "Return," 167–94.

16. Garland, *Son*, 6–8, 11.

17. A trio of exceptions are Kelly, *Creating*; Rosenburg, *Living Monuments*; Dean, *Shook*. A brief but very useful account of Union and Confederate veterans, the value of which is not reflected in the number of times it is cited in this book, is Logue, *To Appomattox*. For examples of excellent books in which the veteran experience is used to explain other aspects of Reconstruction and the Gilded Age, see McConnell, *Glorious Contentment*; Blight, *Race and Reunion*; Blair, *Cities*; Gaines M. Foster, *Ghosts*; Groce, *Mountain Rebels*.

18. *New York Times*, May 14, 1865, reprinted in *Topeka Weekly Leader*, August 30, 1866; *Daily Missouri Democrat*, December 22, 1866; *Confederate Veteran*, May 1893.

19. *Chicago Tribune*, May 5, 1865; *Confederate Veteran*, June 1898; Toomey, *Maryland Line Confederate Soldiers' Home*, 89, 92, 96; *Richmond Daily Dispatch*, January 1, 1884.

20. *Hancock Veteran*, September 9, 1880; Sinisi, "Veterans," 99; *Detroit Tribune's Veteran Soldiers' and Sailors' Hand-Book*, 4–5; Society of the U.S. Military Telegraph Corps,

Reunion Proceedings; *Proceedings of the Ohio Association*; Kirkland, *Civil War Veterans' Organizations*, 19; Bridge, "Shrine."

21. Dana B. Shoaf, "'For Every Man Who Wore the Blue,'" in *Union Soldiers*, ed. Cimbala and Miller, 463–81; *Proceedings of the First and Annual Meetings*, 3; Gaines M. Foster, *Ghosts*, 54.

22. Logue, *To Appomattox*, 93–95; Gaines M. Foster, *Ghosts*, 93–95, 106–7, 114.

23. Lincoln, *Collected Works*, 333.

24. Confederate States of America House of Representatives, *Bill*, 2.

25. Kelly, *Creating*, 93–98; Skocpol, *Protecting Soldiers*, 140–41.

26. Cetina, "History," 213–31; *Annual Report of the Trustees*, 8. 9; William A. Anderson, "Their Last Hurrah," 100.

27. *Report of the Board of Managers . . . 1900*, 201, 210, 197–98.

28. Rosenburg, *Living Monuments*, 19–25, 73.

29. *Confederate Veteran*, January, May 1896, April 1897; *Arkansas Veteran*, May 1914.

30. Logue, "Union Veterans," 423; Rosenburg, *Living Monuments*, 151–52.

31. Davies, "Mexican War Veterans."

32. Linares, "Civil War Pension Law," 8–13, 16, 26–30.

33. McCawley, *Artificial Limbs*, 1–6; Mark E. Rodgers, *Tracing*, 1–10; McClurken, "After the Battle," 276–96.

34. Logue, *To Appomattox*, 124; Costa, *Evolution*, 162; M. B. Morton, "Federal and Confederate Pensions," 73–74.

35. Quoted in Faust, *This Republic*, 199.

36. Stearns, *Be a Man!*; Rotundo, *American Manhood*, 136–37. Bederman, *Manliness and Civilization*, denies that a "crisis" of manhood existed—she uses the term "manliness"—but provides an excellent description of conditions that have led others to come to the opposite conclusion.

37. Ramold, *Baring*, 4–7.

38. Craig Thompson Friend, "From Southern Manhood to Southern Masculinities," in *Southern Masculinity*, ed. Friend, xi–xiii. See also Joe Creech, "The Price of Eternal Honor: Independent White Christian Manhood in the Late Nineteenth-Century South," in *Southern Masculinity*, ed. Friend, esp. 25–31; Kris DuRocher, "Violent Masculinity: Learning Ritual and Performance in Southern Lynchings," in *Southern Masculinity*, ed. Friend, 46–64.

39. Hannah, *Manhood*, 2, 9, 18, 39.

40. Rotundo, *American Manhood*, 178–81.

41. Ibid., 232–39.

42. Pugh, *Sons*, xviii–xix, 110–25.

43. Sandage, *Born Losers*, 5; Stott, *Jolly Fellows*.

44. Pugh, *Sons*, 251; Smiles, *Duty*, 191. See also Smiles, *Character*; Smiles, *Thrift*.

45. Hilkey, *Character*, 33, 80–83, 144–45; Whipple, *Success and Its Conditions*, 20–21.

46. Lewis, *Why Some Succeed*, 481.

47. Owen, *Success*.

48. Steinbeck, *East of Eden*, 14–19, 45, 50–53.

49. Quoted in Linderman, *Embattled Courage*, 280.

50. Gartner and Rockoff, "Veterans." For one Revolutionary War veteran's life and the way that the public viewed him and other survivors, see Alfred F. Young, *Shoemaker*.

51. Warner, "Veteran," 171.

52. Kaplan, *Walt Whitman*, 778. For an analysis of the poem, see Erkkila, *Whitman*, 244–46; Whitman, "Carol."

Chapter 1

1. Bryant, *Cahaba*; *Confederate Veteran*, March 1921.

2. *Daily Cleveland Herald*, July 1, 1865; Jenkin Lloyd Jones, *Artilleryman's Diary*, 360; Dyer and Moore, *Tennessee Civil War Veterans Questionnaires*, 1:175 (hereafter cited as *TCWVQ*); Jordan, *Red Diamond Regiment*, 247; Trenerry, "When the Boys Came Home," 292; *Daily Missouri Democrat*, June 9, August 12, 1865.

3. Fish, "Back to Peace," 436; *Daily Missouri Democrat*, June 9, 1865; U.S. Sanitary Commission, *Soldier's Friend*, 35–36. For a brief, useful account of the logistics of demobilization and the experiences of Union and Confederate soldiers as they traveled home, see Holberton, *Homeward Bound*.

4. U.S. Sanitary Commission, *Soldier's Friend*, 19–20.

5. Jenkin Lloyd Jones, *Artilleryman's Diary*, 362.

6. Jordan, *Red Diamond Regiment*, 247–48, 250; Blanchard, *I Marched*, 149.

7. Trenerry, "When the Boys Came Home," 289–91.

8. *Daily Cleveland Herald*, June 5, 1865.

9. *Bangor Daily Whig and Courier*, July 7, 1865; *North American and United States Gazette*, August 12, 1865; *Boston Daily Advertiser*, August 30, 1865.

10. Wilkinson, *Mother*, 366–67.

11. Stillwell, *Story*, 277–78.

12. *TCWVQ*, 2:814, 4:1495.

13. Phillips, *Diehard Rebels*, 180–81.

14. Oldham, *From Richmond to Texas*, 96–97, 66–67, 85, 98–99.

15. *TCWVQ*, 3:1064–65, 5:2262; Jackman, *Diary*, 169.

16. *TCWVQ*, 2:703, 5:1870–71.

17. Ibid., 1:98, 2:627, 3:929, 972; Wood, *Reminiscences*, 76.

18. Benét, *John Brown's Body*, 294.

19. *TCWVQ*, 3:992.

20. Rotundo, *American Manhood*, 179.

21. Phillips, *Diehard Rebels*, 179–81; *Confederate Veteran*, June, July, August, October, November, December 1895.

22. *TCWVQ*, 5:1944; Fisher, *War*, 154–65; Groce, *Mountain Rebels*, 131–36.

23. *TCWVQ*, 2:548, 711, 3:1119, 5:1803.

24. Kuntz, *Fiddler's Companion*.

25. *TCWVQ*, 1:316, 2:602–3, 697.

26. Ibid., 3:914–15, 1119; Trotter, *Bushwhackers*, 113–19.

27. *TCWVQ*, 2:801, 1:374, 4:1714.

28. Quoted in Carmichael, *Last Generation*, 213.

29. Ephraim Anderson, *Memoirs*, 414; *TCWVQ*, 1:242, 165, 217; Stephenson, *Civil War Memoir*, 383–84.

30. Holt, *Mississippi Rebel*, 343.

31. Reid, *After the War*, 155–56, 239.

32. Dennett, *South*, 34, 266, 45, 67, 63.

33. LeConte, *When the World Ended*, 98–99, quoted in Wetherington, *Plain Folk's Fight*, 234.

34. Garcia, *Céline*, 149, 150, 152.

35. Clemson, *Rebel*, 89.

36. Elmore, *Heritage*, 151.

37. Moore, *War*, 52–53.

38. Bolsterli, *Remembrance*, 107; Stone, *Brokenburn*, 346–47, 349, 363–64.

39. Starbuck, *My House*, 202–4.

40. *Soldier's Friend*, March 1865.

41. *United States Service Magazine*, April 1866; Ordronaux, *Report*, 3.

42. Charles Baker Fields Diary, Virginia Historical Society, April 8, 9, 19, 20, 22, 24, May 6, 1865.

43. Bevens, *Reminiscences*, 249; *TCWVQ*, 4:1362.

44. Linderman, *Embattled Courage*, 267; Stephenson, *Civil War Memoir*, 386–87.

45. *TCWVQ*, 4:1324; Brinton, *Personal Memoirs*, 350; Coe, *Mine Eyes*, 232.

46. *Vermont Watchman and State Journal*, June 30, 1865; *Soldier's Friend*, July 4, 1868.

47. James A. Garfield to Crete Garfield, December 6, 1863, in Garfield, *Wild Life*, 300–301; Fish, "Back to Peace," 441.

48. Russell L. Johnson, *Warriors*, 274; Frank, *Life*, 178–81.

49. *Bureau of Information and Employment*, 2; *Circular*, 4.

50. *Athenaeum*, April 1864.

51. Trowbridge, *Frank Manly*, 10–11.

52. Bardeen, *Little Fifer's War Diary*, 290, 64, 201.

53. *Soldier's Friend*, June 1866. For soldiers' shock at immorality among their comrades, see Reid Mitchell, *Civil War Soldiers*, 73–75.

54. Bull, *Soldiering*, 249; Charles W. Wills, *Army Life*, 370.

55. Quoted in Graf, *On Many*, 423.

56. Jenkin Lloyd Jones, *Artilleryman's Diary*, 365.

57. Officers of 1st United States Veteran Volunteer Engineers, "To All Whom It May Concern," September 24, 1865, William Tucker Letter, Wisconsin Veterans Museum; Benjamin T. Smith, *Private Smith's Journal*, 230; Geer, *Civil War Diary*, 232–33.

58. Kreiser, "Socioeconomic Study"; Fish, "Back to Peace," 437–39.

59. Quoted in Severo and Milford, *Wages*, 130–31.

60. *New York Observer and Chronicle*, January 26, 1865; *Chicago Tribune*, June 21, 1865; *Milwaukee Sentinel*, May 26, 1865; U.S. Sanitary Commission, *Bureau*.

61. *New York Times*, January 23, 1865; *Independent*, June 1, 1865.

62. *New York Times*, January 23, 1865.

63. Severo and Milford, *Wages*, 138–41.

64. *New York Times*, August 19, 31, 1865; *Frank Leslie's Illustrated Newspaper*, November 4, 1865; *Milwaukee Sentinel*, May 26, 1865; *The Knapsack*, November 2, 1865; *Soldier's Friend*, July, February 1866.

65. *Soldier's Friend*, February 1866, October 31, 1868.

66. *Soldier's Friend*, February, June 1866, June 27, 1868, May 1865; *Village Record*, August 2, 1867.

67. *New York Evangelist*, September 21, 1865; U.S. Sanitary Commission, *Soldier's Friend*, 27–28, 32–33; *Soldier's Friend*, February 1866.

68. *Soldier's Friend*, February 1866.

69. *Boston Daily Advertiser*, August 1, 1865.

70. *TCWVQ*, 2:455, 828, 1:242, 3:1169.

71. Phillips, *Diehard Rebels*, 182.

72. McClurken, *Take Care*, 48.

73. Wetherington, *Plain Folk's Fight*, 261–305.

74. *TCWVQ*, 2:602–3.

75. Ibid., 3:1064–65, 2:749–50, 4:1498.

76. *Richmond Dispatch*, December 3, 1893.

77. *TCWVQ*, 2:548, 575, 4:1442, 1:418.

78. Trowbridge, *South*, 115, 117.

79. *TCWVQ*, 3:938, 5:2088–89.

80. Ibid., 3:983.

81. Blair, *Cities*, 55–62.

82. Charles Henry Smith, *Bill Arp's Peace Papers*, 150.

83. Rable, *But There Was No Peace*; Logue, *To Appomattox*, 111–15.

84. Dixon, *Leopard's Spots*, 150–51.

85. Dixon, *Clansman*, 320–21.

86. Beard, *Bristling*, 284–87, 343–48, 301–2, 381–89.

87. Sheehan-Dean, *Why Confederates Fought*, 192–95. For historians' agreement on the Klan's popularity among Confederate veterans, see Gorman, "When Johnny Came," 44–46.

88. U.S. Congress, *Report of the Joint Committee on Reconstruction: Georgia, Alabama, Mississippi, Arkansas*, 38 (hereafter cited as *RJCR*).

89. *RJCR: Florida, Louisiana, Texas*, 37, 39; *Topeka Weekly Leader*, February 15, 1866; Smallwood, Crouch, and Peacock, *Murder*.

90. *RJCR: Virginia, North Carolina, South Carolina*, 24, 31.

91. Ibid., 95.

92. Andrews, *South*, 318–19.

93. *RJCR: Virginia, North Carolina, South Carolina*, 7–8, 179.

94. Ibid., 276–77.

95. Ibid., 184–85, 196.

96. *RJCR: Florida, Louisiana, Texas*, 80; *RJCR: Virginia, North Carolina, South Carolina*, 271–72; *RJCR: Georgia, Alabama, Mississippi, Arkansas*, 6.

97. *RJCR: Georgia, Alabama, Mississippi, Arkansas*, 16–17; Rubin, *Shattered Nation*, 169–71.

98. *RJCR: Virginia, North Carolina, South Carolina*, 68.

99. Wilkins, *"War Boy,"* 33, 81.

100. *TCWVQ*, 2:719, 1:338–40.

101. Ibid., 4:1387, 1418.

Chapter 2

1. Bugbee, "Last Review," 28.

2. *Confederate Veteran*, February 1899.

3. Charles Edgeworth Jones, *Family Reunion*.

4. U.S. House of Representatives, *Investigation of the National Home*, 264.

5. *Soldier's Friend*, September 19, 1868.

6. "The Empty Sleeve at Newport," 534. The hero—or antihero—of William Dean Howells's *A Foregone Conclusion* loses his arm in the war, which proves to be a somewhat superficial attraction to the woman he eventually and not particularly happily marries. The amputation becomes a plot device rather unrelated to any sort of permanent moral or personal effect on the veteran (Beck, "Civil War Veterans," 80–81).

7. Soldiers and Sailors Home Fair, *Great Fair!*

8. *Soldier's Friend*, July 25, 1868.

9. Quoted in Wetherington, *Plain Folk's Fight*, 234; Figg and Farrell-Beck, "Amputation," 454, 459.

10. R. B. Rosenburg, "'Empty Sleeves and Wooden Pegs': Disabled Confederate Veterans in Image and Reality," in *Disabled Veterans*, ed. Gerber, 206–12; Williams, *My Old Confederate Home*, 9–11, 18–20.

11. Robert I. Goler and Michael G. Rhode, "From Individual Trauma to National Policy: Tracking the Uses of Civil War Veteran Medical Records," in *Disabled Veterans*, ed. Gerber, 163–84; Goler, "Loss."

12. Figg and Farrell-Beck, "Amputation," 461–62; McDaid, "'How a One-Legged Rebel Lives,'" 122.

13. Davis, *Camp-Fire Chats*, 197.

14. S. Weir Mitchell, "The Case of George Dedlow," in *Autobiography*, 149.

15. Gannon, "'And, If Spared,'" n.p.

16. McCampbell, *Ex-Confederate Soldiers' Home*, 5, 4; Waddill, *Song*, 7, 9, 10.

17. Wooley, *Irritable Heart*, 40–41.

18. Surgeon's Daily Records, 1867–77, 29, 11, 24, 16–17, Clement J. Zablocki Veterans' Affairs Medical Center Library; Admission Applications, 1867–72: National Home for Disabled Volunteer Soldiers, Northwestern Branch, Milwaukee Public Library.

19. *Neighbor's Home Mail*, May, November 1877, January, May 1878; *Ohio Soldier*, September 29, 1888.

20. *Ohio Soldier*, June 22, 1888.

21. *Confederate Veteran*, April 1899.

22. *Milwaukee Sunday Telegraph*, July 16, 1882; *Ohio Soldier*, April 7, 1888; *Petition and Statements*, 1–3.

23. *Home Bulletin*, January 15, 1887.

24. "Danger in Exercise," *Medical and Surgical Reporter*; Wooley, *Irritable Heart*, 39.

25. Pizarro, Silver, and Prause, "Physical and Mental Health Costs."

26. Jarvis, *Male Body*, 66–112.

27. Babington, *Shell-Shock*, 14–17.

28. Patient Records, Mendota Mental Health Institute Papers, Wisconsin Historical Society.

29. McClurken, *Take Care*, 120–33.

30. *Ohio Soldier*, March 28, 1891.

31. Emery, *It Takes People*, 91–93.

32. Wetherington, *Plain Folk's Fight*, 235–37.

33. *Milwaukee Sentinel*, January 13, 1880.

34. Scurfield, "Post-Traumatic Stress Disorder," 188.

35. Williams-Searle, "Cold Charity," 157–86.

36. *Soldier's Friend*, June 1865.

37. McDaid, "'How a One-Legged Rebel Lives,'" 135; Gantz, *Such*, 95–100.

38. Frances Clarke, "'Honorable Scars': Northern Amputees and the Meaning of Civil War Injuries," in *Union Soldiers*, ed. Cimbala and Miller, 361–94.

39. *Saturday Evening Post*, February 10, 1866.

40. Reed, *One Arm*. The same poem—with "one-legged" replacing "crippled" in the last line—was published as "The One-Legged Soldier" by James Walsh, Co. E., 19th Massachusetts and Co. K, 37th Massachusetts Infantry, Disabled at Petersburg; as "One-Arm Soldier, Co. D, 3d Mass. Cavalry, Disabled at Winchester, Virginia"; and as "The One-Armed Boy, Wounded at Petersburg, Va.," all in American Broadsides and Ephemera, Series 1, American Antiquarian Society.

41. Robson, *How a One-Legged Rebel Lives*, 3. See also McDaid, "With Lame Legs," 22.

42. Cochrane, *History*, 700–702.; *John F. Chase*; *New York Times*, June 18, 1886; Lynn S. Brown, *Gulfport*, 92–97; Weeks, *Gettysburg*, 78.

43. *Harper's Weekly*, July 29, November 4, 1865; *Soldier's Friend*, June 1865.

44. "Exhibition of Left-Hand Penmanship," William Orland Bourne Papers, New York University.

45. Padilla, "Army," 20–66.

46. Katz, *In the Shadow*, 88–102; Rosemarie Garland Thompson, *Extraordinary Bodies*, 35.

47. Bellows, "Provision Required," 10.

48. *Bellefonte (Pennsylvania) Democratic Watchman*, September 3, 1869.

49. Henry W. Bellows to Stephen G.[*sic*] Perkins, August 15, 1862, in U.S. Sanitary Commission, *Documents*, 2.

50. Knapp, "*Sanitaria*," n.p.

51. John Ordronaux, "Proposed Scheme of Relief for Military Invalids," in U.S. Sanitary Commission, *Documents*, 6–8; Stephen H. Perkins, "Report of the Pension Systems, and Invalid Hospitals of France, Prussia, Russia, and Italy, with Some Suggestions upon the Best Means of Disposing of Our Disabled Soldiers," in U.S. Sanitary Commission, *Documents*; Bellows, "Provision Required," 5, 10.

52. Bellows, "Provision Required," 10; *New York Observer and Chronicle*, August 3, 1865; *Soldier's Friend*, April 1866; *Scientific American, New Series*, February 4, 1865; Padilla, "Army," 70–84.

53. Cetina, "History," 283–85; *National Soldiers' Home near Dayton, Ohio*, 14; *Harper's Weekly Supplement*, February 18, 1871.

54. U.S. House of Representatives, *Investigation of the National Home*, 71, 218.

55. *Soldier's Friend*, April 1866; *Prairie Farmer*, March 17, August 4, 1866; *Daily Missouri Democrat*, August 19, 1865; *Colman's Rural World*, June 15, 1865; *Chicago Tribune*, May 1, 1865.

56. McDaid, "'How a One-Legged Rebel Lives,'" 126; Gorman, "When Johnny Came," 37–38.

57. Illinois Soldiers' College and Military Academy, *Illinois Soldiers' College*; *Catalogue of the Officers and Students*, 23.

58. *Soldier's Friend*, August 8, 1868; *Catalogue of the Officers and Students*, 14; "Hansen Military Academy."

59. Cahn, *Teenie Weenies Book*.

60. McMurtrie, *Disabled Soldier*; *Your Duty*, n.p.

61. Corbett, *Out at the Soldiers' Home*, 74; Ramold, *Baring*, 124–25, 141–43.

62. *Milwaukee Sentinel*, December 22, 1869.

63. U.S. House of Representatives, *Investigation of the National Home*, 605, 612–13; *National Police Gazette*, December 18, 1886.

64. *Confederate Home Messenger*, November 1910, April 1911.

65. *Report of the Soldiers' Home Trustees*, 6.

66. Lender and Martin, *Drinking*, 116–22; H. Wayne Morgan, *Yesterday's Addicts*, 9–10, 16–23; Musto, *American Disease*, 73–77.

67. Hendin and Hass, *Wounds*, 183–84; Falvo, *Medical and Psychological Aspects*, 326–27; Corbett, *Out at the Soldiers' Home*, 74–75; Range and Vinovskis, "Images of Elderly in Popular Magazines," 137–38; Kelly, *Creating*, 159–60; Logue, "Union Veterans," 431–32 n. 41.

68. Dean, *Shook*, 87, 98–108, 168–70; Figley and Southerly, "Psychosocial Adjustment," 167–80; Kulka et al., *Trauma*, 86–138, 139–88; Hendin and Hass, *Wounds*, 183–84; Goodwin, "Etiology," 6–11; Heinemann et al., "Prescription Medicine Misuse," 301–16.

69. White, "Lessons," 33–37.

70. *Proceedings of the Northwestern Soldiers' Home Association*, 25, 24.

71. Parsons, *Manhood Lost*, 58, 12, 41.

72. Page, "Gray Jacket," 29, 30, 33.

73. U.S. House of Representatives, *Investigation of the National Home*, 169.

74. Faville, "Canteen," 11.

75. *Home Bulletin*, December 12, 1887.

76. U.S. House of Representatives, *Investigation of the National Home*, 136, 137.

77. Record D, National Home Northwestern Branch, 1–110, 547–56, 681–90, 187, Clement J. Zablocki Veterans' Affairs Medical Center Library.

78. Ibid., 12–13, 584, 183, 289, 177.

79. Ibid., 254, 550, 556, 552; *Surgeon's Daily Records*, 4:5, Northwestern Branch, National Home for Disabled Volunteer Soldiers, Clement J. Zablocki Veterans' Affairs Medical Center Library.

80. Logue, "Union Veterans," 416; Northwestern Branch, National Home for Disabled Volunteer Soldiers, General, Special, and Circular Orders, 1908, Clement J. Zablocki Veterans' Affairs Medical Center Library; Kelly, *Creating*, 144; Record D, 1–10, 547–56, 681–90, 3, 4.

81. Henry Ives File, Sample Case Files, Records of the Public Health Service, Northwestern Branch, National Home for Disabled Volunteer Soldiers, Record Group 90, National Archives and Records Administration.

82. "Softening of the brain" was a popular term for "paralytic dementia," or an actual softening of the brain tissue, encephalomalcia (*Dorland's Illustrated Medical Dictionary*, 1540).

83. Although I accept late-nineteenth-century physicians' rather general and simplistic diagnoses of "alcoholism," experts now believe that people can abuse alcohol without being dependent or addicted to it, although abuse even without addiction can cause serious health and behavioral problems. Knott describes several levels of "alcohol dependence syndrome," with "alcoholism"—periods of intoxication followed by withdrawal—the "acute phase" (*Alcohol Problems*, 21–25, 40–43; see also Mendelson and Mello, *Medical Diagnosis*, 5–8).

84. *Hospital Record*, 1:5. Statistics come from a sampling of three volumes of the *Hospital Record*: 1:1–155, 4:1–78, 281–90, 391–400, 5:1–10, 101–10, 201–10, 301–10, 401–10, 501–10.

85. Ibid., 1:5, 75, 106, 154, 4:12, 449.

86. Courtwright, "Opiate Addiction"; "Temperance," *The Independent* 25 (March 25, 1869): 1,060. On Vietnam, see, e.g., Kuzmarov, "Myth." Ironically, the Victorian concern over addiction to narcotics reflected an uneasiness with modernization represented by the powerful drugs and technologies used to deliver them—from easy-to-swallow pills to easy-to-use syringes—marketed widely by pharmaceutical companies late in the century (Hickman, "'Mania Americana'").

87. Greenlee, *Alcohol*, [4]; "Old Soldier's Experience," 55.

88. *New York Times*, January 3, 1895; U.S. House of Representatives, *Investigation of the Soldiers' Home*, 21.

89. U.S. House of Representatives, *Investigation of the Soldiers' Home*, 725; Cetina,

"History," 444. Twenty-first-century beers with equivalent alcohol content would be light beers, which generally contain around 4.0 percent alcohol.

90. Minutes of the Proceedings of the Board of Managers of the National Asylum for Disabled Volunteer Soldiers, 1:328, Clement J. Zablocki Veterans' Affairs Medical Center Library; U.S. House of Representatives, *Investigation of the Soldiers' Home*, 726, quoted in Cetina, "History," 443.

91. "The 'Canteen' in Soldiers' Homes," 555–56; Cetina, "History," 451.

92. *Report of the Board of Managers* (1903), 89; *Annual Reports of the Board of Managers and Inspection of Branches of the National Home for Disabled Volunteer Soldiers, 1907*, 158; *Hospital Record*, 4:12, 449.

93. H. Wayne Morgan, *Drugs*, 65–74; Musto, *American Disease*, 77–79; H. Wayne Morgan, "Abuse of Chloral Hydrate," in *Yesterday's Addict*, 145–46.

94. *Report of the Board of Managers of the National Home for Disabled Volunteer Soldiers, 1894*, 208–9.

95. Hickman, *Secret Leprosy*, 52–54.

96. H. Wayne Morgan, *Drugs*, 74–83; Lender and Martin, *Drinking*, 122–24; Clark, *Perfect Keeley Cure*, 17–18; Keeley, *Opium*, 79; Warsh, "Adventures."

97. Cetina, "History," 441; *New York Times*, January 3, 1895; *Togus*, 46; *Confederate Veteran*, March, November 1893.

98. Clark, *Perfect Keeley Cure*, iii (the *Telegraph* quote is from a clipping glued to the back of the copy of Clark's book in the Milwaukee Public Library); H. Wayne Morgan, *Drugs*, 74; *Proceedings of the Northwestern Soldiers' Home Association*, 19.

99. *Report of the Board of Managers* (1894), 209; Lender and Martin, *Drinking*, 123–24; Samuel Hopkins Adams, *Great American Fraud*, 121; *Minutes of the Board of Managers*, 2:599. For a brief but illuminating account of an American's efforts to establish the Keeley Cure in England, see Crellin, "Alcoholism." Various articles and letters published in *Medical News* in 1892 debated the effectiveness of the cure, with most doctors suggesting that although it might not damage patients, it did not in and of itself conquer alcoholism. See esp. Randall, "Psychologic Aspect." For a positive and even defensive article, see Haskell, "Keeley Cure."

100. *Minutes of Proceedings of the Board of Managers of the National Asylum for Disabled Volunteer Soldiers*, 2:599; Record D, 548; *Plain Facts*, 7–9.

101. U.S. House of Representatives, *Investigation of the Soldiers' Home*, xi.

102. Ibid., 38.

103. Ibid., 28, 29, 107, 34.

104. Ibid., xi, 37.

105. Ibid., 511, 655, 654.

106. Ibid., 117, 118.

107. Ibid., 32.

108. Ibid., v–vi.

109. Charles W. Morehouse Diary, March 13, 1912, Minnesota Historical Society.

110. Ibid., April 3, 1912.

111. Ibid., March 28, 29, 1912.

112. Ibid., March 5, April 8, 12, 13, June 9, 1912.

113. Ibid., April 9, 1912.

114. Ibid., April 11, 14, 25–27, November 23, 1912.

115. Gautier, *Harder Than Death*, 50, 53.

Chapter 3

1. "Gettysburg," United Confederate Veterans Records, R. E. Lee Camp No. 1; Douthat, *Gettysburg.*

2. Catton, "Army of the Cumberland."

3. Simon Bronner, "Reading Consumer Culture," in *Consuming Visions*, ed. Bronner, 13–53; Edwards, *New Spirits*, 89–96; McGovern, *Sold American.*

4. O'Leary, *To Die For*, 43.

5. Stephen T. Morgan, "Fellow Comrades," 237; *Ohio Soldier*, March 17, July 21, August 4, 1888.

6. *Ohio Soldier*, September 15, 1888; Rowell, *Yankee Artillerymen*, 265–71.

7. *Milwaukee Sunday Telegraph*, May 30, 1880; Noonan, "Politics," 29, 31, 43.

8. *Pacific Veteran*, July 30, 1886, reprinted in *Home Bulletin*, June 5, 1886.

9. Gaines M. Foster, *Ghosts*, 133–41.

10. *Confederate Veteran*, April 1900.

11. Allison, *History*, n.p.

12. Svenson, "'Devoted,'" 50.

13. *Confederate Veteran*, August 1898.

14. *The Reunion of the Blue and the Gray at Vicksburg, Mississippi* (Vicksburg, ca. 1890), Box 46, United Confederate Veterans Records, R. E. Lee Camp No. 1, Virginia Historical Society.

15. *Souvenir.*

16. *Confederate Veteran*, August 1899.

17. McCrory, *Grand Army*, 36.

18. *Milwaukee Sunday Telegraph*, July 6, 13, 1884.

19. Tappan, *Passing*, 99–111.

20. Timothy B. Smith, *Golden Age*, 14–15, 51; Faust, *This Republic*, 85, 95–98.

21. "National Cemetery," 181–84.

22. Weeks, *Gettysburg*, 30–33.

23. Kaser, *At the Bivouac*; Timothy B. Smith, *Golden Age*, 2–8, 34–36.

24. Smith, *Golden Age*, 61.

25. Ibid., 64.

26. Weeks, *Gettysburg*, 61, 68, 79.

27. Ibid., 91–95.

28. *Ohio Soldier*, September 24, 1887.

29. Boynton, "National Military Park"; Timothy B. Smith, *This Great Battlefield*, 101.

30. LaFantasie, *Gettysburg Requiem*, 286–301.

31. *Milwaukee Sunday Telegraph*, May 13, October 7, 1883.

32. Ibid., May 13, 1883.

33. *Confederate Veteran*, March 1898, June 1893, January 1895.

34. Simon J. Bronner, "Object Lessons: The Work of Ethnological Museums and Collections," in *Consuming Visions*, ed. Bronner, 217–54; William Y. Thompson, "Sanitary Fairs"; Gallman, "Voluntarism."

35. *Grand Army Fair*; *What Will You Do?*, n.p.

36. *Antiques Roadshow*, April 10, 2006.

37. Dunkelman, *Brothers*, 264–65; *Ohio Soldier*, September 1, 1888; Roberts, "G.A.R. Museum"; Mary Ann Brown, "Ohio Veterans' Memorial Halls"; Tappan, *Passing*, 35.

38. *Catalogue of Exhibits*, n.p.

39. *Confederate Veteran*, September 1893.

40. Ibid., September 1895, October, November 1897.

41. Ibid., January 1893.

42. "South's Museum."

43. *Confederate Veteran*, August 1897.

44. R. E. Lee Camp Soldiers' Home, "War Relics and Antiquities" (n.p., 188X), Box 45, United Confederate Veterans Records, R. E. Lee Camp No. 1.

45. *Confederate Home Messenger*, June, November 1909, June 1910, January 1908.

46. Toomey, *Maryland Line Confederate Soldiers' Home*, 23, 115–38.

47. Bridge, "Shrine"; *Libby Prison War Museum*, n.p.

48. *Ohio Soldier*, February 25, 1888; *Soldiers' Tribune*, April 5, 1888.

49. *Ohio Soldier*, February 11, 1888; *Soldiers' Tribune*, March 8, 1888.

50. *Libby Prison War Museum*, n.p.; *Confederate Veteran*, July 1893.

51. Bridge, "Shrine."

52. Edwards, *New Spirits*, 54–56.

53. Sauers, *"To Care,"* xv–xviii. In 1906, the publishers changed the title to *The National Tribune, National Guardsman, the American Standard*; twenty years later, after acquiring the official newspaper of the American Expeditionary Force during the Great War, it became the *National Tribune: Stars and Stripes*. The words were reversed in the 1960s to *Stars and Stripes: The National Tribune*.

54. *Ohio Soldier*, August 20, 1887.

55. *Milwaukee Sunday Telegraph*, July 2, December 3, November 19, 1882.

56. *Ohio Soldier*, February 14, 1891; *National Tribune*, April 26, 1883.

57. *Neighbor's Home Mail*, February 1883, December 1878, December 1880, May 1881.

58. *Confederate Veteran*, July, December 1893.

59. Ibid., March, May 1894, June 1895, June 1898.

60. Ibid., May 1899, January 1900.

61. Ibid., October, November 1894, June 1895, January, December 1897.

62. *American Tribune*, September 21, 1888; *Ohio Soldier*, June 20, 1891.

63. *Confederate Veteran*, May 1893; *Confederate Home Messenger*, May 1909; *National Tribune*, September 13, 1883; *Catalogue No. 336 of United Confederate Veterans and Sons of United Confederate Veterans Uniforms* (Cincinnati: Pettibone, n.d.), Virginia Historical Society; *American Tribune*, August 23, 1889.

64. *American Tribune*, December 28, 1888; EBay, June 22, February 12, June 30, 2006.

65. Corbett, *Out at the Soldiers' Home*; EBay, August 27, October 30, 2005, September 25, May 15, 2006; advertisement, *Insights*, 2; *Confederate Home Messenger*, April 1910. See also Stefano, *Pictorial Souvenirs*. Although none of the NHDVS wares are featured in Stefano's book, it offers examples of virtually all of the styles of plates, cups, pitchers, and other ceramic and glassware sold by the homes.

66. Rainwater and Felger, *American Spoons*, 15–16, 38, 82–88, 258–59; Burgess, *Collector's Guide*, 10, 33, 35, 58, 59.

67. *American Tribune*, August 23, 1889; *Confederate Home Messenger*, July, August 1908; Green, "Protecting Confederate Soldiers," 1087, quoted in O'Leary, *To Die For*, 43–44; EBay, October 21, 2005, March 31, 2006. "Brewster, Gordon & Co., Wholesale Grocers" appears in a one-third-page ad in the *Rochester City Directory*, 882. The "Roster of Soldiers in the 'War of the Rebellion'" on the Monroe County Library System Web site lists Lucas Brewster and John, Peter, Robert, and William Gordon, all of whom survived the war.

68. EBay, February 24, 2006, January 21, 2008, August 20, 2005.

69. *Ohio Soldier*, January 16, 30, 1892, July 4, May 23, 1891.

70. Elizabeth Corbett to Enos Comstock, September 8, 1943, Elizabeth Corbett Papers, Milwaukee Public Library; Corbett, *Out at the Soldiers' Home*, 74–75, 156–57, 186–91; *Wright's Milwaukee County and Milwaukee Business Directory*, 323–29; Descriptive Book, Robert Chivas Post No. 2, Records of Milwaukee, Wisconsin, Grand Army of the Republic Posts, 1865–1943, Milwaukee County Historical Society; Record D, National Home Northwestern Branch, 729, Clement J. Zablocki Veterans' Affairs Medical Center Library; George J. Crosby to George Crosby, March 1, 1903, George J. Crosby and Family Papers, 1776–1945, Minnesota Historical Society; Joshua L. Baily, "Prohibition in Kansas," *Friends' Intelligencer*, March 3, 1900; Cetina, "History," 442.

71. U.S. House of Representatives, *Investigation of the Soldiers' Home*, 32.

72. Ibid., 118.

73. Ibid., 598, 612, 603, 466, 467; Record D, 729.

74. U.S. House of Representatives, *Investigation of the National Home*, 199–200.

Chapter 4

1. *Daily Cleveland Herald*, May 20, 1870; Butler, "National Home," 683.

2. Goldberg, *Citizens and Paupers*, 3, 4, 31–76.

3. *Milwaukee Sentinel*, November 27, 1870, December 24, 1868, February 14, 1878; Marten, "'Place.'"

4. *Annual Report of the Northwestern Branch, National Home for Disabled Volunteer Soldiers, 1875*, 7–8; *Milwaukee Sentinel*, December 23, 1878; *Soldiers' Home*, 6.

5. *Milwaukee Sentinel*, July 7, 1869, July 1, 1872, June 29, 1873, July 5, 1879, July 6, 1880.

6. Ibid., November 19, 1867, February 24, 1868, February 1, September 12, 1871, April 20, 1874, January 31, February 22, March 22, January 17, 1872, December 31, 1877; *Program for the Eleventh Promenade Concert*, July 18, 1877, Clement J. Zablocki Veterans' Affairs Medical Center Library, Milwaukee, Wiscosin.

7. *Milwaukee Sentinel*, July 18, 1872, August 2, 1870, July 16, 1886, June 17, 1869, August 1, 5, 1872, July 1, 1875, July 14, 1877, July 14, 1882, July 31, 1873; *National Soldiers' Home near Milwaukee*, n.p.

8. Conover, "Dayton (O.) Soldiers' Home," 339; Stevens, "National Soldiers' Home," 288.

9. *Handbook*, 18, 36–38, 31.

10. Rosenburg, *Living Monuments*, 107–10; *Confederate Home Messenger*, April 1911, June 1910, January 1911.

11. "Sirens and Symbols: Clarksville Residents Reflect on the Texas Confederate Home."

12. *Arkansas Veteran*, July 1916; *Milwaukee Sentinel*, October 8, 1883; U.S. House of Representatives, *Investigation of the National Home*, 72.

13. On the butter issue, see *Ohio Farmer*, April 22, 1897, April 14, 1898.

14. *Milwaukee Sentinel*, April 13, 1867.

15. Ibid., May 9, 16, 1874.

16. *Milwaukee Daily News*, May 26, 1874; *Milwaukee Sentinel*, May 27, 1874.

17. *Milwaukee Daily News*, June 7, 11, 1874.

18. Ibid., May 15, 23, 1874; *Milwaukee Sentinel*, May 9, 21, 1874.

19. *Home Bulletin*, December 3, 10, 17, 1887.

20. Christopher Miller, "Milwaukee's First Suburbs," 107–8; *Relief Guard*, October 11, 1890.

21. *Journal of the Senate*, 20.

22. U.S. House of Representatives, *Investigation of the National Home*, 81, 82.

23. Ibid., 84.

24. Ibid., 134–35, 81–82.

25. *Milwaukee Sentinel*, February 25, 1889.

26. U.S. House of Representatives, *Investigation of the National Home*, 89.

27. Ibid., 138–39.

28. *Milwaukee Sentinel*, December 24, 1885.

29. [Illegible] to Fitzhugh Lee, January 23, 1892, Robert E. Lee Camp, Confederate Soldiers' Home, Applications for Admission, 1884–1941, Library of Virginia; D. B. Pound to William Terry, May 10, 1886, Robert E. Lee Camp, Confederate Soldiers' Home, Letters, 1885–94, Virginia Historical Society.

30. *Milwaukee Sentinel*, October 7, 1882.

31. Ibid., September 23, October 4, 1883.

32. Ibid., September 23, October 19, 1883.

33. U.S. House of Representatives, *Investigation of the National Home*, 57.

34. Ibid., 167.

35. Haskell, *"Pension Reform."*

36. *Milwaukee Sentinel*, October 10, November 5, 1883.

37. Ibid., August 16, 1884.

38. Ibid., August 20, 1884.

39. Kelly, *Creating*, 141–49.

40. *Proceedings of the Northwestern Soldiers' Home Association*, 22.

41. Alcott, "My Red Cap." For a less uplifting but nevertheless positive fictional account of a veteran and his state home, see Phelps, "John True's Decoration Day."

42. A. C. Smith to James G. Davidson, February 13, January 26, 1907, September 15, 1906; advance sheet of the *Veterans' Voice*; Jesse Cornish, "To My Comrades" (Waupaca, 1906), all in Box 1, Folder 6, Wisconsin, Governor: Records on the Wisconsin Veterans' Home, 1887–1921, Wisconsin Historical Society.

43. *Morning Oregonian*, January 17, 1894.

44. Rosenburg, *Living Monuments*, 104–31; *Atlanta Constitution*, October 4, 1901, quoted in Green, "Protecting Confederate Soldiers," 1087; Williams, *My Old Confederate Home*, 115–16.

45. *National Police Gazette*, July 14, 1883.

46. New York State Soldiers' and Sailors' Home, Board of Trustees, *Investigation*, 14–17.

47. Ibid., 38, 24–42, 49.

48. Ibid., 50, 51–53, 79.

49. Ibid., 62–63.

50. Ibid., 81–83.

51. Ibid., 141.

52. U.S. House of Representatives, *Investigation of the National Home*, 56.

53. Ibid., 72, 119, 215.

54. Ibid., 223, 224.

55. Ibid., 585–86.

56. *Plain Facts*, 4–6, 12.

57. U.S. House of Representatives, *Investigation of the National Home*, 93, 265, 74.

58. *Proceedings of the Northwestern Soldiers' Home Association*, 24.

59. McConnell, *Glorious Contentment*, 124–41.

60. Green, "Protecting Confederate Soldiers," 1088; Williams, *My Old Confederate Home*, 119–21, 147–56.

61. Katz, *In the Shadow*, 88–102; Fischer, *Growing Old*. A large literature examines the psychological and emotional burdens of veterans and others as they age and move into nursing homes; see, e.g., Reinardy, "Decisional Control"; Ghusn, Stevens, and Attasi, "Profile."

62. T. H. Flow, "My Life and Observations at the Home," in *Insights*, 50.

63. Henry Clinton Parkhurst, "The Soldier Home Troops," [1910], n.p., Henry Clinton Parkhurst Collection, State Historical Society of Iowa.

64. Ibid.

65. Ibid.

66. Ibid.

67. Ibid.

68. Henry Clinton Parkhurst, "The Bug House," n.d., n.p., Parkhurst Collection.

69. Henry Clinton Parkhurst, "Iowa Soldiers' Home," n.d., n.p.

70. Ibid.; Parkhurst, "Soldier Home Troops."

71. Flow, "My Life," 39–51.

72. Record of William R. Williams, Alice Williams to [Commandant, R. E. Lee Camp Confederate Home], n.d., Robert E. Lee Camp, Confederate Soldiers' Home, Applications for Admission, 1884–1941.

73. McClintock, "Civil War Pensions."

74. *Report of the Directors*, 6; R. P. Gold to J. E. Graves, [June] 10, 1912, R. P. Gold to Mr. Beard, June 5, 1912, Robert E. Lee Camp, Confederate Soldiers' Home, Applications for Admission, 1884–1941, quoted in *They Just Fade Away*, [2]; Fannie B. Wooldridge to J. E. Graves, March 28, 1909, Robert E. Lee Camp, Confederate Soldiers' Home, Applications for Admission, 1884–1941.

75. Benjamin J. Rogers to W. R. Ezell, [January?] 27, 1904, Ezell Family Papers, Virginia Historical Society.

76. George Crosby to George Crosby Jr., March 1, 1903, June 4, 1897, October 27, 1899, George J. Crosby and Family Papers, Minnesota Historical Society.

77. Temple H. Dunn to "My Dear Bettie," September 14, 1904, Folder 1, Temple H. Dunn Papers, Indiana State Library.

78. Ibid.

79. Ibid., September 1904.

80. Ibid., August 19, September 3, December 2, 1905, July 7, 1906.

81. Ibid., May 21, August 19, September 3, December 2, 1905, July 7, 1906.

82. Ibid., June 27, 1907.

83. *Arkansas Veteran*, December 1915.

84. "Our Togus Home," in *Bubbles*, 4.

85. *State of Idaho Soldier's Home History*, 4–5; Schuellerman, *Life*, 1.

86. Joseph Julius Buck Journal, October 12, 1901, Collection of Linda Lee Weiner.

Chapter 5

1. U.S. House of Representatives, *Investigation of the National Home*, 55–56; *Ohio Soldier*, June 16, 1888.

2. Gambone, *Greatest Generation*, 6–7.

3. *Republican Campaign Text-Book*, 121; Vogel, "Redefining Reconciliation," 74–80.

4. *Grand Army Advocate*, April 18, 1889; McConnell, *Glorious Contentment*, 124–41; Logue, *To Appomattox*, 97–99.

5. Quoted in *Ohio Soldier*, October 7, 1888.

6. *Confederate Veteran*, January 1893.

7. *Atlanta Constitution*, February 11, 1901.

8. Green, "Protecting Confederate Soldiers," 1083–84.

9. Charles W. Johnson, *Veteran*, 5, 6, 7–8, 12–13, 18–19.

10. Other commentators also compared returning Union soldiers to Cromwell's army; see, e.g., *New York Daily Tribune*, June 14, 1865.

11. Theodore Bacon, *Veteran Soldier's Duty*, 3, 11, 12.

12. McConnell, *Glorious Contentment*, 152–62.

13. Purcell, *Sealed*, 72–75.

14. *Home Bulletin*, July 31, 1886.

15. *Puck*, December 20, 1882, September 18, 1889.

16. *Daily Missouri Democrat*, February 18, 1866.

17. Bentley, *Address*, 13; *Soldiers' Tribune*, February 2, 1888; *List of Pensioners*.

18. *Ohio Soldier*, September 17, 1887, September 27, 1890; *Home Bulletin*, December 5, 1885; Circular for Milo B. Stevens and Company, General War Claim Attorneys, Pension Materials, Wisconsin Veterans Museum.

19. *Get a Pension: Office of Charles J. Alden, Pension Claim Agent and War Claim Att'y*, Pension Materials, Wisconsin Veterans Museum.

20. *Neighbor's Home Mail*, February 1878.

21. W. H. Wills, *Rally, Soldiers!*, n.p.

22. *American Tribune*, September 7, 1888, May 30, 1890.

23. *National Tribune*, April 26, 1883; Oliver, *History*, 53, 50, 76, 99–102.

24. U.S. House of Representatives, *Investigation of the National Home*, 75–76; Oliver, *History*, 100.

25. W. H. Wills, *Rally, Soldiers!*, n.p.

26. *American Tribune*, November 30, 1888; *Milwaukee Sunday Telegraph*, March 6, 1881.

27. Grover Cleveland, "Veto of the Dependent Pension Bill," in *Principles and Purposes*, 132, 137, 139.

28. Leonard Woolsey Bacon, "Raid"; Sloane, "Pensions and Socialism," 181–82; Charles Francis Adams, *Civil-War Pension*. Adams's booklet was a republication of a series of articles, "Pensions—Worse and More of Them," *World's Work* 23 (1911–12): 188–92, 327–33, 385–98.

29. *New York Times*, June 13, July 10, August 19, May 25, 1890.

30. Quoted in *American Tribune*, March 14, 1890.

31. *Puck*, May 29, August 28, 1889, September 20, 1893, December 20, 1882. See also Hansen, "New Images," 652–53.

32. Church, "How?" 425–27.

33. Hall, *Indignity*, 5, 6, 7, 8–9, 11.

34. Blanck, "Civil War Pensions," 123; Bentley, *Address*, 9; "The Pension Sharks," *The Nation*, March 28, 1889, 258.

35. Skocpol, *Protecting Soldiers*, 121–23.

36. Blanck, "Civil War Pensions," 124.

37. Katz, *In the Shadow*, esp. 18–54.

38. *Puck*, September 20, 1893; Sloane, "Pensions and Socialism," 181–82.

39. Bierce, *Phantoms*, 187, 273.

40. Halttunen, *Confidence Men*, esp. 1–32.

41. *Confederate Veteran*, November 1893, October 1896, December 1897.

42. *Soldier's Friend*, November 1865.

43. *Home Bulletin*, March 27, 1886, September 19, 1885; *Milwaukee Sunday Telegraph*, October 19, 1884.

44. Dunkelman, *Brothers*, 260.

45. *History of the National Home*, 43.

46. Hamilton, "Tramps," 38; Depastino, *Citizen Hobo*, 17–18.

47. Depastino, *Citizen Hobo*, 11–17, 19–29; Keyssar, *Out of Work*, 134–35.

48. Depastino, *Citizen Hobo*, 51–58.

49. *American Tribune*, July 12, 19, 1889.

50. Faust, *This Republic*, 102–36.

51. Gould, *Veteran's Bride*, 111–12.

52. Chopin, "Wizard," 230–44.

53. Ambrose Bierce, "A Resumed Identity," in Bierce, *Phantoms of a Blood-Stained Period*, 303–8.

54. *Milwaukee Sunday Telegraph*, January 15, 1882; *New York Times*, July 14, 1872; *Milwaukee Sunday Telegraph*, October 28, 1883.

55. *American Tribune*, January 4, 1889.

56. *Milwaukee Sunday Telegraph*, January 13, 1884; *Confederate Veteran*, May 1900; *Relief Guard*, August 16, 1890.

57. *Milwaukee Sunday Telegraph*, November 14, 1880.

58. Ibid.

59. McConnell, "William Newby Case."

60. J. G. Way to "Officers of the Soldiers Home," April 20, 1886, Robert E. Lee Camp, Confederate Soldiers' Home, Applications for Admission, Library of Virginia.

61. *Souvenir*, 20; O'Leary, *To Die For*, 46.

62. *Grand Rapids Reunion* quoted in *Ohio Soldier*, April 21, 1888.

63. Ridpath, *Citizen Soldier*, 52–53, 54–55.

64. *Ohio Soldier*, August 20, 1887; J. W. Turner, "Mother," n.p.

65. *Soldiers' Tribune*, December 29, 1887, April 5, 1888; *American Tribune*, September 19, 1890.

66. Gibson, *Liberality*, 3–4.

67. Gillam, "Their War-Records"; Gillam, "Substitute Question"; *Ohio Soldier*, August 17, 1887.

68. Beath, *History*, 7.

69. Russell L. Johnson, "Civil War Generation"; Lee, "Wealth Accumulation"; Lee, "Health."

70. *Soldier's Friend*, November 1865; Prentice, *Why?*, n.p.

71. *Flag of Our Union*, May 5, 1866; "A Distinction with a Difference," *Punchinello*, June 25, 1870, 205.

72. *Whitewater Register* quoted in *Milwaukee Sunday Telegraph*, October 18, 1885.

73. Brothers Cobb, *Veteran*.

74. Beck, "Civil War Veterans," 99–124. The veterans in *The Gilded Age* by Mark Twain and Charles Dudley Warner are virtually unchanged by their experience; they were the same grasping, unsympathetic characters before and during the war as they were after they had served (Beck, "Civil War Veterans," 22–23).

75. Jewett, "Decoration Day."

76. U.S. Civil Service Commission, *History*, 1–3.

77. Beath, *History*, 28.

78. *American Tribune*, October 14, 1897; *To the Veteran*, n.p.

79. Tanner, "Heroic Service," 61.

80. *Rules and Regulations*, 2; April 11, 1902, December 7, 1897, June 7, 21, March 1, 1898, March 21, 1899, Minutes, 1897–1904, Records of the Union Veterans' Union, John A. Logan Regiment, No. 2, Minnesota Historical Society; *Relief Guard*, August 16, July 26, 1890.

81. *Relief Guard*, August 2, 1890.

82. *Remarks Explanatory*, 4, 6.

83. *Ohio Soldier*, March 12, 1892.

84. Faust, *This Republic*, 229.

85. Thomas H. Brown, *Dedicated*, n.p.; *Grand Army Advocate*, June 6, 1889.

86. Costa, *Evolution*, 212, 165.

87. *Soldier's Friend*, September 1866.

88. Redington, "Their Pensions," 2.

89. Raum, "Pensions and Patriotism," 205.

90. *Ohio Soldier*, January 7, 1888.

Chapter 6

1. Grant, "Reimagined Communities," 514–15; *Neighbor's Home Mail*, October 1878.

2. *Soldiers' Tribune*, January 19, 1888.

3. Robert L. Rodgers, *History*, 3–4.

4. Costa and Kahn, *Heroes and Cowards*, 5–6, 168–69, 184–86.

5. Fredrickson, *Inner Civil War*, 166–80.

6. Pettegrew, "'Soldier's Faith,'" 55; Fahs, "Feminized Civil War," 1488–89.

7. It is important not to exaggerate the unity of Civil War veterans, particularly in the North. Logue warns that especially in politics, old soldiers were often deeply divided. Their apparent unanimity was promoted by the GAR, soldiers' papers, and pension attorneys, who sought to rally veterans behind the Republican Party on issues other than pensions. Nevertheless, even in elections involving the reviled Grover Cleveland, veterans rarely voted with one mind ("Union Veterans").

8. Quoted in Gambone, *Greatest Generation*, 29.

9. *Plain Facts*, 3; Reel, *National Police Gazette*.

10. Clarke, "'Let All Nations See.'"

11. Ayers, *Promise*, 26–28, 335–38.

12. Carmichael, *Last Generation*, 213–36.

13. Blair, *Cities*, 127–34.

14. Hoganson, *Fighting*, esp. 21–40.

15. Linderman, *Embattled Courage*, 271–74.

16. Reardon, "Writing Battle History."

17. Faust, *This Republic*, 258–61; Timothy B. Smith, *Golden Age*, 19–20.

18. *Roster of Wisconsin Volunteers*, 1:iii; *Official Roster*, 1:v.

19. Dickens and Kenzer, "Confederate Memorial Literary Society's Roll of Honour." For an analysis of the Tennessee veterans' responses, see Bailey, *Class*.

20. Fahs, *Imagined Civil War*, 311, 314.

21. *Milwaukee Sunday Telegraph*, March 25, 1883. For a first-person memoir of a

much more formal annual campfire held by veterans of an Iowa regiment every autumn, see Harwood, "GAR Campfires."

22. McConnell, *Glorious Contentment*, 166–85.

23. Quoted in Linson, *My Stephen Crane*, 37; Watkins, *Co. Aytch*, 218.

24. Hess, *Union Soldier*, esp. 181–85; Fussell, "Reflections," 6.

25. Quoted in Ramold, *Baring*, 55.

26. Linderman, *Embattled Courage*, 267–69; Warren, *Scars*, 9–17.

27. Quoted in Warren, *Scars*, 13, 14; Pettegrew, "'Soldier's Faith,'" 58.

28. Holmes, *Occasional Speeches*, 15, 8, 9.

29. Dunkelman, *Brothers*, 2, 4–5.

30. Beath, *History*, 4–5, 23.

31. Catton, *Waiting*, 189–90.

32. *American Tribune*, April 11, 1890; E. P. Bartlett, "Extract from an Address of Gen. E. P. Bartlett, Deputy Commander-in-Chief of the Union Veterans' Union, Delivered at the Division Encampment of Illinois held in Chicago, June 14, 15 and 16, 1905," Records of the Union Veterans' Union, Minnesota Historical Society; *New York Times*, October 11, 1902.

33. *Confederate Veteran*, September 1900, April 1899.

34. *Programme*, 1, quoted in McCrory, *Grand Army*, 25.

35. Allison, *History*, n.p.

36. Carnes, "Middle-Class Men," 37–66; Lovering, *Services*; Hill, *Grand Army Tactics*.

37. Wilson, *Baptized*, 25.

38. Ibid., 18–36; *Confederate Veteran*, February 1895.

39. *Big Eat of the Old Guard, R. E. Lee Camp, No. 1, C. V., January 17, 1893*, R. E. Lee Camp Records, Box 45, Virginia Historical Society.

40. *Ohio Soldier*, September 8, 1888; Van Nest, *Ceremonial*. Van Nest's more generic version of the fake ceremony focused its ridicule more on rituals, secrecy, and the ultramanliness of the members' behavior than on the military aspect. See Van Nest, *Burlesque Degree*.

41. McConnell, *Glorious Contentment*, 48–49; Weeks, *Gettysburg*, 107–8; Marsh, *Greatest Burlesque*, 5, 7, 3.

42. Neff, *Honoring*, 179–224.

43. C. O. Brown, *Battle-Fields*, 13.

44. "Shiloh's Battlefield," *Frank Leslie's Weekly*, reprinted in *American Tribune*, March 28, 1890.

45. Benson, *"Yank" and "Reb,"* 39, 14, 56, 39–42, 93, 109. See also the account of the 1881 visit of Pennsylvania veterans to Virginia and the reciprocal visit by Confederates in *Reunions of the Ex-Soldiers*.

46. *National Tribune*, April 17, 1884.

47. *Indianapolis Herald*, reprinted in *Milwaukee Sunday Telegraph*, October 17, 1880.

48. Kirkland, *Civil War Veterans' Organizations*, 19; Bridge, "Shrine"; *Proceedings of the Ohio Association*; U.S. Army Quartermaster Corps, *Martyrs*; Kellogg, *Life and Death*; Cloyd, "Civil War Prisons."

49. *Milwaukee Sunday Telegraph*, March 6, 1881.

50. Weeks, *Gettysburg*, 98; *Confederate Veteran*, March 1896.

51. Rydford, *Kansas Place-Names*, 411; *Official Souvenir: McPherson County, July 4, 1917*, n.p.; Loftin, "Geraldine, Texas"; *Prairie Farmer*, May 11, 1872; *Grantville*.

52. *Blue and Gray*, January, May 1894.

53. Fawcett and Hepper, *Veterans*; Robinson, "Early Days," 265; *St. Cloud Colony*; Fisk, *Founding Story*; James Meade Adams, *Pioneering*; Walters, "Union Colony."

54. *Fitzgerald Daily News*, June 21, September 1, 1909; Chalker, "Fitzgerald"; Blauvelt, "Reunion"; "Northern Veterans." The enthusiasm characteristic of "booster" advertising and "informational" pamphlets appeared in an 1896 publication, Shrader, *New Canaan!*

55. Gosson, *Post-Bellum Campaigns*, 12, 25, 27, 28.

56. Benson, *"Yank" and "Reb,"* 9, 10; Graham, *Ninth Regiment*, 463–92.

57. Williams, *My Old Confederate Home*, 174–75; Blauvelt, "Reunion"; Chalker, "Fitzgerald," 404.

58. *Blue and Gray*, March 1894.

59. *Confederate Veteran*, November 1893.

60. Kennedy, *Address*, 5; Lang, *Address*, 9.

61. *Milwaukee Sunday Telegraph*, July 3, 1881, reprinted in *Bangor Daily Whig and Courier*, June 13, 1887.

62. *Ohio Soldier*, February 28, 1891.

63. Benson, *"Yank" and "Reb,"* 113; *Ohio Soldier*, December 19, 1891.

64. Quoted in Madison, "Civil War Memories," 205–6; *Ohio Soldier*, March 14, 1891.

65. Coski, *Confederate Battle Flag*, 66–71; *Arkansas Veteran*, October 1914.

66. Speierl, "Civil War Veterans," 41; *Information*.

67. McCrory, *Grand Army*, 37; *Milwaukee Sunday Telegraph*, November 29, 1885. This brief discussion is based on Steele, *Barnes's Brief History*.

68. *Confederate Veteran*, April 1894.

69. Ibid., March 1896.

70. Ibid., May 1895.

71. Prince, "Rebel Yell."

72. *American Tribune*, August 2, 1889.

73. Crane, "Veteran."

74. Blight, *Race and Reunion*, 247; for Blight's typically insightful analysis of Bierce, see 244–51.

75. Bierce, *Phantoms*, 17, 19.

76. Ambrose Bierce to Walter Neale, May 22, 1912, in *Much Misunderstood Man*, 223; Bierce, *Phantoms*, 340.

77. Bierce, *Phantoms*, 110.

78. Hess, *Union Soldier*, 173–80.

79. Whitman, *Walt Whitman*, 281–82.

80. Whitman, *Complete Prose Works*, 74.

81. Robert L. Rodgers, *History*, 3–4.

Bibliography

Manuscripts

American Antiquarian Society, Worcester, Massachusetts
    American Broadsides and Ephemera, Series 1, http://www.newsbank.com/readex/
Huntington Library, Pasadena, California
    Papers of Paul James Lindberg, 1868–93
    Hancock Veteran
    Pacific Veteran
Indiana State Library, Indianapolis
    Temple H. Dunn Papers
Library of Virginia, Richmond
    Robert E. Lee Camp, Confederate Soldiers' Home, Applications for Admission,
        1884–1941 (online)
    Robert E. Lee Camp, Confederate Soldiers' Home, Letters, 1885–94
Milwaukee County Historical Society, Milwaukee, Wisconsin
    Cornelius Wheeler Papers
    Records of Milwaukee, Wisconsin, Grand Army of the Republic Posts, 1865–1943
Milwaukee Public Library, Milwaukee, Wisconsin
    Admission Applications, 1867–72: National Home for Disabled Volunteer Soldiers,
        Northwestern Branch, Milwaukee, Wisconsin
    Elizabeth Corbett Papers
Minnesota Historical Society, St. Paul
    George J. Crosby and Family Papers, 1776–1945
    Charles W. Morehouse Diary, 1912
    Records of the Union Veterans' Union, John A. Logan Regiment, No. 2, St. Paul,
        Minnesota
National Archives and Records Administration, Great Lakes Region, Chicago
    Records of the Public Health Service, Northwestern Branch, National Home for
        Disabled Volunteer Soldiers, Record Group 90
New Jersey Historical Society, Newark
    Newark High School *Athenaeum*
New York University, New York
    William Oland Bourne Papers
    http://memory.loc.gov/ammem/ndlpcoop/nhihtml/cwnyhsarcm.html#wb
Perry-Castenada Library, University of Texas at Austin
    Arkansas Veteran, 1913–17
State Historical Society of Iowa, Des Moines
    Henry Clinton Parkhurst Collection

U.S. Army Heritage and Education Center, Carlisle, Pennsylvania
Frederick Edward Bury Papers
Virginia Historical Society, Richmond
Ezell Family Papers
Charles Baker Fields Diary
Robert E. Lee Camp, Confederate Soldiers' Home, Letters, 1885–94
United Confederate Veterans Records, R. E. Lee Camp No. 1, 1883–1936
Linda Lee Weiner Private Collection
Joseph Julius Buck Journal (photocopy)
Western Reserve Historical Society, Cleveland, Ohio
Confederate Home Messenger, 1907–11
Wisconsin Historical Society, Madison
Carrie Richards McIntyre Papers
Patient Records, Mendota Mental Health Institute Papers, Vol. 11, Ser. 2171
Sauk County Clerk, Soldiers' Funeral Expenses, 1891–1902
Wisconsin, Governor: Records on the Wisconsin Veterans' Home, 1887–1921
Wisconsin Veterans' Home, Minute Book, 1887–96
Wisconsin Veterans' Museum, Madison
Pension Materials, 1864–1914
William Tucker Letter, MSS331
Clement J. Zablocki Veterans' Affairs Medical Center Library, Milwaukee, Wisconsin
Minutes of the Proceedings of the Board of Managers of the National Asylum for Disabled Volunteer Soldiers
Northwestern Branch, National Home for Disabled Volunteer Soldiers, General, Special, and Circular Orders, 1908
Program for the Eleventh Promenade Concert, July 18, 1877
Record D, National Home Northwestern Branch
Surgeon's Daily Records, 1867–77

Government Documents

Annual Reports of the Board of Managers and Inspection of Branches of the National Home for Disabled Volunteer Soldiers, 1907. Washington: Government Printing Office, 1907.

Confederate States of America House of Representatives. *A Bill to Be Entitled an Act to Provide for Wounded and Disabled Officers and Soldiers an Asylum to be Called "The Veteran Soldiers Home."* Richmond, 1863.

Eleventh Census of the United States, Special Schedule, Surviving Soldiers, Sailors, and Marines, and Widows, etc., Milwaukee County and Walworth County. National Archives Microfilm, Reel 111.

Journal of the Senate of the State of Mississippi at a Special Session, January, February, and March, 1902. Nashville: Brandon, 1902.

List of Pensioners on the Roll: January 1, 1883. Washington, D.C.: U.S. Government Printing Office, 1883.

New York State Soldiers' and Sailors' Home, Board of Trustees. *Investigation of the Charges of Mismanagement and Cruelty, at the Soldiers' and Sailors' Home, Bath, N.Y.* N.p., 1883.

Official Roster of Soldiers of the State of Ohio in the War of the Rebellion, and the War with Mexico. 12 vols. Akron, Ohio: Werner, 1886–95.

Record of Service of Michigan Volunteers in the Civil War, 1861–1865. 46 vols. Kalamazoo, Mich.: Ihling and Everard, [ca. 1903–].

Report of the Board of Managers of the National Home for Disabled Volunteer Soldiers. Washington, D.C.: U.S. Government Printing Office, 1894.

Report of the Board of Managers of the National Home for Disabled Volunteer Soldiers for the Fiscal Year Ended June 30, 1900. Washington, D.C.: U.S. Government Printing Office, 1900.

Report of the Board of Managers of the National Home for Disabled Volunteer Soldiers. Washington, D.C.: U.S. Government Printing Office, 1903.

Report of the Directors of the Soldiers' Home of Louisiana to the General Assembly. New Orleans: Nixon, 1867.

Report of the Soldiers' Home Trustees for the Year Ending June 3, 1910. Atlanta: Byrd, 1910.

Roster of Wisconsin Volunteers, War of the Rebellion, 1861–1865. 2 vols. Madison, Wis.: Democrat, 1886.

U.S. Congress. *Report of the Joint Committee on Reconstruction.* 39th Cong. 1st sess., 1866, H.R. 30.

U.S. House of Representatives. *Investigation of the National Home for Disabled Volunteer Soldiers.* 48th Cong., 2nd sess., 1886, H.R. 2676.

———. *The Investigation of the Soldiers' Home at Leavenworth, Kans.* 54th Cong., 2nd sess., 1897, H.R. 3035.

Newspapers and Periodicals

Arkansas Gazette (Little Rock)
Atlanta Constitution
Blue and Gray: The Patriotic American Magazine (Philadelphia)
Chicago Tribune
Daily Missouri Democrat (St. Louis)
Fitzgerald (Georgia) Daily News
Frank Leslie's Illustrated Newspaper (New York)
Harper's Weekly (New York)
The Knapsack (Philadelphia)
The Liberator (Boston)
Little Corporal (Chicago)
Milwaukee Sentinel
The Nation (New York)
New York Daily Tribune
New York Times
Richmond Dispatch
Southern Historical Society Papers
Sword and the Pen (Boston)
Topeka (Kansas) Weekly Leader
Youth's Companion (Boston)

Veterans' Newspapers and Soldiers' Home Newsletters

American Tribune (Indianapolis)
Arkansas Veteran (Sweet Home)

Confederate Home Messenger (Pewee Valley, Ky.)
Confederate Veteran (Nashville, Tenn.)
Grand Army Advocate (Des Moines, Iowa)
Hancock Veteran (New York)
Home Bulletin (Norfolk, Va.)
Milwaukee Sunday Telegraph
National Picket Guard (Chillicothe, Ohio)
National Tribune (Washington, D.C.)
Neighbor's Home Mail (Phelps, N.Y.)
Ohio Soldier (Chillicothe, Ohio)
Pacific Veteran (San Francisco)
Relief Guard (St. Paul, Minn.)
Soldier's Friend and Grand Army of the Republic (New York)
Soldiers' Tribune (Lyons, Kans.)

Online Newspapers and Periodicals

American Periodical Series Online
Arthur's Home Magazine (Philadelphia)
Boston Daily Advertiser
Christian Observer (Louisville)
Christian Union (New York)
Colman's Rural World (St. Louis)
Daily Inter Ocean (Chicago)
Flag of Our Union (Boston)
Friends' Intelligencer (Philadelphia)
Hours at Home: A Popular Monthly of Instruction and Recreation (New York)
The Independent (New York)
Medical and Surgical Reporter (Philadelphia)
National Police Gazette (New York)
New York Evangelist
New York Observer and Chronicle
Ohio Farmer (Cleveland)
Prairie Farmer (Chicago)
Puck (New York)
Punchinello (New York)
The Round Table: A Saturday Review of Politics, Finance, Literature (New York)
Scientific American, New Series (New York)
United States Service Magazine
Western Christian Advocate (Cincinnati)
Zion's Herald and Wesleyan Journal (Boston)

Nineteenth Century U.S. Newspapers, Gale Digital Collections

Bangor (Maine) Daily Whig and Courier
Daily Cleveland Herald
Morning Oregonian (Portland)
North American and United States Gazette (Philadelphia)

Saturday Evening Post (Philadelphia)
Southern Planter and Farmer (Richmond)
St. Paul Daily News
Vermont Watchman and State Journal (Montpelier)
Yankton Press (Dakota Territory)

Pennsylvania State University Digital Library

Bellefonte Democratic Watchman
Huntingdon Globe
Village Record

Published Primary Sources

Adams, Charles Francis. *The Civil-War Pension Lack-of-System: A Four-Thousand-Million Record of Legislative Incompetence Tending to General Political Corruption.* Washington, D.C.: n.p., 1912.

Adams, James Meade. *Pioneering in Cuba: A Narrative of the Settlement of La Gloria, the First American Colony in Cuba, and the Early Experiences of the Pioneers.* Concord, N.H.: Rumford, 1901.

Alcott, Louisa May. "My Red Cap." *Sword and the Pen*, December 7, 1881, 3–4; December 8, 1881, 3–4; December 9, 1881, 3–4; December 10, 1881, 3–4.

Allison, Nathaniel Thompson, ed. and comp. *History of Cherokee County Kansas and Its Representative Citizens.* Chicago: Biographical, 1904. http://skyways.lib.ks.us/genweb/archives/cherokee/cherokee-1904ndx.html. Accessed April 7, 2007.

Anderson, Ephraim. *Memoirs: Historical and Personal, Including the Campaigns of the First Missouri Confederate Brigade.* 2nd ed. Ed. Edwin G. Bearss. Dayton, Ohio: Morningside, 1972.

Andrews, Sidney. *The South since the War, as Shown by Fourteen Weeks of Travel and Observation in Georgia and the Carolinas.* Boston: Ticknor, 1866.

Annual Report of the Northwestern Branch, National Home for Disabled Volunteer Soldiers, 1874. Milwaukee: National Soldiers' Home, 1875.

Annual Report of the Northwestern Branch, National Home for Disabled Volunteer Soldiers, 1875. Milwaukee: National Soldiers' Home, 1876.

Annual Report of the Trustees of the Soldiers' Home in Massachusetts, at Chelsea. Boston: Stillings, 1884.

Ayling, Augustus D. *A Yankee at Arms: The Diary of Lieutenant Augustus D. Ayling, 29th Massachusetts Volunteers.* Ed. Charles F. Herberger. Knoxville: University of Tennessee Press, 1999.

Bacon, Leonard Woolsey. "A Raid upon the Treasury." *Forum* 6 (January 1889): 540–49.

Bacon, Theodore. *The Veteran Soldier's Duty to His Country.* Rochester, N.Y.: Rochester Union and Advertiser, 1884.

Bancroft, Hubert Howe. *The Book of the Fair.* Chicago: Bancroft, 1893.

Bardeen, Charles William. *A Little Fifer's War Diary.* Syracuse, N.Y.: Bardeen, 1910.

Beard, O. T. *Bristling with Thorns: A Story of War and Reconstruction.* New York: Worthington, 1883.

Beath, Robert B. *History of the Grand Army of the Republic.* New York: Bryan, Taylor, 1889.

Beaudot, William J. K., and Lance J. Herdegen. *An Irishman in the Iron Brigade: The Civil War Memoirs of James P. Sullivan, Sergt., Company K, 6th Wisconsin Volunteers*. New York: Fordham University Press, 1993.

Beecham, Robert K. *As If It Was Glory: Robert Beecham's Civil War from the Iron Brigade to the Black Regiments*. Ed. Michael E. Stevens. Madison, Wis.: Madison House, 1998.

Bellows, Henry W. "Provision Required for the Relief and Support of Disabled Soldiers and Sailors and Their Dependents: Sanitary Commission No. 95." In *Documents of the U.S. Sanitary Commission*. Vol. 1. New York: n.p., 1866.

Benét, Stephen Vincent. *John Brown's Body*. 1928; reprint, Chicago: Dee, 1990.

Benson, Comrade C. H. *"Yank" and "Reb": A History of a Fraternal Visit Paid by Lincoln Post, No. 11, G.A.R., of Newark, N.J., to Robt. E. Lee Camp, No. 1, Confederate Veterans and Phil. Kearney Post, No. 10, G.A.R., of Richmond Va., October 15th to October 18th, Inclusive*. Newark, N.J.: Neuhut, 1884.

Bentley, J. A. *An Address by Hon. J. A. Bentley, Delivered, before the Grand Army of the Republic, at Philadelphia, Grand Army Day, October 11, 1879*. Microform, Pamphlets in American History, Civil War, 320.

Bevens, William E. *Reminiscences of a Private: William E. Bevens of the First Arkansas Infantry, C.S.A.* Ed. Daniel E. Sutherland. Fayetteville: University of Arkansas Press, 1992.

Bierce, Ambrose. *Can Such Things Be?* New York: Cape and Smith, 1909.

———. *A Much Misunderstood Man: Selected Letters of Ambrose Bierce*. Ed. S. T. Joshi and David E. Schultz. Columbus: Ohio State University Press, 2003.

———. *Phantoms of a Blood-Stained Period: The Complete Civil War Writings of Ambrose Bierce*. Ed. Russell Duncan and David J. Klooster. Amherst: University of Massachusetts Press, 2002.

Blanchard, Ira. *I Marched with Sherman: Civil War Memoirs of the 20th Illinois Volunteer Infantry*. San Francisco: Huff, 1992.

Bolsterli, Margaret Jones, ed. *A Remembrance of Eden: Harriet Bailey Bullock Daniel's Memories of a Frontier Plantation in Arkansas, 1849–1872*. Fayetteville: University of Arkansas Press, 1993.

Boynton, H. V. "The National Military Park." *Century Illustrated Magazine* 50 (September 1895): 703–8.

Brinton, John H. *Personal Memoirs of John H. Brinton, Civil War Surgeon, 1861–1865*. Carbondale: Southern Illinois University Press, 1996.

Brobst, John F. *Well, Mary: Civil War Letters of a Wisconsin Soldier Volunteer*. Ed. Margaret Brobst Roth. Madison: University of Wisconsin Press, 1960.

Brown, A. G. P. *To the Senate and House of Representatives of the United States of America*. Indianapolis: Silent Army of Deaf Soldiers, Sailors, and Marines, ca. 1889.

Brown, C. O. *Battle-Fields Revisited*. Kalamazoo, Mich.: Eaton and Anderson, 1886.

Brown, Thomas H. *Dedicated to the Grand Army of the Republic: A Compilation of the Laws of the Several States Relating to State Aid for Civil War Veterans*. Sioux Falls, S.D.: n.p., ca. 1900. Microform, Pamphlets in American History, Civil War, 870.

Bubbles Blown by Boys in Blue at the National Military Home, Togus, Maine. Togus, Me.: Casey, 1878.

Bugbee, Emily F. "The Last Review." *Little Corporal* 1 (August 1865): 28.

Bull, Rice C. *Soldiering: The Civil War Diary of Rice C. Bull, 123rd New York Volunteer Infantry*. Ed. K. Jack Bauer. San Rafael, Calif.: Presidio, 1977.

Bureau of Information and Employment: U.S. Sanitary Commission, Supplement to No. 90. Washington, D.C.: McGill and Witherow, 1865.

Butler, Maria Barrett. "The National Home for Disabled Volunteer Soldiers." *Harper's New Monthly Magazine* 73 (October 1886): 683–96.

"The Canteen in Soldiers' Homes." *Friends' Intelligencer* 59 (August 1902): 555–56.

Catalogue of Exhibits in Grand Army Memorial Hall. Chicago: Grand Army Hall and Memorial Association of Illinois, 1919.

Catalogue of the Officers and Students of the Illinois Soldiers' College, Fulton, Ill. Fulton, Ill.: Booth, 1870.

Carlino, Don Santiago. *The Soldier Tramp.* Microform, Pamphlets in American History, Civil War, 4.

Cather, Willa. "The Sculptor's Funeral." In *Willa Cather: Collected Short Fiction, 1892–1912*, ed. Virginia Faulkner. Lincoln: University of Nebraska Press, 1970.

Chamberlain, Joshua Lawrence. *The Passing of the Armies: An Account of the Final Campaign of the Army of the Potomac.* Lincoln: University of Nebraska Press, 1998.

Chopin, Kate. "A Wizard from Gettysburg." In *Bayou Folk.* Boston: Houghton Mifflin, 1894.

Church, William Conant. "How Shall the Pension List Be Revised?" *North American Review* 156 (April 1893): 416–31.

Circular to the Branches and Aid Societies Tributary to the U.S. Sanitary Commission, May 15, 1866: U.S. Sanitary Commission, No. 90. Washington, D.C.: McGill and Witherow, 1865.

Clark, Charles S. *The Perfect Keeley Cure: Incidents at Dwight and "Through the Valley of the Shadow" into the Perfect Light.* 3rd ed. Milwaukee: Clark, 1893.

Clemson, Floride. *A Rebel Came Home: The Diary and Letters of Floride Clemson, 1863–1866.* Rev. ed. Ed. Charles M. McGee Jr. and Ernest M. Lander Jr. Columbia: University of South Carolina Press, 1989.

Cleveland, Grover. *Principles and Purposes of Our Form of Government as Set Forth in Public Papers of Grover Cleveland.* Comp. Francis Gottsberger. New York: Peck, 1892.

Cobb, Brothers, Members of Post 30, G.A.R., Department of Massachusetts. *The Veteran of the Grand Army.* Boston: Richardson, 1871.

Cochrane, Harry Hayman. *History of Monmouth and Wales.* East Winthrop, Me.: Banner, 1894.

Coe, Hamlin Alexander. *Mine Eyes Have Seen the Glory: Combat Diaries of Union Sergeant Hamlin Alexander Coe.* Ed. David Coe. Cranbury, N.J.: Associated University Presses, 1975.

Confederate Soldiers' Home of Georgia. Atlanta: Franklin, 1901.

Confederate Soldiers' Home of Georgia. Atlanta: Franklin, 1902.

"Confederate Veteran Alumni Reunion." *Alumni Bulletin of the University of Virginia* 5 (July 1912): 226–82.

Conover, C. R. "Dayton (O.) Soldiers' Home." *American Magazine* 8 (1884): 339.

Constitution and By-Laws. Norfolk, Va.: Philadelphia Brigade Association, 1896.

Corbett, Elizabeth. *Out at the Soldiers' Home: A Memory Book.* New York: Appleton-Century, 1941.

Crane, Stephen. "The Veteran." *McClure's* 7 (August 1896): 222–24.

"Current Topics." *Albany Law Journal: A Weekly Record of the Law and the Lawyers* 52 (December 21, 1895): 385.

"Danger in Exercise." *Medical and Surgical Reporter* 63 (September 13, 1890): 318.

Davis, Washington. *Camp-Fire Chats of the Civil War*. Chicago: Gehman, 1886.

Day, Horace. *The Opium Habit, with Suggestions as to the Remedy*. New York: Harper, 1868.

Dennett, John Richard. *The South as It Is: 1865-1866*. Ed. Henry M. Christman. New York: Viking, 1965.

The Detroit Tribune's Veteran Soldiers' and Sailors' Hand-Book. Detroit: Detroit Tribune, 1889.

Dixon, Thomas, Jr. *The Clansman, an Historical Romance of the Ku Klux Klan*. New York: Doubleday, Page, 1905.

———. *The Leopard's Spots*. New York: Doubleday, Page, 1902.

Douthat, Robert W. *Gettysburg: A Battle Ode Descriptive of the Grand Charge of the Third Day, July 3, 1863*. New York: Neale, 1905.

Downing, Alexander G. *Downing's Civil War Diary*. Ed. Olynthus B. Clark. Des Moines: Iowa State Department of History and Archives, 1916.

Dyer, Gustavus W., and John Trotwood Moore, comps. *The Tennessee Civil War Veterans Questionnaires*. 5 vols. Easley, S.C.: Southern Historical Press, 1985.

Elmore, Grace Brown. *Heritage of Woe: The Civil War Diary of Grace Brown Elmore, 1861-1868*. Ed. Marli F. Weiner. Athens: University of Georgia Press, 1997.

"The Empty Sleeve at Newport; or, Why Edna Ackland Learned to Drive." *Harper's Weekly*, August 26, 1865, 534.

Faville, M. C. "A Canteen." *Outlook*, July 14, 1900, 654–56.

Fisk, Robert A. *The Founding Story of the Soldier Colony That Would Be Our City of St. Cloud Today as Told by Historian Minnie Moore-Wilson and the Kissimmee Valley Gazette of Kissimmee, Florida, from April 16, 1909 to December 31, 1909*. St. Cloud, Fla.: Fisk, 2006.

Folsom, Charles F. "Some Obscure Mental Symptoms of Disease, Read June 13, 1882." *Massachusetts Medical Society: Medical Communications*, Doc. 1, 1881.

Foster, D. N. *History of the Indiana State Soldiers Home at Lafayette, Indiana*. n.p., ca. 1900.

Gaddis, Edgar T. *Pensions, Etc.: A Manual of Useful Information*. Washington, D.C.: Gaddis, 1906.

Gantz, Jacob. *Such Are the Trials: The Civil War Diaries of Jacob Gantz*. Ed. Kathleen Davis. Ames: Iowa State University Press, 1991.

Garcia, Céline Frémaux. *Céline: Remembering Louisiana, 1850-1871*. Ed. Patrick J. Geary. Athens: University of Georgia Press, 1987.

Garfield, James A. *The Wild Life of the Army: Civil War Letters of James A. Garfield*. Ed. Frederick D. Williams. East Lansing: Michigan State University Press, 1964.

Garland, Hamlin. "The Return of the Private." In *Main-Travelled Roads*. New York: Harper, 1899.

———. *A Son of the Middle Border*. New York: Macmillan, 1917.

Gautier, George R. *Harder Than Death: The Life of George R. Gautier, an Old Texan, Living at the Confederate Home, Austin, Texas*. Austin: n.p., 1902.

Geer, Allen Morgan. *The Civil War Diary of Allen Morgan Geer, Twentieth Regiment, Illinois Volunteers*. Ed. Mary Ann Andersen. Denver: Appleman, 1977.

George, C. J. *William Newby: The Soldier's Return: A True and Wonderful Story of Mistaken Identity*. Cincinnati: Krehbiel, 1893.

Gibson, Henry R. *Liberality, Not Parsimony: This Is Our True Pension Policy*. Washington, D.C.: U.S. Government Printing Office, 1900.

Gillam, Victor. "The Substitute Question Again." *Judge*, October 29, 1892, 286–87.

———. "Their War-Records Contrasted." *Judge*, August 20, 1892, 124–25.

Gosson, Louis C. *Post-Bellum Campaigns of the Blue and Gray, 1881–1882*. Trenton, N.J.: Naar, Day, and Naar, 1882.

Gould, Alta Isadore. *The Veteran's Bride, and Other Poems*. Grand Rapids, Mich.: Farrell, 1894.

Graham, Matthew J. *The Ninth Regiment New York Volunteers (Hawkins' Zouaves)*. New York: Coby, 1900.

Grand Army Fair: Catalogue of the Curiosities, Relics, and Mementoes, Comprising the Collection to be Found in the Police Museum. [Boston?], Mass.: n. p., 1873 through 1880.

Grantville: The G.A.R. Colony and Soldiers' Home, San Diego, California. San Diego: Junipero Land and Water, n.d.

Greenlee, D. R. *Alcohol: Its Use in the Soldiers' Home*. Minneapolis: n.p., 1900.

Hall, Edward H. *An Indignity to Our Citizen Soldiers: A Sermon Preached in the First Parish Church, Cambridge, June 1, 1890*. Cambridge, Mass.: Wilson, 1890.

Hamilton, Gail. "Tramps." *Harper's Bazaar*, September 18, 1875, 602.

Handbook and Guide for Visitors to the Home. Dayton, Ohio: Central Depot, 1896.

Haskell, W. G. "The Keeley Cure for Inebriety." *The Arena* 80 (July 1896): 222–27.

———. *"Pension Reform" as Viewed at the National Home for Disabled Volunteer Soldiers*. Gardiner, Me.: Haskell, ca. 1891.

Hay, W. C. *Reminiscences of the War*. Atlanta: Confederate Soldiers' Home of Georgia, 1920.

Hill, Robert F. *Grand Army Tactics of the United States Assimilated to the Tactics of the Regular Army and State Troops, Together with Instructions for Post and Ceremonial Services and Parades, for the Use of the G.A.R. and S.O.V.* Kalamazoo, Mich.: Hill, 1884.

History of the National Home for Disabled Volunteer Soldiers; with a Complete Guide-Book to the Central Home, at Dayton Ohio. Dayton, Ohio: United Brethren, 1875.

Holmes, Oliver Wendell. *The Occasional Speeches of Justice Oliver Wendell Holmes*. Comp. Mark DeWolfe Howe. Cambridge: Belknap Press of Harvard University Press, 1962.

———. *Touched with Fire: The Civil War Letters and Diary of Oliver Wendell Holmes, Jr., 1861–1864*. Ed. Mark de Wolfe Howe. Cambridge: Harvard University Press, 1946.

Holt, David. *A Mississippi Rebel in the Army of Northern Virginia: The Civil War Memoirs of Private David Holt*. Ed. Thomas D. Cockrell and Michael B. Ballard. Baton Rouge: Louisiana State University Press, 1995.

Hopkins, Owen Johnston. *Under the Flag of the Nation: Diaries and Letters of Owen Johnston Hopkins, a Yankee Volunteer in the Civil War*. Ed. Otto F. Bond. Columbus: Ohio State University Press, 1998.

Illinois Soldiers' College and Military Academy. *Illinois Soldiers' College and Military Academy, Will Open Its First Session . . .* Fulton, Ill.: n.p., 1866.

Information Desired Respecting Histories in Use in Alabama Schools and Colleges. Montgomery, Ala.: Joint History Committee of the Confederate Veterans Organizations of Alabama, 1902. Microform, Pamphlets in American History, Civil War, 603.

Insights to Life at the Ohio Soldiers' and Sailors' Home. Sandusky, Ohio: Miller, 1917.

Jackman, John S. *Diary of a Confederate Soldier: John S. Jackman of the Orphan Brigade*. Ed. William C. Davis. Columbia: University of South Carolina Press, 1990.

Jewett, Sarah Orne. "Decoration Day." *Harper's New Monthly Magazine* 85 (June 1892): 84–91.

John F. Chase, Inventor and Temperance Lecturer. Augusta, Me.: n.p., ca. 1886.

Johnson, Charles W. *The Veteran of 1861–5 and the Citizen of 1887.* Minneapolis: Harrison and Smith, 1887.

Jones, Charles Edgeworth. *A Family Reunion.* Augusta, Ga.: n.p., 1898.

Jones, Jenkin Lloyd. *An Artilleryman's Diary.* Madison: Wisconsin History Commission, 1914.

Kaplan, Justin, ed. *Walt Whitman: Poetry and Collected Prose.* New York: Library of America, 1982.

Keeley, Leslie E. *Opium: Its Use, Abuse and Cure; or, From Bondage to Freedom.* Chicago: Banner of Gold, 1897.

Kellogg, Robert H. *Life and Death in Rebel Prisons.* Hartford, Conn.: Stebbins, 1865.

Kennedy, Robert P. *Address of General Robert P. Kennedy, Delivered Decoration Day, at Spring Grove Cemetery, Cincinnati, May 31st, 1880.* Cincinnati: n.p., ca. 1880. Microform, Pamphlets in American History, Civil War, 436.

Knapp, Fred N. *"Sanitaria"; or, Homes for Discharged, Disabled Soldiers.* Washington, D.C.: n.p., 1865.

Lang, T. F. *Address of Col. T. F. Lang, Baltimore, MD., [and] Oration by Hon. M. Brosius, Lancaster, PA., on Decoration Day, at Loudon Park Cemetery.* Baltimore: Wilson Post Musical Association, 1880.

LeConte, Emma. *When the World Ended: The Diary of Emma LeConte.* Ed. Earl Schenck Miers. New York: Oxford University Press, 1957.

Lewis, H. A. *Why Some Succeed while Others Fail.* Cleveland: Wright, Moses, and Lewis, 1887.

Libby Prison War Museum: Catalogue and Program. Chicago: Libby Prison War Museum Association, ca. 1893.

Lincoln, Abraham. *Collected Works of Abraham Lincoln.* Ed. Roy P. Basler. Vol. 8. Springfield, Ill.: Abraham Lincoln Association, 1953.

Loftin, Jack O. "Geraldine, Texas." *Handbook of Texas* online, http://www.tshaonline .org/handbook/online/articles/GG/hrg42.html. Accessed September 14, 2010.

Lovering, Joseph F. *Services for the Use of the Grand Army of the Republic.* Boston: Stillings, 1881.

Marsh, H. P. *The Greatest Burlesque of the Day! The G.A.R. Exposed! By Drumhead.* Rochester, N.Y.: Smith, 1887.

McCampbell, S. J. N. *The Ex-Confederate Soldiers' Home, Richmond, Virginia, in Verse.* Richmond: n.p., 1909.

McCook, John J. "Leaves from the Diary of a Tramp." *The Independent,* December 5, 1901, 2760–67.

Memorial of Sterling Price Camp to the Legislature of Texas, Asking for Aid for the Confederate Home at Austin. Austin: n.p., ca. 1890.

Miller, Charles D. *Report of the Great Re-Union of the Veteran Soldiers and Sailors of Ohio Held at Newark, July 22, 1878.* Newark, Ohio: Clark and Underwood, 1879.

Mitchell, S. Weir. *The Autobiography of a Quack; and, The Case of George Dedlow.* New York: Century, 1900.

Moore, Dosia Williams. *War, Reconstruction, and Redemption on Red River: The Memoirs of Dosia Williams Moore.* Ed. Carol Wells. Ruston, La.: McGinty, 1990.

Morton, Joseph W., ed. *Sparks from the Campfire; or, Tales of the Old Veterans.* Philadelphia: Keystone, 1890.

Morton, M. B. "Federal and Confederate Pensions Contrasted." *Forum* 16 (September 1893): 68–74.

"The National Cemetery at Gettysburgh." *Hours at Home: A Popular Monthly of Instruction and Recreation*, December 1865.

National Soldiers' Home near Dayton, Ohio. Dayton, Ohio: Central National Home for D.V.S., 1881.

National Soldiers' Home near Milwaukee. Milwaukee: National Soldiers' Home, 1881.

"Northern Veterans Making Southern Homes." *Illustrated American*, March 21, 1896, 368–70.

Official Souvenir: McPherson County, July 4, 1917. N.p., 1917.

Oldham, Williamson S. *From Richmond to Texas: The 1865 Journey Home of Confederate Senator Williamson S. Oldham*. Ed. W. Buck Yearns. Dayton, Ohio: Morningside, 1998.

"An Old Soldier's Experience." *Phrenological Journal and Science of Health* 70 (January 1880): 55.

Ordronaux, John. *Report to the U.S. Sanitary Commission on a System for the Economical Relief of Disabled Soldiers*. New York: Sanford, Harroun, 1864.

Owen, William D. *Success in Life, and How to Secure It; or, Elements of Manhood and Their Culture*. Chicago: Howe, Watts, 1882.

Page, Thomas Nelson. "The Gray Jacket." *The Century* 44 (May 1892): 27–33.

———. *The Novels, Stories, Sketches and Poems of Thomas Nelson Page*. Vol. 2, *The Burial of the Guns*. New York: Scribner's, 1908.

"Pensions—Worse and More of Them." *World's Work* 23 (1911–12): 188–92, 327–33, 385–98.

Peters, S. S., comp. *Odes, Hymns and Songs of the Grand Army of the Republic*. Columbus, Ohio: Veteran, 1883.

Petition and Statements of U.S. Maimed Soldiers' League, for the Enactment of Senate Bill No. 833. Philadelphia: n.p., 1890.

Phelps, Elizabeth Stuart. "John True's Decoration Day." *The Continent: An Illustrated Weekly Magazine*, May 30, 1883, 679–89.

Plain Facts in Relation to the Management of the Soldiers' Home, Togus, Maine. Boston: Togus Syndicate, 1895.

Prentice, Clarence J. *Why Can We Not Be Brothers? or, We Know That We Were Rebels*. Louisville, Ky.: Faulds, 1865.

Proceedings of the First and Annual Meetings of the Survivors' Association of the State of South Carolina. Charleston: Walker, Evans, and Cogswell, 1870.

Proceedings of the Northwestern Soldiers' Home Association. Fullerton, Neb.: Nance County Journal, 1895.

Proceedings of the Ohio Association of Union Ex-Prisoners of War in the Reunion Held at Dayton, O., July 29, 30, and 31, 1884, with Register of Members. Columbus: Ohio State Journal, 1884.

Proctor, Edna D. "The Soldier's Release." *Youth's Companion*, November 23, 1865, 186.

Programme and Plan of Organization of the Wisconsin Soldiers and Sailors Re-Union, and Reception of General U. S. Grant, and Other Distinguished Union Generals, June 7th to 12th, 1880. Milwaukee: n.p., 1889.

"The Ragged Old Soldier." *Acme Haversack* 4 (January 1890): 26.

Randall, G. M. "Psychologic Aspect of the 'Keeley Cure.'" *Medical News*, January 16, 1892, 80–81.

Raum, Green B. "Pensions and Patriotism." *North American Review* 153 (August 1891): 205–14.

Redington, J. C. O. "Their Pensions Shall Be Paid in Full." *Acme Haversack* 3 (September 1889): 2.

Reed, George M. *The One Arm and One Leg Soldier, Wounded at the Battle of Shiloh, Sunday Morning, April 6th, 1862*. N.p., ca. 1865.

Reid, Whitelaw. *After the War: A Tour of the Southern States, 1865–1866*. Ed. C. Vann Woodward. New York: Harper and Row, 1965.

Remarks Explanatory of the Beneficent Workings of the Grand Army of the Republic. Brooklyn, N.Y.: Bureau of Employment and Emergency Fund, 1884.

The Republican Campaign Text-Book for 1884. New York: Republican National Committee, 1881.

Reunions of the Ex-Soldiers of the North and South, Held at Luray, Virginia, July 21, 1881 and at Carlisle, Pennsylvania, September 28, 1881. Carlisle, Penn.: Herald and Mirror, 1881.

Ridpath, James Clark. *The Citizen Soldier: His Part in War and Peace*. Amo, Ind.: n.p., 1891.

Robson, John S. *How a One-Legged Rebel Lives: Reminiscences of the Civil War*. Durham, N.C.: Educator, 1898.

Rochester City Directory. Rochester, N.Y.: Drew, Allis, 1885.

Rodgers, Robert L. *History [of the] Confederate Veterans' Association of Fulton County, Georgia*. Atlanta: Sisson, 1890.

Rowell, John W. *Yankee Artillerymen: Through the Civil War with Eli Lilly's Indiana Battery*. Knoxville: University of Tennessee Press, 1975.

———. *Yankee Cavalrymen: Through the Civil War with the Ninth Pennsylvania Cavalry*. Knoxville: University of Tennessee Press, 1971.

Rules and Regulations of the Union Veterans' Union of the United States. Washington, D.C., 1886. Microform, Pamphlets in American History, Civil War, 412.

The St. Cloud Colony. Washington, D.C.: Seminole Land and Investment, ca. 1912.

Sandburg, Carl. *Always the Young Strangers*. New York: Harcourt, Brace, 1952.

Savage, I. W. *A History of Republic County, Kansas*. Beloit, Kan.: Jones and Chubbic, 1901.

Schuellerman, Charles W. *The Life of a Pree Varicator Formerly of Swamppoodle, Pennsylvania; Now of Pennsylvania Soldiers' and Sailors' Home, Erie, Pennsylvania*. Erie, Pa.: Rea, 1905.

Shelton, William Henry. "Uncle Obadiah's Uncle Billy." *Century* 46 (June 1893): 307–12.

Sherwood, Kate Brownlee. *Camp-Fire, Memorial-Day, and Other Poems*. Chicago: Jansen, McClurg, 1885.

Shrader, Jay. *The New Canaan! Fitzgerald and the Old Soldier Colony in Irwin County, Ga.* Savannah: Morning News, 1896.

Sloane, William M. "Pensions and Socialism." *The Century* 42 (June 1891): 179–89.

Smalley, Eugene V. "The United States Pension Office." *The Century* 28 (July 1884): 427–34.

Smiles, Samuel. *Character*. New York: Harper, 1872.

———. *Duty: With Illustrations of Courage, Patience, and Endurance*. New York: Harper, 1881.

———. *Thrift*. New York: Harper, 1892.

Smith, Benjamin T. *Private Smith's Journal: Recollections of the Late War*. Ed. Clyde C. Walton. Chicago: Lakeside, 1963.

Smith, Charles Henry. *Bill Arp's Peace Papers*. New York: Carleton, 1873.

Smith, Thomas W. *"We Have It Damn Hard Out Here": The Civil War Letters of Sergeant Thomas W. Smith, 6th Pennsylvania Cavalry*. Ed. Eric J. Wittenberg. Kent, Ohio: Kent State University Press, 1999.

Society of Loyal Volunteers. *Prospectus and Constitution*. Washington, D.C.: n.p., 1892.

Society of the U.S. Military Telegraph Corps. *Reunion Proceedings of the Society of the U.S. Military Telegraph Corps*. Chicago, 1884. Microform, Pamphlets in American History, Civil War, 418.

Soldiers and Sailors Home Fair. *Great Fair! Academy of Music, Philadelphia*. Philadelphia: King and Baird, 1865.

The Soldiers' Home: Annual Report of the Northwestern Branch, National Home for Disabled Volunteer Soldiers, 1874. Milwaukee: National Soldiers' Home, 1875.

Souvenir, Department of Kansas, Grand Army of the Republic, Thirty-sixth National Encampment. N.p., 1902.

Starbuck, Mary Eliza. *My House and I: A Chronicle of Nantucket*. Boston: Houghton Mifflin, 1929.

State of Idaho Soldier's Home History. Boise: n.p., ca. 1915.

Steinbeck, John. *East of Eden*. Intro. David Wyatt. New York: Penguin, 1992.

Stephenson, Philip Daingerfield. *The Civil War Memoir of Philip Daingerfield Stephenson, D.D.* Ed. Nathaniel Cheairs Hughes Jr. Conway, Ark.: University of Central Arkansas Press, 1995.

Stevens, Emerson O. "The National Soldiers' Home." *New England Magazine* 22 (May 1900): 285–303.

Stillwell, Leander. *The Story of a Common Soldier of Army Life in the Civil War, 1861–1865*. 2nd ed. Erie, Kan.: Hudson, 1920.

Stone, Kate. *Brokenburn: The Journal of Kate Stone, 1861–1868*. Ed. John Q. Anderson. Baton Rouge: Louisiana State University Press, 1955.

Tanner, Mrs. Corporal. "Heroic Service, or Civil Service: Shall Faithful Soldiers or Delving Book Worms Be Promoted?" *Acme Haversack* 3 (September 1889): 61.

Thanet, Octave. "An Old Grand Army Man." *McClure's* 11 (June 1898): 162–69.

They Just Fade Away. Hampton, Va.: Syms-Eaton Museum, n.d.

To the Senate and House of Representatives of the United States of America. Indianapolis: Army, 1889.

To the Veteran of the Civil War, His Son and Grandson. Chicago: Headquarters Division of Illinois, Union Veterans' Union, 1903.

Tracy, Marguerite. "The Broken Toy Soldier." *St. Nicholas: An Illustrated Magazine for Young Folks* 25 (December 1897): 2.

Trowbridge, J. T. *Frank Manly, the Drummer Boy*. Boston: Gill, 1876.

———. *The South: A Tour of Its Battle-Fields and Ruined Cities*. 1866; New York: Arno and the New York Times, 1969.

Turner, J. W. *Mother, Is the Battle Over? Can I Come Home from Canada?; or, The B.J.'s Lament*. Detroit: Whittemore, 1865.

U.S. Army Quartermaster Corps. *The Martyrs Who for Our Country Gave Up Their Lives in the Prison Pens in Andersonville, Ga.* Washington, D.C.: U.S. Government Printing Office, 1866.

U.S. Sanitary Commission. *Bureau of Employment for Disabled and Discharged Soldiers and Sailors*. Philadelphia: n.p., 1865.

——. *Documents of the United States Sanitary Commission*. 3 vols. New York: n.p., 1866–71.

——. *The Soldier's Friend*. Philadelphia: Perkinpine & Higgins, 1865.

Van Nest, J. P. *Burlesque Degree; or, Initiation of a Candidate*. Wooster, Ohio: Van Nest, 1885.

——. *Ceremonial of the "Munchers of Hard Tack"; or, "Jordan Is a Hard Road to Travel."* Greenville, Ill.: DeMoulin, 1888.

Waddill, E. M. *The Song of the Soldiers' Home, Raleigh, N.C.* Raleigh: Edwards and Broughton, 1895.

Warner, Charles Dudley. "The Veteran." *Current Literature* 12 (February 1893): 171.

Watkins, Sam R. *Co. Aytch: A Confederate Memoir of the Civil War*. New York: Macmillan, 2003.

Weld, Stephen Minot. *War Diary and Letters of Stephen Minot Weld, 1861–1865*. Boston: Massachusetts Historical Society, 1979.

What Will You Do for the Soldiers' Home Bazaar to Be Held at Boston in the Autumn of 1881? Boston: Bazaar, 1881.

Whipple, Edwin P. *Success and Its Conditions*. Boston: J. R. Osgood; Boston: Houghton Mifflin, 1899.

Whitman, Walt. "A Carol of the Harvest." *Galaxy* 4 (September 1867): 605–9.

——. *Complete Prose Works*. New York: Appleton, 1910.

——. *Walt Whitman: Selected Poems, 1855–1892*. Ed. Gary Schmidgall. New York: Stonewall Inn, 2000.

Wilkins, Benjamin Harrison. *"War Boy": A True Story of the Civil War and Re-Construction Days*. Tullahoma, Tenn.: Wilson, 1938.

Wills, Charles W. *Army Life of an Illinois Soldier*. Carbondale: Southern Illinois University Press, 1996.

Wills, W. H., and Co. *Rally, Soldiers! To the Aid of Your Good Cause*. Washington, D.C.: n.p., ca. 1883.

Wood, William Nathaniel. *Reminiscences of Big I*. Ed. Bell Irvin Wiley. Jackson, Tenn.: McCowat-Mercer, 1956.

Wright's City Directory of Milwaukee for 1891. Milwaukee: Wright, 1891.

Wright's Milwaukee County and Milwaukee Business Directory, 1896. Milwaukee: Wright, 1896.

Your Duty to the War Cripple. New York: Red Cross Institute for Crippled and Disabled Men, 1918.

Secondary Sources

Adams, Michael C. C. "Retelling the Tale: Wars in Common Memory." In *War Comes Again: Comparative Vistas on the Civil War and World War II*, ed. Gabor Boritt. New York: Oxford University Press, 1995.

Adams, Samuel Hopkins. *The Great American Fraud*. Chicago: American Medical Association, 1907.

Anderson, William A. "Their Last Hurrah: The 19th Michigan Infantry Remembers the Civil War." *Michigan History Magazine* 82 (July–August 1998): 95–100.

Ayers, Edward L. *The Promise of the New South: Life after Reconstruction*. New York: Oxford University Press, 1992.

Babington, Anthony. *Shell-Shock: A History of the Changing Attitudes to War Neurosis.* London: Cooper, 1997.

Baehr, Carl. *Milwaukee Streets: The Stories behind Their Names.* Milwaukee: Cream City Press, 1995.

Bailey, Fred A. *Class and Tennessee's Confederate Generation.* Chapel Hill: University of North Carolina Press, 1987.

Bederman, Gail. *Manliness and Civilization: A Cultural History of Gender and Race in the United States, 1880–1917.* Chicago: University of Chicago Press, 1995.

Blair, William A. *Cities of the Dead: Contesting the Memory of the Civil War in the South, 1865–1914.* Chapel Hill: University of North Carolina Press, 2004.

Blanck, Peter. "Civil War Pensions and Disability." *Ohio State Law Journal* 62, no. 1 (2001): 109–238.

Blanck, Peter, and Chen Song. "Civil War Pension Attorneys and Disability Politics." *University of Michigan Journal of Law Reform* 35 (Fall 2001–Winter 2002): 137–216.

———. "'Never Forget What They Did Here': Civil War Pensions for Gettysburg Union Army Veterans and Disability in Nineteenth-Century America." *William and Mary Law Review* 44 (February 2003): 1109–71.

Blight, David W. *Race and Reunion: The Civil War in American Memory.* Cambridge: Harvard University Press, 2001.

Bridge, Jennifer R. "A Shrine of Patriotic Memories." *Chicago History* 32 (Summer 2003): 4–23.

Bronner, Simon J., ed. *Consuming Visions Accumulation and Display of Goods in America, 1880–1920.* New York: Norton for the Winterthur Museum, 1989.

Brooks, Tim. *Lost Sounds: Blacks and the Birth of the Recording Industry, 1890–1919.* Champaign: University of Illinois Press, 2005.

Brown, Lynn S. *Gulfport: A Definitive History.* Charleston, S.C.: History Press, 2004.

Brown, Mary Ann. "Ohio Veterans' Memorial Halls." *Pioneer America Society Transactions* 14 (1991): 47–54.

Browning, Judkin. "'I Am Not So Patriotic as I Was Once': The Effects of Military Occupation on the Occupying Soldiers during the Civil War." *Civil War History* 55 (June 2009): 217–43.

Bryant, William O. *Cahaba Prison and the "Sultana" Disaster.* Tuscaloosa: University of Alabama Press, 1990.

Burgess, Arene Wiemers. *Collector's Guide to Souvenir Plates.* Atglen, Pa.: Schiffer, 1996.

Cahn, Joseph M. *The Teenie Weenies Book: The Life and Art of William Donahey.* La Jolla, Calif.: Green Tiger, 1986.

Carmichael, Peter S. *The Last Generation: Young Virginians in Peace, War, and Reunion.* Chapel Hill: University of North Carolina Press, 2005.

Carnes, Mark C. "Middle-Class Men and the Solace of Fraternal Ritual." In *Meanings for Manhood: Constructions of Masculinity in Victorian America*, ed. Mark C. Carnes and Clyde Griffen. Chicago: University of Chicago Press, 1990.

Catton, Bruce. "The Army of the Cumberland: A Panorama Show by William D. T. Travis." *American Heritage* 19 (December 1967): 40–50.

———. *Waiting for the Morning Train: An American Boyhood.* Garden City, N.Y.: Doubleday, 1972.

Chalker, Fussell M. "Fitzgerald: Place of Reconciliation." *Georgia Historical Quarterly* 55 (Fall 1971): 397–405.

Cimbala, Paul A. "Lining Up to Serve: Wounded and Sick Union Officers Join Veteran Reserve Corps during Civil War, Reconstruction." *Prologue: Quarterly of the National Archives and Records Administration* 35 (Spring 2003): 1–12.

Cimbala, Paul A., and Randall M. Miller, eds. *Union Soldiers and the Northern Homefront*. New York: Fordham University Press, 2002.

Clarke, Frances. "'Let All Nations See': Civil War Nationalism and the Memorialization of Wartime Voluntarism." *Civil War History* 52 (March 2006): 66–93.

Clausins, Gerhard P. "The Little Soldier of the 95th." *Journal of the Illinois State Historical Society* 51 (Winter 1958): 380–87.

Clinton, Catherine, and Nina Silber, eds. *Battle Scars: Gender and Sexuality in the American Civil War*. Oxford: Oxford University Press, 2006.

Coski, John M. *The Confederate Battle Flag: America's Most Embattled Emblem*. Cambridge: Harvard University Press, 2005.

Costa, Dora L. *The Evolution of Retirement: An American Economic History, 1880–1990*. Chicago: University of Chicago Press, 1998.

Costa, Dora L., and Matthew E. Kahn. *Heroes and Cowards: The Social Face of War*. Princeton: Princeton University Press, 2008.

Courtwright, David T. "Opiate Addiction as a Consequence of the Civil War." *Civil War History* 24 (June 1978): 101–11.

Crellin, John K. "Alcoholism and Drug Addiction in the 'Nineties: An American in London." *British Journal of Addiction* 75, no. 2 (1980): 153–62.

Davies, Wallace E. "The Mexican War Veterans as an Organized Group." *Mississippi Valley Historical Review* 35 (September 1948): 221–38.

Dean, Eric. *Shook over Hell: Post-Traumatic Stress, Vietnam, and the Civil War*. Cambridge: Harvard University Press, 1999.

Depastino, Todd. *Citizen Hobo: How a Century of Homelessness Shaped America*. Chicago: University of Chicago Press, 2003.

Dickens, W. Jackson, Jr., and Robert C. Kenzer. "The Confederate Memorial Literary Society's Roll of Honour." *Civil War History* 43 (March 1997): 59–69.

Dorland's Illustrated Medical Dictionary. Philadelphia: Saunders, 1988.

Dunkelman, Mark H. *Brothers One and All: Esprit de Corps in a Civil War Regiment*. Baton Rouge: Louisiana State University Press, 2006.

Edwards, Rebecca. *New Spirits: Americans in the Gilded Age, 1865–1905*. New York: Oxford University Press, 2006.

Emery, Janet Pease. *It Takes People to Make a Town: The Story of Concordia, Kansas, 1871–1971*. Salina, Kan.: Arrow, 1970.

Erkkila, Betsy. *Whitman the Political Poet*. New York: Oxford University Press, 1989.

Escott, Paul D. *Military Necessity: Civil-Military Relations in the Confederacy*. Westport, Conn.: Praeger, 2006.

Fahs, Alice. "The Feminized Civil War: Gender, Northern Popular Literature, and the Memory of the War, 1861–1900." *Journal of American History* 85 (March 1999): 1461–94.

———. *The Imagined Civil War: Popular Literature of the North and South, 1861–1865*. Chapel Hill: University of North Carolina Press, 2001.

Falvo, Donna R. *Medical and Psychological Aspects of Chronic Illness and Disability*. Gaithersburg, Md.: Aspen, 1991.

Faust, Drew Gilpin. *This Republic of Suffering: Death and the American Civil War*. New York: Vintage, 2008.

Fawcett, Winifred, and Thelma Hepper. *Veterans of the Civil War Who Settled in Potter County, Dakota Territory*. Gettysburg, S.D.: Fawcett and Hepper, 1993.

Figg, Laurann, and Jane Farrell-Beck. "Amputation in the Civil War: Physical and Social Dimensions." *Journal of the History of Medicine and Allied Sciences* 48 (October 1993): 454–75.

Figley, Charles R., and William T. Southerly. "Psychosocial Adjustment of Recently Returned Veterans." In *Strangers at Home: Vietnam Veterans Since the War*, ed. Charles R. Figley and Seymour Leventman. New York: Brunner/Mazel, 1990.

Fischer, David Hackett. *Growing Old In America*. New York: Oxford University Press, 1977.

Fish, Carl R. "Back to Peace in 1865." *American Historical Review* 24 (April 1919): 435–43.

Fisher, Noel C. *War at Every Door: Partisan Politics and Guerrilla Violence in East Tennessee, 1860–1869*. Chapel Hill: University of North Carolina Press, 1997.

Fleche, Andre. "'Shoulder to Shoulder as Comrades Tried: Black and White Union Veterans and Civil War Memory." *Civil War History* 51 (June 2005): 175–201.

Foster, Gaines M. *Ghosts of the Confederacy: Defeat, the Lost Cause, and the Emergence of the New South, 1865 to 1913*. New York: Oxford University Press, 1987.

Frank, Stephen M. *Life with Father: Parenthood and Masculinity in the Nineteenth-Century American North*. Baltimore: Johns Hopkins University Press, 1998.

Fredrickson, George M. *The Inner Civil War: Northern Intellectuals and the Crisis of the Union*. New York: Harper and Row, 1965.

Friend, Craig Thompson, ed. *Southern Masculinity: Perspectives on Manhood in the South since Reconstruction*. Athens: University of Georgia Press, 2009.

Furnas, J. C. *The Life and Times of the Late Demon Rum*. London: Allen, 1965.

Furney, Muriel. *A Comprehensive History of Washington Soldiers' Home and Colony, 1891–1971*. Monroe, Wash.: Reformatory Industries, 1971.

Fussell, Paul. "Reflections on the Culture of War." In *Battle: The Nature and Consequences of Civil War Combat*, ed. Kent Gramm. Tuscaloosa: University of Alabama Press, 2008.

Gallman, J. Matthew. "Voluntarism in Wartime: Philadelphia's Great Central Fair." In *Toward a Social History of the American Civil War: Exploratory Essays*, ed. Maris Vinovskis. New York: Cambridge University Press, 1990.

Gambone, Michael D. *The Greatest Generation Comes Home: The Veteran in American Society*. College Station: Texas A & M University Press, 2005.

Gartner, Scott Sigmund, and Hugh Rockoff. "Veterans in Civil Life, by Period of Service: 1865–1999." In *Historical Statistics of the United States, Earliest Times to the Present: Millennial Edition*, ed. Susan B. Carter, Scott Sigmund Gartner, Michael R. Haines, Alan L. Olmstead, Richard Sutch, and Gavin Wright. New York: Cambridge University Press, 2006. http://dx.doi.org/10.1017/ISBN-9780511132971 .Ed229–482. Accessed September 14, 2010.

Gerber, David A., ed. *Disabled Veterans in History*. Ann Arbor: University of Michigan Press, 2000.

Goldberg, Chad Alan. *Citizens and Paupers: Relief, Rights, and Race, from the Freedmen's Bureau to Workfare*. Chicago: University of Chicago Press, 2007.

Goler, Robert I. "Loss and the Persistence of Memory: 'The Case of George Dedlow' and Disabled Civil War Veterans." *Literature and Medicine* 23 (Spring 2004): 160–83.

Goode, Paul R. *The United States Soldiers' Home: A History of Its First Hundred Years*. Washington, D.C.: privately published, 1957.

Goodwin, Jim. "The Etiology of Combat-Related Post-Traumatic Stress Disorders." In *Post-Traumatic Stress Disorders of the Vietnam Veteran*, ed. Tom Williams. Cincinnati: Disabled American Veterans, 1980.

Gordon, Lesley J. *"I Never Was a Coward": Questions of Bravery in a Civil War Regiment*. Milwaukee: Marquette University Press, 2005.

Graf, Alan D. *On Many a Bloody Field: Four Years in the Iron Brigade*. Bloomington: Indiana University Press, 1997.

Grant, Susan-Mary. "Reimagined Communities: Union Veterans and the Reconstruction of American Nationalism." *Nations and Nationalism* 14, no. 3 (2008): 498–519.

Green, Elna C. "Protecting Confederate Soldiers and Mothers: Pensions, Gender, and the Welfare State in the U.S. South, a Case Study from Florida." *Journal of Social History* 39 (Summer 2006): 1079–1104.

Groce, W. Todd. *Mountain Rebels: East Tennessee Confederates and the Civil War, 1860–1870*. Knoxville: University of Tennessee Press, 1999.

Ghusn, Husam F., Ellen S. Stevens, and Farah Attasi. "A Profile of Aging Veterans." *Clinical Gerontologist* 19, no. 4 (1998): 51–62.

Halttunen, Karen. *Confidence Men and Painted Women: A Study of Middle-Class Culture in America, 1830–1870*. New Haven: Yale University Press, 1982.

Hampel, Robert L., and Charles W. Ornsby Jr. "Crime and Punishment on the Civil War Homefront." *Pennsylvania Magazine of History and Biography* 106 (April 1982): 223–44.

Hannah, Eleanor L. *Manhood, Citizenship, and the National Guard: Illinois, 1870–1917*. Columbus: Ohio State University Press, 2007.

Hansen, Bert. "New Images of a New Medicine: Visual Evidence for the Widespread Popularity of Therapeutic Discoveries in America after 1885." *Bulletin of the History of Medicine* 73 (Winter 1999): 629–78.

"Hansen Military Academy." http://www.cityoffulton.us/news/hansen-military-academy.html. Accessed June 20, 2009.

Harwig, D. Scott. "The Reunion of the Philadelphia Brigade and Pickett's Division, July 1887." *Civil War Regiments* 6, no. 3 (2000): 139–53.

Harwood, Edith W. "GAR Campfires." *The Palimpsest* 70 (Spring 1989): 14–17.

Heck, Frank H. *The Civil War Veteran in Minnesota Life and Politics*. Oxford, Ohio: Mississippi Valley Press, 1941.

Heinemann, Allen W., T. E. McGraw, M. J. Brandt, E. Roth, and C. Dell'Oliver. "Prescription Medicine Misuse among Persons with Spinal Cord Injuries." *International Journal of the Addictions* 27 (March 1982): 301–16.

Hendin, Herbert, and Ann Pollinger Hass. *Wounds of War: The Psychological Aftermath of Combat in Vietnam*. New York: Basic Books, 1984.

Herek, Raymond J. *These Men Have Seen Hard Service: The First Michigan Sharpshooters in the Civil War*. Detroit: Wayne State University Press, 1998.

Hess, Earl J. *The Union Soldier in Battle: Enduring the Ordeal of Combat*. Lawrence: University Press of Kansas, 1997.

Hickman, Timothy A. "'Mania Americana': Narcotic Addiction and Modernity in the United States, 1870–1920." *Journal of American History* 90 (March 2004): 1269–94.

———. *The Secret Leprosy of Modern Days: Narcotic Addiction and Cultural Crisis in the United States, 1870–1920*. Amherst: University of Massachusetts Press, 2007.

Hilkey, Judy. *Character Is Capital: Success Manuals and Manhood in Gilded Age America*. Chapel Hill: University of North Carolina Press, 1997.

Hoganson, Kristin L. *Fighting for American Manhood: How Gender Politics Provoked the Spanish-American and Philippine-American Wars*. New Haven: Yale University Press, 1998.

Holberton, William B. *Homeward Bound: The Demobilization of the Union and Confederate Armies, 1865-1866*. Mechanicsburg, Pa.: Stackpole, 2001.

Hyman, Tony. "Hyman's National Cigar Museum." http://www.cigarhistory.info/ Themes/Patriotic.html. Accessed March 28, 2008.

Jarvis, Christina S. *The Male Body at War: American Masculinity during World War II*. DeKalb: Northern Illinois University Press, 2004.

Johnson, Russell L. "The Civil War Generation: Military Service and Mobility in Dubuque, Iowa, 1860-1870." *Journal of Social History* 32 (Summer 1999): 791-820.

———. *Warriors into Workers: The Civil War and the Formation of Urban-Industrial Society in a Northern City*. New York: Fordham University Press, 2003.

Jordan, William B., Jr. *Red Diamond Regiment: The 17th Maine Infantry, 1862-1865*. Shippensburg, Pa.: White Mane, 1996.

Kaser, James A. *At the Bivouac of Memory: History, Politics, and the Battle of Chickamauga*. New York: Lang, 1996.

Katz, Michael B. *In the Shadow of the Poorhouse: A Social History of Welfare in America*. Rev. ed. New York: Basic Books, 1996.

Kelly, Patrick J. *Creating a National Home: Building the Veterans' Welfare State, 1860-1900*. Cambridge: Harvard University Press, 1997.

Keyssar, Alexander. *Out of Work: The First Century of Unemployment in Massachusetts*. New York: Cambridge University Press, 1986.

King, James L., ed. *History of Shawnee County, Kansas, and Representative Citizens*. Chicago: Richmond and Arnold, 1905.

Kirkland, Turner E. *Civil War Veterans' Organizations, Reunions, and Badges*. Union City, Tenn.: Pioneer, 1991.

Knott, David A. *Alcohol Problems: Diagnosis and Treatment*. New York: Pergamon, 1986.

Kreiser, Lawrence A., Jr., "A Socioeconomic Study of Veterans of the 103rd Ohio Volunteer Infantry Regiment after the Civil War." *Ohio History* 107 (Summer-Autumn 1998): 171-84.

Kulka, Richard A., William E. Schlenger, John A. Fairbank, Richard L. Hough, B. Kathleen Jordan, Charles R. Marmar, and Daniel S. Weiss. *Trauma and the Vietnam War Generation: Report of Findings from the National Vietnam Veterans Readjustment Study*. New York: Brunner/Mazel, 1990.

Kuzmarov, Jeremy. "The Myth of the 'Addicted Army': Drug Use in Vietnam in Historical Perspective." *War and Society* 27 (October 2007): 121-41.

LaFantasie, Glenn W. *Gettysburg Requiem: The Life and Lost Causes of Confederate Colonel William C. Oates*. New York: Oxford University Press, 2006.

Lashley, Tommy G. "Oklahoma's Confederate Veterans Home." *Chronicles of Oklahoma* 55 (Spring 1977): 34-45.

Lee, Chulhee. "Health, Information, and Migration: Geographic Mobility of Union Army Veterans, 1860-1880." *Journal of Economic History* 68 (September 2008): 862-99.

———. "Wealth Accumulation and the Health of Union Army Veterans, 1860-1870." *Journal of Economic History* 65 (June 2005): 352-85.

Lembcke, Jerry. *The Spitting Image: Myth, Memory, and the Legacy of Vietnam*. New York: New York University Press, 1998.

Lender, Mark E., and James Kirby Martin. *Drinking in America: A History*. New York: Free Press, 1987.

Linderman, Gerald F. *Embattled Courage: The Experience of Combat in the American Civil War*. New York: Free Press, 1987.

Linson, Corwin K. *My Stephen Crane*. Syracuse: Syracuse University Press, 1958.

Logue, Larry M. *To Appomattox and Beyond: The Civil War Soldier in War and Peace*. Chicago: Dee, 1996.

———. "Union Veterans and Their Government: The Effects of Public Policies on Private Lives." *Journal of Interdisciplinary History* 22 (Winter 1992): 411–34.

Logue, Larry M., and Michael Barton, eds. *The Civil War Veteran: A Historical Reader*. New York: New York University Press, 2007.

Kuntz, Andrew. "The Fiddler's Companion." http://www.ibiblio.org/fiddlers/RP_RZ .htm. Accessed December 23, 2005.

Madison, James H. "Civil War Memories and 'Pardnership Forgittin'' 1865–1913." *Indiana Magazine of History* 99 (September 2003): 198–230.

Marten, James. "Exempt from the Ordinary Rules of Life: Sources on Maladjusted Union Civil War Veterans." *Civil War History* 47 (March 2001): 57–71.

———. "Nomads in Blue: Disabled Veterans and Alcohol at the National Home." In *Disabled Veterans in History*, ed. David A. Gerber. Ann Arbor: University of Michigan Press, 2000.

———. "Not a Veteran in the Poorhouse: Civil War Pensions and Soldiers' Homes." In *Wars within a War: Controversy and Conflict over the American Civil War*, ed. Gary Gallagher and Joan Waugh. Chapel Hill: University of North Carolina Press, 2009.

———. "'A Place of Great Beauty, Improved by Man': The Soldiers' Home and Victorian Milwaukee." *Milwaukee History* 22 (Spring 1999): 2–15.

McCawley, Patrick J. *Artificial Limbs for Confederate Soldiers*. Columbia: South Carolina Department of Archives and History, 1992.

McClintock, Megan J. "Civil War Pensions and the Reconstruction of Union Families." *Journal of American History* 83 (September 1996): 456–80.

McClurken, Jeffrey W. *Take Care of the Living: Reconstructing Confederate Veteran Families in Virginia*. Charlottesville: University of Virginia Press, 2009.

McConnell, Stuart. *Glorious Contentment: The Grand Army of the Republic, 1865–1900*. Chapel Hill: University of North Carolina Press, 1992.

———. "The William Newby Case and the Legacy of the Civil War." *Prologue* 30 (Winter 1998): 247–55.

McCrory, Thomas J. *Grand Army of the Republic: Department of Wisconsin*. Black Earth, Wis.: Trails, 2005.

McDaid, Jennifer Davis. "'How a One-Legged Rebel Lives': Confederate Veterans and Artificial Limbs in Virginia." In *Artificial Parts, Practical Lives: Modern Histories of Prosthetics*, ed. Katherine Ott, David Serlin, and Stephen Mihm. New York: New York University Press, 2002.

———. "With Lame Legs and No Money: Virginia's Disabled Confederate Veterans." *Virginia Cavalcade* 47 (Winter 1998): 14–25.

McGovern, Charles F. *Sold American: Consumption and Citizenship, 1890–1945*. Chapel Hill: University of North Carolina Press, 2006.

McMurtrie, Douglas C. *The Disabled Soldier*. New York: Macmillan, 1919.

Mendelson, Jack H., and Nancy K. Mello, eds. *Medical Diagnosis and Treatment of Alcoholism*. New York: McGraw-Hill, 1992.

Mitchell, Reid. *Civil War Soldiers: Their Expectations and Their Experiences*. New York: Viking, 1988.

Morgan, H. Wayne. *Drugs in America: A Social History, 1800–1980*. Syracuse: Syracuse University Press, 1981.

———. *Yesterday's Addicts: American Society and Drug Abuse, 1865–1920*. Norman: University of Oklahoma Press, 1974.

Morgan, Stephen T. "Fellow Comrades: The Grand Army of the Republic in South Dakota." *South Dakota History* 36 (Fall 2006): 229–59.

Morris, Roy J. *Ambrose Bierce: Alone in Bad Company*. New York: Crown, 1995.

Musto, David F. *The American Disease: Origins of Narcotic Control*. Expanded ed. New York: Oxford University Press, 1987.

Neff, John R. *Honoring the Civil War Dead: Commemoration and the Problem of Reconciliation*. Lawrence: University Press of Kansas, 2005.

Neugent, Robert J. "The National Soldiers' Home." *Historical Messenger* 31 (Autumn 1975): 88–96.

Noonan, Thomas. "Politics, Patriotism, and Veteran Recognition: The Twenty-third GAR Encampment in Milwaukee, 1889." *Milwaukee History* 30 (Spring–Summer/Fall–Winter 2007): 32–59.

O'Leary, Cecilia Elizabeth. *To Die For: The Paradox of American Patriotism*. Princeton: Princeton University Press, 1999.

Oliver, John William. *History of the Civil War Military Pensions, 1861–1885*. Madison: Bulletin of the University of Wisconsin, History Series, 1917.

Paludan, Philip Shaw. *"A People's Contest": The Union and Civil War, 1861–1865*. Lawrence: University Press of Kansas, 1996.

Parsons, Elaine Frantz. *Manhood Lost: Fallen Drunkards and Redeeming Women in the Nineteenth-Century United States*. Baltimore: Johns Hopkins University Press, 2003.

Pettegrew, John. "'The Soldier's Faith': Turn-of-the-Century Memory of the Civil War and the Emergence of Modern American Nationalism." *Journal of Contemporary History* 31 (January 1996): 49–73.

Phillips, Jason. *Diehard Rebels: The Confederate Culture of Invincibility*. Athens: University of Georgia Press, 2007.

Pizarro, Judith, Roxane Cohen Silver, and JoAnn Prause. "Physical and Mental Health Costs of Traumatic War Experience." *Archives of General Psychiatry* 63 (February 2006): 193–200.

Prince, K. Stephen. "A Rebel Yell for Yankee Doodle: Selling the New South at the 1881 Atlanta International Cotton Exposition." *Georgia Historical Quarterly* 42 (Fall 2008): 340–71.

Pugh, David G. *Sons of Liberty: The Masculine Mind in Nineteenth-Century America*. Westport, Conn.: Greenwood, 1983.

Purcell, Sarah J. *Sealed with Blood: War, Sacrifice, and Memory in Revolutionary America*. Philadelphia: University of Pennsylvania Press, 2002.

Rable, George. *But There Was No Peace: The Role of Violence in the Politics of Reconstruction*. Athens: University of Georgia Press, 2007.

Rainwater, Dorothy T., and Donna H. Felger. *American Spoons: Souvenir and Historical*. New York: Nelson, 1968.

Ramold, Steven J. *Baring the Iron Hand: Discipline in the Union Army*. DeKalb: Northern Illinois University Press, 2010.

Range, Jane, and Maris A. Vinovskis. "Images of Elderly in Popular Magazines: A Content Analysis of Littell's Living Age, 1845–1882." *Social Science History* 5 (Spring 1981): 123–70.

Reardon, Carol. "Writing Battle History: The Challenge of Memory." *Civil War History* 53 (September 2007): 252–63.

Reel, Guy. *The National Police Gazette and the Making of the Modern American Man, 1879–1906*. New York: Palgrave, 2006.

Reinardy, James R. "Decisional Control in Moving to a Nursing Home: Postadmission Adjustment and Well-Being." *The Gerontologist* 32 (February 1992): 96–103.

Roberts, Russell. "G.A.R. Museum Is a Treasury of War Relics." *Civil War Times Illustrated* 29 (September–October 1990): 22–24.

Robinson, Doane. "Early Days in Potter County." In *South Dakota Historical Collections*, vol. 12. Pierre, S.D.: State Department of History, 1924.

Rodgers, Mark E. *Tracing the Civil War Veteran Pension System in the State of Virginia: Entitlement or Privilege*. Lewiston, N.Y.: Mellen, 1999.

Rosenburg, R. B. *Living Monuments: Confederate Soldiers' Homes in the New South*. Chapel Hill: University of North Carolina Press, 1993.

Rotundo, E. Anthony. *American Manhood: Transformations in Masculinity from the Revolution to the Modern Era*. New York: Basic Books, 1993.

Rubin, Anne Sarah. *A Shattered Nation: The Rise and Fall of the Confederacy, 1861–1868*. Chapel Hill: University of North Carolina Press, 2005.

Rydford, John. *Kansas Place-Names*. Norman: University of Oklahoma Press, 1972.

Sandage, Scott A. *Born Losers: A History of Failure in America*. Cambridge: Harvard University Press, 2005.

Sauers, Richard A., comp. *"To Care for Him Who Has Borne the Battle": Research Guide to Civil War Material in the National Tribune*. Vol. 1, 1877–1884. Jackson, Ky.: History Shop, 1995.

Scurfield, Raymond M. "Post-Traumatic Stress Disorder and Healing from the War." In *America and the Vietnam War: Re-Examining the Culture and History of a Generation*, ed. Andrew Wiest, Mary Kathryn Barbier, and Glenn Robins. New York: Routledge, 2010.

Severo, Richard, and Lewis Milford. *The Wages of War: When America's Soldiers Came Home—From Valley Forge to Vietnam*. New York: Simon and Schuster, 1989.

Shaffer, Donald R. *After the Glory: The Struggles of Black Civil War Veterans*. Lawrence: University Press of Kansas, 2004.

Sheehan-Dean, Aaron. *Why Confederates Fought: Family and Nation in Civil War Virginia*. Chapel Hill: University of North Carolina Press, 2007.

Short, Joanna. "Confederate Veteran Pensions, Occupation, and Men's Retirement in the New South." *Social Science History* 30 (Spring 2006): 75–101.

Simpson, John A. *S. A. Cunningham and the Confederate Heritage*. Athens: University of Georgia Press, 1994.

Sinisi, Kyle S. "Veterans as Political Activists: The Kansas Grand Army of the Republic, 1880–1893." *Kansas History* 14 (Summer 1991): 89–99.

Skocpol, Theda. *Protecting Soldiers and Mothers: The Political Origins of Social Policy in the United States*. Cambridge: Harvard University Press, 1992.

Smallwood, James M., Barry A. Crouch, and Larry Peacock. *Murder and Mayhem: The*

War of Reconstruction in Texas. College Station: Texas A & M University Press, 2003.

Smith, Timothy B. *The Golden Age of Battlefield Preservation: The Decade of the 1890s and the Establishment of America's First Five Military Parks*. Knoxville: University of Tennessee Press, 2008.

———. *This Great Battlefield of Shiloh: History, Memory, and the Establishment of a Civil War National Military Park*. Knoxville: University of Tennessee Press, 2004.

"The South's Museum." *Southern Historical Society Papers* 24 (January–December 1896): 354–81.

Speierl, Charles F. "Civil War Veterans and Patriotism in New Jersey Schools." *New Jersey History* 110 (Fall–Winter 1992): 40–55.

Starnes, Richard D. "'The Stirring Strains of Dixie': The Civil War and Southern Identity in Haywood County, North Carolina." *North Carolina Historical Review* 74 (July 1997): 237–59.

Stearns, Peter N. *Be a Man! Males in Modern Society*. 2nd ed. New York: Holmes and Meier, 1970.

Steele, Joel Dorman. *Barnes's Brief History of the United States*. New York: Barnes, 1885.

Stefano, Frank, Jr. *Pictorial Souvenirs and Commemoratives of North America*. New York: Dutton, 1976.

Stott, Richard. *Jolly Fellows: Male Milieus in Nineteenth-Century America*. Baltimore: Johns Hopkins University Press, 2009.

Svenson, Sally E. "'Devoted to Patriotic Reminiscence': The New Hampshire Veterans' Association Campground at the Weirs." *Historical New Hampshire* 54 (Spring–Summer 1999): 41–56.

Tappan, Franklin D. *The Passing of the Grand Army of the Republic*. Worcester, Mass.: Commonwealth, 1939.

"Sirens and Symbols: Clarksville Residents Reflect on the Texas Confederate Home." Online Exhibits: George Washington Carver Museum and Cultural Center. http://www.ci.austin.tx.us/carver/online_exhibits/sir_confederate_home.htm. Accessed September 13, 2010.

Thompson, Rosemarie Garland. *Extraordinary Bodies: Figuring Physical Disability in American Culture and Literature*. New York: Columbia University Press, 1997.

Thompson, William Y. "Sanitary Fairs of the Civil War." *Civil War History* 4 (March 1958): 51–67.

Togus, Down in Maine: The First National Veterans Home. Charleston, S.C.: Arcadia, 1998.

Toomey, Daniel Carroll. *The Maryland Line Confederate Soldiers' Home and Confederate Veterans' Organizations in Maryland*. Baltimore: Toomey, 2001.

Trenerry, Walter N. "When the Boys Came Home." *Minnesota History* 38 (June 1963): 287–97.

Trotter, William R. *Bushwhackers! The Civil War in North Carolina: The Mountains*. Winston-Salem, N.C.: Blair, 1998.

Turner, Fred. *Echoes of Combat: The Vietnam War in American Memory*. New York: Anchor, 1996.

U.S. Civil Service Commission. *History of Veteran Preference in Federal Employment, 1865-1955*. Washington, D.C.: U.S. Civil Service Commission, 1955.

Vinovskis, Maris A. "Images of Elderly in Popular Magazines: A Content Analysis of *Littell's Living Age*, 1845–1882." *Social Science History* 5 (Spring 1981): 123–70.

Vogel, Jeffrey E. "Redefining Reconciliation: Confederate Veterans and the Southern Responses to Civil War Pensions." *Civil War History* 51 (March 2005): 67–93.

Ware, John M., ed. *Standard History of Waupaca County, Wisconsin*. 1917. http://www.rootsweb.com/~wiwaupac/index.htm. Accessed September 14, 2010.

Warren, Craig A. *Scars to Prove It: The Civil War Soldier and American Fiction*. Kent, Ohio: Kent State University Press, 2009.

Warsh, Cheryl Krasnick. "Adventures in Maritime Quackery: The Leslie E. Keeley Gold Cure Institute of Fredericton, N.B." *Acadiensis* 17 (Spring 1988): 103–30.

Weeks, Jim. *Gettysburg: Memory, Market, and an American Shrine*. Princeton: Princeton University Press, 2003.

Wegner, Ansley Herring. "Phantom Pain: Civil War Amputation and North Carolina's Maimed Veterans." *North Carolina Historical Review* 75 (July 1998): 286–96.

Wetherington, Mark V. *Plain Folk's Fight: The Civil War and Reconstruction in Piney Woods Georgia*. Chapel Hill: University of North Carolina Press, 2005.

White, William L. "The Lessons of Language." In *Altering American Consciousness: The History of Alcohol and Drug Use in the United States, 1800–2000*, ed. Sarah W. Tracy and Caroline Jean Acker. Amherst: University of Massachusetts Press, 2004.

Wilkinson, Warren. *Mother, May You Never See the Sights I Have Seen: The Fifty-seventh Massachusetts Veteran Volunteers in the Army of the Potomac, 1864–1865*. New York: HarperCollins, 1991.

Williams, Rusty. *My Old Confederate Home: A Respectable Place for Civil War Veterans*. Lexington: University Press of Kentucky, 2010.

Williams-Searle, John. "Cold Charity." In *The New Disability History: American Perspectives*, ed. Paul K. Longmore and Lauri Umansky. New York: New York University Press, 2001.

Wilson, Charles Reagan. *Baptized in Blood: The Religion of the Lost Cause, 1865–1920*. Athens: University of Georgia Press, 1980.

Wooley, Charles F. *The Irritable Heart of Soldiers and the Origins of Anglo-American Cardiology: The U.S. Civil War (1861) to World War I (1918)*. Aldershot, Eng.: Ashgate, 2002.

Wounds of War: The Psychological Aftermath of Combat in Vietnam. New York: Basic Books, 1984.

Wylie, Alexander. *Veteran and Affiliated Organizations Arising from the Civil War*. Mendota, Ill.: Mendota Reporter, 1966.

Young, Alfred F. *The Shoemaker and the Tea Party: Memory and the American Revolution*. Boston: Beacon, 1999.

Young, John Preston, and A. R. James. *Standard History of Memphis, Tennessee*. Knoxville, Tenn.: Crew, 1912.

Dissertations

Beck, Avent Childress. "Civil War Veterans in the Fiction of Samuel Clemens, William Dean Howells, Henry Adams, and Henry James." New York University, 2003.

Cetina, Judith Gladys. "A History of Veterans' Homes in the United States, 1811–1930." Case Western Reserve University, 1977.

Cloyd, Benjamin Gregory. "Civil War Prisons in American Memory." Louisiana State University, 2005.

Gannon, Barbara A. "The Won Cause: Black and White Comradeship in the Grand Army of the Republic." Pennsylvania State University, 2005.

Gorman, Kathleen Lynn. "When Johnny Came Marching Home Again: Confederate Veterans in the New South." University of California–Riverside, 1994.

Hagaman, Robert A. "Personal Battles: The Lives of Maryland's Black Civil War Veterans, 1840–1920." Northern Illinois University, 2004.

McClurken, Jeffrey W. "After the Battle: Reconstructing the Confederate Veteran Family in Pittsylvania County and Danville, Virginia, 1860–1900." Johns Hopkins University, 2002.

Miller, Christopher. "Milwaukee's First Suburbs: A Re-Interpretation of Suburban Incorporation in Nineteenth-Century Milwaukee County." Marquette University, 2007.

Padilla, Jalynn Olsen. "Army of 'Cripples': Northern Civil War Amputees, Disability, and Manhood in Victorian America." University of Delaware, 2007.

Walters, Glenda Jane. "Union Colony in the Confederate South: Lynn Haven, Florida, 1910–1920." Florida State University, 1995.

Unpublished Papers

Blauvelt, Gerrit L. "Reunion and Old Northern Soldiers: Union Veterans' Colonies in the Post-Reconstruction South." University of Florida, 2008.

Gannon, Barbara A. "'And, If Spared, and Growing Older': Post-War Comradeship in the Grand Army of the Republic (GAR)." Paper presented at the Southern Historical Association Meeting, 2007.

Linares, Claudia. "The Civil War Pension Law." Working Paper 2001-6, Center for Population Economics, University of Chicago.

Miscellaneous

Antiques Roadshow. April 10, 2006. Christopher Mitchell, appraiser. http://www.pbs.org/wgbh/roadshow/archive/200504A45.html. Accessed March 1, 2008.

EBay. Various dates.

Index

U.S. Christian Commission, 52, 249
U.S. Medical Department, 78–79
U.S. Pension Building, 199–200
U.S. Sanitary Commission, 13, 34, 52, 95, 96–97, 139, 224, 249
University of Virginia, 99

"The Veteran" (short story), 280–81
Veteran Brand groceries, 155
Veterans: employment, 4–5, 49, 52, 55–59, 91–95, 103, 233, 239, 236–41; poverty among, 5–6, 14–15, 20, 56–57, 60–62, 76–77, 91, 95, 170–72, 176–77, 185–87, 196, 222–23; in literature, 8–9, 28–29, 31–32, 40–41, 49, 52–53, 66–67, 75, 76, 80–82, 92–93, 95, 100, 105–6, 176–77, 224–25, 235–36, 254, 280–82, 284–85, 291 (n. 9), 292 (n. 40), 301 (n. 74); and families, 8–9, 29, 38, 45, 46–48, 52, 190–96, 256; organizations, 11–12, 18–19, 145; civilians' perceptions of, 18, 19–21, 24, 34, 46–49, 51–57, 76–77, 104, 106, 183–86, 187–95, 197–98, 199–200, 204–5, 213–19, 229, 245–49; politicization of issues related to, 20–21, 29, 166–69, 181–82, 200–203, 228, 303 (n. 7); perceptions of themselves, 28–29, 187–98, 199, 229–36, 252–60; adjustment to peace, 49–55; and sex, 108, 189; and battlefields, 133–38; newspapers, 147–52; in advertising, 154–55; and crime, 167–68, 217; and mental illness, 169–70; lost identity, 224–26; distinguishing themselves from civilians, 246–47, 252–60, 279–85; and combat, 252–60; colonies, 270–72. *See also* Alcohol: and veterans; Disabled veterans; Grand Army of the Republic; National Home for Disabled Volunteer Soldiers; Reunions; Soldiers' homes; United Confederate Veterans; Violence
"The Veteran's Vision" (poem), 284
Vicksburg, 63, 88, 131, 268, 270
Vietnam veterans, 6, 90, 102, 103–4, 111
Violence, 2; committed by veterans, 2, 10–11, 62, 65–72, 89–90, 103, 188, 189; committed against veterans, 2, 41–44

Walker, Willard, 248
Warner, Charles Dudley, 30
War of 1812 veterans, 15
Weeden, E. S., 210
Western Lunatic Asylum (Virginia), 88
Wheeler, Cornelius, 114,
Whipple, Edwin Percy, 27
Whitman, Walt, 31–32, 204, 284–85
Widows. *See* Pensions
Wills, David, 134
Wills, W. H., 210–11
Wilmington, N.C., 70
Wilson, Charles Reagan, 262
Wisconsin State Hospital for the Insane, 87–88
Wisconsin State Legislature, 166–67
"A Wizard from Gettysburg" (short story), 224–25
Woman's Relief Corps, 140
Women's Christian Temperance Union, 102
Woolson Spice Company, 156
Worcester, Mass., 132–33, 140
World War I veterans, 100
World War II, 236; veterans, 87, 100, 248